T0107786

L. M. RULLA S.J. - SR. J. RIDICK S.S.C. - F. IMODA S.J.

ENTERING AND LEAVING VOCATION: INTRAPSYCHIC DYNAMICS

Second reprint

EDITRICE PONTIFICIA UNIVERSITÀ GREGORIANA
ROMA 1988

1976 – First Edition
1980 – First Reprint
1988 – Second Reprint

Con approvazione ecclesiastica

© 1976 - E.P.U.G. - ROMA

EDITRICE PONTIFICIA UNIVERSITÀ GREGORIANA
EDITRICE PONTIFICIO ISTITUTO BIBLICO
Piazza della Pilotta, 35 - 00187 Roma, Italy

This Research Project
was supported
by:

The National Science Foundation of the U.S.A. (NSF GS-1203),

The Foundations' Fund for Research in Psychiatry (FFRP 65-332),

and

The Social Science Research Council of the University of Chicago.

PREFACE

In the parable of the sower (St. Matthew 13, 1-23), our Lord tells us that His messages, His calls are received by men with different dispositions and thus yield different results. Why these different personal dispositions?

Why do quite a few young vocationers present signs of insufficient growth in their vocational commitment during the years immediately following the initial formation in vocational settings?

Why do some of these vocationers — and many of them in recent times — leave their vocational commitment?

Why do quite a few priests and religious of both sexes, who initially did not show the foregoing signs of insufficient vocational growth, later on settle down in what could be called a state of "early retirement" or of "nesting" in vocation, i.e., in the state of more or less apathetic routine in which only half of their potentials are used for the Kingdom?

Many complex elements enter into the picture when one tries to find some clues toward an answer to the previous questions. The primacy of supernatural factors is not denied nor diminished here. Neither is the relevance of the ideas, functions and structures of the vocational institutions overlooked. But, what about the dispositions of men of which our Lord speaks?

Again, the complexity of the issues involved is staggering. The present book intends to bring a modest contribution to the multifaceted task of offering some clues related to these issues. The intrapsychic dynamics of vocationers, conscious and subconscious are the focus of our analyses. They consider people who entered or left vocation after Vatican Council II. These persons were followed for six to eight years after entrance into vocational settings. The findings presented here are part of a project of study still in process. The first author would like to cordially thank those young vocationers who generously participated in the endeavor. His repeated, personal encounters with them have been a source of personal enrichment and profound inspiration. Thanks are also due to those responsible for their formation, who have kindly cooperated throughout.

This book intends to offer some help to all the priests and religious of both sexes who want to grow in their vocational commitment. Also, it hopes to contribute somehow to the difficult tasks related to such a growth : people in charge of formation, vocational directors, spiritual fathers, teachers, superiors, may find some help in their efforts for the good of their brethren. After all, one sees what he knows. And the knowledge which can be acquired by the reading of the present findings may be applied to different situations and cultures. The structural approach to the study of the vocationer followed in this project is somehow transsituational and transtemporal. Actually, it may be applied to any kind of Christian commitment.

Readers who do not have a professional background specifically related to this book may read all the parts which are in normal print and thus get the relevant messages ; while, hopefully, professionals with their attentive skill will also consider the sections in small print. The latter are indispensible for a proper understanding of the approach and findings presented.

Acknowledgements — About ten years were required to accomplish the present task. Many people have contributed to it. However, without the generous, unfailing dedication of Mrs. Julie Lobbia, this study would not have been possible : the authors are deeply indebted to her. Special thanks are extended to Sister Julie Shainauskas, S. S. C., for the admirable key role she played in editing this work.

Salvatore R. Maddi, Professor at the University of Chicago, was talentedly involved in the initial phases of our enterprise and we want to express our gratitude to him. Donald Fiske, of the University of Chicago, and Frank Slaymaker, of Loyola University of Chicago, have contributed with their professional advice or supervision to overcome the many difficulties related to the theoretical and statistical aspects of our endeavor. John Iannantuoni and Louise Rehling of the computation center of the University of Chicago and Paul T. Costa, Jr., and Anthony Arnold were especially helpful in planning some computer analyses. Jackie Bertoletti, Kathy Yakaitis, and Lori Lobbia generously participated in scoring and analyzing data.

We are indebted to Father Hervé Carrier, S. J., rector of the Gregorian University, to Daniel X. Freedman, chairman of the Department of Psychiatry at the University of Chicago, and, in a special way, to Jarl E. Dyrud, associate chairman of the same department, for their continuous support.

Finally, we would like to thank our students of the Institute of Psychology of the Gregorian University in Rome ; we have greatly benefited from their contributions coming from their international backgrounds. Our work with them has been and is a source of encouragement that the ideas and findings presented here are of help to the young vocationers of our present time.

This work has been supported, in part, by the National Science Foundation of the U.S.A. (NSF GS-1203), the Foundations' Fund for Research in Psychiatry (FFRP 65-332), and the Social Science Research Council of the University of Chicago.

Chicago, Illinois
September, 1975

Luigi   M. Rulla, S. J.
Sister Joyce Ridick, S. S. C.
Franco Imoda, S. J.

TABLE OF CONTENTS

PART III.   EPILOGUE

LIST OF CHARTS

XV

LIST OF APPENDIXES

XVIII

XIX

INTRODUCTION

The research presented in this book was started about ten years ago by the first author. The general aim was to study the personalities of people intending to become Catholic priests and nuns, hoping to obtain from this study information that would improve their selection and training. Two major objectives were sought at that time.

The first major aim of this study was to determine the personality characteristics of people entering Catholic vocational training, by comparing groups of students entering training for several Catholic orders or seminary with a group of students entering Catholic lay colleges. The following testing instruments were adopted: the Minnesota Multiphasic Personality Inventory of Hathaway and McKinley, the 16 Personality Factors of Cattell, the Vassar Attitude Inventory (Mary Conover Mellon Foundation), the General Goals of Life Inventory of the Educational Testing Service, the Activities Index of G. Stern, the Thematic Apperception Test of Morgan and Murray, and the Incomplete Sentences Blank (College Form) of Rotter. To gain further understanding of the initial personalities of religious vocationers, the comparison of biographical information concerning these religious or seminarians and lay college students was planned.

The second major aim of the research was to determine the nature and degree of personality changes that take place during the period of formation for the priestly or religious vocation. This was accomplished by assessing personality three times during the first four-year training period: at entrance into the formation centers usually after high school, toward the end of the second year and of the fourth year of formation. The assessment was done by using the above-mentioned tests. Personality changes were studied by comparing these three assessments with each other and with an assessment of per-

1

sonality done on the lay college students just previous to their graduation. The personality changes were to be considered in the light of the influence exercised by the institutional and the peer group pressures.

People belonging to different vocational institutions in the Midwest, East, and West of the USA were invited to participate in the project. These subjects represented the entire group of vocationers entering the different institutions each year. The entering groups of several consecutive years were studied. Table 3.1 outlines the sample of this research. The initial numbers of the entire sample are as follows: Males, Religious or Seminarians 257, Control Group (Catholic College Lay Students) 107; Females, Religious 446, Control Group (Catholic College Lay Students) 136. Thus, the subjects from the religious institutions were 703 and from the lay institutions 243, for a total of 946.

At its inception ten years ago, an exploratory and positivistic approach was taken in the study: to collect data, to search for facts and then to allow them to speak for themselves. For the implementation of this project the collaboration of S. R. Maddi of the University of Chicago was asked; also the financial support of grants by the Social Science Research Council of the University of Chicago, by the Foundations' Fund for Research in Psychiatry, and by the National Science Foundation was obtained.

However, after a few years, the first author of the present book started to realize that the foregoing approach was hardly conducive to a proper understanding of many core characteristics of priestly and religious vocation, like the self-transcendence of Christian asceticism and of apostolic effectiveness. It is true, the personality of vocationers acts only as a natural " disposition " to the charism of supernatural grace; still, grace builds on these " dispositions ". Are there and what are the personality characteristics upon which supernatural charism acts to foster processes like entrance, perseverance and effectiveness in religious vocation? For these processes, is it possible to sort out some motivational psychodynamic trends which are trans-cultural, trans-situational and thus, perhaps, inherent in human nature? Why do people drop out of vocation? Is it possible to predict the " possibility " of adjustment of young

2

vocationers to various different groups or vocational environments? Is it possible to énucleate some transsituational patterns of vocational conflicts, which are different from the ones of gross and non-directly vocational psychopathology? How do these conflicts influence or are they influenced by entrance, dropping out or perseverance, effectiveness or lack of it, adjustment or maladjustment to groups and environments?

An answer to these foregoing questions could hardly come from the exploratory, positivistic approach with which the project had been started. Nor do the current general theories of personality seem to offer a useful answer: first of all, because they " are generally lacking in clarity and explicitness, and they have not been sufficiently formalized to allow for the generation of hypotheses by formal axiomatic deduction " (Wiggins, 1973, p. 447); thus, it is difficult to subject these theories to empirical tests. Secondly, current personality theories do not offer a thorough examination of the rational and empirical links between their conceptualization and the measuring operations directed toward it (Fiske, 1971).

Similar considerations are valid, at least in part, also for some of the psycho-social theories of non-religious vocations, like the ones by Super (1963), Tiedeman and O'Hara (1963), Holland (1966), Roe (1956, 1964), Ginzberg et al. (1951), Bordin, Nachmann and Segal (1963), Sartre (in Simons, 1966). Even when the limitations discussed about the general theories of personality are not found in theories of non-religious vocations, it is nevertheless true that all of these theories show a common factor: self-actualization, self-fulfillment is the basic motivation underlying all vocational choices. But, as it has been discussed elsewhere (Rulla, 1971), priestly and religious vocations go beyond self-actualization and specifically stress also self-transcendence. Any conceptualization about a vocation requires that its core be explicitly identified.

The foregoing discussion suggests a conclusion: the optimal strategy in answering the proposed questions concerning religious vocation is the concurrent development of a new, fresh theoretical conceptualization and of measuring operations which are explicitly linked to them. After all, there is nothing more practical than an appropriate theory, which can be tested by empirical research.

3

Following this line of reasoning, the need for some theoretical formulation for religious vocation became more cogent, since no such theory seemed to be available. The impact of Vatican Council II made this need more felt. Some theoretical propositions were formulated and empirically tested by means of new measuring operations linked to them (Rulla, 1967). The results of this pilot study were promising at least for the first three propositions which were related to the process of entrance into the vocational setting. This fact encouraged further thinking which led to the writing of a psycho-social theory of priestly and religious vocation (Rulla, 1971) with implications and applications for vocational perseverance, effectiveness, celibacy, group dynamics, leadership and various facets of institutional life and community renewal. Further empirical findings seem to support this theoretical frame of reference (Imoda, 1971; Maddi and Rulla, 1972; Rulla and Maddi, 1972; Ridick, 1972).

The present book adopts the same frame of reference and aims to make further contributions toward finding answers to some of the previously outlined questions.

It focuses on the personality of the vocationers. Here some definitions are necessary. Personality " is defined as the way the person interacts with the world outside him and the world within him " (Fiske, 1971, p. 3). These interactions are seen as *processes*, that is, ongoing activities in persons, as " dispositions " to the influence of supernatural and natural factors. However, the theoretical approach followed in this book distinguishes two types of processes, of dispositions: transitory dispositions which show that the person is in different states at different times and situations; and enduring dispositions which override the effects of the transitory ones and determine some continuity in the behavior of the subjects. This distinction is not new in the psychological literature; see, for instance, the concept of " regnant processes " by Murray (1938), neglected for a time and now reconsidered (Klinger, 1971); a similar conceptualization is made by Smith (1968) when he distinguishes transitory self-percepts from the more or less stable self-concept. The distinction is not new, but its translation in researchable theory is not an easy task (Dahlstrom, 1972).

4

Still, this distinction is far from being just a theoretical one; its practical implications are far-reaching. For instance, only if it is possible to recognize the enduring dispositions of a person will it be possible to predict with some reliability the perseverance or effectiveness of entering vocationers as well as their potentialities of adapting themselves to different vocational environments or different groups. Thus, it will be possible to consider, on a scientific basis, the nature of the help that could be offered to them.

The theory followed in this book seeks to estimate the enduring dispositions of the subjects and to separate them from the transitory ones.

The reader will get a better understanding of the scope of the present study when a presentation of this theoretical frame of reference is offered. This is the topic of the following section.

PART I

THE THEORETICAL
AND METHODOLOGICAL BACKGROUND

CHAPTER 1

THE THEORETICAL FRAMEWORK:
THE THEORY OF SELF-TRANSCENDENT CONSISTENCY

This chapter is a brief, over-simplified outline of the basic propositions and tenets followed in this book. In general, no rationale for these constructs is given here, nor explanation of distinctions or of implications, nor referral to the numerous research data on which the conceptualizations are based. These issues are too complex to be discussed in a short presentation. However, because they deal with some critical vocational problems, the serious reader is advised to refer to the original sources (Rulla, 1971, 1967) for an appropriate understanding of the tenets proposed. For the convenience of the reader, in the following presentation referral will be made to the pertinent pages in the 1971 publication.

For the conceptualization proposed here, priestly and religious vocation can be considered together; therefore, the two terms will be used interchangeably (pp. 20-26, 69-73).

According to a theological perspective, a religious vocation is characterized by: (1) the fact and the primacy of God's invitation; (2) the totality of the claim such an invitation lays upon the person; (3) the newness of the obligations specified by this claim (pp. 20-26).

The personality or self of the vocationers can be considered according to the following components (pp. 29-43):

Ideal self: — *Institutional Ideals* (II): The perceptions a person has of the ideals his vocational institution values for its members; therefore, the II represents the individual's role concept.

— *Self Ideals* (SI): the ideals a person values for himself, i.e., what he would like to be or do.

Actual self: — *Present Behavior* (PB) or *manifest self-concepts:* the subject's cognitions about his own present

9

behavior, i.e., what he thinks he usually is or does.
— *Latent Self* (LS): the personality characteristics revealed by projective type instruments. It is assumed that this type of instrument reveals what characteristics, conscious or subconsciuous, a person actually possesses, not merely those which he thinks he has or would like to have (pp. 78-80).
— *Social Self:* the self considered as a social object.

The " Ideal Self " includes the II and the SI; these two components taken together form the self-ideal in a given situation or self-ideal-in-situation (SI-II).

At the conscious level, the ideals proclaimed by the person in his " ideal self " may present the characteristics of values or the ones of attitudes.

Values are enduring abstract ideals of a person, which may be ideal end-states of existence (terminal values or ends) or ideal modes of conduct (instrumental values or means) (Rokeach, 1968, a, b, 1973; Lovejoy, 1950; Hilliard, 1950). In religious vocation, examples of terminal values are the imitation of Christ and the union with God; examples of instrumental values are especially the three evangelical counsels of poverty, chastity, and obedience (pp. 69-73).

Attitudes are dispositions expressing a state of readiness to respond (Allport, 1935, 1954; McGuire, 1969). They differ from values: values are relatively general action tendencies while attitudes pertain to the more specific and changeable activities. A grown person probably has hundreds of attitudes, but only dozens of instrumental values and perhaps only a few terminal values (p. 41). Thus, attitudes may stem from and serve values: e.g., attitudes of nurturance may stem from and serve the value of Christian charity. However, attitudes may become values for the individual especially in the form of, instrumental values which may be poorly compatible with religious vocation; for instance, nurturance may be motivated by succorance, by affective dependency; i.e., the attitudes of nurturance do not stem from and serve the value of charity but the *need* of succorance; in such a case, the individual gives in order to receive through the affective dependency: he *values*

" to be with people " because, in the final analysis, he *needs* to get from them more than to give to them.

The attentive reader by now has realized that attitudes may stem from values and/or from needs (concrete examples of values, attitudes and needs are found in the glossary). Perhaps he has also seen the possibility that vocational values or attitudes proclaimed by vocationers in self-report questionnaires as representing their self-ideals and their reasons for entering religious life, may be, at least in part, a subconscious expression of an underlying need which is in opposition, is inconsistent with the proclaimed self-ideal. The foregoing example of " being with people " is a case in point. Another example taken from cases seen in private practice may be the following one: a vocationer who proclaims the orientation of deference characteristic of obedience will endorse values like " doing my duty " and " having fine relations with other people "; however, maybe he is forced, driven to proclaim such an obedient orientation as a defense against a strongly repressed, unacceptable orientation of rebelliousness stemming from a subconsciuous need of aggressive autonomy. In such a case, there is an *inconsistency* between the values and attitudes proclaimed and the subconsciuos needs, i.e., there is a subconscious inconsistency between the ideal-self and the actual-self of that person, between what he would like to be as a vocationer and what actually he is. Furthermore, note that the individual may be responsive to that inconsistency without being aware of it. Research has shown that such lack of awareness may be unawareness of the existence of the inconsistency itself, or unawareness of any associated stress or unawareness of the inconsistency-resolving activity (see Tannenbaum, 1967 and 1968, and Brock, 1968, who review also research of McGuire, 1960, Brock, 1963, Brock and Grant, 1963, Cohen, Greenbaum and Mansson, 1963).

These *subconscious* inconsistencies or conflicts between the actual self and the ideal-self are present when the individual is prompted subconsciously to respond simultaneously in different and incompatible ways because of the opposition between the needs of his latent-self (LS) and the vocational attitudes and/or values of his ideal-self. Similarly, *conscious* inconsistencies or conflicts are present when the opposition is

11

between the conscious part of the actual self, i.e., the present behavior or PB, and the ideal self.

Parallel with the inconsistencies, there can be conscious or subconscious vocational consistencies between the actual-self and the ideal-self.

In the theory (pp. 82-85), four types of intrapersonal, intraphysic vocational consistencies and inconsistencies have been differentiated. They are based on the relationships among three basic elements of personality: the vocational *values* (terminal and instrumental) of a person, his *attitudes* and his *needs*. Vocational values are assumed to be always present in a person who enters a religious vocation; if they are not present, the strength of the vocational inconsistencies is even greater (pp. 60-66); the same can be said when the individual has pseudo-values, i.e., subjective values (which he may have created) inconsistent with the objective vocational values; an example of a pseudo-value was the above-mentioned proclaimed ideal " to be with people " presented as charity, but stemming prevailingly from a need to get some gratification.

A person can have any one of the four types of vocational consistencies or inconsistencies, which can be described as follows:

— social consistency (SC): when his need, e.g., for nurturance (conscious or subconscious) is consonant with the vocational values and with his prevailing attitudes for nurturance;
— psychological consistency (PsC): when the need for nurturance (conscious or subconscious) is consonant with the vocational values, but dissonant with his prevailing attitudes for nurturance;
— psychological inconsistency (PsI): when the need for nurturance (subconscious) is dissonant with vocational values and with his prevailing attitudes for nurturance;
— social inconsistency (SoI): when the need for nurturance (subconscious) is dissonant with vocational values but not with his prevailing attitudes for nurturance.

The foregoing four types are at the two extreme, opposite poles of a continuum where there are other intermediate types, which are described in Chapter 3 of this book under " Typology ". These extreme types of the continuum are considered to be particularly important for vocational adjustment or

12

growth because they are *central*, i.e., functionally significant for vocational commitment and thus, capable of influencing the perseverance or the apostolic effectiveness of a person in vocation. The concept of centrality will be further discussed in Chapter 3.

According to the common tenets of depth psychology and the results of relevant research presented in the 1971 publication on pages 110-113 and 129-134, the theory states that *subconscious* inconsistencies exercise a particularly negative influence upon the vocational commitment. Furthermore, such a commitment is especially affected when these inconsistencies are the dominant motivation which characterizes a person (pp. 43 and 382).

From the theoretical tenets presented up to this point, it is seen that the theory has two basic elements: (1) the *self-transcendence* of the self-ideal, especially of the vocational terminal and instrumental values; (2) a pursuit of these ideals which is accomplished and supported by a *consistent* self. Thus, this theoretical framework can be identified as a theory of self-transcendent consistency. Self-transcendence and consistency in turn will dispose to and foster self-fulfillment, effectiveness and perseverance (pp. 48-51, 126-129, 307-321 and Table IV). The relationships among these elements is schematically represented in Chart 1:

CHART 1

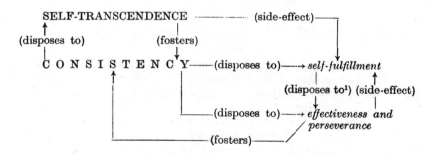

---

[1] Self-fulfillment will lead to effectiveness and perseverance according to whether or not the *part* of the self fulfilled may be integrated with objective vocational values (cfr. Chapter 7).

The preceding presentation of the theory of self-transcendent consistency has dealt prevailingly with the intrapersonal aspects of personality, with the way the person interacts with the world within him. However, the way he interacts with the world outside him is very important also. The theory considers at length (pp. 99-120, 251-380) this interpersonal relationship of the individual with his vocational institution and his peer groups. Having made reference to the original source for a discussion of these interpersonal aspects, here it suffices to state that mere gratification of vocationally dissonant needs, both in the intra- and inter-personal dimension, may have a " positive " influence on perseverance, but it does not have a positive influence on effectiveness: people may remain in vocation prevailingly because some of their vocationally dissonant needs are gratified, e.g., their need for security or for power; but this will not have a positive influence on their " effectiveness " as priests or religious, that is, on their visible manifestation of the values of Christ; at most, this will support their " efficiency " as administrators, as teachers, etc. Vocational effectiveness is fostered when both vocationally consonant needs and vocational values and attitudes are fulfilled (pp. 102-120; Table V). Theoretical positions and research findings seem to support this reasoning (Winch, 1955a, b, 1958; Thibaut and Kelley, 1959; Miller, 1963; Fouriezos, Hutt and Guetzkow, 1950; Rokeach, 1968b).

It is now possible to present the five basic propositions for the intrapersonal aspect of the vocational theory of self-transcendent consistency (pp. 47-67). In the light of the previous discussion, they should be more meaningful to the reader.

1. Religious vocation is an implementation of the self-ideal rather than of the self-concept.
2. Religious vocation is an implementation of the self-ideal-in-situation.
3. The self-ideal implemented in the commitment to a religious vocation is characterized more or only by instrumental and terminal values rather than by attitudes, and the content of this self-ideal is made up of normative variables to a greater extent than is true of the self-concept.
4. Perseverance and effectiveness of religious vocation correlate with the type, degree and number of aware or unaware

central consistencies and inconsistencies of the actual self with the vocational attitudes and/or vocational values.

5. The aware or unaware central inconsistencies of the actual self with the vocational attitudes and/or vocational values which affect perseverance and effectiveness of religious vocation, at the beginning of vocational crises are more present among attitudes than among instrumental or terminal values; and, within these behavioral parameters, more among normative than among preference variables. If there is a worsening of the vocational crisis, such inconsistencies will increase in number and strength and will gradually change the instrumental values essentially related to one or more of the three evangelical counsels.

(For a definition of some terms, like norm and preference values and attitudes, see glossary.)

As can be seen from the foregoing propositions, factors influential in the beginning of religious vocation are not necessarily equivalent to those that are influential in staying in and working effectively. More will be said in this regard in Chapter 4.

This brief presentation of the vocational theory of self-transcendent consistency has not dealt with many of its tenets; among them is one of paramount significance for a proper understanding of the research presented in this book: the structural approach. Because of its relevance, this aspect will be discussed in a separate section, which follows immediately.

CHAPTER 2

THE THEORY AS A STRUCTURAL APPROACH
TO THE STUDY OF VOCATION

It was stated in the introduction that this research was started with an exploratory, positivistic approach. Later on the formulation of a theoretical frame of reference (Rulla, 1971) led to a structural approach which seems to be less imperfect for understanding some of the complex issues related to religious vocation.

Human behavior shows salient regularities as well as salient discontinuities. They were mentioned in the introduction as enduring or as transitory dispositions of the self to the influence of supernatural and natural factors.

To account for salient behavioral regularities and discontinuities, personality theorists and researchers have proposed two assessment models or strategies (Dahlstrom, 1972): the multidimensional and the typological. The discussion and the examples offered by Dahlstrom may help to explain this distinction.

Let us consider three qualitatively different interactions between a man and a woman: (1) the man insults the woman at the top of his voice for fifteen minutes without allowing her to utter a word. (2) The man beats, slaps the woman several minutes on end. (3) The man struggles with the woman at the brink of a precipice several hundred feet high; finally, the woman falls over the brink to her death on the rocks.

A researcher may try to make a lawful sense of the foregoing behaviors by following either the multidimensional or the typological model. If he chooses the multidimensional strategy, he will say that the three qualitatively different interactions depend on the quantitative variations of an underlying set of dimensions or variables: e.g., he will locate the verbal abuse, the physical abuse, and the homicidal actions of the man along a quantitatively increasing value or scale of underlying variables like aggression and trust-mistrust.

16

If the researcher follows the typological strategy, he could take the homicidal behavior previously described under 3 and seek patterns among the variables by which to describe some order or regularity. Thus, using examples suggested by Conrad (1966) for typing violence, throwing a woman over a brink may turn out to be: (1) the murder of his wife by her husband enraged at the discovery of her marital unfaithfulness (situational violence under extreme provocation); (2) the consequence of the delusions of a psychotic who believed the woman was part of a conspiracy against him (pathological violence); (3) the accidental releasing of his girl friend by a fiancé who was attempting to scare her while rough-housing with her on a picnic (accidental violence). Here, different patterns of underlying motivation are set and behavior, descriptively similar, are psychodynamically differentiated according to some types: situational, pathological, and accidental violence.

Both models, multidimensional and typological, have their advantages and disadvantages. For instance, in contrast with multidimensional analysis, typological analysis might allow the exclusion of aggression and mistrust in case 3 of accidental violence where, perhaps, they could be unimportant determinants. On the other hand, the multidimensional analysis may offer the possibility of obtaining a quantitative scaling of behavior along a dimensional intensity of aggression and mistrust; this quantitative assessment may, perhaps, enable the researcher to find lawful relationships between provocations and aggressive acts along the lines of the frustration-aggression formulation done by the Yale group (Dollard et al., 1939).

Both models lead to some patterning, to some taxonomy, but by following two different paths: in the multidimensional strategy, statistical techniques of correlation allow the discovery of clusters of intercorrelation among scaled variables (e.g., aggression, trust, etc.); in turn, these intercorrelations may indicate recurring patterns or configurations among these variables. In the typological strategy, these recurring patterns or configurations among the variables are previously abstracted from data and/or observations and then empirically tested. However, it seems that, within the realm of typological strategy, a further distinction is necessary. This distinction is discussed by authors like Loevinger (1966 a, b; 1969) and Kohlberg (1969, 1971 a).

In the typological approach, the patterns among the variables are abstracted from data and/or observations. However, there can be two kinds of abstraction and, therefore, two kinds of typological strategy: one that is based on *content*; a second that is based on *structure*. Actually, we think that the same two kinds of abstraction can be applied to the multidimensional strategy. The discussion which follows will first present examples of content typology and of structural typology. Then, it will suggest the application of the structural approach to both the multidimensional and the typological strategies.

An example of the content typology is the one proposed by Erikson (1959, 1963) with its eight stages of ego development. Examples of the structural typology are the logical-developmental stages described by Piaget (1963) and the moral-developmental stages proposed by Kohlberg (1958, 1969, 1971 b, 1973).

Let us discuss briefly this distinction between a typology of content and a typology of structure by using the models theorized by Erikson and by Kohlberg respectively. Note that for our purposes, consideration here will be restricted to the formal aspects of the models the authors have employed rather than to the content of their insights.

Erikson characterizes, if not defines, successive stages of ego development by eight successive nuclear conflicts: basic trust versus mistrust; autonomy vs. shame and doubt; initiative vs. guilt; industry vs. inferiority; identity vs. role confusion, etc. (cfr. Appendix B-3). These stages describe the focal concerns of persons in different periods of their development; thus, trust-mistrust is the central concern in infancy, identity-role confusion the central concern in adolescence, etc. Here the *content*, the *what* is what characterizes the developing person, is what characterizes his developmental period.

Kohlberg presents six universal stages of development in moral thought. These six stages of moral development are divided into three major levels, the preconventional, the conventional, and the postconventional or autonomous. The preconventional level characterizes childhood; the postconventional level is first evident in adolescence. Note that the six moral stages are *structures* of thought through which the

18

child moves sequentially. Therefore, here it is not what but *how* a person thinks that characterizes his developmental level.

While the stages proposed by Erikson tell us *what* a person thinks about, whether he is preoccupied, for instance, with trust or autonomy or guilt, Kohlberg's moral stages tell us *how* that person thinks concerning autonomy or guilt and so forth. That is: in the content or " what " typology, stages tell us what is in the person's mind; in the structural or " how " typology, stages tell us only how he thinks about what is on his mind; for instance, if he thinks about autonomy according to a conventional or a postconventional level. This " how " is determined by the structures that characterize his mind, which act as " structured wholes ": each stage implies a deep organization uniting a variety of superficially different kinds of response.

There is another basic difference between Kohlberg's and Erikson's typologies. Kohlberg's stages are an hierarchical integration. " This implies that higher stages include lower stages as components reintegrated at the higher level " (1971 b, p. 186). Erikson's stages are not hierarchical in the same way. Resolutions of identity conflicts are not also resolutions of trust or autonomy conflicts, that is, each of the earlier conflicts persists rather than being integrated into or being hierarchically dominated by the next. As a consequence, when we want to describe the central concerns of a person in a developmental period, we have a picture of content which is multidimensional i.e., it is represented by many quantitative measures, a different one for each conflict. In this sense, there is no difference with the multidimensional strategy described before. The Erikson stages are purifications and exaggerations of typical life histories. " They are not universal abstractions from data " (Kohlberg, 1971 a, p. 1077). The abstraction is based on the content, on the " what " which concerns the self, rather than on the structure of the self, on the " how " it concerns it.

The theory of self-transcendent consistency combines both the " how " and the " what ", the structure of the self and its content. However, the " what " is assessed as predictor of vocational events like entrance, dropping out, etc., only in function of the " how "; thus, the theory adopts a structural model. Let us explain.

19

The vocational consistencies or inconsistencies of the theory tell us *what* the vocationer feels about, whether he is preoccupied or not with aggression or sex or domination and so forth. They also tell us *how* he feels, whether he is motivated consistently or inconsistently concerning aggression or sex or domination as they relate to his vocational attitudes and/or values. However, the what is assessed as predictor, for instance, of dropping out, only in function of the how; for example, aggression or sex (the " what ") are assessed as predictors of dropping out or not, only in function of the " how ", i.e., of whether they motivate a person inconsistently or consistently with regard to his vocational attitudes and/or values; to put it in terms of the structures of the self: aggression or sex are assessed as predictors of dropping out or not, only if there is a significant inconsistency or consistency between the actual-self and the ideal-self of the individual. Proposition 4 of the theory spells out more precisely this *how*, i.e., the specific patterns of relationship between the actual-self and the ideal-self which influence perseverance and effectiveness. Similarly, Propositions 1 and 2 state the pattern of relationship between specific structures of the self which fosters entrance into a religious vocation: here, the relationship specifying the choice of religious vocation would be the one between the self-ideal and the institutional-ideal (self-ideal-in-situation or SI-II) (Rulla, 1967) in contrast with the relationship between self concept and institutional ideal (PB-II) which rather specifies the choices of non-religious vocationers.

Thus, the structural approach considers mán as a composite of a definite number of structures, of subsystems of the self: the actual-self, the ideal-self, and their components (cfr. p. 7); these subsystems are distinct, but dynamically related among themselves by some qualitative patterns; these patterns are specific for each vocational event they influence. Therefore, these events are predicted according to specific *qualitative* structural patterns of the self which are not subject to the quantitative variations of cultural or situational influences and, therefore, are more enduring dispositions. The structural approach to the study of vocation sorts out trends and dispositions which may be considered as transcultural and transsituational. Of course, these dispositions are more or less

20

influenced by different environments, but the environments act always through these structural dispositions, regardless of the different contents which characterize them. For instance, a historical period of rapid, sometimes radical changes of socio-cultural elements may lead to confusion about vocational values and attitudes, i.e., about the self-ideal-in-situation; these social changes would increase the *number* of structural vocational inconsistencies and thus would increase the dropping out; however, they would not change the basic psychodynamic *mechanism* of dropping out. These same mechanisms are considered to be the relevant dispositions for dropping out of males or females, of seminarians or religious, of people who belong to different religious orders, to different countries, etc., either in the same historical period or in different ones. In this sense, the structural approach followed in this research project is, perhaps, a qualitatively new contribution to the research done up to now in the field of religious vocation.

The structural approach to the study of vocation may be applied according to the two previously described strategies: the multidimensional and the typological. This is what is done in the present book: various vocational events are interpreted or predicted by assessing the content, the " what " in function of specific patterns of the structures of the self, of the " how ", as they are formulated in the theory of self-transcendent consistency.

The concrete ways in which the two strategies are applied in the book will be described when the various issues (entrance, dropping out, etc.) will be considered. Here, only the guidelines of them will be presented.

Chapters 5 and 6 apply the structural approach according to the multidimensional strategy: clusters of intercorrelation among scaled variables, like trust, affiliation, domination, etc., are used to see the recurring patterns of relationship among the subsystems of the self (e.g., ideal-self and its components, etc.), which—according to the theory—are supposed to influence entrance into vocation. In other words: the " what " of trust, affiliation, helps to see the " how ", i.e., to see the patterns of relationship among the subsystems of the self which influence entrance.

Chapters 7, 8, and 9, will, at least in part, use the struc-

21

tural approach according to a typological strategy: types of vocational consistencies or inconsistencies are sorted out according to the structural conceptualization of the theory. As in chapters 5 and 6, these types of consistencies or inconsistencies are characterized by recurring, specific patterns among the subsystems of the self; they represent the " how " which determines the relevance of the " what ", i.e., the importance of the different variables like affiliation, domination. Furthermore, these types are assessed in *each* individual separately.

Thus, the consistencies or inconsistencies underlying the entering or the leaving of vocation are related only to the actual expectations (from *personal* values and attitudes) and needs of each individual and prescind from the norms which characterize a vocational group or a socio-cultural milieu. Therefore, the results of this structural-typological strategy are even more transituational, transcultural, transtemporal than the ones obtained by means of the structural-multidimensional strategy.

Of course, the actual relevance of the different types of consistencies or inconsistencies in influencing entering, leaving vocation, etc., depends on their " centrality " (cfr. Chapters 1 and 3). However, since centrality means the psychological significance of the consistency or inconsistency of a variable for an *individual* person, it can be used only in the typological strategy which studies each individual separately, as it is used, at least in part, in chapters 7, 8, and 9. Therefore, it cannot be utilized as such in chapters 5 and 6 which deal with groups; a different operationalization of the concept of centrality, i.e., of functional significance is necessary for the group study. The operationalization used in these chapters will have the following characteristics.

First of all, only *inconsistencies or conflicts* will be studied because of the reasons discussed in chapters 4, 5 and 6.

Secondly, such inconsistencies or conflicts will be considered to be " central " when a *statistically* significant analysis shows that the inconsistent variable discriminates two groups in one direction for the *latent*-self while the same or a clinically similar variable discriminates the two groups in the opposite direction for the *ideal-self*; for instance, for people who enter religious life a central inconsistency for succorance is present when, for this variable, they are higher in the latent-self but lower in the ideal-self when compared to people who do not enter. This double and opposite statistically significant difference between the two groups for the latent-self vs. the ideal-self is necessary in order to allow a more reliable interpretation of the data. In fact, in this study the structures of the self in the latent-self and in the ideal-self are assessed by different sets of measurements, and research shows that there is incontrovertible evidence for lack of complete congruence among these measurements. However, by using the foregoing double and opposite statistical significance, it is possible to implement what Fiske (1971) calls "the wisest strategy" of measuring personality available at present, i.e., to treat each mode of measurement as a construct in its own right.

Thirdly, the foregoing central inconsistencies or conflicts will be considered more acceptable in the interpretation of the findings if the variables which are centrally inconsistent are more than one, especially if they form a clinical cluster.

Fourthly, subconscious needs which are particularly *dissonant* with the vocational values or attitudes proclaimed by individuals are apparently greater liabilities for vocation.

At the end of these introductory chapters, it is important to make explicit a basic assumption underlying both the theoretical and empirical tasks of understanding religious vocation. A set of distinct average scores on personality tests, though valuable, is rather far from being a complete picture of a vocationer's personality. Man is not only, nor especially, a composite of an indefinite number of *separate* psychological tendencies, nor is vocation sufficiently explained in terms of role, professional career or other concepts related to cross-sectional aspects of personality. This is particularly true if the focus of inquiry is the significance of the basic vocational motivations for entrance, perseverance and effectiveness in vocation. The various individual motivational characteristics should be estimated in terms of the dynamic relationships among the major parts of the personality: it is the dynamic balance or imbalance among such parts which determines the predominant motivation of a person.

The study of religious vocation, in this sense, cannot be separated from, because it is actually part of the general inquiry into the meaning of human existence.

23

CHAPTER 3

EXPERIMENTAL PROCEDURES AND DESIGN

A. THE SUBJECTS

As already mentioned in the introduction, the experimental subjects of this study were religious of both sexes and seminarians; lay students of both sexes from Catholic colleges served as control groups. The age of the subjects was 18 to 20. The numbers of the participants were already given in the Introduction. Table 3.1 shows the distribution of groups of subjects by institution and training center or setting. Notice that in the case of the religious male subjects, there are two training centers or settings which belong to the same religious institution (Institution I) and one training center for seminarians (Institution II). Similarly, in the case of the female subjects, training centers or settings 1 and 2 belong to the same religious institution (Institution I) while training center 3 belongs to another (Institution II). The lay control students came from four different centers: two for males and two for females.

The subjects of the experimental group came from the Midwest, East, and West of the United States; the ones of the Control group, prevailingly from the Midwest. However it was assured that the representative samples for the control group would match with the religious population in age, high school grades, Catholic and rural-urban background; also, an appropriate matching in socio-economic class was obtained by considering the father's occupation and education. The foregoing data were abstracted especially from the biographical inventory (Appendix B-4).

B. THE PSYCHOLOGICAL INSTRUMENTS AND THEIR RATIONALE

1. *The Modified Activities Index*

A modification of the Activities Index (Stern, 1958, 1970) was devised in order to measure the self-concept, self-ideal, and institutional ideal of the subjects.

24

The Activites Index (AI) in its standard form yields information about 30 needs corresponding to the list developed by Murray (1930) through answers given by subjects to 300 items presented in a like-dislike format. In the modification (MAI) devised for this study, each item is responded to three times by the subject with different instructional sets, so that for each of the variables, information is obtained about the present behavior (MAI-PB) of the respondent, his self-ideal (MAI-SI), and the perception of the institution's ideal (MAI-II). This modification should allow the determination of how each subject sees himself, how he would like to be, and how he perceives the demands of the institution. In this way, information about both *self-concept* and *self-ideal* of subjects is made available. More will be said later when discussing the theoretical reasons for the selection and use of these tests; suffice it here to report with reference to the list of Murray's needs, a quotation by Jackson who has developed a test recently using this same conceptualization. Jackson maintains that the systems of variables emphasized in Murray's (1938) theory of personality possesses the advantages " of conveying broadly, if not exhaustively, the spectrum of personality needs, states, and dispositions, of possessing a carefully worked out and polished definition and of having a good deal of theoretical and empirical underpinnings " (Jackson, 1970, p. 67; Wiggins, 1973, p. 410).

For the special purposes of this research and because of their special relevance to religious life, seven other scales were added to the list of those used by Stern in the Activities Index (AI), e.g., piety, mortification, obedience. For these new scales, some of the items present in Stern's Index were used and additional items were written. Appendix B-1 lists all the scales of the MAI, including the six special scales used in this study.

Because of the basic modification of the instructional sets and the addition of the seven scales, reliability and validity could not be assumed on the basis of the previous extensive work of Stern. Measures of internal consistency and stability had to be obtained for the MAI. Using a sample of 52 male religious and a sample of 48 lay control students, a rank order correlation coefficient (rho) and a Pearson product moment correlation were obtained among the three sets of data (PB, SI, II) for each scale in order to provide information concerning linearity of relationships. Tables 3.2, 3.3, 3.4 and 3.5 show the coefficients for both the religious and lay groups. This analysis establishes the extent to which the breakdown of the AI into its three components (PB, SI, II) leaves intact the three components' homogeneity as measuring devices.

Using the same samples, an item analysis was also performed

to determine the power of each item to discriminate between the two groups, religious and lay, in each of the scales considered. A Pearson product-moment correlation of .25 or more was considered necessary for the item inclusion. Table 3.6 shows the results of this analysis.

For another analysis of internal consistency, the protocols of a subsample of 100 subjects constituted of equal numbers of men from religious and lay college groups were submitted to an item analysis in order to determine the point bi-serial r between each item and its total scale score. In this analysis, because of the limited number of items in each scale, Guilford's (1954) procedure for correcting this correlation for the contribution of the item under analysis to the total score was used. With such an analysis, the presence of a significant correlation is an indication that the item is to be included in the scale. Table 3.7 shows the number and percentages of item/total correlations falling at different significant levels for the MAI-PB, MAI-SI, MAI-II versions of the MAI. There is a high similarity between the results obtained for the 30 original scales of the AI and for the seven religious scales. Correlations of individual items with their scales beyond the point .005 level appear in the overwhelming majority of cases and item/total correlations failing to reach significance are limited to a very few cases.

However, the decision to drop an item not significant in one version of the test depended on its contribution to the other versions of the MAI. A further analysis revealed that 66% (19 scales) of the original 29 scales contain only items significantly correlated with their total scale scores across all three versions of the test, and that the same was true for 55% (4 scales) of the seven religious scales. 28% (8 scales) of the original 29 scales and 17% (1 scale) of the religious scales contained one item that did not correlate significantly with their total scale score in only one version of the test.

Finally, 10% (3 scales) of the 29 original scales and 14% (1 scale) of the seven religious scales contained two items that did not correlate significantly with the total scale score in only one version of the test. As it was found that every one of the items failing to correlate significantly with its total scale score on one version of the test was significantly correlated with its total scale score on the other two versions of the test, the decision was made to keep these items in the test.

To assess the stability or generalizability over time of the MAI, a subsample of 36 females from both religious and lay college groups was given the test on two different occasions separated by one month. The range of the product-moment correlations between test and retest on the 29 original scales was from .30 to .84 with a mean of

.70 for the MAI-PB, from .37 to .86 with a mean of .70 for MAI-SI, and from .37 to .87 with a mean of .67 for MAI-II. The medians were between .71 and .72 for MAI-PB, .68 for MAI-SI, and .67 for MAI-II. The range of the product-moment correlations for the test-retest for six of the seven religious scales was from .34 to .81 with a mean of .69 for MAI-PB, from .31 to .85 with a mean of .61 for MAI-SI, and from .50 to .84 with a mean of .64 for MAI-II. The medians were between .70 and .72 for MAI-PB, .62 and .69 for MAI-SI, and .59 and .63 for MAI-II. The statistical significance of these correlations was also tested and they all appeared statistically significant on the 35 scales mentioned with p-values exceeding the .0005 level in all cases except eight. Because of its low test-retest correlations, one of the seven religious scales was dropped.

2. The General Goals of Life Inventory (GGLI) and The Modified General Goals of Life Inventory (MGGLI)

In order to obtain information about values, the General Goals of Life Inventory (GGLI) of the Educational Testing Service (1950) was given to each subject. The format of the test is a twenty items forced choice, yielding a rank ordering of ideals pertaining to biological, social, and religious concerns. An additional item was added concerning intellectual endeavor. A modified form of this test was also given following the same patterns as already explained for the MAI. In Appendix B-2, the reader will find the list of the 21 variables as well as this modified form where each of the 21 items was responded to three times by the subject to obtain information about his present behavior (MGGLI-PB), his self-ideal (MGGLI-SI), and his perception of the institution's ideals (MGGLI-II) for the particular value corresponding to each of the 21 items.

To assess the stability of this modified form of the test, a sub-sample of 25 religious women took the MGGLI on two occasions separated by approximately a month. The range of the percentages of correspondence between test and retest on the 21 scales was from .68 to 1.0 with a mean of .88 for the MGGLI-PB, from .68 to 1.0 with a mean of .90 for MGGLI-SI, and from .68 to 1.0 with a mean of .86 for MGGLI-II. The medians were .88 for MGGLI-PB, .92 for MGGLI-SI, and .88 for MGGLI-II. The statistical significance of these percentages was also tested and all the p-values found were less than .01 except for one scale which was less than .06.

3. The Projective Techniques

a) The Thematic Apperception Test (TAT)

Two projective techniques were administered in the study to obtain information at a less conscious level of the self. The first consisted of the administration of six cards of the Thematic Apperception Test (TAT) (cards 1, 2, 6GF, 12M, 14, 19 for males and cards 1, 2, 6GF, 8GF, 12F, 19 for females) prepared by Morgan and Murray (1935) and a group picture from Henry and Guetzkow (1951). For details in the administration procedure, see the following section "Procedure of Testing" in this same Chapter 3.

The stories given by the subjects on each card were analyzed separately according to a scoring system for the presence (1) or absence (0) of a list of needs, emotional styles, defenses, and conflicts. The list of needs follows Murray's (1938) classification and his definitions were used for scoring. Emotional styles and defenses are found in the psychoanalytic literature and Erikson's (1950) conceptualization was used for the list of conflicts. In Appendix B-3, the reader will find a sample of the scoring sheet for the TAT with the list of needs, emotional styles, and conflicts. The analysis of each protocol, requiring approximately 1 ½ hours, was made separately by Rulla and Maddi without knowledge of the group to which the subject belonged. A comparison of their results was subsequently made to resolve scoring disagreements or confirm independent agreements. Periodic controls were instituted to check interscorer agreement. Such agreement was established analyzing the interscorers' consistency over 30 protocols. For the emotional styles, the range of independent agreement was from 78 to 98 percent with a mean of 86.95 percent and a median falling between 80 and 90 percent. The scoring of needs showed an agreement ranging from 55 to 94 percent with a mean of 82.95 percent and a median of 88 percent. The range of agreement for defenses was from 63 to 95 percent with a mean of 81.83 percent and a median falling between 89 and 85 percent. All these levels of agreement were found to be statistically highly significant.

Having established interscorer agreement or internal consistency in terms of generalizability over scorers (Cronbach, 1971), the generalizability over the components of each measurement was to be established. A sample of 20 males and 20 females from both religious and lay groups were selected for an analysis of homogeneity. Considering each card as an item in a total test consisting of seven cards, the reliability coefficients obtained using the Kuder-Richardson 20 (K-R 20) ranged for the emotional styles from .46 to .81 with a median between .68 and .74. The K-R 20 values for needs ranged from .25 to .88 with a median of .75, and for the defenses the K-R 20 values were from .22 to .86 with a median of .60. The values of the K-R 20 for the eight conflicts finally ranged from .38 to .84 with a median between .73 and .79. All these results were statistically significant and can be considered surprisingly good for a projective instrument.

b) The Rotter Incomplete Sentences Blank (ISB)

The second projective technique used was the Incomplete Sentences Blank (ISB) of Rotter (1950).

The scoring of this test was made according to the same list of variables as for the TAT by the same persons, Rulla and Maddi, using the completed sentence as a unit of analysis instead of the story given on a card. Such scoring was made for each subject immediately after the scoring of the TAT. Again, the scoring was made independently at first without knowledge of the group to which a protocol belonged, and then notes were compared to resolve disagreements. To establish interscorer agreement while working independently, 25 protocols were selected at different times during scoring. Percentages of agreement ranged from 75 to 88 percent for the emotional styles, with a mean of 83 percent and a median of 85 percent. Agreements for the needs ranged from 47 to 91 percent with a mean of 83.50 percent and a median of 85 percent. The range of agreement on the defenses was from 67 to 90 percent with a mean of 83 percent and a median of between 75 and 80 percent. For the conflicts, the range of agreement was from 75 to 92 percent with a mean of 85.30 percent and a median of 85 percent. All the above levels of agreement were statistically significant.

4. *The Biographical Inventory*

The Biographical Inventory was given to obtain information on basic biographical data concerning the individual and his family, religion and the religiosity of parents, the nature and amount of schooling, ethnic origin, socio-economic status, and geographic location, etc. This inventory provides other information, also, about the subject's perceptions of some basic intrafamilial relationships, i.e., father-mother-siblings, about the influence of significant persons in his environment.

For the test of stability of the 15 variables of the Biographical concerning family relationships (Appendix B-4, question 55), a test-retest procedure was undertaken. Twenty-eight subjects, representing both males and females, were tested about 3 weeks apart. Pearson r correlation coefficients were computed. As 5 of the 15 scales measuring relationships of the subjects with mother did not reach a statistically significant correlation in this analysis, they were excluded from this study. These scales were: Trusting—Distrustful, Understanding—Unsympathetic, Critical-Forgiving, Envious—Appreciative, Openminded—Closedminded. The stability coefficients for relationships with the mother, on the 10 retained variables, ranged from .41 to .97 with a mean of .65 and a median of .63; for relationships with the father, the range was from .47 to .82, with a mean of .68 and a median of .70; for relationships between parents, the coefficients ranged from .34 to .94 with a mean of .67 and a median of .74.

Although the information is suitably coded to yield quantitative measurements, only a small part of the data are considered in this book. Appendix B-4 is a form of this Inventory.

5. *The Rationale for the Use of the Instruments*

Turning now to the question why these particular instruments were adopted for the present study, we will explain some of the logical connections between the instruments selected and the relevant conceptualization outlined in chapter 1. The importance of the logical step, making explicit the connection between the conceptual frame of reference, its concepts and the operationalization of the constructs used, has been frequently and recently emphasized (Fiske, 1971, 1973).

Three major focuses of the theoretical framework adopted in this study will be considered here: first, the emphasis on self-transcendent consistency; second, the dynamic motivational approach with its specific attention to the conscious as well as to the subconscious motivation; and, third, the structural approach with its emphasis on " centrality " and other qualitative dimensions.

a) The Emphasis on Self-transcendent Consistency

One of the characteristics underlying the theoretical conceptualization followed in this work is its emphasis on what has been defined as self-transcendent consistency. The choice of religious vocation is conceived to be related not so much to what the person is or how he sees himself, but rather to what he would like to be, to what he *ideally* would like to do with the help of God. Also, perseverance and effectiveness of religious vocation are seen to correlate with consistencies and inconsistencies of the actual self with the vocational attitudes and/or vocational values (Rulla, 1971, pp. 50, 56).

30

The division of the self into *actual* and *ideal* self flows directly from this conceptualization. On the one hand, self-transcendence is made possible and actualized through the presence and functions of a self-ideal as distinct from the actual self while, on the other hand, consistency implies a functional coherence between the actual and ideal components of the self.

The problem of finding an operational definition of this conceptualization had to be solved. The Activities Index (AI) with its three hundred item format, based on like-dislike answers, appeared to be ill-fitted to the characteristic dimensions of Religious life constituting the very object of inquiry. Such a format with its like-dislike choice of answers immediately placed the test in a theoretical frame of reference which focused on and had as an underlying assumption a purely self-fulfilling view of the human person and vocation. Little space was left for the respondent to express that self-transcendent tendency believed to be inherent in the typically human capacity to make a " project " of his life by establishing a self-ideal in the light of personal and/or institutional social sets of values. Little room was left for any consideration regarding the action of the Supernatural Grace of God acting through these higher functions of man.

A modification of the test was therefore necessary which would provide an appropriate expression and assessment of the *ideal* dimension of the person as distinct from the *actual* one. Hence, the introduction of the new sets of responses: PB, SI, II and the substitution of the choice-format " consistent ", " inconsistent ", " irrelevant ", for the previous " like ", " dislike ".

Such a modification of the test, therefore, offers the means of measuring the ideal-self dimension of the person as distinct from the actual one. A look at the component elements of this ideal-self is thus necessary.

As the ideal-self is constituted by both *attitudes* and *values*, it was important to make use of two different tests measuring independently these two sets of self-attributes in a way which would be consistent with the reasoning reported above. Accordingly, the modification of set and format was applied both to the GGLI (values) (MGGLI) and to the AI (attitudes) (MAI). In this way, measurements were available of the ideal-self as expressed in values or end-states of existence and of the ideal-self as expressed in attitudes (cf. chapter 1). Furthermore, as *attitudes* are conceived to be response predispositions including both an *affective-conative* component and a more *cognitive* component, the MAI-SI provided a fitting measurement for the first of these aspects, the affective-conative, and the MAI-II for the second, the more cognitive component.

31

Having indicated the relationship between *ideal-self* and its measuring instruments, let us now turn to the conceptualization and measurement of the *actual-self*.

Two sets of measurements were used to assess two aspects of the actual-self: self-concept, and latent-self.

First, the *self-concept* part of the actual-self was measured by the MAI-PB. This set of measurements is particularly directed at the assessment of *traits* conceived as consistently manifested patterns of behavior expressing a response *capability*. The concept of trait or capability as constituent of the actual-self is to be distinguished from the concept of attitude, mentioned above when discussing the ideal-self.

By way of digression, let us mention here that the combination of capability (PB) and predisposition (SI-II) are conceived to constitute a *habit*. The importance of a precise formulation and assessment of these concepts can be evaluated in the light of their relevance to basic problem areas as moral conduct, on the one hand, and the field of psychopathology, on the other. Arnold (1960) has discussed the relationship between the concept of habit and the concepts of virtue and vice, and Freud (1943) has always used the notion of trait both in relation to the notion of symptom and that of character trait.

For a more detailed discussion of all the above conceptualizations, see Rulla (1971, pp. 37-40; see also, Wallace, 1966, 1967). It is important to note here that traits as well as attitudes in the total dynamics of the personality may be expected and are found to have both needs and values at their motivational and operational roots. An accurate assessment of traits and attitudes may be of central importance when the focus of interest is on the relative weight of need or value motivation.

The second component of the actual-self, the *latent-self*, was measured by the TAT and Rotter ISB, which are known to assess the prevailingly subconscious aspects of the self.

b) The Dynamic-motivational Approach

The second general aspect of the conceptualization to be discussed in connection with the selection of specific instruments is the dynamic motivational approach with its emphasis on subconscious processes. The theoretical framework followed in this study stresses and makes constant reference (see chapter 1) to the distinction between conscious and subconscious self-attributes and processes.

This view, taking into account and generally attributing greater weight to subconscious processes, in particular to subconscious inconsistencies, has been treated elsewhere (Rulla, 1971; Wylie, 1957).

The assessment value of the TAT has been discussed extensively (Murstein, 1963; Zubin, Eron, and Schumer, 1965; Rabin, 1968; Fiske and Pearson, 1970). Today, clinicians and research workers seem to agree that the TAT is not " fantasy " in the sense of " primary process "; that it reveals not only impulses, needs, or affects projected on the character with whom the storyteller identifies, but also defensive and adaptive processes. Lazarus (1961) suggested that as the intensity of needs is increased, various ego controls will be brought into play as a result of the organism's stress. Among the ego control processes that are assumed to modify fantasy expression of needs are anxiety (McClelland et alii, 1953; Feshback, 1961), guilt (Clark, 1952) and mechanisms of defense determined by them. Pittluck (1950) showed the influence of anxiety motivating mechanisms of defense and found that the tendency to use these mechanisms was negatively related to the tendency to act out.

Other elements were also found to influence TAT content. Subjects can " control " to some extent the amount of self-attributes in the stories (Murstein, 1965; Kaplan and Eron, 1965; Ismir, 1963; Tutko, 1964). The subjects' interpretations and expectations concerning situations and the examiner may influence their products (Levy, Schumer and Zubin, 1964; Fiske, 1971).

It seemed, therefore, that the assessment of a need in TAT material should be done not in terms of raw scores but rather in terms of its percentages over all the variables scored including mechanisms of defense, guilt, and depression which may have a defensive purpose. The scoring of the TAT in this study adhered to these criteria including needs, emotions, and defenses as well as conflicts. For details concerning emotions and needs, see Appendix B-5. The definitions of defenses are well known throughout the depth-psychology literature.

An important feature of the present approach is the special attention used in keeping the definition of the variables constant when such variables were used across tests, that is, in different instruments, measuring different levels of the self. For instance, the TAT scoring on the variable like succorance was done while constantly keeping in mind Murray's definition (see Appendix B-5) of that dimension, the same definition being at the basis of Stern's construction of the corresponding scale of the AI and, therefore, of the MAI.

An objection could be raised here concerning the use of the variables at different levels of personality. Research, particularly about the need for achievement (McClelland, 1958; Lindzey and Heinemann, 1955, McClelland et al. 1953; De Charms, Morrison, Reitman and McClelland, 1955), has demonstrated that, whereas fantasy measures tap personal goals, structured self-descriptive measures, aiming at the measurement of the same need, tap social goals. As a consequence, objectors hold that the correlation between two types of measurements is absent or mild.

The answer to this objection is that, aside from the fact that these studies do not consider ego-control factors and anxiety levels, their results may be favorable rather than unfavorable to the methodological implementation of the theoretical assumptions made here. The assumption in this book is that religious vocation requires an integration of the " persona " with personality and, therefore, a consistency between personal and social goals.

We have here an instance of the implementation of the structural approach mentioned in Chapter 2. There, its connection with the self-transcendent consistency theory is presented; here, we see how it has been operationally applied.

c) The Structural Approach

In the framework of the assumption delineated at the end of chapter 2 concerning the dynamic unity of the person, the structural approach, endeavoring to evaluate personal psychodynamics, focuses on the individual as a composite of a definite number of structures or subsystems of the self.

The theoretical approach adopted here combines, in its assessment procedures, the " how " and the " what "—the structure of the self and its content. The " what " is assessed as characterizing vocational events only in function of the " how ".

In this section we will attempt to show how we have implemented this point of view in the measurement procedures of individual psychodynamics. How the structural approach was implemented when dealing with groups has already been indicated in chapter 2 and will be further explained in chapters 5 and 6. Here we will consider the individual approach to personality that will be used predominantly in chapters 7, 8, and 9.

In the previous section of this chapter we have already seen how the adoption and use of specific instruments (MAI-PB, SI, II, TAT, Rotter ISB) resulted in the measurements of the different subsystems of the self (i.e., actual-self and ideal-self).

We have also pointed out that a continuity of dimensional content (e.g., aggression, nurturance) was maintained across tests or subtests so that the obtained measurements were suitably applied to the study of the relationships between different substructures of the personality.

The core measurement of this relationship focused on the continuum consistency/inconsistency. By its very nature this focus on consistency/inconsistency reveals the structural approach.

The task at hand was to determine and find an appropriate measurement for certain structural aspects or qualities affecting the consistency/inconsistency of each content variable in every individual. This determination should be made in view of obtaining a quantitative measurement of the psychodynamic weight of each consistency/inconsistency as expressed in specific content variables. Although these measurements were formulated in quantitative terms, they were basically determined by and therefore, expressive of qualitative structural features of the self and its substructures. To give an example, if we were to find that a person obtained a score of 15 for his inconsistency on aggression, we would have to keep in mind that this score was not the sum of 15 items endorsed by him on a test scale of 20 items measuring aggression. Instead, this score was the quantitative expression of a specific psychodynamic content (e.g., aggression) assessed in function of certain structural qualities as level, type, and degree of internal inconsistency between his actual and ideal-self.

It is to these structural qualities of consistency/inconsistency that we now turn in order a) to identify them, b) to indicate their theoretical relevance, and c) to explain how they were used in the specific assessing strategies adopted in this book.

Having already mentioned the structural characteristic of the concept of consistency/inconsistency (chapter 2), we will consider the following structural qualities in this section: *centrality, type, level,* and *degree.*

Centrality. A simple way of using the data obtained from the different tests would be to evaluate, for each content variable (e.g., aggression, nurturance), the degree of discrepancy (inconsistency if high, consistency if low) between substructures of personality such as actual-self and ideal-self. This step was considered not only necessary but insufficient as well. As many authors have pointed out (McClelland, 1961; Hovland, 1960; Sears, 1968; Maddi, 1968; etc.), under some conditions, inconsistency is tolerated and even sought out. Therefore, our search is to establish not only the presence of any inconsistency but also whether the consistency/inconsistency is relevant for perseverance and effectiveness in religious life. In other words, we should be able to establish if this consistency/inconsistency is *central* in the psychodynamics of the individual, i.e., if it has a *functional* significance for the vocational life of the individual under consideration. After a brief indication of the rationale of the concept, we will present its operational definition.

The factors which are crucial and determinant in making a consistency/inconsistency functionally significant for the individual have often been presented in the literature, but as separate units, i.e., not as operationally interdependent and dynamically convergent toward the same process. A conceptualization presented elsewhere (Rulla, 1971, pp. 73ff.) where three factors were selected and integrated in a dynamic framework, is now summarized:

" 1. A self-attribute may determine a functionally significant consistency or inconsistency if ... it is relevant for the achievement of personal goals.

2. ... the same self-attribute should show ego-centrality, i.e., a centrality for self-esteem (French-Sherwood, 1965; Smith, 1968); this ego-centrality may be present at a conscious or at a subconscious level. Thus, for instance, a functionally significant inconsistency for vocation may be present if the individual has a positive affect (self-esteem centrality, conscious or at least subconscious) toward, e.g., aggression which he may consider not to be instrumental to the attainment of religious vocation: what is attractive (aggression in self-esteem centrality) is not acceptable to the person for his own ideals for religious vocation (aggression as his vocational goal); in other words, his emotional wanting is dissonant with his rational wanting.

3. However, for a consistency or an inconsistency to be functionally significant, a third factor, mentioned by Arnold (1960) and by Kelman and Baron (1968) is necessary. This third factor is the adequacy or inadequacy of the individual's coping mechanisms toward the achievement of his vocational goals. Thus, in the case of inconsistency, the unacceptable attraction, which is the result of the other two factors, becomes really functionally significant in the life of a person if it is *kept* in the center of his attention; but this is possible only if there is a relevant inadequacy of the person's coping mechanisms toward such unacceptable attraction; for instance, referring to the previous example about aggression, the coping mechanisms of the individual do not succeed to avoid the fact that aggression remains in the center of attention of his emotional wanting, which is dissonant with his rational wanting.

We can conclude that functionally significant consistency or inconsistency for religious vocation is present when there is consistency or inconsistency among the three factors 1) of vocational goals, 2) of self-esteem, and 3) of adequacy or inadequacy of coping mechanisms for the same variable. Seen in this perspective, functionally significant inconsistencies can be equated with conflicts, at least in the sense that in both *an unacceptable attraction remains in the center of attention* ".

The operational identification of the three factors determining the functional significance of consistency/inconsistency was basically made by using the same three substructures of personality already mentioned (LS, PB, SI-II). Chart 2 will guide our reasoning by showing the three factors and their corresponding operational identification.

CHART 2

THE THREE FACTORS OF FUNCTIONALLY SIGNIFICANT
CONSISTENCIES AND INCONSISTENCIES

THE FACTORS	THEIR OPERATIONAL IDENTIFICATION
1 - Relevance of a self-attribute for the achievement of one's goals.	1 - SI-II congruence or lack of congruence for one of the "general attitudes", e.g. aggression.
2 - Centrality (conscious or subconscious) of the *same* self-attribute (e.g. aggression) for maintaining a positive self-conception or self-esteem.	2 - PB-(SI-II) congruence or discrepancy for conscious centrality. - LS-(SI-II) congruence or discrepancy for subconscious centrality.
3 - Adequacy or inadequacy of person's coping mechanisms in handling the *same* self-attribute (e.g. aggression) toward the achievement of his goals.	3 - The proportion to which the *same* self-attribute is present in the actual self (conscious, i.e. PB, or subconscious, i.e., LS) of the individual in comparison with his other self-attributes.

(Rulla, 1971, p. 76)

1) The vocational relevance of these general attitudes for a person was operationally identified by means of the congruence between his self-ideal (SI) and his role concept (II) for each one of the general attitudes. This congruence had been empirically established by Rulla (1967) and has been confirmed by the findings presented in chapters 5 and 6 of this book. Accordingly, the relevance of congruence was assumed in the present assessment procedures, and the operational identification of this factor consisted in taking into consideration the personal dimension of the ideal self expressed as a unit in the SI-II. Computationally, an average score of the SI and II was obtained to represent this factor. SI-II will appear again in the operational identification of the second factor. For the reasons given in chapter 1 as well as in Rulla (1971, pp. 60-66), it was decided to use only general attitudes (like abasement, achieve-

ment, etc.) and to exclude vocational values as means to detect *initial* vocational consistencies and inconsistencies.

 " 2) The centrality of the *same* self-attribute for self-esteem. Commonly used techniques for measuring self-esteem include self-report questionnaires and the congruence (or high correlation) or the discrepancy (or low correlation) between actual- and ideal-self qualities. The degree of congruence (or correlation) between the manifest-self concepts (PB) and the self-ideal-in-situation (SI-II) for each self-attribute can be indicative of this dimension on the conscious level. On the subconscious level, such a centrality is implicitly expressed in the LS-(SI-II) congruence or discrepancy, as the following discussion will show.

 3) The adequacy or the inadequacy of the person's coping mechanism in using the *same* self-attribute toward the achievement of his goals " (Rulla, 1971, p. 77).

The assumption adhered to is that there is a dynamic interdependence of the attributes of a person. As many authors have observed (Secord, 1968; French and Sherwood, 1965; Aronson, 1968; Brehm and Cohen, 1962; Festinger, 1957, 1964; McGuire, 1966, 1969) an individual has a trend in self-reports to increase what he considers the desirable self-attributes and to diminish the undesirable ones. The same can be said, at least to some extent, for the content of the projective tests (see, e.g., Murstein, 1965; Levy, Schumer and Zubin, 1964; Kaplan and Eron, 1965; etc.).

Accordingly, all scoring was based on percentages rather than raw scores (see Rulla, 1971, pp. 77-80). These scores were taken as indicative of the adequacy or inadequacy of the person's coping mechanisms in handling the same self-attribute toward the achievement of his goal. These percentage scores were accepted as suitable measurements of the third factor of centrality, both on the conscious and subconscious level.

We can see at this point where we stand in reference to an operational identification of functionally significant consistencies and inconsistencies. Chart 3 will help us to synthesize the foregoing discussion and prepare for the operational definition.

CHART 3

TYPES OF FUNCTIONALLY SIGNIFICANT INTRAPERSONAL VOCATIONAL CONSISTENCIES
AND INCONSISTENCIES

	I	II	III	IV
Mean over all evaluations →	Need and Attitude	Need and Attitude	Need Attitude	Attitude Need
Types of Consistencies and Inconsistencies	SC for Con. SoI for Dis.	SoI for Con. SC for Dis.	PsC for Con. PsI for Dis.	PsI for Con. PsC for Dis.

N.B. SC = Social Consistency   SoI = Social Inconsistency
PsC = Psychological Consistency   Con. = Self-attribute consonant with vocational values
PsI = Psychological Inconsistency   Dis. = Self-attribute dissonant with vocational values

(Rulla, 1971, p. 85)

The *first factor* is represented by the presence of the general attitude in every column of the figure: the SI-II is the measured dimension of the ideal-self corresponding to " attitude ".

The *second factor* is indicated by the difference between the first two columns (I and II) and the other two (III and IV): in the first two columns, the discrepancy of need and attitude (be it conscious: PB-(SI-II), or subconscious: LS-(SI-II)) is low so that need and attitude are correlated, whereas in the other two columns (III and IV) need and attitude are discrepant.

The *third factor* is finally indicated by the difference of columns I and III, on the one hand, and columns II and IV, on the other. Columns I and III represent the cases in which the need score is above the mean of all scores, whereas columns II and IV represent the cases in which the need score is below the mean of all scores.

The operational definition is, however, still incomplete.

We have come to the point of placing consistencies and inconsistencies into patterns resulting from theoretically relevant combinations of substructural units of personality. What is particularly important, however, is that such patterns are expressed as measureable relationships and that such measurements are an appropriate expression of the factors determining the centrality or functional significance of any consistency/inconsistency. Given the measureability of these relationships, it is now possible to raise the question about how to decide which of these consistencies/inconsistencies is central and which one is not: Is there any variable whose consistency/inconsistency is not central? More precisely: How large should a correlation/discrepancy be between actual-self and ideal-self to consider factor 2 operative in determining centrality? How far should a need be above/below the mean of all needs to consider factor 3 operative in determining centrality? A cut-off point had to be established. A decision was made based on the rationale already explained concerning the basic unity of personal psychodynamics and the interdependence of variables (chapter 2; the previous section of this chapter; Rulla, 1971, pp. 77-78). It was decided to consider as *central* a consistency/inconsistency only if factor 2 (correlation/discrepancy) *and* factor 3 (need) will reach somewhat extreme scores, that is, higher or lower than the mean of at least 1/3 of a standard deviation (1/3 SD) of the distribution of all the content variables considered. In such a way, variables that were average or near average for consistency/inconsistency *and* average or near average for need/strength were *not* considered as central or functionally significant.

The first outcome of this operational definition of centrality was to qualify every content variable: some content variables appeared to be central and were retained as measurements of functionally significant dimensions of the psychodynamics of the individual's personality; others, which did not qualify for centrality, were dropped as irrelevant or non-functionally significant in the person's psychodynamics. Therefore, the content (the " what ") was assessed in function of the structure (the " how "), that is, the centrality of the consistency/inconsistency of the total personal psychodynamics.

Type. Chart 3, which was used to show the operational definition of centrality, is also used to determine and operationally define the type of consistency/inconsistency. There were 14 content variables used to define these types of consistency/inconsistency; they are listed in Appendix C-1.

We have seen that every content variable analyzed for centrality falls into one of the four columns of Chart 3, corresponding to a pattern of relationships between actual- and ideal-self. The bottom row of cells is labeled as " Types of Consistencies and Inconsistencies. " To be able to decide if a particular variable (e.g., aggression) when present with a high need and high attitude (Column I) would result in a Social Consistency or a Social Inconsistency, a decision had to be made concerning its dissonance *with vocational values,* terminal and/or instrumental (cfr. chapter 1). Obviously, a person with high need and high attitude on aggression will differ from a person with low need and low attitude on aggression, even though in both cases the discrepancy between actual-self (need) and ideal-self (attitude) is low. If we consider aggression as vocationally dissonant, then the pattern of high need and high attitude will define a social inconsistency (SoI); if we consider aggression as vocationally consonant or less dissonant, then high need and high attitude will define a social consistency (SC).

By a content analysis of the definitions of variables scored on projective techniques and of the items constituting the MAI scales, a decision was reached concerning the vocational neutrality or dissonance of each of these content variables with regard to vocational values. As vocational values let it be remembered that we refer here to the two terminal values of Union with God and Imitation of Christ as well as to the three instrumental values represented by the three evangelical counsels of poverty, chastity and obedience. These five values constituted the touchstone for establishing the vocational dissonance or vocational neutrality of specific variables. Accordingly, several variables were recognized as definitely dissonant—non-neutral—such as, aggression, abasement, etc., whereas others were considered less dissonant and more consonant—neutral— with vocational values, e.g., order, achievement. However, the psychodynamic value of each content variable was established within the total structural framework: for instance, aggression was to be considered psychodynamically an asset if present as a central consistency, and as a liability if present as a central inconsistency.

More details about this distinction of variables in terms of their vocational neutrality or dissonance will be found in Appendix C-2.

Once the dissonance or neutrality was determined, each content variable was qualified by a type of consistency/inconsistency: SC, SoI, PsC, PsI.

A coefficient was applied to each of these types so as to assign a measurement to this qualitative aspect of consistency/inconsistency. Concrete details of these coefficients are explained in Appendix C-2.

Level. A difference in level was determined by the fact that a specific consistency/inconsistency was found to be at the conscious level, PB-(SI-II), or at the subconscious level, LS-(SI-II). In this study, the PB was obtained from a questionnaire, the MAI; the subconscious level was conceptually differentiated into preconscious and unconscious: both are part of the psyche whose contents are not at the time in the conscious; but the second cannot be made conscious by ordinary rational methods (like a good examen of conscience, a meditation), while the preconscious can. The preconscious level was assessed by the Rotter ISB (LSR); the unconscious, by the TAT (LST). In fact, the Rotter is a slightly more structured test than the TAT, because the individual is asked to complete sentence stems presented by the experimenter. Therefore, it *may* tap a level of awareness somewhere between the TAT and the questionnaires. However, more precise techniques are necessary to assess a difference of level, especially for inconsistencies. These techniques are considered in the following discussion about the " degree " of consistency/inconsistency.

This difference of level, representing a structural aspect of the person's psychodynamics, was operationally defined by using a set of coefficients applied to the specific consistency/inconsistency. The weight of the coefficients assigned was based on the assumption that subconscious factors have greater influence than conscious ones on the overall individual's psychodynamics. Such an assumption is founded on empirical and clinical observations (cfr. chapter 4). Concrete details of this operationalization appear in Appendix C-3.

Degree. Two different aspects of degree of consistency/inconsistency were considered: first, the degree of consistency/inconsistency between the actual- and the ideal-self; second, the degree

42

of consistency/inconsistency *within* the actual-self, i.e., between the different substructures of the actual-self (the intra-actual-self degree of consistency/inconsistency). Measurements of the first aspect were obtained by computing the differences between the SI-II scores and the PB, LSR, and LST scores respectively. Three scores were, therefore, obtained: one expressing the degree of consistency/inconsistency for a particular variable between the ideal-self (SI-II) and the conscious actual-self (PB); the second, expressing the degree of consistency/inconsistency between the same ideal-self (SI-II) and the subconscious actual-self as the LSR of the Rotter; the third, expressing the degree of consistency/inconsistency between the same ideal-self (SI-II) and the subconscious actual-self as the LST of the TAT.

After having controlled these scores for centrality, according to the procedures explained above, the scores emerging as central were submitted to a further analysis. This analysis introduced us to the second aspect of the degree of consistency/inconsistency— the intra-actual-self degree. The three scores obtained via the above-mentioned operation represented different aspects of the actual-self in their relationship to the ideal-self. However, they also represented possible different relationships *within* the actual-self. An example may help. An individual might, at this point, appear to have a central inconsistency for aggression at the subconscious level for the LS of the TAT (LST) or of the Rotter (LSR), and at the same time to have a central consistency for aggression at the conscious level (PB). In such a case, there is a conscious consistency for PB and (SI-II) versus a subconscious inconsistency for LS and (SI-II), a pattern of obvious inconsistency within the actual-self. It would indeed make quite a difference psychodynamically to have an unconscious consistency for aggression instead of an unconscious inconsistency, when there is a consistency at the conscious level for the same variable. This structural difference was, therefore, to be taken into account and measured.

Now, if we consider that each of the two relationships, PB-(SI-II) and LS-(SI-II), can be present as consistency or as inconsistency, we could see that arithmetically there are 16 combinations possible (4 × 4). However, the possible combinations were reduced to 8 because of the obvious impossibility of having both, a consistency and an inconsistency at the same level at the same time.

Accordingly, the 8 possible combinations are as follows:

CHART 4

RANKING OF POSSIBLE
INTRA-ACTUAL-SELF CONSISTENCIES/INCONSISTENCIES

1 — PB-(SI-II) Consistency	and	LS-(SI-II) Inconsistency
2 — ⎯⎯⎯⎯⎯⎯⎯⎯⎯		LS-(SI-II) Inconsistency
3 — PB-(SI-II) Inconsistency	and	LS-(SI-II) Inconsistency
4 — PB-(SI-II) Inconsistency		⎯⎯⎯⎯⎯⎯⎯⎯⎯
5 — PB-(SI-II) Inconsistency	and	LS-(SI-II) Consistency
6 — PB-(SI-II) Consistency		⎯⎯⎯⎯⎯⎯⎯⎯⎯
7 — ⎯⎯⎯⎯⎯⎯⎯⎯⎯		LS-(SI-II) Consistency
8 — PB-(SI-II) Consistency	and	LS-(SI-II) Consistency

(Rulla, 1971, p. 88)

In view of the theoretical frame of reference proposed in this book (chapter 1), combinations 1 and 2 of the foregoing ranks are considered functionally significant vocational inconsistencies. Combinations 3, 4, and 5 can be called conflicts because the individual is still prompted to respond simultaneously in different and incompatible ways, i.e., by SI-II versus PB or LS. Combinations 6, 7, and 8 are functionally significant vocational consistencies. It will be noticed that—as mentioned in chapter 1—the foregoing ranking of combinations constitutes a continuum from inconsistency (1) to consistency (8).

A degree of intra-actual-self consistency/inconsistency was identified. A coefficient was applied to each combination constituting this ranking to express the relevance of this intra-actual-self consistency/inconsistency in the dynamics of the personality. In Appendix C-4, the reader will find a more detailed explanation of how the coefficients were determined and applied.

At this point, we seem to have achieved the task of operationally defining the structural aspects or qualities affecting the consistency/inconsistency of the substructures of the self: centrality, level, type, and degree. The measurements of these qualities can now be integrated. Before describing this integration, it is important to notice that the *level* of inconsistency can now be more precisely assessed because, according to the 8 rankings of chart 4, what is known to the subject in his PB-(SI-II) dimension is contrasted with his LS-(SI-II) dimension. Thus nn. 1 and 2 of chart 4 strongly suggest an unconscious inconsistency, while nn. 3, 4, and 5, a preconscious one. The reader may more easily visualize this implication by looking at chart 5. As already mentioned, it was decided to call nn. 1 and 2 "inconsistencies", and nn. 3, 4, and 5 "conflicts."

CHART 5

SUBSTRUCTURES OF THE SELF
AND THEIR MEASURING INSTRUMENTS

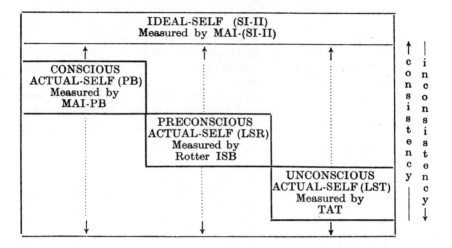

An assessment of the contribution of each content variable to the psychodynamics was obtained by adding three coefficients: a) the one for intra-actual-self consistency/inconsistency; b) the one for type (SC, SoI, PsC, PsI) of consistency/inconsistency; and c) the one for level (conscious, preconscious, unconscious.) Appendix C-5 presents the synthesis of the sums of the three coefficients for each pattern of intra-actual-self consistency/inconsistency. This table is a further development of the ranking on page 44 by including level and type.

The result of the sum of these three coefficients was multiplied by the degree of the functionally significant consistency/inconsistency expressed by the difference between the actual-self and the ideal-self-in-situation, as discussed previously.

At this point, the reader will be able to see how it was possible to compile a chart for each individual (see Appendix C-6) with a summary outline including qualitative information—inconsistencies, consistencies, and conflicts—and quantitative information—the numbers expressing the values for each content variable listed under its qualitative heading.

The sum of all the scores for inconsistencies, conflicts, and consistencies produced a final comprehensive measurement of each individual's psychodynamics. This total sum was used in calculating the various percentages.

For reasons that will be explained in chapter 7, we computed and labeled: the *degree of compliance* as the percentage of all the inconsistencies and the defensive consistencies over the total sum of the final comprehensive measurement; for the concept of defensive consistencies, see Appendix C-2; the *degree of identification* as the percentage of all the conflicts over the total sum; and the *degree of internalization* as the percentage of all the non-defensive consistencies over the total sum.

Using these three new summary scores, three indexes were developed. First, an *index of adaptation* was calculated by applying the formula $\frac{C - A}{A + C}$ where A was the degree of compliance and C, the degree of internalization. Such an index expresses the relative weight, therefore, the prevalence of the tendency toward internalization over the tendency toward compliance and vice versa. The concepts of need motivation versus value motivation come to mind in connection with the concept of prevalence of compliance over internalization and vice versa. But we have to postpone any further elaboration until chapter 7.

Second, an *index of possible growth* was calculated using the degree of identification which was first divided by 2 and then by 100. The first operation's rationale will be explained in greater detail in chapter 7. Suffice it to say that this identification score was considered to be a comprehensive measurement of two processes: internalizing identification and non-internalizing identification. It was decided to assign half of the score to the first and the other half to the second process. The division by 100 was adopted as a mathematical procedure to convert the scores into decimals for the purposes of comparison with the index of adaptation.

Third, an *index of vocational maturity* was obtained by means of an algebraic sum of the index of adaptation and the index of possible growth. This Index of Vocational Maturity was a partial expression of the total psychodynamics of the individual in terms of the structural qualities of his consistencies/inconsistencies and was measured using the content variables, such as aggression, achievement, etc., listed in Appendix C-1.

Further details of the procedures used to render the three indexes more objective will be found in Appendix C-7.

C. TYPOLOGY

At several points in the previous discussions, we have encountered the concept of types and we have seen patterns emerge. The question arises: How many types of individual psychodynamics were discernible in the assessment procedures followed in this work? A definite typology exists and originates in the theoretically relevant combination of the different structural aspects of the self. Such typology may be seen under two different aspects. The first aspect is the typology defined by the patterns of particular variables, like abasement, achievement, etc.; such typology corresponds to the different forms that a variable can take in the psychodynamics of an individual when one considers the combination of structural aspects as consistency/inconsistency, level, type, and degree.

The second aspect of the typology is defined by the specific pattern characterizing an individual person. How many types of persons in terms of the structural psychodynamics can be identified by these assessment procedures? Appendices C-5 and C-8 will help us to provide an answer to these questions.

For both typologies, the structural elements entering the composition of the particular typology were: four types of consistency/inconsistency (SC, SoI, PsC, PsI), three levels (conscious, preconscious, unconscious), eight degrees (see Chart 4).

The typology of variables. Appendix C-5 indicates that there are 28 types or patterns in which a specific variable can appear in the personal psychodynamics. Each variable will appear with the structural quality of a specific degree which will place this variable in one row (from 1 to 8) of the appendix. For each degree, the level (conscious, preconscious, unconscious) specifies other possible types. For instance, if we look at degree 1 (corresponding to conscious consistency and subconscious inconsistency), we see that two patterns can be identified: a) conscious consistency and preconscious inconsistency (first and second columns), and b) conscious consistency and unconscious inconsistency (first and third columns). Each of these allows for other patterns as PsI and SoI. How many types of variable patterns can we, therefore, define? As we have considered the conscious consistency as fulfilling its dynamic function independently of its character of PsC or SC, four types of variable patterns are possible for degree 1.

If one were to consider the preconscious and unconscious levels in combination, the patterns could be considered more numerous because the same person could be found to have: a) conscious consistency and preconscious inconsistency; b) conscious consistency and unconscious inconsistency; or c) conscious consistency and both, preconscious and unconscious inconsistency. Even though these different patterns were taken into account through the coefficients, psychodynamically, the third one was not considered different enough as to warrant the addition of a new type. In other words, the fact that an inconsistency is at the preconscious level does not seem to add anything significant to the fact that there is already an unconscious inconsistency. Following a reasoning similar to the one used for degree 1, four types are also possible for degree 2 as well as for degrees 3, 5, 7, and 8. Two types are possible for degrees 4 and 6. The total of possible types is 28.

The typology of individuals. The typology of individuals differs from that of variables in that an individual's psychodynamics are defined only by functionally significant vocational inconsistencies or consistencies (Rulla, 1971, p. 88). Accordingly, referring again to Appendix C-5, the types that would correspond to degrees 3, 4, and 5 are excluded from the typology of individuals as not functionally significant. Conflicts are important but not central in the individual's psychodynamics and, therefore, cannot be taken to define and typify such psychodynamics. Four types are defined at degrees 1 and 2 in a way similar to the definition of variable patterns. Two types are defined at degree 6 and two types at degrees 7 and 8. Why not four types at degrees 7 and 8? It was reasoned that, psychodynamically, the pattern of a preconscious consistency with (8) or without (7) conscious consistency would have to be considered equal to the pattern of an unconscious consistency with (8) or without (7) conscious consistency. Consequently only two types were considered at the degrees 7 and 8.

The types of individual intrapsychic psychodynamics will, therefore, sum up to 14: 8 types of inconsistencies and 6 types of consistencies.

The typology discussed above is expressive of the patterns of intrapsychic psychodynamics of variables or of the individual. A brief mention should be made about a typology of interpersonal dynamics. This typology will be defined by the same factors involved in the intrapsychic typology plus an additional factor characteristic of interpersonal dynamics—the fulfillment or lack of fulfillment of the values, attitudes and needs of the individual on the part of the group. This factor is considered as influencing the intrapersonal consistency of the individual and, therefore, is seen as fulfilling or not fulfilling the individual (Rulla, 1971, pp. 89-129).

Four types of interpersonal consistencies and inconsistencies can be described:

— *social consistency* (*SC*). There is fulfillment of a need, of vocational values, and of the need's corresponding attitude of the individual by the group;

48

— *psychological consistency (PsC)*. There is fulfillment of a need, of vocational values, but not of the corresponding attitude.
— *psychological inconsistency (PsI)*. No fulfillment of a need; fulfillment of vocational values and of the attitude corresponding to the need;
— *social inconsistency (SoI)*. No fulfillment of a need nor of its corresponding attitude; only fulfillment of vocational values.

Appendix C-8 shows the interaction among the four types of the intrapersonal (Ia) dimension and the four types of the interpersonal (Ir) dimension as related to perseverance and effectiveness in the religious life. Sixty-four patterns or types of influence are indicated. Appendix C-8, however, only considers four types for the intrapersonal dynamics. If we combine Appendix C-5, which summarizes all intrapsychic typology, and Appendix C-8, which summarizes interpersonal typology, we will see that for each pattern found in Appendix C-5, four patterns are available in the interpersonal dimension (summarized in the right-hand columns of Appendix C-5).

The variable-patterns typology that had 28 possibilities at the intrapsychic level will, therefore, have 28 × 4 or 112 possibilities at the interpersonal level.

The individual typology which presented 14 possible types at the intrapsychic level will present 14 × 4 or 56 possible patterns or types when intra- and interpersonal factors are considered.

D. Procedure of Testing

The selection of subjects, test design, test choice and evaluation discussed above intended to control confounding of results by irrelevant effects. Further random variables, possibly playing a role in test results, needed to be controlled in order to assure further static-free evaluation of personality. The *testing procedure* itself was so arranged to minimize the effects of " setting ", namely, the general context in which the subject takes the test.

The testing was first offered to the lay students on their college campuses, and to the religious in their training centers. Their participation in the study, free and optional, was asked as if it were a normal and valuable part of their academic experience, emphasis being placed on how it would " contribute to a greater understanding of educational practices ", as well as to their personal growth. It was made clear that those who participated would obtain results

49

concerning their own performance at the end of the study. The educational institutions themselves supported this rationale since they, too, would profit from the general conclusions of the study.

Religious groups were approached as a whole, whereas, the entering classes at the lay colleges were too large for such a procedure. Therefore, random sampling of entering lay college students was made, with care being taken to assure a representative sample of the entire class in age, high school grades, socioeconomic class, Catholic and rural-urban background. Virtually all religious subjects and 70-74% lay college students approached agreed to participate.

So as to facilitate frank and " involved " cooperation, prospective students were guaranteed anonymity. Furthermore, it was made clear to them that the personal information they offered would not be communicated to their peers, superiors or the scientific community in any manner whereby they may be identified.

The religious groups then participated in 3 testing sessions at different intervals of their four-year formation or training. Each session lasted about three days, the between-test time intervals being so arranged as to minimize fatigue and boredom. The three sessions occurred at the following times:

1) About 10 days after arrival into the religious training center (at entrance);
2) Almost 2 years later;
3) Almost 4 years following entrance.

Thus, the same tests were given three times to each group of religious.

For lay college groups, 2 testing sessions, each of about 3 days' duration were used: the first, at the end of the first week on campus; the second, at the beginning of the senior year.

The test content has been introduced above and will be elaborated on more fully in the issues to come, also. Suffice it here to say that all the directions were clearly and carefully explained in an identical manner. The TAT was group administered.

The examiner, too, was the same in nearly all cases. Father Rulla, not a part of each educational institution involved, collected the data.

E. FAMILY DYNAMICS AND DEPTH INTERVIEWS

Two types of interviews were used in this research: the Family Dynamics Interview (FI) and a Depth Interview (DI). Both of them were given by the first author.

50

The Family Dynamics Interview was administered to the religious separately from the Depth Interview, while both were done together with the lay college students.

The interviewer would prepare the FI by privately reviewing the information given by the individual in the Biographical Inventory administered at entrance into the vocational setting. The FI would take place about four months after the Biographical Inventory had been filled out. Thus, it was assumed that the person had, at least in part, forgotten the more detailed information concerning the family interaction presented by him in the Biographical Inventory.

Each FI took about a half-hour. It followed a relatively structured guide as to specific content. Examples of these procedures appear in Appendix B-5. This interview focused upon incongruences in the information obtained in the Biographical Inventory, with the view toward clarifying major family conflicts, major familial influences on the subject, and the degree of insight the subject had concerning family dynamics.

The Depth Interview (DI), the second for religious groups and the first for lay college students, took place for all subjects after about four years of training. In preparing for the Depth Interviews, the interviewer would skim through the results of the previously accomplished FI and the aspects of the Biographical Inventory most relevant to early life. In addition, he would familiarize himself with the major findings from some of the tests given to the subjects in the three testing periods: at entrance, after two and after about four years of training in the religious settings or lay colleges.

The tests considered in this intuitive analysis and their variables are outlined in Appendix B-6. The analysis of the Minnesota Multiphasic Personality Inventory (MMPI) by Hathaway and McKinley (1951) included both the *profiles* of its validity and clinical scales and the scores of other special scales; two sets of variables, for a total of 101, were assessed: a set of more psychopathological variables like the subscales described by Harris and Lingoes (1955); the anxiety and repression scales (Welsh, 1956), etc.; a second set of more psychodynamic scales like the ones devised by Finney (1965, 1966 a and b), which are more focused on drives or needs, mechanisms of defense, and the recurring patterns of personal interaction that an individual sets up with others.

Other tests used were: the 16 Personality Factors of Cattell (1957), for which, as for the MMPI, the *profiles* were evaluated as well as the second order factors considered descriptive of core tendencies; the PB (Present Behavior) scales of the MAI, previously described; four of the generalized tendencies of the Vassar Attitude

51

Inventory (Webster, Sanford, & Freedman, 1957), conceived as underlying and integrating particular attitudes and values in the person; one scale (flexibility) from the California Personality Inventory (Gough, 1956).

The total of variables assessed by all the foregoing tests was 162 at each of the three testing periods. This evaluation was made by means of an intuitive analysis which considered: 1) at entrance, for each variable of each individual, the difference between the score of the variable for the individual and the mean obtained for that variable in the entering group to which the individual belonged; 2) for the second or third testings, the mean for the entire group of the difference between the first testing and the second one or between the second testing and the third one; this mean of the change of the group for a variable was then algebraically compared with the difference found in each individual between the first and second testings or the second and the third testings for that variable.

This perusal of the more objective findings provided hypotheses as to the major conflicts, defenses, attitudes or values, traits, and specific needs, plus the bases of these in early experience. Once all this information had been assimilated by the interviewer, the DI would begin.

The first part of the DI was guided according to the judgments required in the Depth Interview Supplement, which appears in Appendix B-7. As can be seen, first to be determined were certain features of interaction between the subject and his Father Master or Superiors and his peers. The subject's answers to questions permitted decisions as to amount of interaction that took place, and how the subject evaluated the Superiors or peers in these interactions. Note that the majority of these interactions (e.g., communication, affection, interactional conflict) is the same which had been evaluated in the Biographical Inventory and the FI. By keeping in mind the information about the subject's relationship with parents and siblings available in the Biographical Inventory and the FI, the interviewer attempted to determine whether the relationships with the Superiors and/or peers were of the transference variety, and if so, what the content of the transference could be. At the end of this part of the interview, the interviewer questioned and made judgments concerning the range of personality variables and patterns mentioned at the bottom of the Depth Interview Supplement.

The next part of the DI was a more unstructured exploration concerning the nature and content of conflicts in order to determine the degree of awareness of his problems and characteristics that existed in the subject. Here, once again, the information from the previously administered tests, as well as from the Biographical Inventory and the FI, were used as a basis for inferring the substance of conflicts, as in the first part of the DI. If the subject was found to be conscious of his conflicts, this part of the interview was brief. If he did not show awareness, he was gradually confronted with the evidence of his conflicts gleaned from the tests, Biographical Inventory and FI. In borderline cases, care was taken not to reveal underlying unconscious material in any manner that could provoke a traumatic decompensation.

The final part of the interview explored the sex life of the subject, and dealt with his fantasies and actions prior to and during religious formation. More specifically, questions were asked about dating, fears of the other sex, self image as a man or woman, masturbatory practices, and latent or overt homosexuality. In general, questions began with indirect phraseology, proceding to a more direct format according to the appropriateness of the situation.

The time required for each personal interview was about two hours.

A definite aim of the DI was to discover the degree of developmental maturity (cfr. chapter 7) present in the personality at entrance into training, and the course of this degree of maturity during the training period. The interview was also intended to close the subject's participation in the study with as much benefit to him as was possible, in terms of information about himself and exploration of future plans and problems.

Immediately following the interview, the interviewer completed a form requiring him to judge the intensity in the subject of the emotional styles, specific needs and defenses, used in analysing TAT protocols. In addition to this and of special note is the fact that the interviewer had to rank in order of intensity the developmental stages or conflicts among the eight described by Erikson (1950, 1959), which he had found in the interview.

The final step was the writing of a clinical summary concerning psychopathological, psychogenetic, and especially dynamic considerations. An outline for the DI appears in Appendix B-8.

F. Analysis of Data

As noted in chapter 2, the present book approaches the problem of religious vocation through a structural approach according to the multidimensional or a typological strategy. There are five Issues dealt with, and in each one, the "what" of the scaled variables are used to see the "how," i.e., the patterns of relationship among the subsystems of the self which are supposed to determine behavior in the problems analysed. Specifically, the analysis of data was oriented toward this objective.

More generally, the research considered both assessment "of", i.e., understanding of vocational phenomena, and assessment "for", i.e., some prediction of them. These assessments consist of some method of data combination, clinical or statistical. In clinical combination, the judgment of the examiner or researcher is the major organizer and combiner, i.e., data are combined largely by the cognizing activity of a clinician. The second, statistical combination, leaves the combining of data not to the mind of a human being, but to that of a computer or statistician.

Data *combination* should be distinguished from *measurement*. Measurement or data *collection* is that process wherein chosen subjects are given a test intended to tap particular characteristics of personality through the test responses the subject might give. These psychological test responses are data measurement, "indices", which serve as "input" to the assessment system. Data are thus collected, then combined and evaluated.

Two different methods can be used in collecting data: judgmental and mechanical. Any testing procedure which involves human judgment (e.g., interview, TAT) is judgmental measurement. A technique of data collection, on the other hand, which does not rely on human judgment can be called mechanical (e.g., MAI, GGLI).

In short, data collection (measurement) may be either judgmental or mechanical, and data combination may be either clinical or statistical. What are the best strategies, then, of data collection and data combination?

This issue has been debated by many authors (e.g., Holt, 1958; Meehl, 1954, 1965; Goldberg, 1968). A recent useful clarification and explication has come from Sawyer (1966).

Sawyer combines both measurement and combination to form a joint classification of predictive methods. The eight possible methods of prediction take the following tabular form:

SAWYER'S CLASSIFICATION OF PREDICTIVE METHODS
(Sawyer, 1966)

| *Mode of data collection* | *Mode of data combination* | |
	Clinical	Statistical
Judgmental	1. Pure Clinical 20%	2. Trait Ratings 43%
Mechanical	3. Profile Interpretation 38%	4. Pure Statistical 63%
Both	5. Clinical Composite 26%	6. Mechanical Composite 75%
Either or Both	7. Clinical Synthesis 50%	8. Mechanical Synthesis 75%

These methods can be defined in the following manner:

1. The *Pure Clinical* method consists of judgmental measurement and clinical data combination. Clinical Interviews are of this type.

2. *Trait Ratings* involve judgmental measurement and statistical combination. The clinical interviewer gives his judgmental ratings to a statistician for combination.

3. *Profile Interpretations* utilize mechanically measured and clinically combined data. MMPI profiles are classical examples.

4. The *Pure Statistical* prediction is that wherein mechanically measured data are combined in a statistical manner.

5. The *Clinical Composite* method includes an input of judgmentally and mechanically measured data, which are then integrated by a clinician.

6. In the *Mechanical Composite* the input is of both judgmentally and mechanically measured data, which are then integrated statistically.

7. In the *Clinical Synthesis* method judgmental and/or mechanical data are fed into a computer. The results in turn are given to a clinician as a new piece of input information. The clinician then has three choices: 1) to discard the information of the computer; or 2) to incorporate it into the clinical impression or 3) to abandon his clinical impression and retain instead the computer-produced one.

8. The *Mechanical Synthesis* method is similar in complexity to number 7, but has, it seems, little practical value (Wiggins, 1973).

Sawyer applied this schema to 45 published studies to determine whether a given prediction method was superior, inferior or equal to other methods employed in the study. A total of 75 comparisons between prediction methods were made, and Sawyer then computed comparable percentages — indices of superiority of the prediction methods (see percentages in the chart).

The hierarchy of prediction methods thus takes the following form:

1) n. 6 — Mechanical Composite (n. 8 is equivalent, however dropped because of its unnecessary involuted procedures).
2) n. 4 — Pure Statistical.
3) n. 7 — Clinical Synthesis.
4) n. 2 — Trait Ratings.
5) n. 3 — Profile Interpretation.
6) n. 5 — Clinical Composite.
7) n. 1 — Pure Clinical.

Wiggins (1973) notes in Sawyer's percentages two limitations: 1) the percentages are based on comparisons of a given method with many other methods and 2) the number of comparisons on which the percentages are based differs widely from method to method. However, he asserts that "certain conclusions that would not be contradicted by more detailed analyses" can be made (p. 197).

Of these conclusions, Sawyer states explicitly that the judgmental measurement with *either* method of data combination, is the weakest source of measurement or input data. As for data combination, regardless of the type of input data, a statistical combination is more accurate. Sawyer concludes that the "best" method of prediction is one in which both judgmentally and mechanically measured data are statistically combined.

The reader having thus before him a schema of possible methods of data analysis, can now readily judge for himself where most known vocational studies fall. As for the present book, the data analyses of its five Issues fall into the following categories suggested by Sawyer:

Issue I   deals with the conscious process of entering with a Purely Statistical method of prediction (n. 4 of Sawyer).

Issue II   discusses the subconscious motivations underlying entrance and prevailingly uses Clinical Synthesis, which Holt (1958) calls "sophisticated clinical prediction" (n. 7 of Sawyer).

Issue III   considers the strength and the content of the conscious and subconscious motivation to enter. Here, different procedures are used: the Mechanical Composite, the Profile Interpretation, and the Clinical Composite, which correspond to nn. 6, 3, and 5 of Sawyer, respectively. A fourth procedure is the Clinical Synthesis (n. 7 of Sawyer).

Issue IV   concerns the trend of the entering intrapsychic dynamics to persist; it uses the same first three methods adopted for Issue III.

Procedures nn. 6, 7, 3, and 5 of Sawyer are used for *Issue V* which consider the problem of dropping out.

A more detailed explanation of analysis methods will be found within each issue. All in all, as can be seen, the methods applied to the different issues are generally of the more reliable type.

Before ending this section on analysis of data, two final remarks are a propos: one regards the use of a rather sophisticated statistical method — this method, used in some of the issues, combines the Multivariate Analysis of Variance and the Discriminant Function Analysis (Bock, 1963). These are especially helpful in the interpretation of mean differences since they allow consideration not only of the significance level of each variable, but also the magnitude of that variable's unique contribution towards discriminating between the two groups. The Discriminant Function provides a partial control for variable intercorrelation. Few studies to date concerning vocation have employed this type of statistical precision.

Finally a cautionary word should be made. Despite all efforts to the contrary, our specific values, preferences, insights, biases and prejudices naturally urged us to underscore some results while glossing over others, particularly those of a less psychodynamic orientation.

PART II

ISSUES

CHAPTER 4

GENERAL PREMISES

First, let us state once and for all that the present investigation always assumes the good faith, the sincerity of the people who volunteered to participate as subjects for the project. The whole theoretical approach of this study stresses the relevance of depth, subconscious psychology. Therefore, there can be no question here of sin, of malice, etc.

Secondly, the readers are cautioned that a full evaluation and interpretation of the issues discussed in this book should be based on a careful reading of the theoretical and methodological explanations and justifications presented in the Introduction and in Part I.

Thirdly, this research focuses on vocational, not on psychopathological, issues. Therefore, it refers to the individuals not as neurotics or as psychotics, etc., but as people who do not manifest symptoms of mental disease but still have subconscious inconsistencies which may affect their vocational perseverance and effectiveness. As a matter of fact, many of the subjects considered in this study had been psychologically screened before their admission into the religious houses. This was especially true for the male Religious, even though also for them the screening was usually limited to questionnaires filled out by the entering individuals or by observers.

Fourthly, the theoretical frame of reference adopted in this book evaluates the vocational events, like entrance, dropping out, etc., not only in terms of content but also and especially in terms of structural dimensions of the self; thus, as was already discussed in chapter 2, transcultural, trans-situational, and transpersonal conclusions are possible. An example will clarify this asset of the research.

It is likely that different people in different groups, in different countries, at different times have different reasons for dropping out of religious training; these reasons may be different intrapsychic contents. Thus, some people can drop out because of personal difficulties with obedience, others because of difficulties concerning chastity, etc. If obedience, chastity, are considered only when they are linked to patterns of relationship among structures of the self, like the ideal-self, latent-self, etc., then transcultural, trans-situational and trans-temporal conclusions are possible; in fact, these structures of the self do not change with different people, in different educational settings and at different times. Periods of critical changes in the Church may change the frequency with which the foregoing structural patterns will appear in individual vocationers, but will not change their importance in catalyzing the process of dropping out.

Fifthly, this investigation usually studied the *entire*, intact entering groups of religious or seminarians, not just samples taken from the groups.

Sixthly, several theoretical and methodological statements have been made in Part I of this book. Now, in starting the discussion of specific issues, these statements need to be explicated in the context of the issues considered. In other words, we now pass from the general "Propositions" of the theory (cfr. Chapter 1) to some specific hypotheses which can empirically support or disprove those "Propositions".

Rulla (1967, 1971) has hypothesized that a person enters religious vocation because he wants to implement his personal ideals in the context of a particular religious institution. In this sense, it may be said that religious vocation is an implementation of the self-ideal in a given situation. This self-ideal-in-situation is the result of two components: the ideals the person has for himself, self-ideal (SI), and the ideals of the institution *as they are perceived by the individual* (II). However, this self-ideal-in-situation (SI-II) will remain the psychological pivot of the future life and religious vocation only if it is objective and free. It is objective when the content predominant in its two components for each individual corresponds to the essential ideals proposed by the vocational institution; concretely, such content corresponds at least to the two terminal values of imitation of Christ and union with God as well as to the three instrumental values of poverty, chastity (as

62

distinct from celibacy) and obedience; the latter in religious vocation become vows, while — in the words of Vatican Council II — for priestly vocation they are the three " most necessary virtues of the priestly ministry " (Presbyterorum Ordinis, NN. 15 to 17).

The self-ideal-in-situation is not free when its content is the consequence of some underlying subconscious conflicts or inconsistencies of the person which " drive ", force him in his motivation; in such a case, the person's ideal is consciously conceived but unconsciously held.

The objectivity and freedom of this self-ideal-in-situation may be impaired by interference coming from the following four sources (Rulla, 1971, pp. 57-58, 272-293): 1) *lack of knowledge* concerning the ideals of the institution. 2) *Identification* with the vocational institution. Because of his desires to identify with the chosen vocational setting, the individual projects these desires on the institution; thus, he perceives the institutional ideals as quite similar to his own ideals. Research findings support this view both for groups in general (e.g., Vroom, 1960, 1966) and for religious groups (Rulla, 1967; Maddi and Rulla, 1972; Rulla and Maddi, 1972). It should be noted that this similarity and attraction relationship between the individual and his reference groups is a two-way street. Not only does real similarity produce liking, but liking also enhances the perceived similarity of the reference group which is an exaggeration of the real similarity to the extent that the subject likes his group of reference (Byrne and Blaylock, 1963; Campbell, Converse, Miller, and Stokes, 1960; Sampson and Insko, 1964).

3) Influence of *intrapsychic conflicts or inconsistencies*. A person may enter religious life in part to defend himself against or to gratify underlying subconscious needs, which are less acceptable for a vocational commitment. In such a case, an inconsistency or conflict would be present between the self-ideal-in-situation proclaimed by the individual and his actual-self, either as manifest self or as latent self. However, according to the findings of Wylie (1957) the inconsistency between the individual's self-ideal and his less readily symbolizable, i.e., rather subconscious, actual self (or self-concept in Wylie's terminology) induces more anxiety and defensiveness than the one between the same self-ideal and a more readily symboliz-

able, more conscious actual-self. Similarly, according to depth psychology thinking—especially psychoanalytic—subconscious conflicts determine greater fear, anxiety, guilt, shame, and defensiveness than conscious conflicts. In turn, higher degrees of the foregoing emotional threats lead to greater maladjustment (Janis, 1969; Levitt, 1967; Beier, 1951; Osler, 1954; Easterbrook, 1959; Berkun, Bialek, Kern and Yagi, 1962). Thus, for instance, in the case of religious vocation, dropping out may fellow (Ridick, 1972).

4) *Pressure* from the *group*, the styles of *leadership* and the *institutional structure*. This fourth source of interference with the objectivity and freedom of the self-ideal-in-situation may be influenced by the previously described third source. In fact, subconscious conflicts may affect not only the self-ideal-in-situation but also the way in which the group is structured or perceived; an example in point may be the type of leaders who are chosen by the members of the group: the underlying subconscious conflicts or inconsistencies may influence such a choice. If the self-ideal-in situation and the structure or perception of the group are defensive processes against subconscious conflicts, the effects upon the self-ideal-in-situation may be different from those upon the group (Imoda, 1971). In fact, it is characteristic of conflicts to produce various different types of defenses

The objectivity and freedom of the self-ideal-in-situation (SI-II) are affected differently by the foregoing four sources: lack of knowledge, non-defensive identification, intrapsychic conflicts or inconsistencies, and group pressure.

When only the first and/or second conditions are present, there is not a significant conflict between ideal-self and actual-self; therefore, a reappraisal of his SI-II by the individual is possible; during the first phase of religious life, he is helped toward this reappraisal via persuasive communications, interpersonal interaction with leaders, peers, etc. This reappraisal may lead to dropping out or to pursuing the vocational commitment; either decision is the result of a free, mature process.

When the third source of interference is also present, the conflict between the ideal- and actual-self is of such a nature that a free, objective reappraisal of the SI-II is more difficult. This becomes particularly true when the subconscious inconsistencies or conflicts influence not only the SI-II of each individual, but the group elements of the fourth source as well. In such a case, the individual is in a conflictual state with regard to his vocational commitment and he may more easily drop out. Brock has been doing an interesting series of studies (Brock, 1965; Brock and Blackwood, 1962) testing such theories as Festinger's social comparison and cognitive dissonance, Stotland's identification and Kelman's identification formulations in situations that allow the subject either to change his own attitude or to distort the perception of his group of reference, with the latter proving to be a strong tendency.

From the foregoing considerations, it would seem that in the final analysis, it is the third source of interference, especially in the form of *subconscious* vocational inconsistencies, which would make possible or less possible an objective reappraisal of the SI-II. Along this line, Rulla (1971) has suggested that dropping out of religious life is in part a function of the inconsistencies between the ideal-self-in-situation and the actual-self when these inconsistencies are determined by subconscious needs which are especially incompatible with the vocational commitment.

On the basis of the previously mentioned theorizing and findings, many questions may be asked concerning people who enter into a vocational setting. The present book deals with the following questions:

1) Do people enter because of what they consciously think and feel themselves to be or because of what they consciously would like to be?

2) Should one take at face value the proclaimed motivation to enter or, in addition, should possible subconscious elements be considered?

3) If the conscious motivation to enter is not the entire motivation, i.e., if a subconscious psychodynamics is also present, to what degree does it affect the entering people? And what are the contents which characterize this psychodynamics?

4) Does the entering intrapsychic dynamics tend to persist in the individuals who remain in vocation?

5) Does the same psychodynamics tend to influence leaving the vocation as well as vocational effectiveness?

Some answers to these five questions are sought in the five issues considered in this book. Each one of the issues will be discussed separately for the female and for the male group.

CHAPTER 5

THE CONSCIOUS MOTIVATION TO ENTER:
THE GERMINATIVE SELF-IDEAL-IN-SITUATION
OR SI-II

The title of this chapter should not mislead the reader. Let us recall that religious vocation is a supernatural grace. Therefore, the psycho-social elements considered in this and in the following chapters prescind from, but are subordinate to the pervasive influence of the supernatural element. However, religious vocation may be seen as and is the encounter of two freedoms: of God and of man. Therefore, it is also a dialogue between God and man. The part played by man supported by grace in his vocational dialogue with God can be considered as a fundamental option, that is, as "an orientation freely imposed on our whole life" (Fransen, 1957).

The aim of this chapter is very limited: it does not intend to consider whether or not content characteristics of personality exist which distinguish people entering the religious vocation from the rest of the general population. In this regard, some authors (e.g., Darmanin, 1973) are inclined to give a rather positive answer; however, the majority of the reviewers of the pertinent literature (e.g., D'Arcy, 1968; Potvin and Suziedelis, 1969; Rooney, 1968, 1972; Dittes, 1971; Godin, 1975) think that the findings are rather inconsistent and ambiguous.

Our objective is only to look for an answer to the question: in the realm of *conscious* motivation to enter a vocational setting, do people enter because of what they think they are or because of what they would like to be? This question translated in the terms of the theory of self-transcendent consistency pits the values and attitudes against the traits. Here some definitions and explanations are necessary.

Following the tenets commonly accepted by the experts, attitudes and values are thought to express a response predisposition. For the reasons discussed in presenting the theory (1971, p. 39), *two* components of such predispositions are distinguished: 1) a rather cognitive component which refers to how an object *is perceived by a person*; this cognitive component is operationalized as " institutional ideal " or II; and, as such, it constitutes an interpersonal rather than an intrapersonal unit of analysis (Allen, 1968) because it expresses, at least in part, the influence the vocational institution exerts upon the person; and 2) a rather affective-conative component in the context of a vocational commitment; this component expresses the positive or negative attraction the person has toward that object (affective part) and the tendency to act according to such an attraction (conative part); the self-ideal or SI operationalizes this conative-affective component. As Kernan and Trebbi (1973) and Ostrom (1969) have shown, these cognitive, affective, and conative parts are distinct, albeit interrelated facets of a person's response tendency.

Whereas, attitudes and values mean only the *predisposition* to act, traits (Wallace, 1966, 1967) indicate the *capability* to act; that is, they are a sign that the predisposition may be translated into action. In the theory, traits are operationalized as " present behavior " (PB), i.e., as manifest self-concepts, or a subject's cognitions about his own present behavior: what a person thinks he is or usually does.

The combination of SI and II is the self-ideal-in-situation (SI-II), which expresses the predisposition of attitudes and of values, i.e., what people would like to be in a given situation. The combination of self-concepts about one's present behavior (PB) with his perception of the institutional-ideals (II) is the self-concept-in-situation (PB-II), which means what people think they are or do in a given situation.

Why would people choose religious vocation because of their SI-II rather than because of their PB-II? Many considerations seem pertinent in answering this question.

Feldman and Newcomb (1969) summarize the results of seven studies: Stern, 1961; Weiss, 1964; Becker and Mittman, 1962; Webb, 1963; Pervin, 1966; Standing, 1963; Chickering, mimeo. These studies asked the entering freshmen of lay colleges what they thought were the expected demands, characteristics, and opportunities of their college environment. These 'expected' environments were compared with the "actual" environments as revealed by the students already acquainted with their colleges. Both the "expected" and the "actual" college environments were assessed by means of the College Characteristics Index (Stern, 1970) which measures the conception students have of their environmental pressures according to thirty scales; these scales are intended to be parallel with the first thirty scales used in the present research in the Modified Activities Index or MAI (cfr. chapter 3 under "Instruments and Their Rationale"). Therefore, the structure of the self measured by the College Characteristics Index is quite similar to the one tackled by the "Institutional Ideal" or II in the present book. Both the College Characteristics Index and the II stress the role concept, i.e., the perception the individuals have of their role.

The results of the foregoing seven studies showed that the entering students expected more from the institutions than those who had been studying there already. Generalizing from these studies as well as from other research findings (Stern, 1966 a, b; Webb, 1963; Pace, 1965-1966), Feldman and Newcomb conclude that entering freshmen of lay colleges describe their environment both realistically and unrealistically. Their view of the college environment is based on a general, stereotyped, and somewhat idealized image of college life. Similar results were obtained by Stern (1970) and other investigators (Wood, 1963; Fisher, 1961; Scoresby, 1962; Standing and Parker, 1964) for several colleges, non-catholic and catholic, as well as by Pace (1963, 1965-66, 1966 a, b), Brown (1967), Berdie (1966, 1967), Gaff (1967) and Fisher (1966) by using the College and University Environment Scales. Standing (1962) also shows the same phenomenon among transfer students, as does Buckley (1969) for entrance to the State University of New York system after two years of the community college. "Prior experience is evidently discounted as an exception to the myth" (Stern, 1970, p. 93, footnote 3 on errata sheet).

There seem to be several good reasons for predicting that people who enter a religious vocational setting also have a rather idealized image of religious life. First of all, because

68

the mission to which they are called "transcends all human energies and human wisdom" (Vatican Council II, Presbyterorum Ordinis, No. 15), their view of vocational life may be easily both unrealistic and idealized, at least in part. In *this* sense, entering vocationers and entering lay college students may be expected to be similar.

Secondly, there is a set of considerations which suggest further similarity between the two groups, religious and lay people entering their respective training centers: 1) both lay and religious people are like "novices": "In general terms, the freshman in college is a novice in an unfamiliar social organization, and is, therefore, confronted with the values, norms and role structures of a new social system and various new subsystems" (Feldman and Newcomb, 1969, p. 89). Both lay and religious undergo an experience which usually involves desocialization (pressures to unlearn *some* past values, attitudes, and patterns of behavior) as well as socialization (pressure to learn and to participate in the new social structure). 2) As a number of investigators (Silber, Hamburg, et al., 1961; Freedman, 1965; Douvan and Kaye, 1962; Wallace, 1963) have noted, young persons entering lay college both expect and want to change and develop. They conceive of college as a vocational *preparation*, as a specific instrumental scheme for job initiation, but not yet as a specific occupational commitment. Actually, the choice of the school is frequently based upon inappropriate or transitory needs and attitudes. The same may be said of people entering religious centers. Both lay and religious, especially in the first months, are people in training, in search, in preparation; they are not real "vocationers", at least in the sense of being already vocationally or occupationally committed.

On the basis of the foregoing findings and considerations, one could expect that both lay and religious young people who enter their educational institution would present a rather idealized II or "institutional ideal". Furthermore, if the II is somewhat idealized, it seems reasonable to hypothesize that the attractive force to the institution resides more in the ideals the individuals have (SI) than in how these individuals see themselves to be (PB). In fact, if the institution is idealized, there is already a difference between what the person thinks himself to be and what he thinks the institution wants him to be. Therefore, because the person is choosing an idealized institution, he is reaching for something beyond his self-concept or PB. However, if a person sees himself as poor (PB) and does not desire to become better (SI), it is highly improbable that he would choose an institution which he perceives as expecting his improvement (II). Therefore, if this person chooses that institution, he does so because the institution matches with his ideals rather than because it does not fit with his behavior. Thus, in the final analysis, people would be consciously attracted to their own institution by what they ideally would like to be more than by what they think themselves to be. If these assumptions are true, then for these individuals the correlation between SI and II should be more frequently significant than the correlation between PB and II. Consequently, the following hypotheses for the *conscious* motivation of religious or seminarians entering a vocational setting can be stated:

1) For entering religious vocationers, the correlations SI-II are more frequently significant than the correlations PB-II.
2) The first hypothesis is valid for the SI-II of both the values and the attitudes of the entering subjects.
3) The foregoing two hypotheses hold also for students entering lay colleges.

Tests and measurements

To measure the self-concept (PB), the self-ideal (SI), and the institutional-ideal (II), a modification of the Activities Index or AI (Stern, 1958, 1970) was used for attitudes, while a modification of the General Goals of Life Inventory (GGLI of the Educational Testing Service, 1950) was employed for values. The characteristics of the modification of the Activities Index (MAI) as well as the ones of the modification of the GGLI (MGGLI) have been described in chapter 3.

The correlations SI-II and PB-II were performed by employing a Pearson product-moment correlation technique. A chi-square measurement was used to determine: 1) if the proportion of significant SI-II correlations over significant PB-II correlations was significantly higher; 2) if the foregoing proportion was not significantly different between religious and lay entering subjects.

70

The Female Group

For the study of both males and females, the groups of religious entering their vocational settings were compared with separate groups of students entering Catholic lay colleges. The religious and the lay groups were closely similar for the following variables: age, socio-economic level, Catholic and urban-rural background, and high school grades. A similar matching of religious and lay groups according to these five variables was used in the study of the other issues of this book; therefore, such a matching will not be mentioned in discussing these remaining issues. For further information concerning procedures of testing, cfr. chapter 3. Frequently the entering subjects belonged to consecutively entering classes; each class was separated from the next by about one year.

In the present issue, for the study of *values*, the female sample included 39 religious, who represented the entire group entering a religious institution. They were compared with 84 female lay subjects randomly selected from the girls entering a Catholic lay college in the same year as the religious. Thus, 123 entering females were considered for values.

For the assessment concerning *attitudes*, the religious sample was made up of: 1) the entire two consecutive entering groups of an institution; 2) the entire group entering the same institution but in a different setting; 3) the entire three consecutive groups entering a different institution. The total of religious subjects was 297. The lay sample was represented by randomly selected girls entering two different Catholic colleges in the same years as the religious; that made a total of 136 people. Thus, 433 subjects were studied for attitudes.

Results

Tables 5.1 and 5.2 show the findings for the correlations SI-II and PB-II for values; Tables 5.3 and 5.4, the corresponding data for attitudes.

For values: the chi-square results indicate that both for entering religious and lay people, the proportion of significant SI-II correlations over significant PB-II correlations was significantly higher:

chi-square for Religious = 11.55; level of significance: $P < .001$
chi-square for Lay   = 6.43; level of significance: $P < .02$

The corresponding results for attitudes also show that SI-II is significantly higher than PB-II:

chi-square for Religious = 24.99; level of significance: $P < .001$
chi-square for Lay   = 23.17; level of significance: $P < .001$

Finally, the findings were not significant for both values and attitudes when an answer to the following question was sought: Is the proportion of significant SI-II over significant PB-II for religious significantly different from the same proportion for lay people?

To answer this question, a test of significance of the difference between the two proportions was made:

The result for values was: $z = 1.08$; not significant.
The result for attitudes was: $z = -.11$; not significant.

The Male Group

Subjects

The sample for the study of *values* was formed by 54 religious who represented the entire two consecutive groups entering an institution and the whole group entering the same institution in another setting. The lay freshmen were randomly selected from the people entering one college; they totaled 56 subjects. The year of entrance of the initial groups of religious and the one of the lay people coincided. The subjects considered for values altogether totaled to 100 people.

Attitudes were studied by assessing 247 subjects: 140 of them were religious, 107 lay people. The religious belonged to the same institution but to three different settings; they represented the entire three consecutive entering groups of two settings (three groups for each setting) and the whole entering group of a third setting. The lay freshmen were randomly selected from two Catholic colleges at a time coinciding with the entrance of religious people.

Results and Discussion

The data related to the correlations SI-II and PB-II are in Tables 5.5 and 5.6 for values, and in Tables 5.7 and 5.8 for attitudes.

The results for the male group are exactly the same as the ones seen for the female group. This is true for the proportion of significant SI-II correlations over significant PB-II correlations, with the former being significantly higher than the latter.

For values:
chi-square for Religious = 4.76; level of significance. $P < .05$
chi-square for Lay   = 6.15; level of significance: $P < .02$

72

For attitudes:

chi-square for Religious = 8.82; level of significance: $P < .005$

chi-square for Lay = 20.00; level of significance: $P < .001$

For males as for females, there is no significant difference between religious and lay people for the proportion of significant SI-II correlations over significant PB-II correlations:

for values: $z = .14$; not significant

for attitudes: $z = -.30$; not significant

To confirm the greater strength of the association of the SI-II relationship over the PB-II, both for female and male groups, a sign-test was performed; the following results were obtained:

			(two-tail probability)
Females	Values	Religious	$< .001$
		Lay	$< .001$
	Attitudes	Religious	$< .001$
		Lay	$< .001$
Males	Values	Religious	$< .004$
		Lay	$< .002$
	Attitudes	Religious	$< .001$
		Lay	$< .001$

The three hypotheses of this investigation received full support. These results prompt considerations, some more general, others more specific to religious vocation.

The subjects studied here are people of college age who, at least in part, were unfamiliar with the social organization or institution which they chose to enter. Therefore, first of all, these people were confronted with a new experience of desocialization and of socialization. Secondly, they were not real " vocationers ", i.e., not yet individuals totally or, at least, realistically committed to the vocation or occupation offered by the chosen organization.

It would seem that people with the foregoing characteristics tend, first of all, to choose the institution on the basis of ideals rather than of personal conscious realities; in fact, at least on the conscious level, they seem to choose the institution because of what they would like to be rather than because of what they are, i.e., because of the ideal-self (SI-II) rather than because of the conscious actual-self-in-situation (PB-II).

73

Secondly, since the ideals (SI) of these individuals correlated with the ideals of the institution (II) more frequently than the concepts these subjects had of their present behavior or capabilities (PB), it would seem that the view of the chosen institution is somewhat idealized by these subjects. This interpretation of a somehow idealized view of the chosen institution is confirmed by the findings of the numerous studies quoted by Feldman and Newcomb (1969) as well as by Stern (1970), as they were discussed at the beginning of the present chapter. Furthermore, such an interpretation is in line with the fact substantiated by several authors (Byrne and Blaylock, 1963; Campbell, Converse, Miller, and Stokes, 1960; Sampson and Insko, 1964) that the similarity and attraction relationship between the subject and his reference group is a two-way street: the two elements form a reverberating circuit in which they mutually enhance each other. In other words, and in the context of our discussion, the attraction for a reference group or for an institution enhances the perceived similarity between the individual and the group or institution, i.e., this similarity is an exaggeration of the real one; now, here the similarity was especially with the ideals of the person rather than with his conscious real capabilities.

The foregoing two interpretations seem to be true for people entering Catholic colleges and Catholic vocational settings. In the present research 680 subjects of both sexes, selected from 10 different settings in the Midwest, East and West of the USA, show these patterns. These results were obtained by using the structural approach to the study of personality, i.e., by analyzing the relationships among three structures of the self. Therefore, perhaps they may be generalized beyond socio-cultural and temporal situations for Catholic people who present the characteristics described above. The data available in the present study do not allow both interpretations to be extended to non-Catholic people, a possibility which is, however, suggested by the previously mentioned numerous studies reviewed by Feldman and Newcomb (1969) and by Stern (1970).

More specifically, with regard to religious vocation, it seems to be true that the SI-II is the basic conscious disposition for entering a vocational setting: according to the operational definitions followed in the present study, the ideal-self was more relevant than the self-concept-in-situation for 437 subjects, men and women, who entered 6 different settings located in the Midwest, East and West of the USA. This is in line with the proposed vocational theory according to which: "religious vocation is an implementation of the self-ideal-in-situation" rather than of the self-concept-in-situation. Of course, as it was stated in the original formulation (Rulla, 1971) "such a proposition is meant to be more assertive than exclusive" (p. 51). Whether this tends to become a fact prevalent for religious vocation in comparison with non-religious vocation, cannot be asserted on the basis of the data available in this paper because, as we have seen, the subjects studied here are not yet real "vocationers".

It remains a fact that the prevalence of the SI-II over PB-II seems to be true for people entering a religious vocational setting. This prevalence of the self-ideals over the self-concepts coincides with the call to self-transcendence which is appropriate (even though not exclusive) for the religious mission. Furthermore, such a prevalence may be the psychological disposition which most favorably opens a person to the influence of supernatural grace: to become what *ideally* he would like to be *with the help of God*. In this sense, the SI-II is the germinative, conscious motivation to enter religious vocation: it has great potentials for growth toward self-transcendence and, as a *side-effect* of it, toward self-fulfillment, self-actualization.

However, precisely because it is based on "ideals", such a motivation may be, in part at least, non-realistic. Man is not motivated only by ideals, but also by needs, i.e., by action tendencies resulting from a deficit of the organism or from natural inherent potentialities which seek exercise or actuality: e.g., sex, affiliation, etc. (cfr. Appendix B-3). These tendencies, at least in part innate and universal to man (Allport, 1935, 1961; Murray, 1938; Etzioni, 1968), are inextricably mingled in every act of man; the attitudes and the values of a person's SI-II may be influenced by needs, because human motivation is inextricably the result of three levels of psychic life: the psycho-physiological, the psycho-social, and the rational or spiritual. Man is a differentiated existing unity (Nuttin, 1962). Therefore, a realistic view of the motivation to enter a vocational setting prompts the second question outlined in the general premises about such a motivation: should one take at face value the proclaimed ideals to enter or, in addition, should other factors be considered? This question leads us to the study of the second issue proposed in this book.

Summary of Findings

1) Individuals (680 subjects of both sexes) who entered 4 different Catholic lay colleges and 6 different settings for religious vocation showed the tendency to choose the institution on the basis of personal ideals rather than of personal conscious realities.

2) This pattern in choosing goes together with a somehow idealized view of the institution.

3) Specifically for religious, the foregoing findings were true for 437 subjects, male and female, who entered 6 different settings located in the Midwest, East and West of the USA.

4) This prevalence of self-ideals over self-concepts may be an asset for the vocational growth; in fact, it may foster both the openness of the person to the influence of supernatural grace and the person's self-transcendence in the accomplishment of his mission. However, man is not motivated only by ideals.

CHAPTER 6

THE SUBCONSCIOUS MOTIVATION TO ENTER:
THE VULNERABLE SI-II

The previous chapter has shown that individuals enter religious vocation with a conscious motivation which tends to idealize both themselves and the institution. Entrance is motivated more by personal ideals (SI) than by conscious personal realities (PB); furthermore, role concepts (II) tend to correlate highly with the personal ideals (SI). Because the reality of the individual's capabilities (PB) is somehow over-ridden by the SI and the II, the motivation to enter is—at least in part—not objective.

This partial " idealization " and lack of objectivity of the entering vocationers may be either the consequence of their lack of knowledge concerning the institution or the expression of their germinative desire to identify themselves with the ideals of the institution in order to better themselves, to modify their present way of life for a more valued future. The first reason is readily understandable. The second one, too, is quite probably present; this is suggested by the fact that the choice is made more on the basis of what the individuals would like to be than on what they are.

However, the fact that the SI-II correlations are more frequently significant than the correlations PB-II prompts further consideration and questions. The decision to enter is especially the result of the ideals chosen (II) and desired (SI); these ideals (SI-II) are made by attitudes and/or values. Now, instrumental values and attitudes may serve at least four functions: utilitarian, ego-defensive, value-expressive, and know-ledge (Katz, 1960; Katz and Stotland, 1959). A closely related conceptualization is suggested by Smith, Bruner and White (1956).

People strive to maximize the rewards in their environment and to minimize the punishments. If they hold an attitude or a value to reach these aims, then the attitude or the value serves an *utilitarian* function. If they hold them to protect themselves from acknowledging unacceptable truths about themselves or the hard realities in their external world, then an *ego-defensive* function is at work; an example in point may be defensive nurturance: the unacceptable truths about having an exaggerated need to get affection and attention is covered by a proclaimed attitude or value of giving; the giving, however, is only a means to cover up the getting, to make it more acceptable for one's self image. In the *value-expressive* function, the attitudes or the instrumental values have the function of giving expression to the person's terminal, central values. Finally, the *knowledge* function serves man's aspiration to understand his universe, to give adequate structure to it, etc.

While many attitudes or instrumental values are serving a single type of the functions just described, others may serve more than one purpose for the individual; actually, they may serve needs or terminal values which are not homonymous: e.g., an attitude of submissiveness in one person may serve a need for affective dependency, or in another person, it may be a defense against a personally unacceptable need for rebellious autonomy; similarly, for yet another person, the need for achievement may incline that person either to a utilitarian competition or to value-expressive cooperation.

Which ones of the four functions are served by the expressed motivation to enter a vocational setting? Are ego-defensive or utilitarian purposes at work together with value-expressive and knowledge functions? In other words: are the conscious attitudes or values at the service of needs which are not consistent with the vocational commitment? It should be stressed that the entering vocationer may be completely in good faith, i.e., he can use ego-defensive or utilitarian attitudes without being aware of doing it, therefore, in a subconscious way.

Research findings (cfr. Tannenbaum, 1967, 1968, and Brock, 1968, who review also previous research by McGuire, 1960; Brock, 1963; Brock and Grant, 1963; Cohen, Greenbaum and Mansson, 1963) show that the person may be responsive to inconsistent elements of his self without being aware of it.

One can distinguish two kinds of lack of awareness: unawareness of the existence of the inconsistency and of its associated stress; unawareness of the activities, of the behavior the person uses to overcome, to resolve the inconsistency and the related stress.

The foregoing considerations and findings have been conceptualized in the theory of self-transcendent consistency by the following predictions: 1) the role concepts (II) and the self-ideals (SI) of entering vocationers are very close in content; 2) for *some* of the entering vocationers, the ideals of the institution as perceived by the individual (role concepts or II) may become his means not only for implementing his self-ideals (SI) but also for gratifying or for defending himself against underlying subconscious needs, which are less acceptable for a religious vocational commitment; 3) in such a case, the ideal-self (SI and II) of the person is inconsistent with the subconscious part (latent-self or LS) of the actual-self; following the findings of Wylie (1957) and others, as well as the tenets of depth psychology (cfr. p. 11), these subconscious inconsistencies are considered as influencing the motivation of the individual in a considerably greater way than the conscious inconsistencies, like the ones of PB with SI-II or the ones within the ideal-self (e.g., between SI and II); therefore, subconscious inconsistencies are identified as " central or functionally significant inconsistencies " (cfr. Chapters 1 and 3); 4) the behavior of the individual as perceived by him (PB) is in part understandable in the light of the existing subconscious inconsistencies between LS and SI-II; 5) the patterns of defenses used by the person (like compensation, projection, etc.: cfr. glossary under " mechanisms of defense ") and his emotional styles (like the degree of his anxiety, depression, guilt) are a further help in understanding the subconscious motivation underlying the entrance into a religious vocation.

Consequently, the following hypotheses can be formulated concerning people entering a religious vocational setting:

1) In general, there is a good consistency among the components of the ideal-self of the entering vocationers, that is, among the content of the values and the attitudes proclaimed by the individuals in their initial commitment to a religious vocation.

2) The vocational consistency within the ideal-self is undermined by *some* central, subconscious inconsis-

tencies of its components with the latent part of the actual-self (LS).

3) These subconscious inconsistencies between the ideal-self (SI and II) and the latent self (LS) explain *in part* the patterns of behavior (PB), of defenses and of emotional styles presented by entering people.

Tests and measurements

The values and attitudes of the ideal-self were assessed by means of the General Goals of Life Inventory (GGLI) and of the modification of the Activities Index (MAI) respectively. These instruments were discussed in chapter 3.

It should be noted that the MAI measures the rather affective-conative component of attitudes or SI separately from their rather cognitive component or II. In contrast, for the values these two components of the ideal-self, i.e. the SI and the II, are measured together by the GGLI. This " single index " of values is a reasonably robust index of a person's response predisposition. In fact, as the findings of chapter 5 indicate, there is a high and positive intercorrelation between the two components both for values and for attitudes. Several other empirical studies (Rosenberg, 1956; Fishbein, 1963, 1965; Ostrom, 1969; Kernan and Trebbi, 1973) confirm the validity of this " single index " to assess the individual's response predisposition.

The actual-self as perceived by the subjects was assessed by means of the " Present Behavior " (PB) of the MAI. The latent part of the actual-self (LS) was measured by two instruments: the Incomplete Sentence Blank (ISB) of Rotter (1950) and the Thematic Apperception Test (TAT) of Morgan and Murray (1935). Both tests have been described in chapter 3. Here it suffices to recall that both these instruments assessed the same " needs " described by Murray (1938); their scoring definitions were the same as those which guided item selection on the MAI; therefore, the comparison of variables across these tests is feasible. The ISB (Incomplete Sentences Blank) and the TAT (Thematic Apperception Test) were used also to assess the emotional styles and defenses as well as the eight developmental stages or conflicts described by Erikson (1950, 1959) (cfr. chapter 3).

A multivariate analysis of variance (Bock, 1963) was performed for each test in order to compare each religious group to its control group (cfr. end of chapter 3).

Finally, the central, functionally significant inconsistencies between the ideal-self and the latent-self were evaluated according to the operationalization norms discussed at the end of chapter 2.

Norms of data interpretation

In the preceding sections of this book, as in chapters 2, 3, and 4, many guidelines for interpreting the results of the present research have already been stated; their rationale, theoretical and empirical, has also been discussed. Here, a few other norms will be presented; they are particularly relevant for this chapter and the following ones.

1) First of all, let us recall that subconscious inconsistencies are considered significantly more relevant than conscious ones for the psychodynamic balance of an individual; cfr. the introduction to this chapter as well as chapter 4 for the observational, clinical and empirical bases of this position.

2) Following the tenets and findings of many authors, e.g., of Harding (1944, 1948) and of Rokeach (1968, 1973), values as measured by the GGLI are considered to have greater motivational strength than attitudes as tapped by the MAI.

3) With regard to attitudes, their affective-conative component or SI is regarded as their core; therefore, SI is considered a greater motivational force than the rather cognitive component or II. This position is supported by many research findings and theoretical tenets (e.g., McGuire, 1969; Rosenberg, 1956; Fishbein, 1963, 1965; Ostrom, 1969; Kernan and Trebbi, 1973).

4) The eight conflicts or stages described by Erikson (1950, 1959, 1963) are interpreted as antinomies and, thus, as expressing the oscillation of a person between two poles; e.g., the first conflict is considered as the motivational force that drives a person to oscillate toward the pole of trust or toward the pole of mistrust. In this sense, the two poles of the antinomies act like needs; however, as the presentation by Erikson indicates, they may be related to or serve many and different needs.

Subjects

The *Religious Group* consisted of 283 entering females; they are practically the same people studied in chapter 5 for the attitudes. The small difference in number between the sample considered there (297 subjects) and here (283 subjects) is due to spoiled or incomplete test protocols. Also, the 136 subjects of the *Lay Group* were the same as the people assessed for attitudes in chapter 5. The reader is referred to that chapter for a description of the sample.

The entering religious subjects belonged to two Orders of nuns. Both religious Orders screened their candidates according to procedures similar to those used by the two Catholic lay colleges of the Lay Group. Also, for both religious Orders, the primary apostolic work is pre-college education. Because of the time-consuming nature of the TAT and ISB scoring, random sub-samples from the original groups were selected for scoring on these tests: a subsample of 126 out of the 283 subjects for the Religious Group and a subsample of 48 out of the 136 subjects for the Lay Group.

Results and Discussion

The findings are presented in Tables 6.1 through 6.6. Chart 6 summarizes the significant differences between the Religious and the Lay Groups present in the ideal-self for values and attitudes, as well as in the actual-self for its latent (LS) component. Chart 7 summarizes the patterns of behavior (PB), of defenses, and of emotional styles.

The discussion will consider the proposed three hypotheses separately.

The first hypothesis

The values proclaimed by Religious in the GGLI indicate a great difference between them and the Lay Group: 17 out of 21 scales are significantly different. Following the ranking of emphasis indicated by the discriminant function analysis, the Religious Group stresses these values: religious women wish more than do lay to serve their community and God, find their place in life and accept what circumstances bring, so as to achieve immortality. They are not as concerned as lay about making a place for themselves, but rather are interested in greater self-discipline and less pleasure, peace of mind, power or control. They wish to sacrifice themselves

CHART 6

SIGNIFICANT VARIABLES: ENTERING RELIGIOUS FEMALES VS. LAY *

IDEAL SELF			LATENT SELF	
Values	Attitudes		Needs and Conflicts	
General Goals of Life Inventory GGLI	Self-Ideal SI	Institutional Ideal II	Incomplete Sentences Blank ISB	Thematic Apperception Test TAT

Values — General Goals of Life Inventory (GGLI)

- + + Serving my Community
- + + Serving God
- + − Finding my Place in Life
- + − Accepting What Circumstances bring
- + − Achieving Immortality
- + − Making a Place for Myself
- + − Self-discipline
- − − Getting Pleasures
- − − Peace of Mind
- − − Power, Control
- + + Self Sacrifice
- − − Self-Development, Genuine Person
- − − Security
- − − Fine Relations with Others
- + − Doing my Duty
- − − Doing the Best for Myself
- − − Intellectual Endeavor

Attitudes — Self-Ideal (SI)

- + Succorance
- + Deference
- − Dominance
- − Narcissism
- + Fantasied Achievement
- + Abasement
- − Change

- + Piety
- + Obedience
- + Chastity
- + Poverty

Attitudes — Institutional Ideal (II)

- + Order
- + Succorance
- − Natural Science
- + Abasement
- − Understanding
- − Achievement
- − Humanities and Social Science
- − Dominance
- + Fantasied Achievement
- + Energy
- − Harm Avoidance
- + Adaptability
- − Change
- − Reflectiveness
- + Emotionality
- + Deference
- − Ego Achievement

- − Responsibility
- + Poverty
- + Chastity
- + Obedience
- + Mortification
- + Piety

Needs and Conflicts — Incomplete Sentences Blank (ISB)

Needs
- − Avoid Censure and Failure
- − Abasement
- + Counteraction
- + Autonomy
- + Affiliation
- + Harm Avoidance
- + Acquirement
- + Nurturance
- + Understanding
- + Deference
- + Exhibition
- + Achievement
- + Dominance
- + Change
- + Order

Conflicts
- + Integrity vs. Despair
- − Initiative vs. Guilt
- + Identity vs. Diffusion
- + Industry vs. Inferiority
- + Generativity vs. Stagnation
- + Intimacy vs. Isolation
- + Trust vs. Mistrust
- + Autonomy vs. Shame and Doubt

Needs and Conflicts — Thematic Apperception Test (TAT)

Needs
- + Nurturance
- + Counteraction
- + Order
- − Dominance
- + Exhibition
- + Achievement
- + Deference
- − Acquirement
- − Autonomy
- − Abasement
- − Harm Avoidance
- − Succorance
- − Emotionality

Conflicts
- − Identity vs. Diffusion
- − Trust vs. Mistrust
- − Intimacy vs. Isolation
- − Autonomy vs. Shame and Doubt
- − Initiative vs. Guilt
- + Industry vs. Inferiority

* Variables listed according to weight on the Discriminant Function.
+ = Religious higher than Lay.
− = Religious lower than Lay.

more and are also higher than lay in their wish to become a genuine person through self-development. Security and fine relations with others are less important as values for religious women when contrasted with lay women. They prefer to be dutiful and are less willing to simply accept the bad features of the world while doing the best for themselves and those dear to them; they are less interested in the development of their minds in intellectual pursuits.

Undoubtedly, the general picture characterizing the values of the entering religious females is one of highly disciplined and selfless people committed to religious and altruistic concerns.

This picture of ideals is corroborated by the results for attitudes. For the SI, as compared with Lay women, religious women have personal ideals of succorance (dependency) and deference, rather than dominance, narcissism or fantasied achievement. They wish to be abased and humble and want change or novelty less than do lay. They wish to be pious, obedient, chaste and poor more than do lay women of their age.

On the II, religious women endorse higher order and succorance than do lay women, and less natural science. They also perceive the institution as expecting abasement of them, but less understanding (knowledge), achievement, humanities and social science interest or dominance than do the lay women perceive their institutions expecting of them. Religious women perceive fantasied achievement, energy, harm avoidance, adaptability and change to be expected of them, whereas they think that reflectiveness is not so expected of them. Religious women also endorse more emotionality and deference, but less ego achievement in their II. They also believe the institution expects them to help others. They do not think the convent asks them to value responsibility, bu they do see poverty, chastity, obedience, mortification and piety as expected of them by the religious institution, at least more than do lay women in relation to their respective institution.

The ideals proclaimed by the religious for the attitudes of the SI and II are very similar to the picture of self-discipline, of self-lessness and of commitment to the concerns of religious life which was seen for the values on the GGLI. In fact, first of all, the difference with the Lay Group is confirmed: 10 scales out of the 35 scales of the MAI-SI and 24 out of the 35 for the MAI-II are significantly different between the two groups.

Secondly, and more important, the good consistency within the ideal-self stated by the first hypothesis, is shown by the following data: 1) of the 10 variables which significantly differentiate the Religious from the Lay Group for the SI, 8 are consistent with the homonymous variables of the II. This is a particularly relevant

84

result because, as we have seen in chapter 5, the SI-II correlation is an important factor in the decision to enter religious vocation. 2) The content of these 8 scales confirms the general picture of commitment to the ideals of religious life presented by the values in the GGLI and is consistent with them. In fact, the emphasis is on piety, obedience, chastity, poverty, deference, submissiveness vs. dominance and self-criticality.

The second hypothesis

The second hypothesis deals with the following question: should one take at face value the proclaimed, conscious motivation to enter or, in addition, should possible subconscious elements be considered? The presence of inconsistencies of the subconscious, latent part of the self with the components of the ideal-self may offer an answer.

First, a general description of the data from the TAT and ISB is presented. Then a contrast of these findings in the latent-self versus the ones of the ideal-self will follow.

Within the TAT, when the needs loading less strongly on the discriminant function are considered, no immediate sense of inconsistency appears; actually, while entering religious in comparison with lay people have less interest in autonomy, harm avoidance and emotionality, they are also lower in abasement and succorance.

However, a sense of inconsistency becomes specific and evident if one focuses on the needs which in the TAT discriminate more characteristically the two groups, religious and lay people. In fact, on the one hand, religious show the same picture of discipline and selflessness present in the ideal-self: they are higher in nurturance, counteraction, order, deference and lower in dominance. However, paradoxically, they are also higher in exhibition, achievement with its accent on success, and acquirement.

The results of the ISB show a paradoxical pattern of inconsistency partially similar to the one of the TAT. While the entering religious are higher in affiliation, acquirement, exhibition, achievement, and dominance, on the one hand, they are also lower on avoidance of censure and failure, abasement, autonomy and harm avoidance, and relatively high on counteraction, nurturance and deference, change and order, on the other hand.

The inconsistencies present within both the TAT and ISB become more apparent when these data of the latent-self are compared with the ones seen in the ideal-self.

In the first hypothesis, the entering religious people showed values and attitudes which consistently emphasized self-discipline,

85

self-sacrifice, obedience, chastity, poverty, deference, submissiveness vs. dominance. In contrast, in the latent-self, they present a picture which stresses, in both the TAT and the ISB, the needs for exhibition, for acquirement, and for achievement with its accent on success; similarly, for the variable " dominance ", the higher need found in the ISB is inconsistent with the lower corresponding attitude proclaimed in the SI and in the II as well as with some values (e.g., " serving my community " or " self-sacrifice ") stated in the GGLI.

The results concerning the eight developmental stages or conflicts described by Erikson further confirm the existence of subconscious inconsistencies in the religious group. Thus, in the ISB the entering religious are higher for all these eight conflicts. The inconsistencies of these conflicts with the values and attitudes proclaimed in the ideal-self are many; one can think, for instance, of the contrast between the stated disposition to serve, to be obedient and deferent on the one hand, and the conflicts concerning trust vs. mistrust or autonomy vs. shame and doubt, on the other.

On the TAT, only the conflict of initiative vs. guilt is higher for the religious group. This difference between ISB and TAT is perhaps related to the fact that the entering religious in the II perceive their vocational institution as requiring abasement and obedience, and in the SI wish to comply with this perception. If it is assumed that the ISB taps a more conscious level of experience than the TAT, then it seems understandable that the individuals under the influence of abasement and obedience would tend to comply more easily in the ISB and thus to respond in a more socially desireable fashion. Assuming that this interpretation is true, then the TAT would provide a more accurate assessment of the subjects.

Anyway, the conflict of initiative vs. guilt fits quite well with the two clusters of needs previously noted as consistent or as inconsistent with the ideal-self expressed by religious: the needs for nurturance, counteraction, affiliation, order and deference, on the one hand, and in contrast, the needs for exhibition, for achievement, for acquirement, and for dominance, on the other hand. According to Erikson (1950, p. 22), the conflict of initiative vs. guilt permeates many areas of life; furthermore, its origins are to be found during the third developmental stage of man, which is related to infantile sexual identity and thus:

" . . . adds to the inventory of basic social modalities in both sexes that of " making " . . . There is no simpler, stronger word to match the social modalities previously enumerated. The word suggests enjoyment of competition, insistence on goals, pleasure of conquest. In the boy the emphasis remains on ' making ' by head-on attack; in the girl it may change to ' making ' by making herself attractive and endearing. The child thus develops the prerequisite for *masculine* and *feminine initiative,* that is, for the selection of social goals and perseverance in approaching them ". (Erikson, 1959, p. 78).

" The danger of this stage is a sense of guilt over the goals contemplated and the acts initiated in one's exuberant enjoyment of the new locomotor and mental power: acts of aggressive manipulation and coercion which go far beyond the executive capacity of organism and mind and therefore call for an energetic halt on one's contemplated initiative ". (Erikson, 1950, p. 224).

The subconscious needs for exhibition, for achievement, for acquirement, for competitive dominance shown by the entering religious people might have been sown during their third developmental stage of initiative vs. guilt because of unnecessarily exaggerated parental punitiveness or control. In turn, these needs may maintain in the adult the conflict around initiative vs. guilt concerning their expression and gratification. The choice of a religious vocation, then, would subconsciously serve either an ego-defensive or an utilitarian function; i.e., this choice expresses either the defensive reaction against the underlying guilt stirred up by needs (e.g., acquirement) which are subconsciously felt as inconsistent with the values proper to religious vocation (e.g., poverty) or the utilitarian function of subconsciously retaining the initiative for a potential expression of the same needs. Thus, the proclaimed values and attitudes of self-discipline and of unselfish concern for others function *consciously* as value-expressive, i.e., as means to implement the ideal-self; however, *subconsciously* they may function either as a defense against or as means for potential gratification of the inconsistent needs.

However plausible the present interpretation may be with regard to the *content,* the fact remains that, with regard to the *structure* of the self, there are large discrepancies, i.e., central subconscious inconsistencies between the ideals consciously proclaimed by the subjects and their subconscious needs.

Of course, this fact is not true for all the entering females; for instance, since group averages have been compared among the different structures of the self, the suggested conclusion is not generalizable to all the people in the group. However, the fact of the subconscious structural inconsistencies for at least some members of the group remains.

The third hypothesis

The third hypothesis holds that the subconscious inconsistencies explain *in part* the patterns of behavior (PB), of defenses and emotional styles presented by the entering people. Turning now to Chart 7, we find variables relevant to the third hypothesis testing for female religious.

CHART 7

SIGNIFICANT VARIABLES: ENTERING RELIGIOUS FEMALES VS. LAY *

MANIFEST SELF (As perceived)	LATENT SELF (As assessed)	
Traits	Emotional Styles and Defenses	
Present Behavior PB	Incomplete Sentences Blank ISB	Thematic Apperception Test TAT
— Change + Order — Abasement — Adaptability — Sensuality — Emotionality - Narcissism — Nurturance — Practicalness + Energy — Natural Science + Planfulness — Reflectiveness — Objectivity + Piety — Responsibility + Poverty	*Emotional Styles* — Depression, Covert + Anxiety, Overt — Anxiety, Covert + Guilt, Covert + Guilt, Overt + Paranoid Thinking + Depression, Overt *Defenses* — Intellectualization — Regression — Displacement — Projection, Complementary + Reaction Formation + Undoing + Projection, Supplementary + Parentification + Isolation + Compensation	*Emotional Styles* + Depression, Covert + Guilt, Covert + Guilt, Overt — Anxiety, Overt + Paranoid Thinking *Defenses* + Compensation + Reaction Formation + Isolation + Undoing — Displacement + Identification + Parentification — Projection, Complementary — Intellectualization

* Variables listed according to weight on the Discriminant Function.
+ = Religious higher than Lay.
— = Religious lower than Lay.

As is evident, there are a total of 17 out of 35 scales which were significantly different for the religious and the lay women on the MAI Present Behavior (PB) analysis. The religious group perceives less change in their behavior and more order. They see themselves as lower as far as being abased, adaptable, sensual, emotional, narcissistic, nurturant and practical. They claim they are more energetic and not interested as much as lay women in natural science. They claim more planful behavior, but less reflectiveness and less objectivity. They believe themselves to be more pious but less responsible in work and study; they claim higher poverty.

What, generally speaking, can be made of the present behavior as consciously presented by women religious? Can it be related to underlying needs? Sanford, Webster and Freedman (1957) claim that within the present behavior, one may find expression of impulses and/or inhibition of them. It is believed that both impulse expression or impulse inhibition can be defensive or spontaneous, according to the underlying psychodynamics. The present behavior alone, then, cannot be a major or reliable yardstick for psychologically assessing the personality (see the general premises). In fact, individuals with the same manifest behavior may have quite different underlying psychodynamics, e.g., central subconscious consistencies or inconsistencies (Rulla, 1971, pp. 152-154).

In order to more effectively evaluate whether the manifest behavior may be defensive or spontaneous in nature, the present interpretation will thus consider the given conscious self-perception for PB as well as the defenses and emotional styles in the light of the consistencies and inconsistencies which have already been seen to be present in the subjects under study.

The variables significantly differentiating religious from lay women *within* the structure of PB or conscious self-perception can be seen as suggestive of consistencies (similar clusterings) and inconsistencies (opposite clusterings) even on a conscious level. On the one hand, religious women see themselves as consistently higher in order, poverty, piety and self-denial, generally less sensual, vain or emotional, and more energetic, while on the other hand, they indicate they are less reflective, and less responsible, less helpful of others, less objective, and less adaptable, that is, less humble.

How can these consistencies and especially these inconsistencies *within* the self perception (PB) be interpreted if we also consider the consistencies and inconsistencies between values and attitudes (the ideal-self) vs. the needs of the latent self? As seen earlier (p. 84), religious women showed consistent self-ideals centering around self-discipline, self-sacrifice, obedience, chastity, deference, vs. dominance. In the latent self, however, needs for exhibition, achievement, dominance, acquirement are noted. The expression and/or inhibition of these inconsistent needs and ideals may be partially explicative of similar, though not exact inconsistencies noted above in the manifest behavior; there is a tendency toward order, poverty, piety, self-denial, less sensuality, less vanity and emotionality vs. a tendency toward behavior which is energetic, less reflective, less responsible, less helpful of others, less objective, and less humble.

The same can probably be said of the PB if we especially consider the third conflict of initiative vs. guilt, seen in the TAT as differentiating women religious from the lay: the present behavior, as partially expressive of values, attitudes and of underlying subconscious consistent and inconsistent needs, may be seen as related to this conflict. In fact, there is concern with *initiative* in the use of energy more for self than for others, in a proud, less objective, less reflective manner; and all these traits may easily stir up a sense of *guilt*. In turn, this guilt may lead them to counterbalance by means of traits like less narcissism or more order, piety, planfulness, and poverty.

It is important to note, however, that not all the variables presented in the PB are interpretable clearly and precisely in the terms given; the interpretation offered is always subject to appropriate depth investigation through interviews.

The study of possible inconsistencies or conflicts as related to PB can be further pursued by considering the emotional styles as gleaned from the TAT and the ISB analysis (see Chart 7). On the TAT, the religious indicate high covert depression and guilt (overt and covert), but are low on overt anxiety; they are also notably higher in paranoid thinking. On the ISB, the findings suggest internally inconsistent scores on anxiety (high overt, low covert) and depression (lower covert, higher overt), but the emphasis on guilt and paranoid thinking remain intact.

The prevalence of guilt may suggest that whatever the content of underlying inconsistencies, they most likely revolve around patterns of moral worth.

The emphasis on paranoid thinking fits in as an adjunct to this guilt, and could also fall in line with the results already seen for the conscious (chapter 5) and the subconscious motivation of the present chapter: religious women consciously tend to idealize the institution upon entrance. However, subconsciously, they present inconsistencies of these ideals with their needs. It seems understandable, then, that the subjects would feel " dissatisfied ", guilty

90

and would lose objectivity in favor of exaggerated ideation. The inconsistent subconscious tendencies as well as the paranoid thinking and guilt may also lead to inconsistent moments of depression and anxiety as indicated.

Given all of the above findings, one would expect the religious vocationers to indicate or choose the kind of defenses that attempt to *change* or deny rather than *justify* unacceptable, guilt-provoking behavior and thoughts. This is exactly the outcome of the TAT and ISB defense analysis.

The picture of the defenses on the ISB is comparable to that of the TAT. On the ISB, religious women are lower than lay women in intellectualization, regression, displacement, and projection (complementary) and higher in undoing, reaction formation, supplementary projection, parentification, isolation and compensation.

On the TAT, female religious vocationers indicate they use more defenses such as compensation, reaction formation, isolation and undoing, with less displacement. They are also higher than lay women in identification and parentification, but lower in projection (complementary) and intellectualization. The first four defenses mentioned particularly tend to shift guilt and depression-provoking material toward its opposite or change it to some more acceptable material or behavior. The low displacement, projection and intellectualization suggest that they reverse guilt-provoking behavior rather than justify it. The emphasis of religious women on identification is supportive of the other defenses, since it may be considered as a basis for recasting personal wishes and attitudes into those held by people in authority. This is in line with the idealization of the institution found in these same people (chapter 5). The tendency to parentify other people and institutions indicates that the nuclear family may be a source of conflict; some investigation into this area will be done in the following chapters.

The Male Group: The Seminarians

Subjects

The sample consisted of the entire group entering the training center in a Midwestern town. There were 47 subjects; however, due to incomplete protocols, only for the GGLI were all these individuals studied, while for the MAI, the ISB, and the TAT, 45 people were assessed.

The criteria followed in choosing this group deserve a special mention. In chapter 5, many reasons and facts were given to show that people who enter a religious vocational setting are not real " vocationers ": usually, their commitment is not made yet. This can be said to be even more true for the Seminarians chosen for this project. In fact, first of all, they received their college training along with lay students at the same small Catholic college in a Midwestern town and shared classes and academic facilities with them; secondly, although the Seminarians lived together in a community on the campus, they shared meals and recreational facilities with the lay students, also. Therefore, one could expect that their initial commitment to the priestly vocation would be even less evident than the one of people who enter a religious vocational setting and were isolated from continuous interaction with lay students.

The control group for Seminarians was randomly chosen from the lay Catholic males enrolled at the same college. All the entering Seminarians and 70% (for a total of 64 people) of the lay students living on the college campus agreed to participate in the project.

Results and Discussion

Tables 6.7 through 6.12 show the findings. The variables significantly different between the Seminarian and Lay Groups are summarized by charts 8 and 9.

92

CHART 8

SIGNIFICANT VARIABLES: ENTERING SEMINARIANS VS. LAY *

	IDEAL SELF		LATENT SELF	
	Values	Attitudes		Needs and Conflicts	
	General Goals of Life Inventory GGLI	Self-Ideal SI	Institutional Ideal II	Incomplete Sentences Blank ISB	Thematic Apperception Test TAT
	— Making a Place for Myself + Self Sacrifice — Security — Intellectual Endeavor — Coping with Life — Power, Control + Serving my Community + Serving God	— Fantasied Achievement + Practicalness + Deference — Science	— Natural Science + Succorance + Counteraction — Nurturance — Practicalness — Understanding — Humanities and Social Science — Exhibition — Achievement — Aggression	*Needs* — Play — Harm Avoidance + Dominance + Counteraction + Abasement + Avoid Censure and Failure — Recognition — Acquirement	*Needs* — Harm Avoidance — Succorance — Sex + Avoid Censure and Failure = (—Adaptabil.) ++ Autonomy ++ Dominance — Acquirement — Play ++ Abasement +++ Aggression +++ Counteraction +++ Change — Exhibition
		+ Piety	+ Mortification	*Conflicts* — Trust vs. Mistrust	*Conflicts* + Autonomy vs. Shame and Doubt — Trust vs. Mistrust — Generativity vs. Stagnation + Identity vs. Role Diffusion + Industry vs. Inferiority

* Variables are listed according to weight on the Discriminant Function.
+ = Seminarians are higher than Lay.
— = Seminarians are lower than Lay.

The first hypothesis

The ideal-self of the Seminarians, as represented by the values of the GGLI, is different from the one of the lay students for 8 out of the 21 variables. Note that for entering females, the same difference was 17 out of 21.

In comparison with lay people and in order of decreasing emphasis, Seminarians are lower for " making a place for myself getting ahead ", higher in " self-sacrifice for a better world ", less looking for security, for intellectual endeavor, for coping with life's problems as they come, for power or control over people and things; in addition, they value serving their community as well as serving God by doing His will. Therefore, in content terms, Seminarians shun competition, dominance, and personal safety in favor of service to mankind and of deferent submissiveness to God.

This general picture for values is consistent with the ideals proclaimed by the Seminarians for their attitudes. The data speak for themselves. For their own ideal or SI, Seminarians value less fantasies concerning achievement and are more indifferent to tangible personal gains, while they emphasize deference to authority and piety; finally, they show less interest in natural sciences. For the II, Seminarians see their institution as emphasizing mortification, succorance, and nurturance, and as deemphasizing natural sciences, counteraction, tangible personal gains, intellectuality, interest in the humanities and the social sciences, exhibition, achievement, and aggression.

The hypothesis of a good, general consistency among the values and attitudes of the ideal-self is supported. This is particularly true if the two stronger motivational forces of the ideal-self, i.e., the values of the GGLI and the core of the attitudes represented by the SI, are considered together. However, as expected, this ideal-self of the Seminarians is less articulated, less elaborated than the ones of the entering religious, females and males (compare chart 8 with charts 6 and 10).

The second hypothesis

Adopting the same type of analysis used for the female group, we can start with the TAT results. Again as for the females, contrasts are present within the test and especially between it and the ideal-self.

Seminarians show lower needs for harm avoidance, succorance, sex, acquirement, play and exhibition and a higher need for counteraction: a picture of self-discipline and selflessness. In contrast, however, they present greater needs for avoidance of censure and failure, for autonomy, dominance, abasement, aggression and change.

The inconsistencies between the ideal-self and the latent-self are apparent: entering Seminarians consciously emphasized deferent submissiveness to God and to authority and shunned competition and dominance; however, subonsciously, they present greater needs for autonomy, for dominance, for aggression and—in such a context—for counteraction. Similarly, they stress the unselfish ideals of lack of concern for personal security, but—in contrast—they show greater concern about abasement and have greater needs for avoidance of censure and failure. By the same token, they proclaimed readiness to self-sacrifice for a better world and indifference to tangible personal gains, but they present needs for dominance, for aggression, and for avoidance of censure and failure.

In line with the foregoing inconsistencies, one is not surprised to find that the entering Seminarians have a greater conflict of autonomy vs. shame and doubt as the first conflict which differentiates them from lay students. Similarly, in accordance with the foregoing inconsistencies with their ideal-self as well as in line with their higher needs for abasement and for avoidance of censure and failure, Seminarians are higher than their controls for the conflicts of identity vs. role diffusion and of industry vs. inferiority.

Further results for the conflicts described by Erikson show a positive picture for the Seminarian group in comparison with the Lay Group: Seminarians are less disturbed for trust vs. mistrust and for generativity vs. stagnation. This disposition to trust and to engage in constructive endeavor is, first of all, in line with their lower needs for harm avoidance, succorance, sex, acquirement, play, exhibition, and with their greater thrust to counteract; it is consistent with their ideals of self-sacrificing service to mankind, also.

The many inconsistencies between the conscious ideals and the latent-self, which we have seen in the TAT findings for the Seminarians, are not so apparent in the ISB. As a matter of fact, only the inconsistency centering around a greater need to avoid censure and failure seems to be present. The findings for play, harm avoidance, dominance, counteraction, abasement, recognition, acquirement, and the conflict of trust vs. mistrust seem quite consistent with the selflessness and discipline proclaimed in the GGLI, in the MAI-SI, and in the MAI-II.

As it was seen in the discussion for the findings of the religious females, the partially discrepant results between the two fantasy tests, TAT and ISB, may be explained by the fact that these two tests set up different conditions for the revelation of the self: the ISB is a more structured test than the TAT because it asks the person to complete items having definite reference to his own life; thus, in taking this test, the individual may feel more threatened to reveal personally-unacceptable material. Then, it would not be surprising to find that the results of the more structured ISB are in part close to the structured self-reports, while the results of the rather unstructured and less threatening TAT more easily reveal material which is personally-unacceptable because inconsistent with the proclaimed ideals.

Nevertheless, the large discrepancies between the ideal-self and the latent-self are a fact. We will return to these findings when discussing the results of the entering religious males.

The third hypothesis

Chart 9 summarizes the statistically significant variables of Seminarians vs. lay as discussed in this hypothesis.

CHART 9

SIGNIFICANT VARIABLES: ENTERING SEMINARIANS VS. LAY *

MANIFEST SELF (As perceived)	LATENT SELF (As assessed)	
Traits	Emotional Styles and Defenses	
Present Behavior PB	Incomplete Sentences Blank ISB	Thematic Apperception Test TAT
— Play — Natural Science + Adaptability + Harm Avoid. — Aggression — Narcissism	*Emotional Styles* + Depression, Covert	*Emotional Styles* + Anxiety, Covert — Paranoid Thinking — Guilt, Overt + Guilt, Covert
+ Obedience + Piety + Poverty	*Defenses* — Undoing — Projection, Complementary	*Defenses* + Repression — Isolation — Projection, Supplementary — Undoing + Displacement

* Variables listed according to weight on the Discriminant Function.
+ = Seminarians higher than Lay.
= Seminarians lower than Lay.

For PB, whereas female religious were different from lay on 17 out of 35 scales, Seminarians differ from lay men on only 9 scales. In their present behavior, Seminarians perceive in themselves behavior oriented less toward play or natural science, aggression or narcissism, but more toward adaptability, harm avoidance, obedience, piety, and poverty.

A look at these 9 variables indicated a rather consistent self-perception. In summary, the Seminarians claim they are more ready to forego personal gratifying needs, e.g., play, aggression, narcissism, and submit themselves rather to authority and to God, in adaptable, obedient, pious and poor (as an expression of poverty) behavior. Thus, if taken at face value, the PB at first may appear to be a rather " spontaneous " impulse inhibition, at least since no conscious behavioral inconsistencies would suggest otherwise.

However, seen in the light of the underlying subconscious inconsistencies evidenced in hyptohesis 2, these conscious consistencies may take on a new meaning. They do fall in line readily with that part of the latent self which endorses less sex, less recognition, acquirement, play or exhibition, and, perhaps, higher abasement. They also are concordant with the ideal-self which strives for submissiveness to God and authority, sacrifice of self, less competition, less dominance. However, this conscious behavior indicated in the PB seems rather inconsistent with subconscious needs for avoidance of censure and failure, for dominance, autonomy, and aggression. This may suggest that submission to authority and a self-forgetting more conscious exterior may be an attempt to cover over more subconscious drives for autonomy, aggression, and domination, while being at the same time in the service of subconscious needs of avoidance of censure and failure and, perhaps, of abasement. Thus, after consideration of the underlying inconsistencies, the conscious PB does not seem to be as " spontaneous " as, at first look, one would think.

The conflicts indicated in the TAT seem to confirm this interpretation. In fact, Seminarians have to defend themselves against the conflicts of autonomy vs. shame and doubt, identity vs. role diffusion, and industry vs. inferiority.

Since the PB seems rather consistent but may actually be covering over and at the service of subconscious inconsistent needs, we should expect emotional styles and defenses which are repressive or *justifying* in nature. In fact, as seen from chart 9, Seminarians are higher in covert anxiety, guilt and depression, and lower than lay in paranoid thinking and overt guilt. The justifying trend seems to prevail in the adopted defenses; in fact, apart from the use of projection, Seminarians utilize repression and displacement more and isolation or undoing less—quite the opposite of the female religious sample who tend to *change* guilt-provoking behavior by using less displacement and intellectualization and more undoing, reaction formation and isolation.

Once again, let us recall to the reader that not all variables are definitively interpretable as given; the present interpretation is always subject to appropriate depth investigation in interviews.

THE MALE GROUP: THE RELIGIOUS

Subjects

The religious group practically included the same individuals studied in chapter 5 for the conscious motivation of attitudes. These religious totaled 135 entering males. The reader is referred to chapter 5 for a description of the sample.

An appropriate control group of lay students was composed to match the religious subjects. The individuals of the lay group studied with the seminarians were combined with lay Catholic males enrolled at a large college in a Midwestern city. The resulting lay group consisted of 105 subjects, randomly selected from among the entering freshmen; they represented 70% of the people invited to freely participate in the project. The time-consuming nature of the TAT and ISB scoring necessitated the choice of random sub-samples from both the religious and the lay groups. The scoring of these two tests investigated 82 entering religious and 64 lay students.

Results and Discussion

The findings are presented in Tables 6.13 through 6.18. Charts 10 and 11 summarize the variables which significantly differentiate religious from lay people.

CHART 10

SIGNIFICANT VARIABLES: ENTERING RELIGIOUS MALES VS. LAY *

IDEAL SELF			LATENT SELF	
Values	Attitudes		Needs and Conflicts	
General Goals of Life Inventory GGLI	Self-Ideal SI	Institutional Ideal II	Incomplete Sentences Blank ISB	Thematic Apperception Test TAT

General Goals of Life Inventory GGLI
- − Making a Place for Myself
- + Serving God
- − Security
- − Intellectual Endeavor
- − Doing the Best for Myself
- + Achieving Immortality
- − Coping with Life
- + Self Sacrifice
- + Getting Pleasure
- − Self-Discipline
- + Doing my Duty
- + Living for the Pleasure of the Moment
- − Survival
- + Serving my Community
- − Power, Control

Self-Ideal SI
- − Natural Science
- + Humanities and Social Science
- + Nurturance
- − Abasement
- − Order
- − Change
- − Harm Avoidance
- − Fantasied Achievement
- − Impulsiveness
- + Objectivity
- + Adaptability
- + Practicalness
- + Deference
- − Play
- − Narcissism
- − Emotionality
- + Succorance
- + Ego Achievement
- − Sensuality
- + Poverty
- + Piety
- + Mortification
- + Responsibility
- + Obedience
- + Chastity

Institutional Ideal II
- − Natural Science
- + Energy
- + Nurturance
- + Abasement
- − Objectivity
- − Affiliation
- + Practicalness
- + Succorance
- + Counteraction
- + Deference
- + Ego Achievement
- + Adaptability
- + Dominance
- − Fantasied Achievement
- − Play
- + Planfulness
- + Narcissism
- + Change
- + Order
- − Humanities and Social Science
- − Sensuality
- − Harm Avoidance
- + Poverty
- + Mortification
- + Responsibility
- + Chastity
- + Piety
- + Obedience

Incomplete Sentences Blank ISB

Needs
- − Harm Avoidance
- − Acquirement
- − Sex
- − Play
- − Deference
- + Counteraction
- + Aggression
- + Abasement
- − Change

Conflicts
- − Integrity vs. Despair
- − Trust vs. Mistrust

Thematic Apperception Test TAT

Needs
- − Harm Avoidance
- − Acquirement
- + Emotionality
- − Succorance
- − Sex
- − Deference
- − Abasement
- + Dominance
- − Play
- + Exhibition
- − Avoid Censure and Failure
- + Autonomy
- + Aggression

Conflicts
- + Autonomy vs. Shame and Doubt
- − Generativity vs. Stagnation
- + Intimacy vs. Isolation
- − Integrity vs. Despair
- + Industry vs. Inferiority
- + Identity vs. Role Diffusion

* Variables are listed according to weight on the Discriminant Function.
+ = Religious are higher than Lay.
− = Religious are lower than Lay.

The values stated by religious in the GGLI differentiate them from the lay group for 15 out of the 21 variables; this is a remarkable difference if it is compared with the corresponding figures for seminarians who differed from the lay people in only 8 out of 21 variables.

The content of the values include the following characteristics. Male religious strive less to make a place for themselves and rather wish to serve God. To accomplish this they are willing to forego personal security, intellectual pursuits and concern with doing the best only for themselves and those dear to them. With their ultimate goal—immortality in heaven—they strive less than lay men to merely cope with life as it comes. Through self-sacrifice, self-discipline, duty and the renunciation of pleasure, they seem to reach for goals beyond merely their own survival, rather seeking to serve their community, but not to obtain power or control.

Of the foregoing 15 differentiating values of the GGLI, 12 are the same which distinguish the entering religious females from their lay group. Therefore, again, as for the religious females, entering religious males stress values of self-discipline, selflessness, of dedication to humble service to mankind and to God. Furthermore, religious males are unconcerned about themselves and shun competitive power and control, personal safety and vanity.

The consistency of these values of religious with their attitudes is impressive. The stated self-ideals or SI are as follows. Male religious are lower in ideals than lay men for natural sciences, but higher for humanities and social science. They have nurturance and abasement as personal ideals more than do lay men, but espouse ideals of order, change, harm avoidance, fantasied achievement and impulsiveness less than them. Objectivity and adaptability are ideals for male religious and they wish to be indifferent to personal tangible gains; they wish to be deferent. They also tend to idealize less play, narcissism and emotionality than lay college men, but maintain succorance and ego achievement in their repertoire of ideals. To finalize their picture of ideals, they also endorsed less sensuality, but more poverty, piety, mortification, responsibility, obedience and chastity.

The view of the religious concerning their institution is shown by the following data. Again, as for their personal ideals, they see the institution expecting less interest in natural sciences of them. They perceive institutional ideals of higher energy, nurturance, abasement and objectivity and less affiliation or search for tangible personal gains. On the whole thus far, their institutional ideals seem similar to their personal ideals. Male religious, more than lay male collegiates, see their institution expecting more succorant, counteractive, deferent, ego achieving, dominant and adaptable living from them. They see the institution as discouraging fantasied achievement and play, but encouraging planfulness and less narcissism. They are, furthermore, higher in institutional ideals as change and order, lower in humanities and social science, sensuality, avoidance of injury to themselves. As to be expected, they perceive institutional ideals as higher than lay men in poverty, mortification, responsibility, chastity, piety and obedience.

The foregoing findings regarding the ideal-self of values and attitudes may be summarized as follows: 1) there is an evident difference between the religious males and the lay students: in 15 out of the 21 values of the GGLI; in 25 out of the 35 variables of the MAI-SI and in 28 out of the 35 variables of the MAI-II. 2) Entering religious males have a vocational ideal-self which is much more elaborated than the one of the entering seminarians; the religious group differs from the lay group for 15 variables of the GGLI, 25 of the MAI-SI and 28 of the MAI-II, while the comparable figures for seminarians vs. their lay group were 8 for the GGLI, 5 for MAI-SI and 11 for the MAI-II. 3) The just-presented data show a quite clear desire of the religious males to commit themselves to their vocation. This fact is further corroborated by the striking consistency which exists within the components of the ideal-self: first of all, of the 25 variables which significantly differentiate the religious from the lay group for the SI, 18 are consistent with the homonymous variables of the II, only 3 are inconsistent and the remaining 4 do not significantly differentiate the two groups in the II: therefore, these 4 latter variables give a further support to the good consistency within the ideal-self if one recalls that the SI has a greater vocational motivational strength than the II. Secondly, the content of the 22 scales (18 plus 4) for attitudes is highly consistent with the general picture of commitment to the ideals of religious life presented by the values in the GGLI. In fact, the emphasis is on poverty, piety, mortification, responsibility, obedience, chastity, nurturance, acceptance of criticism, deference, as on shunning of personal safety, of narcissism and sensuality.

The first hypothesis of good consistency among the components of the ideal-self seems to be well supported.

The second hypothesis

The striking consistency within the ideal-self is partially seriously undermined by central, subconscious inconsistencies between it and the latent-self.

101

Already within the TAT there is a picture of inconsistency. On the one hand, religious show the same picture of selflessness and of discipline presented in the ideal-self: they are lower in harm avoidance, acquirement, succorance, sex, play, exhibition, and show more self-criticality. However, in contrast, a picture of competitive self-assertion seems to be present also: religious are higher for emotionality, dominance, avoidance of censure and failure, autonomy, aggression, and lower for deference.

On the ISB, a similar discrepancy emerges. Lower harm avoidance, acquirement, sex, play, change, coupled with higher abasement, are present on the one hand; lower deference, higher aggression and counteraction are found on the other hand. Again, signs of competitive self-assertion emerge, even though less striking than the ones of the TAT. As previously discussed for the results of the females and of seminarians, the more apparent—and therefore, threatening—relevance for self-description of the ISB in comparison with the TAT may explain the partial difference between the two tests.

The inconsistencies present within both the TAT and the ISB become more evident when these findings for the latent-self are compared with the ones seen in the ideal-self.

The entering religious proclaimed values and attitudes which consistently emphasize deferent service, obedience, shunning of competitive power and control. In contrast, in the latent-self, they present a picture which stresses less deference and greater aggression, dominance, autonomy, emotionality, and—in this context—greater counteraction. Furthermore, in the ideal-self, religious stated ideals of lesser concern for personal safety and of greater adaptability or humility; in contrast, in the TAT, they show greater concern for avoidance of censure and failure. Similarly, they proclaimed readiness to self-sacrifice for a better world, to self-discipline, and to less narcissistic concerns, but they have greater needs for aggression, emotionality, dominance, autonomy, avoidance of censure and failure.

There is a similarity between the inconsistencies of the ideal-self vs. latent-self shown by the religious males and the ones presented by the seminarians. Therefore, one would expect that there is also a similarity for the conflicts described by Erikson. The data confirm this expectation. Consequently, the following discussion concerning these conflicts will combine seminarians and religious.

Both the religious and the seminarian groups are in a better psychological balance than their corresponding lay groups with regards to the two developmental stages of trust vs. mistrust and of generativity vs. stagnation. Religious are also more balanced for the stage of integrity vs. despair. This positive picture of trust, of promising engagement in constructive endeavor is in line with the consistency found for both religious males and seminarians between their ideals of self-sacrificing service to mankind and their lower needs for harm avoidance, acquirement, succorance, sex, play, and exhibition.

However, the negative picture is the same for religious males and seminarians, also: they present the same conflicts described by Erikson and these conflicts seem to be related to the same central inconsistencies between their ideal-self and latent-self.

First of all, in line with the inconsistencies between humanitarian, cooperative goals, on the one hand, and competitive, aggressive needs, on the other, the main conflict for both seminarians and religious is autonomy vs. shame and doubt. It would seem that for some of the seminarians and religious, the choice of religious vocation may have, in part, served the defensive function of coping with the subconscious conflict over an underlying rebellious autonomy. In committing themselves to humanitarian concerns and obedience to authority, seminarians and religious hope to be able to resolve their inconsistencies in a socially useful manner. This would explain the autonomy pole of the conflict and related inconsistencies. As far as the other pole is concerned, i.e., shame and doubt and related inconsistencies, perhaps the following considerations are pertinent. Religious and seminarians show inconsistency between their ideals of less concern for personal safety and of greater humility, on the one hand, and their greater need to avoid censure and failure, on the other. Thus, perhaps, for some of them, religious vocation may subconsciously serve the utilitarian function to diminish the possibility of censures and of failures and the defensive function of overcoming their feelings of shame and doubt. By committing themselves to ideals of humility and altruistic concerns, they subconsciously hope to obtain the support of the vocational institution to resolve their inconsistencies in a socially useful style of life.

Secondly, in accordance with the foregoing inconsistencies between ideals reflecting lack of selfish concern for oneself, on the one hand, and the needs for avoidance of censure and failure, for abasement, aggression, dominance, and counteraction, on the other, two other secondary conflicts are similar for religious males and seminarians: identity vs. role diffusion and industry vs. inferiority. Indeed, according to Erikson (1959, pp. 142-143), problems concerning identity are likely present in adolescence when the earlier conflict concerning autonomy vs. shame and doubt has not been successfully overcome. In discussing these persons, Erikson says:

103

> In their search for a new sense of continuity and sameness, ado-
> lescents have to refight many of the battles of earlier years,
> even though to do so they must artificially appoint perfectly well-
> meaning people to play the roles of enemies. (1950, p. 228).

Furthermore, according to Erikson (1959, p.92), these persons
are frequently intolerant as a necessary defense against their underlying sense of poor, diffuse identity.

In addition to the foregoing three conflicts, religious present
the one of intimacy vs. isolation. This conflict may be related to
the already seen inconsistencies between readiness to self-sacrifice
and to non-narcissistic, non-sensual concerns, on the one hand,
and the greater needs for emotionality, for dominance, for aggression, for autonomy, on the other. Along the same line, it is interesting to note that the self-descriptions of the MAI (SI and PB) show
that religious not only are high in nurturance but high in succorance as well, which may signify that their tendency in giving may
be in order to get. According to Erikson (1959, pp. 124-125), the
presence of this intimacy vs. isolation conflict for the religious can
be related, at least in part, to the fact that they presented the conflict over identity vs. role diffusion; he suggests that an inability
to resolve the conflict over intimacy vs. isolation is likely when
the one of identity vs. role diffusion had not been successfully
overcome:

> That many of our patients break down at an age which is pro-
> perly considered more preadult than postadolescent is explained
> by the fact that often only an attempt to engage in intimate
> fellowship and competition or in sexual intimacy fully reveals
> the latent weakness of identity.
>
> True " engagement " with others is the result and the test
> of firm self-delineation ... Where a youth does not resolve such
> strain, he may isolate himself and enter, at best, only stereotyped
> and formalized interpersonal relations; or he may, in repeated
> hectic attempts and repeated dismal failures, seek intimacy with
> the most improbable partners.

We have seen that seminarians and religious are quite similar
in their psychodynamics of underlying inconsistencies. However,
they are also quite different: seminarians present a much less articulated and elaborated ideal-self than the religious males; e.g., in
the GGLI, only 8 of the 21 values differentiate seminarians from
their control, whereas 15 out of 21 differentiate religious. In the
same line, none of the 6 religious scales of the MAI differentiate
seminarians from their control, when SI and II are considered together. In contrast, all these 6 scales for the SI and II differentiate

the religious from their control. It is possible that, because the seminarians entered and shared the same college campus with the lay students, they never experienced even an initial, significant commitment to their vocation.

If the foregoing difference means that, in a sense, seminarians never really " entered " their vocation, then it should not be a surprise to find that they dropped out at a significantly higher rate than the religious. Information obtained at the end of the four-year training period of seminarians and of religious indicated that 95% of the former had dropped out, whereas only 47% of the latter had left religious life.

Nevertheless, the similarity of religious and seminarians for the central subconscious inconsistencies remains. According to the tenets and observations, clinical and empirical, of depth psychology, such subconscious inconsistencies are not easily overcome. Therefore, in spite of the consciously proclaimed ideals, one would expect that the existing underlying subonscious inconsistencies may be a potential for future difficulty. In fact, the " Loyola Psychological Study of the Ministry and Life of the American Priest ", sponsored by the National Conference of Catholic Bishops of the USA, show that 202 of the 271 priests studied were psychologically either " undərdeveloped " or " maldeveloped " (Kennedy and Heckler, 1971). Entering vocationers show central subconscious inconsistencies and, apparently, such inconsistencies may persist; the initial conscious vocational commitment is not an assurance that subjects will successfully cope with these inconsistencies in their future religious or priestly life.

The third hypothesis

Finally, we turn to the third hypothesis for the male religious, asking what function these subconscious inconsistencies can have in explaining their present behavior.

Chart 11 indicates the variables relevant to this hypothesis, significantly differentiating religious males from the lay sample. There are 12 out of the 35 scales significant for PB.

CHART 11

SIGNIFICANT VARIABLES: ENTERING RELIGIOUS MALES VS. LAY *

MANIFEST SELF (As perceived)	LATENT SELF (As assessed)	
Traits	Emotional Styles and Defenses	
Present Behavior PB	Incomplete Sentences Blank ISB	Thematic Apperception Test TAT
Traits	*Emotional Styles*	*Emotional Styles*
— Change	— Paranoid Thinking	— Guilt, Covert
— Natural Science	— Depression, Overt	— Paranoid Thinking
+ Humanities and Social Science	— Anxiety, Overt	— Guilt, Overt
— Order		
— Succorance	*Defenses*	*Defenses*
+ Nurturance	— Parentification	— Parentification
+ Practicalness	— Isolation	+ Repression
+ Objectivity	+ Repression	— Isolation
— Narcissism	+ Reaction Formation	+ Displacement
— Sensuality	+ Intellectualization	— Undoing
	— Undoing	
+ Chastity	— Regression	
+ Poverty		

* Variables listed according to weight on the Discriminant Function.

\+ = Religious higher than Lay.

— = Religious lower than Lay.

As is seen, male religious see themselves as endorsing less change and being less interested in natural science, but more so in humanities and social sciences. They are not as orderly or dependent as lay males, and they claim they do help others more. They profess to be less concerned with tangible personal gains for themselves, less narcissistic and less sensual, and see themselves as more objective, chaste and poor.

Similar to the seminarians, the PB of the religious males content-wise generally seems to present a consistent pattern. In a word, their description of self in terms of forgetfulness of self and sensual, dependent relationships for rather objective chaste altruistic concerns is quite impressive, if we stop there.

However, when the results of hypotheses 1 and 2 are integrated, this rather consistent-appearing exterior takes on new shades of meaning. The PB of male religious is similar to their values and attitudes in terms of selflessness and discipline for God and others; as recalled in hypothesis 1, they were higher in values and attitudes as poverty, mortification, chastity, nurturance, deference, service of community and God, and less narcissistic.

Yet, both these ideals and the PB are quite inconsistent with the latent self which indicates higher needs for avoidance of censure and failure, for autonomy, aggression, dominance, emotionality and less deference. Furthermore, as already seen in discussing hypothesis 2, these inconsistent needs are in line with and reinforced by conflicts described by Erikson: autonomy vs. shame and doubt, intimacy vs. isolation, industry vs. inferiority, identity vs. role diffusion.

Now, if we recall the findings obtained for seminarians, we can notice a striking similarity between them and the present ones of the male Religious with regard to the relationship among the substructures of the self. For both seminarians and male Religious, the dimensions of the ideal-self (SI and II) for values and attitudes are quite consistent with their PB and inconsistent with their LS. Therefore, it seems that the data for the PB confirm what has been said in hypothesis 2 concerning SI and II: PB, too, for both seminarians and male Religious, at least in part, is used for utilitarian or for ego-defensive purposes.

With this in mind, one would expect to find the same trends in male Religious as found in Seminarians for defenses and emotional styles, i.e., an indication of a repressive trend or of a trend toward justification rather than change of behavior. This is, in fact, present.

In the ISB analysis, male religious are lower than male lay collegiates in paranoid thinking, depression and anxiety, lower in

107

parentification, isolation and undoing and regression, and higher in repression, reaction formation and intellectualization. As for Seminarians, the prevailing trend toward repressive or justifying attempts is even more evident in the TAT where less overt and covert guilt, less paranoid thinking are present, and greater repression, displacement and intellectualization exist together with less isolation and undoing.

The fact seems to be that the nonemotionality indicated in less guilt, depression and anxiety is consistent with the use of repression. As indicated or suggested earlier in the presentation of consistent, one-sided PB and values and attitudes, underlying inconsistent needs are repressed. The relative absence of parentification, isolation, undoing and regression also indicate a general clamping down on emotional expression, capable thus of producing a conscious presentation of themselves as less sensual, less sexual, less changing, less dependent, less narcissistic, more objective. Rather than paranoid thinking, there is intellectualization of underlying inconsistent needs, i.e., justification of them in terms of socially-honorable goals and implementation.

Finally, once again, let us remind the reader that the present interpretation of variables is always not definitive or all-inclusive. It is always subject to appropriate depth investigation in interviews for final verification.

Summary of Findings and Considerations

1) The individuals studied in this Chapter 6 were practically the same considered in chapter 5: a) 283 female religious who belonged to six different groups entering three different settings; they represented these entire groups and were compared with 136 lay Catholic college girls entering two different colleges; b) 135 male religious who represented the seven groups which entered three different houses of formation; they were compared with 105 freshmen of two lay Catholic colleges.

In addition, the present chapter studied the whole entering groups of 45 seminarians who started their college training; they were matched with 64 lay freshmen of the same college.

For all the lay control groups, the individuals who volunteered to participate in the project representd 70% or more of the total entering population which had been randomly selected and invited.

2) Three hypotheses were formulated:

    1) In general, there is a good consistency among the components of the ideal-self of the entering votioners, that is, among the content of the values and the attitudes proclaimed by the individuals in their initial commitment to a religious vocation.

    2) The vocational consistency within the ideal-self is undermined by *some* central, subconscious inconsistencies of its components with the latent part of the actual-self (LS).

    3) These subconscious inconsistencies between the ideal-self (SI and II) and the latent self (LS) explain *in part* the patterns of behavior (PB), of defenses and of emotional styles presented by entering people.

These three hypotheses were tested by means of multivariate analyses of variance and discriminant function analyses. In general, they received support by the findings, for all the three groups of vocationers: seminarians, female and male religious. These results confirm, expand and clarify the ones of chapter 5.

3) The findings of hypothesis 1 support the data of chapter 5 that the ideals of a person expressed by his self-ideal-in-situation (SI-II) are the basic *conscious* disposition to enter a religious vocation. This initial force in turn may foster the self-transcendence which characterizes the vocational commitment; it also disposes the individual to the action of grace and, as a side effect, to self-actualization, to self-fulfillment (cfr. chapter 1). The foregoing considerations are well supported by the significantly higher ideals shown by the entering vocationers in comparison with their lay control groups.

4) However, the results of hypothesis 2 indicate that the entering vocationers present an " idealization " both of their real personalities and of the institution they choose to enter.

In fact, there are many significant inconsistencies between the latent part (LS) of the actual-self of vocationers on the one hand, and their self-ideal (SI) and institutional ideals (II), on the other. These inconsistencies are reinforced by other similar ones, which appear *within* the actual-self, at least in its latent component (LS).

109

These " idealizations " of selves and of institutions may act according to a feedback mechanism: the similarity which the individual perceives between himself and the chosen institution enhances his attraction to it; in turn, the felt attraction enhances the perceived similarity. There follows an unrealistic exaggeration of the similarity. All these processes lead to an idealistic choice and decision, which, however, are not completely realistic.

The lack of realism seems to stem, at least in part, from the subconscious realities of some needs present in the latent self, which are significantly inconsistent with the conscious realities of the vocational ideals. In fact, there are strong indications from the data (cfr. hypothesis 2 for the three groups studied) that the consciously proclaimed ideals serve only in part the two functions of attitudes described in the beginning of this chapter 6 as value-expressive function and as knowledge function. The data strongly suggest that part of the ideals consciously expressed may serve the other two possible functions of attitudes: utilitarian and ego-defensive. In other words, the choice and the decision to enter are made also as a consequance of subconscious needs, so that people may subconsciously direct themselves to the life in religious vocation as an attempt to gratify themselves (utilitarian function) or as a defensive effort to cope with underlying conflicts or inconsistencies (ego-defensive function).

5) The findings for the three groups discussed in hypothesis 3 suggest that, as it seemed to be true for the proclaimed self-ideal, so also the self-concept concerning the manifest behavior (PB) may be expressive of any one of the four functions of attitudes. Again, this fact is in part the consequence of the existing subconscious inconsistencies between the ideal-self (SI and II) and the latent-self (LS).

In the same line, it is interesting to notice a structural difference between the female religious group and the male groups of religious and seminarians (cfr. hypothesis 3). In women, the PB is somewhat inconsistent *within* itself and partially inconsistent with the ideal-self of values and attitudes, while in men the PB is quite consistent within itself and with the ideal-self. In addition to this fact, and perhaps in relation with it, women use defenses which tend to change rather than to

110

justify guilt-provoking behavior (PB) or thoughts (SI and II); men do the opposite. It is characteristic of conflicts, and of inconsistencies to produce various different types of defenses; and this seems to be the case in the present study because of the underlying subconscious inconsistencies.

6) A conclusion is prompted by the findings and considerations discussed up to now in chapters 5 and 6: in spite of the unquestioned sincerity and generosity of the individuals, the motivations and the manifest behavior *consciously* proclaimed by entering vocationers can not be taken at face value. Other elements should be considered, especially subconscious influences. In fact, people tend to idealize themselves and the institutions.

People enter " idealistically "; and this " idealism " may be realistic if it stems from ideals which are consistent with the actual-self, especially in its latent component; such consistencies dispose to self-transcendence and to the action of supernatural grace. However, in more than a few people, it seems that entering idealism is quite unrealistic because of subconscious inconsistencies. Hence, a germinative SI-II goes frequently together with a vulnerable SI-II, which is neither objective nor free (cfr. chapter 4). Ideals are consciously conceived, but may be subconsciously held.

7) Content-wise, the female religious of the present sample are characterized by the conflict described by Erikson as of initiative vs. guilt. Male vocationers (seminarians and religious) are concerned with the conflicts of autonomy vs. shame and doubt, of identity vs. role diffusion, of industry vs. inferiority, and, only for religious, of intimacy vs. isolation. For a description of these conflicts discussed by Erikson (1950, 1959) see Appendix B-3. The structural approach to the study of vocation followed in this book underlines not so much this content aspect, but rather an interesting structural pattern which emerges in all the three groups studied: the content of the developmental conflicts described by Erikson is often closely related to the content of the structural inconsistencies between the ideal-self and the latent-self. For instance, for the male religious, the conflict of autonomy vs. shame and doubt is in line with their inconsistencies between the proclaimed readiness for goals of self-discipline of self-sacrifice, of defe-

111

rent obedience, on the one hand, and their needs for competitive aggression and avoidance of censure and failure, on the other hand (cfr. pp. 102-103). It would seem that there exists some relationship between the developmental or affective maturity of vocationers and their maturity in making a vocational decision, i.e., between their affective maturity and what could be called their vocational maturity.

8) The findings indirectly support the hypothesis (cfr. chapter 4) that the objectivity and freedom of the SI-II at entrance may be impaired by the four sources of lack of knowledge, identification with the vocational institution, intrapsychic conflicts or inconsistencies, and pressures from the environment. The latter is possible especially in the case of conflictual, inconsistent individuals, who are more vulnerable, i.e., more sensitive to the influence exerted by members of their family, of vocational institutions, e.g., through their teaching organizations.

9) Intriguing questions are raised by the results with regard to the role which values play for perseverance in vocation of the entering people. It would seem that if vocational values are only *moderately* present, the rate of dropping out is significantly increased. The case in point is the group of seminarians when compared with the one of male religious: the two groups differ significantly in terms of values, the seminarians showing much lower values. At the end of four years of training, 47% of the male religious and 95% of the seminarians had dropped out. This is in line with the theoretical position presented in chapter 1 with regard to values and vocational inconsistencies.

However, do the values become a significant asset when they are *strongly* present? What is the mutual dynamic relationship between values and subconscious inconsistencies for the process of dropping out and for vocational effectiveness?

10) The policy to defer the entrance of the applicants into the religious houses has become frequent. The usefulness of this measure is evident, especially in the case in which developmental problems are at stake. But is it useful when unconscious or deeply preconscious vocational inconsistencies are present? Can they improve and to what extent, if they are approached merely by means of greater existential experience? It would seem that if the person is *unconsciously* inconsistent, he would

continue to react to his central inconsistencies with ego-defensive or utilitarian attitudes, which in turn will sustain an unrealistic idealization of the self and of the institution. And all these processes will take place without the person knowing it. Then, how can the existential experience made possible by the deferred entrance be of any real help?

As the reader can easily understand, many of the hypotheses and question touched upon in chapters 5 and 6 need more data in order to be supported, confirmed, answered or clarified. This will be done, in part at least, in the following chapters by investigating if and how much the central consistencies/ inconsistencies influence the developmental-affective and the vocational maturities (chapter 7), if they tend to persist (chapter 8), if they affect leaving vocation (chapter 9).

THE GERMINATIVE AND THE VULNERABLE SI-II: THEIR STRENGTH AND CONTENTS IN ENTERING PEOPLE

One of the conclusions suggested by the findings of chapters 5 and 6 was that the ideals of an entering vocationer as expressed by his SI-II (self-ideal-in-a-given-situation) are frequently unrealistic and thus vulnerable because of *subconscious* forces. What individuals entering a vocational setting thought of their ideals was in part inconsistent with the latent components of their self.

How much of this SI-II is made vulnerable? What kind of variables undermine it more frequently: abasement or aggression or succorance, etc.? The answer to the first question may be found by combining aspects of both the germinative and the vulnerable SI-II and by evaluating their corresponding strengths. In terms of the theory and of the structural approach proposed in this book (cfr. chapters 1 and 2), this means to assess the degree of consistencies and/or inconsistencies present in *each* person. An analysis of the content variables of these consistencies/inconsistencies will help to answer the second question.

Thus, the present chapter will have two separate parts which will deal: 1) with a *quantitative* assessment of the strengths of the consistencies/inconsistencies underlying the SI-II; and 2) with a *qualitative* evaluation of their content.

THE STRENGTH OF THE SI-II

Proper indices were developed to reach the goal aimed at in this first part. Their rationale, their methodological implementation and their limitations will now be considered.

In the previous chapter the meaning of the four possible functions of attitudes was discussed; e.g., when a person expresses an attitude which can be qualified as of achievement, he may do it because he is aiming, consciously or subconsciously, to express vocational values (value-expressive function), or to increase his knowledge (knowledge function), or to obtain a reward (utilitarian function) or defend himself against some underlying and unacceptable need or against some hard realities in the external world (ego-defensive function).

With regard to these four functions of attitudes, two sets of hypotheses have been elsewhere (Rulla, 1971, pp. 150-151 and 307-321) formulated: 1) that the utilitarian and the ego-defensive functions may prevail over the value-expressive and the knowledge functions in the case of compliance and of non-internalizing identification, while the opposite is true in the case of internalization and of internalizing identification; 2) that compliance or non-internalizing identification may prevail in the motivation of a person when he has central subconscious inconsistencies between his ideal-self and his latent-self, while internalizing identification and internalization are fostered by central consistencies between the same component of the self.

The foregoing two hypotheses need explanation and a more precise presentation. According to the theoretical and empirical contribution of Kelman (1958, 1960, 1961), *compliance* can be said to occur when an individual accepts influence from another person or group not because he believes in the content of the proposed attitudes, but simply in order to gain some external reward or to avoid some punishment controlled by that person or group. According to the theory proposed in this book, unconscious or deeply preconscious vocational inconsistencies lead to compliance. In fact, when an individual has such inconsistencies, " his sense of frustration will ' drive ' him to look for actual or potential sources of approval, of acceptance, of rewards and, conversely, to avoid sources of disapproval, of rejection, of punishment. To the extent to which he is ' driven ' by the foregoing central vocational inconsistencies, compliance will take place " (Rulla, 1971, p. 317). Note that external pressure is not indispensable; relief of internal guilt is sufficient (Freedman, Wallington and Bless, 1967).

115

Identification occurs when the individual adopts the behavior of another person or group because this behavior is associated with a satisfying relationship to this person or group. In contrast with compliance, the individual believes in the content of the induced behavior; however, he believes it only or especially because this content is associated with the satisfying relationships. Note that this gratifying relation to the other person may be established by the receiver either in actuality or within his own fantasy. In both instances, the relation is gratifying because it supports *part* of the image the individual has of himself.

When an individual's psychodynamics is chiefly characterized by *not* deeply preconscious vocational inconsistencies (PsI or SoI) and by *conscious* vocational conflicts (PsC), his sense of mild frustration or of tensions will ' incline ' him to look for sources which will enhance his more or less shaky self-image, self-esteem, by means of gratifying self-defining relationships; thus, identification will develop*. However: a) to the extent to which *the part* of the self-image, of the self-esteem gratified by the relationship may be integrated with objective vocational values, to that extent the identifying relationship will lead toward internalization of vocational attitudes and values (internalizing identification); b) as much as the *part* of the self-image gratified by the identifying relation can *not* be integrated with objective vocational values, so much this relation will lead toward compliance or at least away from internalization (non-internalizing identification).

Identification is a powerful process of social influence but it is *highly ambivalent* as a means of affecting internalization of vocational attitudes and values: it may enhance it, but it may hinder it, too (e.g., Kelman, 1961; Schafer, 1968) (Rulla, 1971, p. 317).

It may be hypothesized that vocationally dissonant variables (cfr. Appendix C-2) lead rather to non-internalizing identification, while vocationally neutral variables (cfr. Appendix C-2) lead to internalizing identification.

" *Internalization* can be said to occur when an individual accepts influence because the induced behavior is congruent

---

* Let us recall that in the theory, self-conception, self-esteem were defined in terms of PB-(SI-II) and/or of LS-(SI-II) congruence or discrepancy.

with his value system " (Kelman, 1961, p. 65). Here the *content* of the induced attitude or behavior is intrinsically rewarding since it is consistent with the value-system of the individual, it fits with his psychodynamics (of values, attitudes and needs). Thus the induced attitude or behavior is "internalized", because it is not tied to an "external" source and thus does not depend on social support; the latter was the case for compliance or identification where the induced attitude or behavior was not integrated in a consistent way with the individual's value system, but rather tended to be isolated from the rest of his values. Internalized behavior gradually becomes independent of the external source; in fact, "it becomes part of a personal system, as distinguished from a system of social-role expectations" (Kelman, 1961, p. 66). Of course, the intrinsic reward of internalization is obtained by the individual also *by means of* his interaction with the environment (people, work, etc.). This is not true for identification and even more for compliance where the individual's gratification is attained *because of* the interaction with the environment, under the form either of a gratifying relationship (identification) or of reward-punishment, approval-disapproval processes (compliance).

> When an individual's psychodynamics does not present pre-conscious vocational inconsistencies and is characterized by conscious vocational conflicts or consistencies (PsC or SC), his sense of tension and his ego-strength will dispose him to look for value congruence of his behavior since this congruence is the intrinsically gratifying factor; thus, internalization of vocational attitudes and values is fostered (Rulla, 1971, pp. 317-318).

Kelman points out that the three processes are not mutually exclusive and seldom occur in pure form. However, in many situations a particular process predominates and determines their central characteristic.

The foregoing distinctions may become clear if applied to vocational choice and commitment. This may be done by using the six motivational patterns for behavior in organizations proposed by Katz (1964). Compliance is present when a person enters a vocation or remains in it because of: 1) conformity to the norms of the system: people in the institution accept the fact that membership means "complying" with its rules; 2) instrumental system rewards: membership in the institution entails benefits to the individual; e.g., social and financial security, educational facilities; these benefits provide incentives for entering and remaining in the system; 3) instrumental individual rewards: while system rewards apply to all members, individual rewards of an instrumental character (e.g., a promotion) are obtained by some individuals because of their particular contributions or their privileged positions, etc.

Identification is present when the person enters or persists in religious life because of intrinsic satisfaction from specific role performance: the activity in a role is gratifying in itself because such an activity gives the individual the chance to express his skill, his talents, to gratify his needs (e.g., for achievement, for dominance, etc.); this motivational pattern has to do with the opportunities which the institutional role, or professional roles within the institutions, provide for the expression of individual talents and abilities and for the satisfactions of accomplishment.

In contrast, the commitment to a vocational institution is the result of internalization if the person has taken the values or goals of the institution as his own. Two examples will show the difference between the present and the previous pattern of motivation: a) the religious sister who derives her gratifications from teaching could be equally happy in doing it in many different places—or, even, institutions (lay or religious)—but unhappy as a nurse in anyone; b) on the contrary, the sister who has internalized the values of her vocation or, even the goals of her own institution with its specific problems and potentialities, wants to stay on at her vocation or institution and, furthermore, is willing to accept other assignments than a teaching one.

Finally, identification is again prevailing if the underlying motivation of the vocational commitment is especially based on gratifications derived from primary-group relationships. These are the social-emotional satisfactions which members of a small group obtain from interacting with one another; mutual attraction, approval, support, stimulation, etc., are among the many conscious or subconscious motivations possible in this category. Strictly speaking, this affiliative motivation is "another form of instrumental-reward-seeking, but some of its qualitative aspects are sufficiently different from the instrumental system and individual rewards previously described to warrant separate discussion " (Katz, 1964, p. 143).

From the foregoing discussion, it appears that the combination and the assessment of the strength of compliance, non-internalizing identification, internalizing identification and of internalization which are present in an entering vocationer may give a quantitative evaluation of the relative strength of his germinative and vulnerable SI-II. Accordingly, we considered it useful to devise some measurement which could express if and how much the internalizing forces of the self of the person (internalization and internalizing identification) would outweigh the non-internalizing forces (non-internalizing identification and compliance). As will be discussed in the following paragraphs, we tried to obtain an index of the maturity of a person. It should be emphasized that the aim intended here was an assessment of, not an assessment for (Prelinger and Zimet, 1964; Wiggins, 1973); i.e., our emphasis was on " understanding " the degree of maturity with which people enter religious life rather than on " predicting " how this degree of maturity affects his perseverance or his effectiveness in vocation.

Every reader familiar with the field knows the great complexity related with the task of conceptualizing and of measuring the *maturity of the self*. It is not the purpose of the present discussion to consider in detail this difficult, multifaceted problem. According to Becker (1971), one can approach this task by following three possible directions: an empirical method, which Becker calls " holistic research ", like the one followed by Maslow (1954); a theoretical method, like the one of Heath (1965); finally, an approach which tries to find an experimental verification of a theory already formulated. We chose the last direction and tried to assess maturity according to the degree of compliance, of identification, internalizing or not, and of internalization, in the framework of the theory proposed in chapter 1.

The first question which we had to answer was: is maturity related to the objectivity and freedom of the SI-II and thus, to consistency/inconsistency in the self?

Two conditions characterize the objectivity and freedom of the SI-II (Rulla, 1971, pp. 168-173): 1) the values and the attitudes proclaimed by a person in his SI-II correspond to the real hierarchy of values and objects to which he aims; therefore, those values and attitudes serve the value-expressive function rather than the utilitarian or ego-defensive functions, i.e., internalization or internalizing identification rather than compliance or non-internalizing identification; 2) the foregoing system of subjective values and attitudes (SI-II), in addition to being objectively valid, should also be consistent with the rest of the self, especially with its latent part (LS); because of this consistency with the rest of the self, the SI-II is free; actually, the person is free and can make acts of genuine self-affirmation; as Weigel (1960) has stressed, self-affirmation should be consistent with the structure of the self otherwise it becomes self-denial. And, as the consistency of the self makes *possible* the freedom and the objectivity of the SI-II, so each act of self-affirmation will increase the consistency of the self.

In line with the foregoing considerations, the following definition of maturity was proposed: " the knowledge and the acceptance of one's objective and free SI-II *and* the living of it " (Rulla, 1971, p. 193). However, what is this SI-II, what is the value-attitude system which characterizes it? We took into consideration only two types of value-attitude systems: the one of vocation and the one of normal human development.

The first type emphasizes the vocational values, terminal and instrumental (cfr. chapter 1), and sees maturity especially in the light of them; hence, it was called " vocational maturity ". A related *Index of Vocational Maturity* (IVM) was developed and translated into measurement procedures (cfr. chapter 3, under B). This index expresses the degrees of compliance, identification, and internalization which an individual has at the moment in which he actually enters a vocational setting. Again, let us recall that this index *as such* has no predictive value concerning the future life in vocation. It only helps to understand the amount of consistency/inconsistency which motivates one's vocational choice and decision and thus, the strength of this germinative and vulnerable SI-II considered together; i.e., how much the germinative SI-II outweighs the vulnerable SI-II or vice versa; in a word, how mature, in *psy-*

chological terms, has been one's decision to enter a religious vocation.

The second type of value-attitude system which was considered emphasizes the concept of ego- or self-development. This concept was rendered measureable by the thinking of Harry Stack Sullivan (1953) and of Piaget (1932). Many other theories and researches have followed these two original conconceptualizations: C. Sullivan, Grant and Grant (1957), Isaacs (1956), Peck and Havighurst (1960), Kohlberg (1964), Loevinger (1966 a, b, 1970, 1973), and possibly for some aspects Ausubel (1952), Harvey, Hunt and Schroder (1961), and Rogers (1961). All these authors consider the stages of ego-development as types; that is, they stress the possibility that development may stop below the highest level for many persons, thus generating a corresponding typology (a fact not emphasized by Erikson, 1950, 1959). All the mentioned authors are more or less concerned with a value-attitude system which centers around impulse control, moral development, interpersonal relationships and cognitive preoccupations (Loevinger, 1970). Several of them see human development as a milestone sequence, i.e., as a sequence of different levels of behavior, which tend to rise and then fall off in prominence as one ascends the scale of maturity; these levels differ qualitatively and are " not completely reducible to quantitative differences even though they may be graded continuously " (Loevinger, 1969, p. 92). In the sequence proposed by Loevinger, in contrast to the expositions of Erikson, age-specific aspects are excluded from the definitive descriptions. The milestone sequence outlined by these authors may be interpreted as a value-attitude system of human development which ascends from the stage of compliance to the ones of non-internalizing and internalizing identifications, to the internalization previously discussed in this chapter.

The common elements of a normal developmental sequence offered by the foregoing authors were adopted in this study to express the " developmental maturity " characterizing the entering vocationers. A corresponding *Index of Developmental Maturity* (IDM), which some writers would call an index of " affective maturity ", was developed. This index expresses the degrees of compliance, identification, and internalization

121

of an entering vocationer as they can be inferred by his capacity to handle, to control his major core conflicts. The handling capacity was rated as I if the conflicts appeared to be strong enough to "always" have a debilitating influence on the person's functioning in any one of the following three areas: academic performance, interpersonal relationships, and moral-religious values in general. The same capacity to handle core conflicts was graded as II when any one of these three foregoing areas of functioning was affected "almost always"; as III if affected "frequently"; as IV if "rarely" affected.

Degree I of developmental maturity would correspond to prevailing compliance, degree II rather to non-internalizing identification, degree III rather to internalizing identification, and degree IV to prevailing internalization. Judgments of the capacity of handling core conflict(s) and the corresponding degree of developmental maturity were based on an intuitive, clinical synthesis of test data collected during all three testing sessions of this research and on the information which appeared during the "Depth Interview". The procedures followed in this assessment have been described in chapter 3, under E.

It should be noticed that in judging moral-religious development, the attention and importance given to the three *virtues* of poverty, chastity and obedience were greater in the case of entering vocationers than in the one of lay college people.

What are the similarities and the differences between the two proposed indices of vocational maturity and of developmental maturity?

Both indices intend to rate entering vocationers or lay people of similar age according to a milestone sequence characterized by four stages or types of compliance, of non-internalizing identification, of internalizing identification and of internalization. Both indices are based on a typology of variables (e.g., abasement, aggression, etc.) more than of persons, even though for both of them the attention is focused particularly on the variables which have the greater influence on the person's functioning. In fact, for the index of vocational maturity (IVM) the attention is on the central inconsistencies or consistencies (cfr. chapter 3, under B) and for the index of developmental maturity (IDM) on the main core conflicts.

However, there are differences, between the two indices,

both conceptual and operational. Conceptually, both indices consider as important the system of moral-religious values and attitudes, especially for entering vocationers. Still, the emphasis of the IVM is on the *vocational* values, terminal and instrumental, while this is less true for the IDM. In fact, the evaluation of the inconsistencies, conflicts, and consistencies (chapter 3, B) made to obtain the IVM was strictly related to whether the needs and the attitudes characterizing these inconsistencies, conflicts, etc., were dissonant or neutral with regard to vocational values.

Differences were present also operationally. The IVM considered only 14 of the 162 variables assessed in the IDM. Secondly, the statistical operations of the first index would take into explicit or implicit account 105 variables which were not assessed in the second index. Thirdly, the combination of the objective data obtained from the tests was done in the IVM according to a " mechanical composite " technique, while the IDM emerged from the techniques of " profile interpretation ", " clinical composite " and " clinical synthesis " (cfr. chapter 3, F for a description of these techniques).

The two indices are conceptually and operationally distinct. However, distinctions do not necessarily imply divisions or separations. The distinctions discussed between the two indices do not in any way prejudice the question of correlations or of complex triggering or facilitating effects between the two of them. It is the task of empirical research to find some answer to this question concerning the possible interdependence between the two aspects of maturity, developmental and vocational. This will be done to a very limited extent in the present chapter.

Before passing to the presentation of the research, it is proper to briefly list some limitations, among many possible others, of the two adopted indices.

Both indices consider the relationship of values and of the degree of compliance, of identification and of internalization; but they do it more indirectly than directly; in fact, the statistical procedures by which they are obtained take into consideration the force which values have in their dynamic interaction with attitudes and needs but not their own independent force. Thus, the conflict-free areas of the self perhaps are not sufficiently considered. Furthermore, both indices consider assessment of, not assessment for, i.e., both help to understand the decision to enter rather than to predict; they help to partially evaluate how mature, developmentally and vocationally, the decision to enter a religious vocation has been, but—as such—they do not serve the function of predicting perseverance or effectiveness in vocation. Finally, the IVM has assessed only 14 variables, as needs and as attitudes in their mutual consistent/inconsistent relationship (cfr. Appendices B-3, C-2); however, these 14 variables, taken from Murray's (1938) theory of personality, are agreed upon as covering quite broadly, if not exhaustively, the spectrum of human motivation (Jackson, 1970; Wiggins, 1973).

THE RESEARCH

The Index of Developmental Maturity (IDM)

The results for the index of developmental maturity (IDM) are presented in charts 12 and 13.

CHART 12

DEGREE OF DEVELOPMENTAL MATURITY
PRESENT IN EACH INDIVIDUAL
AT ENTRANCE INTO THE RELIGIOUS INSTITUTION

Group	Degree of Developmental Maturity			
	I	II	III	IV
Religious Males (N = 80)	15% (12) f	45% (36) f	30% (24) f	10% (8) f
Religious Females (N = 128)	12% (16)	48% (61)	26% (33)	14% (18)
Totals (N = 208)	13.5% (28)	46.5% (97)	28% (57)	12% (26)

(Percentages; Number of subjects in parenthesis)

N.B. Degree I: always influenced by main conflict(s).
Degree II: almost always influenced by main conflict(s).
Degree III: frequently influenced by main conflict(s).
Degree IV: rarely influenced by main conflict(s).

CHART 13

DEGREE OF DEVELOPMENTAL MATURITY
PRESENT IN EACH INDIVIDUAL
AT THE BEGINNING OF THEOLOGICAL TRAINING

Group	Degree of Developmental Maturity			
	I	II	III	IV
Beginning Theologians (N = 39)	31% (12) f	48.5% (19) f	18% (7) f	2.5% (1) f

(Percentages; Number of subjects in parenthesis)

N.B. Degree I: always influenced by main conflict(s).
Degree II: almost always influenced by main conflict(s).
Degree III: frequently influenced by main conflict(s).
Degree IV: rarely influenced by main conflict(s).

The 208 subjects considered in chart 12 are all the Religious, males and females, to whom it was possible to give the depth interview (cfr. chapter 3, section E) after four years of training in religious life. They represented 89% of the available sample of males and 93% of the similar sample of females. The last interviews took place in 1972.

The 39 individuals studied in chart 13 are people who had just begun their Catholic theological training. They belonged to a group entirely different from the one of 45 younger seminarians studied in chapter 6 at the beginning of their college training. For these 39 people, the interviews took place in 1973 and 1974.

An important difference between the two groups of chart 12 and the one of chart 13 concerns their geographical distribution. People of chart 12 belonged to the religious setting which in Table 3.1 are indicated as 1 and 2 for men and to settings 1, 2 and 3 for women, therefore, to 5 different settings. These religious came from the Midwest (3 settings), from the West (1 setting) and from the East (1 setting) of the USA. On the contrary, the individuals of chart 13 were 75% of the invited students who belonged to 45 dioceses geographically representing the entire territory of the USA.

The data of charts 12 and 13 speak for themselves: only a very small percentage of the subjects who decide to start a vocational commitment has reached a developmental maturity, which allows them to handle their core conflict(s) in a successful way. A second set of entering vocationers, with percentages which oscillate between 30 and 18, is frequently influenced in a negative way; while a substantial majority is either always or almost always negatively influenced by their core conflict(s).

As the data of chapter 6 indicated, the group of seminarians studied there (45 subjects) had not yet made a real decision concerning a vocational commitment. Perhaps, their living together with lay students on the same college campus was part of the factors leading to a possible uncertainty in their decision. These data and facts should be taken into consideration while looking at the results found for this group. Because of the high rate of dropping out, only 22 members of this entering group of seminarians were able to be interviewed; actually, the interview took place only after two years of training instead of after four years as with the other groups. The data concerning their IDM are: 41% (9 subjects) for degree I, 59% (13 subjects) for degree II. Almost all these 22 subjects dropped out two years after the interview.

The results found in the present study sound quite similar, at least percentage wise, to the ones published in other research. Even though the reader should take into account the different criteria and methodologies followed by the various investigators, perhaps he may be interested in knowing some of these findings: according to Baars and Terruwe (1971), 10-15% of all priests in North America and in Western Europe are mature, 60-70% emotionally immature, 20-25% present serious psychiatric difficulties. According to another perspective, the data of Kennedy and Heckler (1971) concerning priests of the United States indicate that out of 271 subjects: 19 are developed, 50 developing, 179 underdeveloped, and 23 maldeveloped. This sample is not representative of the entire population because only 31% of the religious priests and 24% of the diocesan priests initially selected for the project were eventually interviewed.

All the foregoing figures are quite close to the ones which concern the general population both in Western Europe and in North America. Several studies have been published. Here it suffices to mention some of the most known, like the ones by Srole et al. (1962), by Leighton (1963), by Essen Möller (1956).

Unfortunately, in the present research it was not possible and/or advisable to compare the religious groups with their corresponding lay Catholic college groups of males and females for the IDM. For one, the participation in the final depth interview of the lay college people at the end of the four years of college was too low: 21% of the males and 59% of the females invited. Secondly, and more important, as already indicated, the criteria used in assessing the two groups, religious vs. lay, were different, at least with regard to the living of the three virtues of poverty, chastity and obedience. These two shortcomings were not present for the assessment of the index of vocational maturity (IVM), which was done on the basis of the data obtained at the beginning of the lay college training. Thus, the percentage of the participants was 70% and 72% for the randomly selected males and females, respectively. Furthermore, while in the assessment of the IDM the interviewer knew if the subject was a lay or a religious person, and thus was possibly influenced in his evaluation, the same was not true for the IVM; the latter is based on a computer combination of data obtained from self-report questionnaires and from an evaluation of projective techniques in which the two assessing persons scored the protocols independently and without knowing whether the protocol would belong to a religious or to a lay person. Therefore, for IVM a comparison between religious and lay persons is possible. Actually, this possibility is made even more acceptable because this index was conceived and operationalized according to a structural approach (cfr. chapter 2).

The Index of Vocational Maturity (IVM)

The subjects studied for the IVM were randomly selected from the entire groups starting their training as religious, seminarians, or lay college students. This selection was necessitated by the time-consuming nature of the scoring of the projective tests (TAT and ISB) used with other tests for this index. The female religious totaled 95 and came from two consecutively entering groups of setting 1 of Table 3.1 as well as from a group of setting 2 of the same institution. The 96 male religious also belonged to one institution and precisely to three consecutive groups of setting 1 and to two consecutive groups of setting 2. Seminarians totaled 40 subjects, males and females of lay colleges 52 and 50 respectively; all these subjects were entering freshmen. Thus, the seminarians were 40, the religious males and females were 191, and the controls of both sexes 102, for a total of 333 subjects.

There were three aims intended by using the IVM: 1) to obtain indirectly an evaluation of the strength of the germinative and the vulnerable SI-II of the entering vocationers, i.e., to express in one measurement the amount of consistencies/inconsistencies present in them; 2) to see if and to what extent there was a relationship between the two indices of vocational maturity and of developmental maturity; and 3) to compare among themselves the various groups of entering vocationers (religious, females and males; seminarians) and of freshmen of lay Catholic colleges.

The task related to the first two aims was performed by studying the 91 subjects among the religious males and females as well as among the seminarians for whom it was possible to match the results of the depth interview (IDM) with the ones of the IVM. This was done by comparing for *each one* of the 91 subjects his actual performance in the IDM (e.g., his degree II of developmental maturity) with the score obtained for his IVM (e.g., .15). Table 7.1 gives the data which were matched. Note that the degrees of Developmental Maturity of this sample were as follows: 24% for Degree I, 54% for II, 21% for III and 1% for IV.

A statistical analysis was performed to assess the validity coefficient and the discriminative efficiency of the IVM as compared to the IDM. The phi-coefficient of validity obtained was: .6304, which shows that between the two indices there is a correlation significant at $p < .0001$. Table 7.2 outlines the results for the discriminative efficiency. The overall proportion of " similar " assessments made by the two indices is 87%: $P(VP) + P(VN) = = .165 + .703 = .868$.

The third aim was to compare among themselves the various groups for the IVM. The comparisons made were the following: 1) Religious Males vs. Religious Females; 2) Religious Females vs. Lay Females; 3) Religious Males vs. Lay Males; 4) Seminarians vs. Lay Males; 5) Seminarians vs. Religious Males; 6) All Religious, Males and Females, vs. All Lay, Males and Females; and 7) All Religious, Males and Females, combined with Seminarians vs. All Lay, Males and Females. Each group of the foregoing contrasts was divided into two subgroups: people with " high " IVM and people with " low " IVM. " High " and " low " were determined according to the standards obtained in Table 7.2 and therefore, correspond to individuals with prevailing internalization or internalizing identification vs. individuals with prevailing non-internalizing identification and compliance.

When comparing the various groups according to the two foregoing " high " and " low " degrees of vocational maturity, there was no significant difference between any groups of the seven comparisons considered. These comparisons were made using the simple chi-square and the phi-coefficient method.

128

Having discussed the relative strength of the SI-II in terms of the amount of consistencies/inconsistencies which affects its objectivity and freedom, we will focus on some content variables which structurally express the germinative or vulnerable SI-II.

The subjects considered here were the same 333 individuals described in the previous section. The measurements adopted were those explained in chapter 3, section C: the quantification of the amount of consistencies/inconsistencies and conflicts/defensive consistencies for each variable.

This analysis should highlight the content variables emerging as major difficulties or major strengths in the subjects and will explore any significant difference between the groups concerning these areas of strengths and weaknesses. Although the focus will be on the content, the structural approach is still the basis of the entire analysis, i.e., the variables considered are the ones which recurred most frequently through the structural analysis.

The first concern is with the frequencies of the inconsistencies, conflicts, defensive and non-defensive consistencies expressed as percentages for each group and for the whole sample. Table 7.3 presents the frequencies and percentages for each variable in each of the five groups. If we combine these data for all the groups using summary percentages for each variable, the following appear as most prominent: for inconsistencies—dominance 75%, abasement 73.8%, defendence 71.6%, aggression 56%, succorance 44.6% (in other words, these data indicate that 75% of the 333 people analyzed in this study presented a central inconsistency for dominance, etc.); for conflicts—succorance 41%, harm avoidance 39.6%, counteraction 36.2%, nurturance 31.6%, affiliation 31.2%, defendence 25.8%, and achievement 24.8%; for defensive consistencies—order 69.4%, understanding 66.2%, achievement 61.8%, counteraction 59.5%, affiliation 51.2%, and nurturance 46.8%; for consistencies—exhibition 81%, chastity 62.8%, harm avoidance 34.6%, and aggression 18.2%.

This global picture expressed in terms of *frequencies* corresponds to the data discussed in the previous section concerning vocational and developmental maturity. More specifically, the presence of inconsistencies in 70-75% of this sample corresponds to the data reported earlier in this study.

The next observation is in regards to the comparisons that can be made between the different groups when the variables that significantly differentiate them are considered. Chart 14 shows the contrasts, their direction and the variables contributing to the differentiation among groups.

Chart 14

VARIABLES SIGNIFICANTLY DIFFERENTIATING GROUPS IN TERMS OF STRUCTURAL SELF-CONCEPTIONS

FOR MALE RELIGIOUS AND FEMALE RELIGIOUS *

Inconsistencies	M	F	Conflicts	M	F	Defensive Consistencies	M	F	Consistencies	M	F
Dominance	−	+	Achievement	+	+	Achievement	−	+	Aggression	−	++
			Exhibition	+	−	Dominance	−	+	Exhibition	−	−
			Harm Avoidance	−	+	Order	+	−	Harm Avoidance	++	−
			Nurturance	+	+	Understanding	−	+	Order	++	+
			Understanding	+	−	Chastity	+	−	Chastity	−	−
			Chastity	−	+						

FOR MALE RELIGIOUS AND MALE CONTROLS

Inconsistencies	R	C	Conflicts	R	C	Defensive Consistencies	R	C	Consistencies	R	C
Abasement	+	−	Defendence	+	−	Affiliation	++	−	Harm Avoidance	+	−
Dominance	−	++	Affiliation	−	++	Counteraction	−	+	Chastity	−	+
Harm Avoidance	−		Counteraction	−	−	Understanding	−	−			
			Nurturance	++	−	Chastity	+	−			
			Succorance	−	−						

FOR FEMALE RELIGIOUS AND FEMALE CONTROLS

Inconsistencies	R	C
Defendence	—	+
Affiliation	+	—
Nurturance	+	—
Succorance	—	+

Conflicts	R	C
Defendence	+	+
Aggression	+	—
Counteraction	—	+
Dominance	+	—
Nurturance	+	+
Succorance	—	+

Defensive Consistencies	R	C
Dominance	—	+

Consistencies	R	C
Order	—	+

FOR SEMINARIANS AND MALE RELIGIOUS

Inconsistencies	S	R
Defendence	+	—
Dominance	+	—

Conflicts	S	R
Defendence	—	+
Aggression	—	+
Dominance	—	+
Order	—	+
Succorance	—	+

Defensive Consistencies	S	R
Affiliation	—	+
Order	—	+
Chastity	—	+

Consistencies	S	R
Succorance	+	—

FOR SEMINARIANS AND MALE CONTROLS

Inconsistencies	S	C
Harm Avoidance	—	+

Conflicts	S	C
Aggression	—	+
Counteraction	—	+
Dominance	—	+
Harm Avoidance	+	—
Nurturance	+	—

Defensive Consistencies	S	C
Counteraction	+	—
Dominance	+	—
Order	—	+

Consistencies	S	C
Harm Avoidance	+	—

* Variables listed are all statistically significant.
+ = First group higher than the second group.
— = First group lower than the second group.

Of the 64 variables significantly differentiating the groups, 34 are vocationally neutral and 30 are vocationally dissonant. The difference among the groups is not explained by this content differentiation alone.

Chart 15 is a further summary of the data, listing the frequencies and percentages over all dimensions of the 64 variables contributing to the differentiation among the groups. As previously discussed in this chapter, inconsistencies lead toward compliance as a prevailing trend, consistencies toward internalization, conflicts for vocationally dissonant variables toward non-internalizing identification, and conflicts for vocationally neutral variables toward internalizing identification. Chart 15 follows this conceptualization. Keeping in mind that inconsistencies, defensive consistencies, and conflicts for dissonant variables constitute the vulnerable aspect of the SI-II and that consistencies and conflicts for neutral variables constitute the germinative aspect of the SI-II, Chart 15 indicates that 62.5% of the variables significantly differentiating the groups appear as inconsistencies, defensive consistencies, or conflicts for vocationally dissonant variables (the vulnerable SI-II), whereas 37.5% of the variables significantly differentiating the groups appear as consistencies or conflicts for neutral variables (the germinative SI-II).

A test for the significance of a proportion applied to this result yielded a $z = 2.07$, $p < .04$. The groups appear to be differentiated more in terms of the vulnerable aspect of the SI-II than in terms of the germinative aspect of the SI-II.

Chart 16 shows the breakdown of the variables that contribute to the significant differentiation among the groups into the vocationally neutral and vocationally dissonant (cfr. Appendices C-2 and B-3).

The number of variables corresponding to the vulnerable aspect of the SI-II (cfr. chart 15 and previous discussion) is 22 for the dissonant and 18 for the neutral variables. The number of variables corresponding to the germinative aspect of the SI-II is 8 for the dissonant variables and 16 for the neutral.

Using tests of the significance of a proportion, the following results emerged: 1) the germinative and vulnerable aspects of the SI-II do not differ in terms of neutral variables ($z = .34$, $p < .74$); 2) there is no significant difference within the vulnerable SI-II between dissonant and neutral variables ($z = .64$, $p < .52$); 3) there is a difference, but only approaching significance, within the germinative SI-II between the dissonant and neutral variables ($z = 1.73$, $p < .08$); and 4) the germinative and vulnerable aspects of the SI-II differ significantly in terms of the dissonant variables ($z = 2.89$, $p < .004$).

132

CHART 15

PERCENTAGES AND FREQUENCIES OF VARIABLES
SIGNIFICANTLY DIFFERENTIATING GROUPS

(Variables N = 64)

Contrasts	Inconsistencies and Defensive Consistencies		Conflicts for Dissonant Variables		Conflicts for Neutral Variables		Consistencies		Totals	
	%	f	%	f	%	f	%	f	%	f
Male Religious—Female Religious	9.37	(6)	4.69	(3)	4.69	(3)	7.81	(5)	26.56	(17)
Male Religious—Lay Control	10.94	(7)	3.13	(2)	4.69	(3)	3.13	(2)	21.88	(14)
Female Religious—Lay Control	7.81	(5)	4.69	(3)	4.69	(3)	1.56	(1)	18.75	(12)
Male Religious—Seminarians	7.81	(5)	4.69	(3)	3.13	(2)	1.56	(1)	17.19	(11)
Seminarians—Lay Control	6.25	(4)	3.13	(2)	4.69	(3)	1.56	(1)	15.63	(10)
TOTALS	42.17 (27) 62.50		20.33 (40) (13)		21.88 (14) 37.50		15.62 (24) (10)		100.00	(64)

% = Percentages
f = Frequencies

Chart 16

FREQUENCIES OF VOCATIONALLY DISSONANT
AND NEUTRAL VARIABLES DIFFERENTIATING GROUPS

Contrasts	Inconsistencies		Defensive Consistencies		Conflicts		Consistencies		Totals
	DV*	NV*	DV	NV	DV	NV	DV	NV	
Male Religious—Female Religious	0	1	1	4	3	3	4	1	17
Male Religious—Lay Control	2	1	1	3	2	3	2	0	14
Female Religious—Lay Control	2	2	0	1	3	3	0	1	12
Male Religious—Seminarians	1	1	1	2	3	2	1	0	11
Seminarians—Lay Control	1	0	0	3	2	3	1	0	10
TOTALS	6	5	3	13	13	14	8	2	64

* DV = Dissonant Variables
NV = Neutral Variables

A corollary is suggested by the foregoing findings that the operationalization of non-internalizing identification versus internalizing identification hypothesized at the beginning of this chapter 7, seems to be valid.

A final observation can be made regarding the five groups when considering the number of variables by which each comparison differs. Referring again to chart 15, seventeen variables significantly differentiate male and female religious, whereas only ten variables differentiate seminarians and the lay control group. The other group comparisons fall within this range.

These findings seem to agree with the relatively low degree of difference found between seminarians and lay control (chapter 6) and with other data that will be discussed in chapter 9 concerning the rate of dropping out for male and female religious.

Summary of Findings and Considerations

1) As was discussed at length at the beginning of this chapter, the strength of the germinative and of the vulnerable SI-II (self-ideal-in-a-given-situation) considered together was assessed by means of two indices: the index of vocational maturity and the index of developmental maturity. Both indices aimed at expressing by means of one measurement the amount of compliance, of non-internalizing identification, of internalizing identification, and of internalization present in each one of the entering vocationers or freshmen of lay colleges. Refer to the beginning of this chapter for further explanations of terms as well as of the rationale, the methodological implementation, and the limitations of these two indices.

In the index of *vocational* maturity, these degrees of compliance, of non-internalizing identification, of internalizing identification, and of internalization were considered as expressing the strength of the consistencies/inconsistencies of one's needs and attitudes with regard to vocational values, terminal and instrumental (cfr. chapter 1 and the beginning of the present chapter). In the index of *developmental* maturity, the same degrees of compliance, etc., were considered as expressing indirectly the capacity of the person to handle, to control his main core conflict(s) in any one of the three following areas of daily living: academic performance, moral-religious values,

135

interpersonal relationships. Four degrees of the index of developmental maturity were assessed: degree I of prevailing compliance if the person's handling of the three foregoing areas had been *always* affected, degree II of prevailing non-internalizing identification if this handling had been *almost always* affected, degree III of prevailing internalizing identification if *frequently* affected, degree IV of prevailing internalization if *rarely* affected.

It was assumed that compliance and non-internalizing identification would serve rather the ego-defensive and the utilitarian functions of attitudes while internalizing identification and internalization would serve rather the value-expressive and knowledge functions.

Thus, the data obtained for the two indices can be a partial indication of the developmental or of the vocational maturity which were present in each vocationer at the time of his decision to enter a religious commitment. However, both indices—as such—are assessments of, not assessments for; that is, they help in understanding the motivation to enter but not in predicting the perseverance or effectiveness of the individuals in the vocational life. This fact does not imply that these measurements have no predictive potential; indeed, such potential is implicitly present, but it should be made more explicit in order to acquire an actual predictive capacity. This will be done in chapter 9 when discussing the process of dropping out of vocation.

2) 208 religious, males and females entering their religious institutions, plus 39 seminarians entering their theological training were assessed for the index of developmental maturity. 22 seminarians of another group were also studied; they entered their college training on a lay college campus. Thus, a total of 269 subjects was assessed for the index of developmental maturity.

333 subjects were studied for the index of vocational maturity; they were a random part of the samples considered in chapters 5 and 6, divided as follows: 96 male religious from two settings of the same institution; 95 female religious from two settings of the same institution; 40 seminarians entering

136

their college training; 50 girls and 52 boys representing the freshmen of lay Catholic colleges.

3) The findings for the groups studied for the index of developmental maturity are shown in charts 12 and 13. They speak for themselves: few of the entering vocationers made their vocational decision according to a prevailing internalization, which would allow them to be " rarely " affected by their major conflict(s) in the three areas of academic performance, moral-religious development, and interpersonal relationships. A percentage oscillating between 18 and 30 entered with a motivation characterized by non-internalizing identification, which would " frequently " debilitate their functioning in these three areas of daily living; a substantial majority would be affected " almost always " or " always " in their functioning because of prevailing non-internalizing identification or because of prevailing compliance, respectively.

These data are similar, at least percentage-wise. to the results of other research done in Europe and North America among priests *and* the general population (cfr. this chapter for further information). However, the difference of criteria and of methodology adopted in the various research, cautions against an unqualified comparison of results.

4) When the foregoing results for the index of developmental maturity of *each person* are compared with the ones obtained for the same persons in the index of vocational maturity, one finds that the two sets of data have a significant correlation. This was true for the 91 subjects studied in this comparison. Furthermore, for the *same* comparison, when the individuals with a trend toward internalization, i.e., the ones showing a prevalence of internalizing identification or of internalization, are compared with the ones with a trend to not internalize because of their prevailing compliance or non-internalizing identification, a correspondence of 87% is found between these two sets of measurements.

5) Thus, two procedures of measurement, which methodologically are completely independent, lead to " similar " results: at most, only 10-15% of the vocationers of our sample

137

had made a decision to enter the vocational institution, which was motivated by an internalized self-ideal-in-the-given-situation (SI-II). A substantial majority, oscillating between 60% and 80%, showed an entering motivation characterized by ego-defensive or utilitarian subconscious attitudes; i.e., for these people the choice of religious vocation was not only the means to implement their ideals, but also a *subconscious* attempt either to react defensively against underlying conflicts or to gratify conflictual needs. These attitudes expressed a prevailing compliance or non-internalizing identification related to subconscious forces. The relevance of the *subconscious motivation* underlying the decision to enter the religious institution seems to be quite great.

The frequency of central, unconscious inconsistencies found in our sample confirms the relevance of this subconscious motivation: for variables like dominance, abasement, and defendance (i.e., pride-humility), such inconsistencies are present in about 70-75% of some of the vocationers, for aggression in about 56% of the same or other vocationers of the sample studied, etc. These findings support and quantify the results discussed in chapter 6. In this regard points 4) and 6) considered in the "Summary of Findings and Considerations" of that chapter are particularly relevant. Let us stress again the fact that the values proclaimed on entrance cannot be taken at face value. The subconscious motivation should also be considered.

Also, it is interesting to notice that the data of chart 15 confirm the observation made in chapter 6 that among all the groups studied, the entering seminarians were the least differentiated from their lay controls. The results concerning the subconscious motivation confirm the ones of the conscious one.

6) The data of chapter 6 suggested the possible relationship between the degree of developmental maturity reached by a person and his degree of vocational maturity. The present chapter has shown that a correspondence between the two degrees of maturity is present in 87% of the individuals with regard to their prevailingly internalizing or non-internalizing personality. It would seem that the developmental maturity

and vocational maturity represent two processes which are not dichotomous, but rather strictly interdependent; at least, according to the conceptual and operational definitions followed in this research.

7) There are no significant differences between groups of vocationers and groups of lay college students with regard to their index of vocational maturity. In contrast, the data of chapter 6 had strongly suggested that such a difference existed with regard to their SI-II. This contrast confirms the fact that the SI-II is the psychological force which disposes one to enter a vocation and which opens the person to the call of supernatural grace. However, for the SI-II the difference between vocationers and non-vocationers found in chapter 6 concerned the *conscious* values and attitudes which, in the light of the findings of chapters 6 and 7, appear to be somewhat unrealistically idealized. Thus, an important question remains: to what extent is the SI-II free and objective? how much is the SI-II conflict-free, i.e., how much is it the consequence of a genuine *value* motivation rather than of a motivation significantly influenced by *subconscious* and vocationally inconsistent *needs*?

8) Some light on this issue was spread by the findings discussed here in number 5) concerning the great strength of subconscious motivation at entrance into religious vocation. Further light comes from the data presented in chart 15. They confirm the weight of the subconscious motivation and add another significant indication: they point to the vocationally *dissonant needs* as particularly relevant in the entering motivation *when* one considers them in terms of the substructures of the personality, like inconsistencies, consistencies, etc. In fact, as chart 15 shows, the vulnerable part of the SI-II is more important than its germinative part in differentiating the various groups of lay and religious people studied in this investigation at their entrance into the institutions. Now, this vulnerable part of the SI-II is expressed by the inconsistencies, defensive consistencies and conflicts of vocationally dissonant variables, that is, by forces which are prompted and sustained especially by vocationally dissonant needs (cfr. Appendix C-2).

This relevance of both the vulnerable, conflictual part of the SI-II and of the vocationally dissonant variables is confirmed by the data of chart 16 and related statistical analyses; in fact, the latter show that, while the difference between the germinative and the vulnerable part of the SI-II of the various groups for the vocationally neutral variables is not significant, the same difference is significant for the vocationally dissonant variables.

9) As a consequence of the results and considerations discussed in the foregoing points 5) and 8), one would expect that the unconscious inconsistencies between the attitudes and the needs of vocationally dissonant variables, like aggression, exhibition, etc., do play an important role in influencing the future commitment of the vocationer in terms of his perseverance and vocational effectiveness.

Of course, all these indications coming from the results need an appropriate confirmation from empirical findings. This task will be met in chapter 9 when considering the process of dropping out.

10) At this point of our investigation, two general conclusions are prompted by the findings. First, at their entrance into the vocational institution, the vocationers present in a significant degree shortcomings of personality which, without being signs of psychopathology, are factors that make their *vocational* motivation vulnerable. The important point here is that these vocational shortcomings are already there before the individuals start their training in the institutions; therefore they are not determined by the vocational institutions. A second general conclusion is that the shortcomings considered here come from *subconscious* forces.

But do the institutions usually offer an appropriate help to handle these subconscious forces? It seems that, in general, this is not the case. And yet, these subconscious factors seem to count for the future commitment to religious life. They count because: 1) they tend to persist; 2) they tend to affect the future perseverance in the vocational commitment. The following two chapters will consider these two trends of the entering motivation.

140

CHAPTER 8

THE ENTERING INTRAPSYCHIC DYNAMICS
AND ITS TREND TO PERSIST

One of the considerations prompted by the findings of chapters 6 and 7 was related to the subconscious motivation which underlies the entrance into religious vocation of many persons. People subconsciously choose this vocation *also* as an attempt to defend themselves against some of their subconscious needs or as a means to gratify some others.

More specifically, the results indicated, first of all, that a substantial majority seems to be influenced by this subconscious motivation.

Secondly, they strongly suggested that for many of these persons the ideals proclaimed by them at entrance were significantly more vulnerable than germinative, i.e., leading more to the lack of freedom which characterizes compliance and non-internalizing identification than to processes of growth by means of active internalization; more to entrenchment prompted by conflictual needs, than to the unfolding inspired by free, self-transcendent values. This being reactive more than active because of the demands from subconscious inner needs may be connected to the familial or educational background of the vocationer. As a matter of fact, there is a substantial body of scientific literature which indicates the probable effects of infantile residues from family influence upon the choice of religious vocation.

Early experiences in the family, and socialization processes in the family and schools have been seen as correlated with personally adopted methods of self-control, delay of gratification, of ability to resist temptation (cfr. Bandura and Walters,

1963; Kohlberg, 1964; Hoffman, 1970; Bronfenbrenner, 1961; Berkowitz, 1964; etc.). Similarly as Becker (1964) has suggested after reviewing many studies, "non-moral" types of parental expectations concerning aggression, dependency, etc., are also transmitted to offspring; now, vocational attitudes as considered in this work are such "non-moral" general attitudes. In the same line, one can recall the considerable evidence that parents' values are lived out in young adults (Keniston, 1967; Adams, 1968; Sampson, 1967). The reader may consult interesting, critical reviews of the pertinent literature related either to religious values in general (Fairchild, 1971; Milanesi and Aletti, 1973) or, more specifically, to vocational motivation (Godin, 1975). All these studies underscore the longstanding, persistent influence of the past.

Thirdly, the results pointed to the unconscious nature of the foregoing motivational forces of entering vocationers. Now, as Goethe said, if a person does not know his past, he is condemned to repeat it. Indeed, this is one of the basic tenets of depth psychology with regard to unconscious conflicts (see, for instance, Mahl, 1969). Elsewhere (Rulla, 1971, pp. 129-142. 163-165) the point was made that there exists a psychodynamic, "similarity" between unconscious conflicts in general and the vocational inconsistencies, as defined in this book (chapter 1). It has been contended that people with unconscious or deeply preconscious vocational inconsistencies are relatively unmodified by new information; more precisely: the information coming from the environment may influence them for a short while, but not enduringly. These people use defenses, which prevent them from becoming aware of the true nature of their frustrations and thus, from modifying their behavior through reappraisal and relearning; this incapacity of reappraisal applies also to their unrealistic, non objective self-ideal in the vocational situation (SI-II). Among these defenses a special mention should be made of the "transferences" which may seriously impair the behavior of a person; they will be considered later in this chapter.

These tenets and observations of depth psychology are confirmed by research made according to the perspectives of social psychology. Here, suffices it to recall that a person who has made a difficult ideological decision tends to add attitudes that bolster or justify his choices, thus helping him to avoid painful post decision regret (Aronson, 1968; Brehm and Cohen, 1962; Festinger, 1957, 1964; McGuire, 1969; Secord and Backman, 1974). Similarly, the research by Brock (Brock, 1965; Brock and Blackwood, 1962) has shown that people tend to distort the perception of their reference group, like their religious institutions, rather than to change their attitudes. These subconscious defenses may be expected to be particularly true for persons who have central, unconscious vocational inconsistencies.

The foregoing considerations and empirical data suggest that, very likely, the motivation presented by the vocationers of our sample may persist after their entrance; this is true at least for the vulnerable part of this motivation, which, however, is prevalent among vocationers. The research discussed in this chapter intends to test this hypothesis.

Four types of investigations are offered for this purpose: 1) the results obtained by means of the depth interview and expressed in the index of developmental maturity described in chapter 7; 2) the relationship between the data concerning the family background of the vocationers on the one hand, and the degree of developmental maturity as well as the degree of vocational maturity (cfr. chapter 7) reached by them, on the other hand; 3) an analysis of the transferences developed by the vocationers during their first four years of training in religious life; and 4) the influence of the entering motivation upon the leaving or not of the vocational commitment. The findings of this latter investigation will be presented in the following chapter 9.

THE RESEARCH

1) *The depth interview results*

Charts 17 and 18 show the findings concerning the degree of developmental maturity as obtained by means of the depth interview and related test data (cfr. chapter 3, section E).

CHART 17

DEGREE OF DEVELOPMENTAL MATURITY
PRESENT IN EACH INDIVIDUAL
AT ENTRANCE INTO THE RELIGIOUS INSTITUTION

Group	Degree of Developmental Maturity			
	I	II	III	IV
Religious Males (N = 80)	f 15% (12)	f 45% (36)	f 30% (24)	f 10% (8)
Religious Females (N = 128)	12% (16)	48% (61)	26% (33)	14% (18)
TOTALS (N = 208)	13.5% (28)	46.5% (97)	28% (57)	12% (26)

CHART 18
DEGREE OF DEVELOPMENTAL MATURITY
PRESENT IN EACH INDIVIDUAL
AFTER 4 YEARS OF VOCATIONAL FORMATION

Group	Degree of Developmental Maturity			
	I	II	III	IV
Religious Males (N = 80)	f 21% (17)	f 37% (30)	f 29% (23)	f 12% (10)
Religious Females (N = 128)	13% (17)	44% (56)	27% (35)	16% (20)
TOTALS (N = 208)	17% (34)	40.5% (86)	28% (58)	14% (30)

(Percentages; Number of subjects in parenthesis.)

N.B. Degree I: always influenced by main conflict(s).
Degree II: almost always influenced by main conflict(s).
Degree III: frequently influenced by main conflict(s).
Degree IV: rarely influenced by main conflict(s).

The samples studied in both charts (208 religious, males and females) is the same described on page 125. As the reader can see, the percentages for men and women together in the various degrees of developmental maturity are strikingly similar after four years of training (chart 18) to what they were at the beginning (chart 17). Nor are the percentages separately by sex very different at the two periods of time. The McNemar test for the significance of changes with correction for continuity (Siegel, 1956, p. 63) was performed by using the results of charts 17 and 18 in the following way: degrees I and II combined of Developmental Maturity were contrasted against degrees III and IV combined. The results obtained were as follows:

Religious males	chi square = .17; $p < .70$
Religious females	chi square = .57; $p < .55$
Religious males and females together	chi square = 1.23; $p < .25$

Thus, no significant change occurred in the Degree of Developmental Maturity of the individuals after 4 years of vocational formation.

Indirect additional information relevant to the trend of the entering psychodynamics to persist may be inferred from chart 19. In it, two different groups are compared; they had in common the fact of being a sample coming randomly from the entire territory of the USA. The group of 39 beginning Theologians is the same described on page 125. The 271 priests represented the sample studied by Kennedy and Heckler (1971; cfr. chapter 7).

CHART 19

DEGREE OF DEVELOPMENT
PRESENT IN EACH INDIVIDUAL
OF TWO DIFFERENT GROUPS

Group	Degree of Developmental Maturity			
	I*	II	III	IV
Beginning Theologians (N = 39)	f 31.0% (12)	f 48.5% (19)	f 18.0% (7)	f 2.5% (1)
	Degree of Development			
	Mal-developed	Under-developed	Developing	Developed
Priests** (N = 271)	f 8.5% (23)	f 66.5% (179)	f 18.0% (50)	f 7.0% (19)

(Percentages; Number of subjects in parenthesis.)

*Degree I: always influenced by main conflict(s).
Degree II: almost always influenced by main conflict(s).
Degree III: frequently influenced by main conflict(s).
Degree IV: rarely influenced by main conflict(s).
** (Kennedy and Heckler, 1971)

Each of the various groups of men, of women and of totals for both sexes together presented in charts 17, 18, and 19 was divided in two subgroups: degrees I and II of rather non-internalizing people vs. degrees III and IV of rather internalizing persons. When each one of the groups of chart 17 was compared to its corresponding group of chart 18 according to the two foregoing subgroups of internalizing vs. non-internalizing people, there was no significant difference between any groups. Significance was not present also between men and women. The same was true for a similar comparison between the two groups of chart 19 in spite of the differences in age and in interpreting the interview responses. These comparisons were made using the simple chi square and the Phi-coefficient method.

Although these comparisons must be regarded as only suggestive, the trend of the entering psychodynamics, germinative and vulnerable, to persist seems to be quite strong. Further support for this statement comes from other data obtained in the depth interview of two groups studied here, the religious males and females of charts 17 and 18: the main, core conflict(s) was completely or partially unknown to 86% of the males and to 87% of the females at entrance into the vocational institutions; after four years of vocational training, the same conflict(s) was still unknown in the same degree to 83% of the men and 82% of the women.

2) *The Family Background Data*

A second indication of the trend of the entering motivation to persist over time can be had indirectly through the analysis of data on family conflicts. Do conflicts exist in families of those entering, and does their influence perpetuate itself in religious life? The answer to these questions was sought by using the Index of Developmental Maturity first, and then the Index of Vocational Maturity with the Family Background.

The Comparison of Developmental Maturity with Family Background Data. Data tapping information on family interaction and conflicts at three different periods of the subject's life was gathered from the religious in the Biographical Inventory (BI), the Family Interview (FI), and the Depth Interview (DI), as described earlier (cfr. Chapter 3). The Biographical Inventory, the reader may recall, was given immediately upon entrance and its task n. 55 (see Appendix B-4) provides a self-report of the subject's interaction with father, mother, and siblings, and parental interaction, in terms of polar concepts rated on a continuous scale from 0 to 9 for, e.g., " In conflict... In harmony ". The same information was gathered through the Family Interview four months later, where mother,

146

father, and sibling conflicts were assessed, this time, however, not merely through the subject's self-report, but also through professional assistance, probing and evaluation by the interviewer. The four months' time seems to be adequate to allow the person to forget most of the details as to what he had written on the Biographical Inventory, therefore, a check of congruence between FI results and BI could be made. Finally, four years later, conflicts with parents were again assessed in the Depth Interview. A final analysis was made by the interviewer as to similar variables such as interactional conflicts, affection, communication, etc. The exact method of coding the results so as to ascertain frequency of conflicts in each of the three tests (BI, FI, DI) is explicated in Appendix C-9.

The male group consisted of 102 subjects—80 religious and 22 seminarians—the same people considered in the previous section concerning the results of the depth interviews. There were also 22 seminarians, the same as those described on page 126.

The female group was composed of 128 subjects, also the same studied in the previous section 1) of this chapter.

Does the vulnerable part of the subjects' entering motivation perhaps have some origin in family interactional dynamics? Chart 20 provides information for consideration here.

CHART 20

PARENTAL CONFLICTS IN MALE AND FEMALE RELIGIOUS AND SEMINARIANS
AS INDICATED IN THE BIOGRAPHICAL INVENTORY, FAMILY INTERVIEW, DEPTH INTERVIEW

Groups	Biographical Inventory		Family Interview		Depth Interview	
	Positive	Negative	Positive	Negative	Positive	Negative
Males (N = 102)	78.4% (80)	21.6% (22)	56.2% (45) (sems excluded)	43.8% (35)	8.8% (9)	91.2% (93)
Females (N = 125)	71.2% (89)	28.8% (36)	46.4% (58)	53.6% (67)	11.2% (14)	88.8% (111)
TOTALS (N = 227)	74.4% (169)	25.6% (58)	50.2% (103) (sems excluded)	49.8% (102)	10.1% (23)	89.9% (204)

(Percentages; Number of subjects in parenthesis.)

147

At entrance, 74.4% of the religious were eager to report they had positive (i.e., favorable or affirmative) relations with their parents and 25.6% claimed they were negative (unpleasant, disruptive). Interestingly enough, four months later and with a bit more probing and subsequent insight, 50.2% continued to insist they had such positive relations whereas 49.8% began to claim the possibility of negative or conflictual relationships with their parents. The shift was particularly marked in females who were also a bit more likely to indicate negative family interaction on the BI than were the males. Finally, by the time of the DI, four years later, subjects showed a marked tendency to describe their early family interaction in negative rather than positive terms, a clear tendency in both males and females: positive, 10.1%; negative, 89.9%. This is quite a striking reversal, indeed, especially if one remembers that this reversal was what the subjects themselves admitted. These tendencies of religious students to idealize family interaction as seen in Chart 20 are in keeping with other research indicating idealization of family by religious vocationers (Maitre, 1967).

The data of chart 20 thus suggest that there had been unpleasant early familial experiences of subjects, but also that subjects tend to maintain these less positive experiences in the less conscious parts of their personality where they tend to persist on entrance into religious life and even into their formation years. Are these real, but repressed, negative familial experiences related to developmental maturity?

Chart 21 can be of assistance here. On this chart, as the reader can see, congruences and incongruences are considered.

CHART 21

DEGREES OF DEVELOPMENTAL MATURITY AND PERCENTAGES OF CONGRÜENCE OF REPORT FOR FAMILY CONFLICTS ON THE BIOGRAPHICAL INVENTORY (BI), FAMILY INTERVIEW (FI), DEPTH INTERVIEW (DI)

Developmental Maturity	Male religious and Seminarians (N = 102)						Female Religious (N = 125)					
	Congruence				Incongruence		Congruence				Incongruence	
	positive		negative				positive		negative			
	%	f	%	f	%	f	%	f	%	f	%	f
III and IV	5.88	(6)	7.84	(8)	18.63	(19)	8.8	(11)	15.2	(19)	14.4	(18)
I and II	2.94	(3)	12.75	(13)	51.96	(53)	2.4	(3)	13.6	(17)	45.6	(57)
Totals	8.82	(9)	20.59	(21)	70.59	(72)	11.2	(14)	28.8	(36)	60.0	(75)

% = Percentages in relation to total sample
f = Number of subjects

Here, incongruence is defined as the changing attitude of subjects toward their family situation, that is, it includes those who report their parent/child relationship as "happy," "favorable," "benign," on the BI and who later, with more insight and assistance, can report it as negative, disruptive and troubled on the FI and/or DI. A congruence, on the other hand, is found in the case of those who report positive, happy, favorable relations with their parents throughout the BI, FI, and DI, or who report these relationships constantly as negative, disruptive, throughout the BI, FI, and DI. As indicated by percentages on the chart, male and female religious who tend to be incongruous in their evaluation of early family interaction, more frequently fall in the lower developmental maturity category of I and II, because they were always, or almost always affected by core conflict(s). There is, in fact, a significant difference of the distribution of incongruities on I and II vs. III and IV degrees of developmental maturity. A test for the significance of a proportion applied to the results concerning male subjects (19 vs. 53 of Chart 21) yielded a $z = 4.82$, $p < .001$; when applied to the results concerning female subjects (18 vs. 57 of Chart 21) the obtained $z = 5.31$, $p < .001$.

These findings would not be interesting if the criteria used for judging the developmental maturity of subjects were the same used for the BI, FI, and DI concerning the family. While there may have been some indirect overlap, the assessment of the degrees of developmental maturity focused on *personal* dynamics and was made primarily in terms of objective test data and of the questions which these data prompted for the interviews.

On the other hand, family assessment was made through specific questions regarding communication, conflict, affection *within the family*. Because of this distinction, it is possible to interpret chart 21 as indicating that family conflicts, whether consciously acknowledged (as shown by consistent negative or positive familial attitudes) or partially repressed (as shown by inconsistent reporting of familial attitudes), seem to be somehow related to the degree of developmental maturity in religious students.

The Comparison of Vocational Maturity with Family Background Data. In order to minimize and to test for possible clinician effects on the above results, a similar comparison of family conflicts (congruence/incongruence on BI, FI, DI) was made with the Index of Vocational Maturity, also.

The sample consisted of 70 subjects, 31 female and 39 male religious. They were studied together because: 1) there was a small number of people; 2) since a structural approach was adopted for studying separately *each* person for the two sexes, this combination is acceptable; 3) as we will shortly see, the percentages of transferences are practically equal in the two sexes. These individuals are a subsample of the subjects randomly selected and described in chapter 7 for the study of the Degree of Vocational Maturity. They are also a subsample of the subjects used in the present chapter for the Index of Developmental Maturity; this subsample includes all the subjects for whom it was possible to have *all* the necessary tests: MAI, TAT, Rotter, Biographical Inventory, Family Interview, Depth Interview. The reader may perhaps recall that the evaluation of the Index of Vocational Maturity requires the use of the MAI, TAT, and Rotter, which are not necessary for the assessment of the Degree of Developmental Maturity. The time-consuming procedures for scoring the TAT and Rotter made the random reduction of this subsample inevitable. It should be stressed that the Index of Vocational Maturity is arrived at through a mechanical process of computerized assessment which is completely independent of the analysis of the Family Background and of the Depth Interview.

Chart 22, utilizing the Index of Vocational Maturity, indicates results similar to those found in chart 21 which used the Degree of Developmental Maturity, at least for the test of difference of proportions of incongruities among subjects with high vocational maturity vs. incongruities among subjects with low vocational maturity.

CHART 22

DEGREES OF VOCATIONAL MATURITY AND PERCENTAGES
OF CONGRUENCE OF REPORT FOR FAMILY CONFLICTS
ON THE BIOGRAPHICAL INVENTORY, FAMILY INTERVIEW,
DEPTH INTERVIEW

(Male and Female Religious, N = 70)

Vocational Maturity	Congruence				Incongruence	
	positive	f	negative	f		f
HIGH	5.7%	(4)	4.3%	(3)	11.4%	(8)
Low	4.3%	(3)	11.4%	(8)	62.9%	(44)
TOTALS	10.0%	(7)	15.7%	(11)	74.3%	(52)

N.B. For the Operational Definition of " High " and " Low ", see Table 7.2.

150

8 subjects with high vocational maturity and 44 subjects with low vocational maturity were found having incongruences. The test for the significance of a proportion applied to these data yelded a $z = 6.92$, $p < .001$. Thus repressed and persistent family conflicts seem to inhibit not only developmental, but also vocational maturity.

3) *The Analysis of Transferences*

If family conflicts are repressed but persistent, what happens to them? Do they find an expression in religious life? Can they be detected?

It seems so. These conflicts can become evident in the clinical phenomenon known as transference. Transference occurs when an individual, as an adult, feels and acts as a child, i.e., when he feels and behaves toward another person as he did toward important figures in his past, generally parents, siblings, relatives or educators. Transferences are positive if there is a friendly, attractive attitude toward the other person; they are negative if an unfriendly, hostile attitude exists. [1] The person is generally conscious of his feelings, but lacks awareness as to 1) *what* they are a repetition of (e.g., earlier familial experiences), 2) *that* they are being re-enacted, or 3) *why*. There is, thus, a perpetuation of his conflicts.

The transference can and does occur in religious life, as anyone living therein will attest. Subjects may have attitudes and feelings toward superiors and peers which resemble those toward their own parents or siblings. For the data collection, a transference was assessed as present if the attitudes and feelings of the subjects in the relationship with the superiors or peers were inflexible, unidimensional or in other ways seemingly inconsistent with the amount or nature of actual contact with the other person. Furthermore, this information could be related clinically to what had appeared for the same clinical clusters of variables on the BI, or the FI, or, more frequently, the DI (cfr. Appendix B-7).

Chart 23 summarizes the transferences detected in the religious males and females. Seminarians were excluded from this analysis because, as explained at the beginning of Chapter 6, they were living in settings which were substantially different from the ones of the religious.

---

[1] Since transferences are usually ambivalent, here negative and positive transferences are statistically considered together.

151

CHART 23

COMPARISON BETWEEN TRANSFERENCES OF MALE AND FEMALE RELIGIOUS AND CONGRUENCE OF REPORT FOR FAMILY CONFLICTS ON THE BIOGRAPHICAL INVENTORY (BI), FAMILY INTERVIEW (FI), DEPTH INTERVIEW (DI)

Transferences	Males (N = 80)						Females (N = 125)					
	Congruence positive		Congruence negative		Incongruence		Congruence positive		Congruence negative		Incongruence	
	%	f	%	f	%	f	%	f	%	f	%	f
Yes M: 69% (55) F: 67.2% (84)	3.75	(3)	17.5	(14)	47.5	(38)	3.2	(4)	19.2	(24)	44.8	(56)
No M: 31% (25) F: 32.8% (41)	7.5	(6)	6.25	(5)	17.5	(14)	8.0	(10)	9.6	(12)	15.2	(19)
Totals	11.25	(9)	23.75	(19)	65.0	(52)	11.2	(14)	28.8	(36)	60.0	(75)

% = Percentages in relation to total sample
f = Number of subjects

About 69% of the male religious and 67% of the female religious appeared to develop transference relationships during training, generally with the father master or directress of novices. Furthermore, it is interesting to note the relationship between the development of transferences and the subject's incongruency as to reporting familial interactions. Subjects with transferences tended to be incongruous in the BI, FI, and DI reports, having repressed unacceptable family conflicts at entrance, which were later accepted as present, with the help of the interviewer. The test for the significance of a proportion (two-tailed) yielded a $z = 3.06$, $p < .004$, for male subjects; and a $z = 3.26$, $p < .001$ for female subjects. On the contrary, for those without transferences, no significant difference of the frequencies of congruency vs. incongruency was evident. The test for the significance of a proportion (two-tailed) yielded a $z = .60$, $p < .56$ for male subjects; and a $z = .16$, $p < .88$ for female subjects.

To summarize and integrate the findings of parts 1), 2), and 3) just discussed in this chapter, charts 24 and 25 may be helpful.

CHART 24

PERCENTAGES OF TRANSFERENCES,
HIGH AND LOW VOCATIONAL MATURITY, AND CONGRUENCE
OR INCONGRUENCE OF SUBJECTS' REPORTS
ON THE BIOGRAPHICAL INVENTORY (BI),
FAMILY INTERVIEW (FI), DEPTH INTERVIEW (DI)

(Male and Female Religious, N = 70)

Trans-ferences	Vocational Maturity	Congruence on BI, FI, DI				Incongruence on BI, FI, DI		p*
		positive		negative				
		%	f	%	f	%	f	
YES	High	1.4	(1)	4.3	(3)	10.0	(7)	ns
	Low	2.9	(2)	10.0	(7)	47.1	(33)	<.001
No	High	4.3	(3)	—	—	1.4	(1)	ns
	Low	1.4	(1)	1.4	(1)	15.7	(11)	<.001

* p is the probability of the significance of the relationship between Vocational Maturity and Family Conflicts.
N.B. For the operational definition of " High " and " Low ", see Table 7.2.

153

CHART 25

PERCENTAGES OF TRANSFERENCES, HIGH AND LOW DEVELOPMENTAL MATURITY,
AND CONGRUENCE OR INCONGRUENCE OF SUBJECTS' REPORTS
ON THE BIOGRAPHICAL INVENTORY (BI), FAMILY INTERVIEW (FI), DEPTH INTERVIEW (DI)

Trans-ferences	Degree of Developmental Maturity	MALE RELIGIOUS (N = 80)					FEMALE RELIGIOUS (N = 125)				
		Congruence on BI, FI, DI positive	negative	Incongruence on BI, FI, DI	p*		Congruence on BI, FI, DI positive	negative	Incongruence on BI, FI, DI	p	
		% f	% f	% f			% f	% f	% f		
YES	HIGH (III and IV)	2.5 (2)	5.0 (4)	15.0 (12)	ns		1.6 (2)	8.8 (11)	10.4 (13)	ns	
	LOW (I and II)	1.25 (1)	12.5 (10)	23.5 (26)	.007		1.6 (2)	10.4 (13)	34.4 (43)	<.001	
No	HIGH (III and IV)	5.0 (4)	5.0 (4)	5.0 (4)	ns		7.2 (9)	6.4 (8)	4.0 (5)	.002	
	LOW (I and II)	2.5 (2)	1.25 (1)	12.5 (10)	.02		.8 (1)	3.2 (4)	11.2 (14)	.02	

* p is the probability of the significance of the relationship between Developmental Maturity and Family Conflicts.

As indicated in these charts, entering motivation as assessed in the Developmental Maturity and the Vocational Maturity seems to be related backwards in time to family conflicts as expressed by the incongruities on BI, FI, and DI.

With regard to vocational maturity for both males and females, when considered together, those with low vocational maturity tend to be more incongruous than congruous in describing family interactions; chart 24 shows that p is $< .001$ for people with and without transferences. A similar trend is present for developmental maturity. Chart 25 shows that for males p is .007 and .02; for females, $p < .001$ and .02. Thus, family conflicts may persist as possible origins of low vocational and developmental maturities.

On the one hand, both maturities, as just seen, seem to be backwardly related to family conflicts of childhood and/or adolescence; on the other hand, another interesting aspect of the charts is that, forward in time, both maturities seem to be correlated with transferences which occur after entry into religious vocation. As indicated in the charts, of those who have transferences, more subjects tend to be also in the low maturity categories (concerning vocational maturity, for males and females considered together $p < .001$; in developmental maturity, for males, p is .007; for females $p < .001$) and, at the same time, tend to show more incongruency of report on family conflicts.

The results relating degrees of vocational and developmental maturities with family background and transferences in religious life are either not significant or ambiguous for people who have high degrees in both maturities (charts 24 and 25).

SUMMARY OF FINDINGS AND CONSIDERATIONS

1) The data of the previous Chapter 7 indicated that the vulnerable part of the ideals proclaimed by individuals in a given situation (SI-II) is more important than the germinative part of the same SI-II in differentiating the various groups of religious, seminarians and lay entering freshmen studied in this research. Also, they indicated that the same vulnerable part of the SI-II has a great weight upon the entering motivation since it prevails over the germinative part for 60 to 80% of the entering vocationers of our sample.

This vulnerable part of the SI-II is expressed by *sub-*

conscious, central inconsistencies, defensive consistencies and conflicts of vocationally dissonant variables as they are defined in chapter 1 and in Appendices C-2 and C-4. In fact, such inconsistencies, defensive consistencies and conflicts come from needs and attitudes of the vocationers and make vulnerable i.e., subconsciously undermine the vocational ideals proclaimed by them in their SI-II. The germinative part of the SI-II is expressed by conflicts of vocationally neutral variables and by central consistencies; they may support the germinative part of the SI-II because they are either neutral or consistent with the ideals proclaimed in it.

According to the theorizing of this book (cfr. the beginning of chapter 7), the vulnerable part of the SI-II tends not to internalize vocational values because it is characterized by compliance and by non-internalizing identification, while the germinative part tends to internalize these values because it is characterized by internalization and by internalizing identification.

On the basis of the foregoing data and considerations as well as of observations, of research, and of theoretical tenets coming from depth psychology, social psychology and research on religious or vocational development, it was hypothesized that the vulnerable part of the entering motivation tends to persist in the years following entrance into religious life.

2) 208 religious males and females plus 39 entering students of theology were considered for the part of the research concerning the degree of developmental maturity of vocationers. These samples are described on page 125. An additional sample of 22 seminarians entering a Catholic college as freshmen were studied for one part of our investigation. 70 religious, men and women, the available random sample of the 208 just mentioned, were considered for the investigation regarding the degree of vocational maturity.

3) The trend of the entering motivation to persist was tested in two ways: directly and indirectly.

Directly, the 208 religious, males and females, were assessed according to their degrees of developmental maturity

156

at entrance and after four years of vocational training. As charts 17 and 18 indicate, no significant changes were found after four years both for the vulnerable part (degrees I and II) and for the germinative part (degrees III and IV) of the SI-II. Similarly, 86% of the men and 87% of the women of the same sample were completely or partially unaware of their main conflict(s) at entrance; this unawareness was 83% for the men and 82% for the women after four years. Finally, the results of the comparison between 39 students beginning theology and 271 ordained priests of another research were in the same line of the foregoing findings.

4) The indirect investigation concerning the trend of the entering psychodynamics to persist was made by relating the vulnerable and the germinative parts of the SI-II backwardly in time with family background data and forward in time with the occurrence of transferences in religious life. Transferences were considered as present when the vocationer in his/her interaction with authority figures or with peers would relive the relationship he/she had with his/her parents during childhood or adolescence. This regressed reliving reinforces the vulnerable part of the SI-II and thus leads to its perpetuation, to its persistence.

The findings indicate, first of all, that about 69% of the male religious and 67% of the female religious appeared to develop transferential relationships during training. Secondly, and more important, the results obtained in our investigation as shown in charts 20 to 25 indicate the following interdependent relationships: persisting family conflicts may be among the origins of persisting personal conflicts as shown by the degrees of low developmental and vocational maturities of the entering vocationers; personal conflicts may express themselves in the defensive adoption of transferences which in turn are a reliving of the original family conflicts. These relationships are schematically presented in chart 26.

CHART 26

PERSONAL MATURITY,
DEVELOPMENTAL OR VOCATIONAL

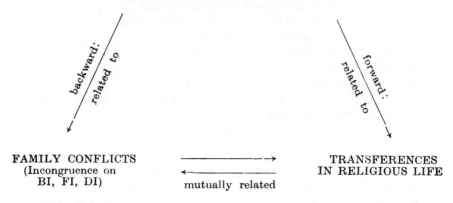

FAMILY CONFLICTS   ——————→   TRANSFERENCES
(Incongruence on   ←——————   IN RELIGIOUS LIFE
BI, FI, DI)   mutually related

From this chart, one can readily begin to see how the entering intrapsychic dynamics may be a longstanding, persisting process. Interestingly enough, this is true for people with prevailingly low degrees of vocational and developmental maturities, while it is not necessarily true for people with high degrees in both maturities.

Thus, there are many and convergent findings, which both directly and indirectly strongly suggest that the vulnerable part of the SI-II, which characterizes the people " low " in maturity, tends to persist. Furthermore, the data from the present chapter and from chapter 7 also suggest that the people with these low degrees of maturity may be as many as 60 to 80% of the entering vocationers.

5) With regard to the results just presented, two considerations are relevant: a) the adaptability and the developmental capacities of human beings are *per se* beyond any quantifiable observation or prediction. The two extreme positions concerning man are untenable: as there are no totally integrated men, but rather men who are on their way to such an integration, so there are no inconsistent people who are totally impotent beings (excluding, of course, the cases of extreme pathology, who are not the subjects of our considerations).

However, the intrinsic power which man, as man, has to change and to improve himself when he uses the supernatural action of grace, *de facto* does not seem to be at work in some persons, especially the ones with unconscious or deeply preconscious inconsistencies. Therefore, here we speak of a *trend* toward persistence of psychodynamics; a trend which characterizes some people, but does not necessarily crystallize them.

b) In the same line, the description of types of people and of their degree of maturity should be qualified. This assessment was done by means of the indices of developmental maturity and of vocational maturity; apart from the limitations of these measurements which were described in chapter 7, it should be noticed that these indices are based on a typology of crucial variables (e.g., exhibition, succorance, etc.) more than on a typology of all aspects of a person, i.e., they focus on the variables which have the greatest influence on the person's functioning, but these variables are not the whole person. A more comprehensive view of the person will be presented in chapter 9, which reaches the same conclusions concerning the persistence of the entering motivation in the light of the process of dropping out of vocation.

6) Since no substantial changes seem to take place in the " maturity " of the majority of people during the first four years of vocational training, the usefulness of this training comes into question. Note that the subjects considered in this chapter completed their training between 1969 and 1972, i.e., under the new, more liberal policies of formation which followed Vatican Council Il. By the same token, the trend toward persistence shown by the psychodynamics of the majority of these vocationers, calls into question the belief in the usefulness of helping these *subconscious* psychodynamics *only* by deferring the entrance into religious life. For this majority, the mere deferring will be of little or of no help.

7) The findings of this chapter prompt some further considerations, which are not directly related to the topic discussed here, but are interesting with regard to vocational problems in general.

After reviewing the pertinent literature, Kohlberg (1969,

1966) concludes that findings contradict any theory that claims that good parent relations are necessary for normal social development, especially in the moral and psycho-sexual areas, while there are some results suggesting that bad parent relations retard or disrupt such development. The findings presented in this chapter (charts 24 and 25) seem to indicate that such a conclusion may be extended to people entering a religious vocation with regard to their developmental and vocational maturities: vocationers who had good parent relations will not necessarily present a good degree of both maturities.

8) Our data would suggest an additional, interesting aspect: there seems to be a difference between repressors of bad relations with parents and non-repressors of bad relations with parents. The former, i.e., people who in their reports concerning their relations with parents are incongruent across the Biographical Inventory, the Family Interview, and the Depth Interview, tend to have a low degree of developmental and vocational maturity; while the latter, i.e., people who do not show such incongruent reporting, less frequently tend to show such a low degree in both maturities, even though they congruently reported bad, negative relations with their parents. More simply: people who are incongruent in their reports are more frequently in the low maturity groups (I and II in chart 24 and " low " for chart 25) than are those who are congruently negative in their reports (P is < .001 for all these three comparisons).

Therefore, perhaps, the degrees of developmental and vocational maturities are negatively influenced when a relation with the parents was not only bad, but also repressed and kept away from awareness; merely a bad parent relationship does not necessarily lead to low maturity. To repress a past, bad parent relationship and to think of it in an optimistic but unrealistic way has a much stronger negative influence upon growth than to openly admit the negative reality.

9) Previously, in this chapter, it was said that the trend of the entering psychodynamics to persist may be investigated by studying its possible influence on the future dropping out of vocationers. This is the topic of the following chapter.

Chapter 9

THE ENTERING INTRAPSYCHIC DYNAMICS
AND ITS TREND TO INFLUENCE LEAVING VOCATION

The great increase during the past ten years in the dropping out of priestly and religious vocation is a well-known fact. The reader interested in some of the disturbing figures concerning this phenomenon may consult Kauffman (1970), Harvey (1973), Fretelliere (1972), Pro Mundi Vita (1971), Modde (1974), Godin (1975). A simple, but very revealing picture of this situation of the entire Church is highlighted by the comment of the General of the Society of Jesus concerning his religious order: each *week* the Society of Jesus has in its records the following figures: 6 people enter, 7 die, and 20 leave (Arrupe, 1972).

This striking phenomenon of massive dropping out of vocation should be seen in the more comprehensive framework of a " vocational anthropology ". Some pertinent considerations have been presented elsewhere (Rulla, 1971, pp. 194-224 and, less directly, 225-384). The problem is multifaceted and a complex one. Many and different factors influence it. Roughly, one could say that the process of leaving religious vocation is at least the result of the interaction among the following five sets of elements: 1) supernatural factors and the person's cooperation with them; 2) personality characteristics of the individuals; 3) pressures coming from the group or the kind of community in which the person lives; 4) factors related to the norms, constitutions and structures of the vocational institutions; and 5) pressures emerging from the historical socio-cultural milieu in general and, more specifically, from the structural functioning of the Church.

Needless to say, the present book does not aim, by any means, to deal with the foregoing five sets of elements. Our purpose is to bring a modest contribution with regard to one of these five factors: the personality characteristics of the individuals. For different aspects related to this complex issue of leaving vocation, the interested reader may consult, first of all, the extensive sociological research done by Greeley (1972) and NORC (1971); also the investigation by Olabuenaga for the Spanish milieu (1970 and Pro Mundi Vita 1971); the one by Stryckman (1971) for the Quebec area; by Schallert and Kelley (1970) as well as by Modde and Koval (1975) for the USA; by Schmidtchen in cooperation with " Institut für Demoskopie in Allensbach " (1973) as well as by Mönikes (1973) for West Germany. In general, these studies stress the following aspects: a person leaves his vocation because of a personal dissatisfaction expressed as a feeling of isolation, of loneliness (Greeley, 1972), coming especially from a lack of fulfillment in pastoral work or from conflictual tensions between values and institutions (e.g., NORC, p. 262); the desire to marry is more a consequence than a determining factor of leaving.

As Godin (1975) keenly points out, a vocational crisis which is centered around values and institutional structures will inevitably influence the opinions expressed in the responses the individuals give in psycho-social investigation as well as the underlying meaning of the language used by them. Hence, the difficulty to establish objective criteria which characterize what is a success and what a failure in the vocational commitment, either as vocational effectiveness or as perseverance. With regard to this difficulty Godin discusses three important studies: by Rashke (1973), by Neal (1970, 1971) and by Carroll (in Bier, ed., 1970, pp. 159-189); let us consider this last study.

Carroll (1970) compared the prediction of vocational success or effectiveness of subjects made at their entrance into vocation by means of psychological tests (MMPI and Sentence Completion Test) on the one hand, with the evaluation of this success of the same subjects expressed after many years by their theology professors, on the other hand; he made a similar comparison between the prediction based on the same psychological tests at entrance and the evaluation made after many years by the peers of the subjects studied. While there was a statistically significant correspondence between the prediction of the psychologist and the evaluation of the professors, no such correspondence was present between the prediction of

162

the psychologist and the evaluation of peers. Parenthetically, but as relevant, an objection to this research raised by William G. T. Douglas, points to the fact that the rating system employed is in danger of reinforcing patterns already established by ecclesiastical superiors: " if we psychologists select people who are judged as good people by those already established, we are implicitly reinforcing present patterns " as well as " getting a picture of what is valued by those who are ecclesiastically established " (Douglas, in Bier, ed., 1970, p. 182).

Is it then impossible to predict vocational perseverance or effectiveness? The just mentioned lack of correspondence of judgments between people responsible for formation and peers indicates that such a prediction becomes very difficult, especially in times in which values and institutional structures are called into question and are evaluated differently by people responsible for formation and by peers. On the other hand, some research like that just mentioned by Carroll, the studies by Rooney (1966), by Weisgerber (1969 and in Bier, ed., 1970, pp. 190-208), the theorizing and findings by Lee (1968, 1969 a, b, 1970, a, b, c, 1973), show that there are elements in the personality of the entering vocationers which support the possibility of *some* prediction.

In this book, we are not directly interested in prediction as a means of selecting candidates to religious life; rather, we intend to better understand possible basic mechanisms of psychodynamics which underlie the processes of entrance as well as of success in religious vocation. This is done by proposing a theory, which is based on a structural approach to personality (cfr. chapters 1 and 2). This structural approach is supposed to have *built-in* criteria to predict vocational perseverance and effectiveness. In fact, one of its crucial aspects is that objective vocational values, terminal and instrumental (cfr. chapter 1), are pitted against what *each* person *perceives* of his own values and attitudes (SI) as well as the ones of the institution (II); role concepts rather than role expectations are considered, i.e., roles as perceived and expected by subjects rather than roles as expected by the institution or by peers. Furthermore, these personal perceptions are evaluated not only in terms of their contents, but rather in view of their being consistent or inconsistent with the prevailing needs of the person. Therefore, the evalutation prescinds from the norms which characterize a vocational group or institution as well as the ones proper to a particular socio-cultural milieu or a historical period; similarly, it prescinds from the norms of a particular validated test. Thus, our approach is somehow trans-situational, transtemporal. Finally, this approach is supposed to have built in itself the elements which indicate the predictable capacity of a person *to internalize* vocational values and attitudes. While the other aspects of our approach have been discussed at length in chapters 1 and 2, this last predictive aspect needs to be clarified and explained. This will be done in the following paragraphs.

The proclamation of values does not necessarily mean the practice of them. In *The Brothers Karamazov*, Dostoyevski says that many people can love all men, but find it next to impossible to love man in the singular; as the studies by Harding (1944, 1948) have proven, the values a person holds speculatively tend to break down when he is confronted with specific situations. What is important for people who enter a religious vocation is their capacity to internalize instrumental values and attitudes according to the objective terminal value-system of vocation. In fact, the important theorizing and the research by Rokeach (1968, 1973) has shown that values have their independent force upon human motivation. The same is true for attitudes, the cornerstone of social psychology (see the comprehensive presentation by McGuire, 1969 and by Freedman, Carlsmith and Sears, 1974). Actually, attitudes may become a value in themselves: some individuals subconsciously can make of the attitude or of the external observance which implements the vocational values, not a means to an end, but an end in itself; for instance, the giving of nurturance may become a demanding succorance, or the letter of the law may prevail over its spirit and sacrifice it to externalism. However, attitudes, as such, have less dynamic impact upon motivation than values; see the research by Homant (1970), Holland (1972) and Rokeach (1973).

The findings of the preceding chapters 5, 6, and 7 have indicated that the self-ideal-in-vocational-situation (SI-II) is the psychological force which disposes one to enter a vocation. However, the same findings indicated also that the values and attitudes of this SI-II may be frequently undermined by subconscious needs which are unconsciously or preconsciously inconsistent with either the values or the attitudes. The results of chapter 8 have strongly suggested that the foregoing psychodynamics of the entering vocationers may persist during religious life, especially for its vulnerable part; in particular, the same data concerning persistence of psychodynamics suggest the close relationship which may exist between needs and homonymous attitudes as they were assessed in the Index of Vocational Maturity.

From the foregoing findings and considerations, it appears that the attitudes of the SI-II may exert their own force upon the motivation of the entering vocationers. However, this force may present three aspects: 1) the force which an attitude, e.g., for dominance, exerts *with* either his homonymous need for dominance, or *with* a similar value, like the instrumental value of the General Goals of Life Inventory: " Power, control over people and things ", or *with* both, homonymous need and value; 2) the force which an attitude exerts independently from the homonymous need or from a similar value; e.g., an attitude for achievement may serve the homonymous need or the value of cooperation with others; however. it may also be independent from both and serve a vocationally inconsistent need for competitive aggression (Hollander, 1971). In this second instance, the attitude for achievement is somewhat bound with the inconsistent need for aggression and thus, it may not be easily integrated with its homonymous need and/or with the value of charitable cooperation.

3) Actually, this difficulty in integration is even greater if a third aspect of the force of the attitude is considered; such a resistance to integration is exerted when two conditions are *both* present: first of all, when in time an attitude has acquired its own strength; here the conceptualization of various authors may be recalled: the concept of *emotional* attitude as an emotional *habitual* disposition, a concept elaborated especially in the works of Arnold (1960, 1969, 1970), and, in part, of Peters (1958, 1965, 1970); the functional autonomy of motives described by Gordon Allport (1937, 1961) and expressed in his definition of attitudes as " readiness to respond " (1935, 1954, and the scholarly discussion by McGuire, 1969); Hartmann's (1950, 1952, 1955, 1958) conceptualization regarding the function

of defenses. Secondly, the resistance to the integration of the attitude is even greater when central inconsistencies or consistencies between homonymous needs and attitudes are present in the psychodynamics of the person; in fact, because these inconsistencies or consistencies are central, i.e., significantly important for the person, for his self-concept, he will more or less subconsciously resist any homonymous or heteronymous force which tends to change them. Ostrom and Brock (1969), Edwards and Ostrom (1969) express a similar concept when they state that linking a particular attitude to more important values should make it more resistant to change than linking it to less important values.

But, it is especially the important theorizing of Rokeach (1973) which should be mentioned here. Amplifying and modifying the contribution of authors like McDougall (1926), Mead (1934), Hilgard (1949), Cooley (1956), Rogers (1959), Secord and Backman (1965), Aronson (1969), Nel, Helmreich and Aronson (1969), Rokeach contends that the self-conceptions, conscious and unconscious, are more central to a person than his values and his attitudes. Self-conceptions are all one person's· cognitions, conscious and unconscious, negative and positive, as well as the affective connotations of these cognitions about that person's total conception of himself. Any dissonance within these self-conceptions may affect behavior. Furthermore, " ...paradoxically, ...under certain conditions values may be easier to change than attitudes. Values are less central than self-conceptions but more central than attitudes. If a person's values are in fact standards employed to maintain and enhance self-conceptions, then a contradiction between values and self-conceptions can be most effortlessly resolved by changing the less central values " (Rokeach, 1973, p. 217).

In the theory of religious vocation formulated in 1971 and summarized in chapters 1, 2, and 3 of the present book, these self-conceptions discussed by the foregoing authors are operationalized as central inconsistencies, central consistencies and conflicts. One would expect that the greatest resistance to integration into the self-system will come from the *central* motivations. The following ranking of resistances to integration may be hypothesized for a religious vocationer: the greatest resistance will be offered by the central inconsistencies of vocationally dissonant variables because by definition they are central, i.e., functionally significant for the person, are unconscious and have dissonant variables (cfr. chapter 1 and Appendices C-2 and C-4); in decreasing degree, the resistance will be presented by central consistencies of dissonant variables, by central inconsistencies of neutral variables (central and only neutral) by central consistencies of neutral variables, by conflicts (non-central and dissonant or neutral). Note that here we do not consider the influence which values exert on the psychodynamics independently i.e. on their own merit; e.g. while the central inconsistencies and consistencies of a scrupulous vocationer tend to resist any change his values continue to exert their own, independent influence upon his total psychodynamics and the person may grow in them even though this growth will hardly touch the part of this behavior affected by his central inconsistencies and consistencies. As has been discussed elsewhere (Rulla, 1971, pp. 102 ff.) the person's sanctification is not intrinsically affected but his vocational effectiveness and perseverance may be affected.

The research presented up to now in this book has considered only the first two possible aspects of the force of the attitudes; more precisely it has considered directly the force which the attitudes have together with their homonymous or heteronymous needs in consistent or inconsistent relationships; the force of attitudes in their dissonant or neutral relevance to vocational values has been assessed indirectly (cfr. chapter 6 and Appendix C-2). In the original theorizing (Rulla, 1971) attitudes, values and needs were considered as independent but convergent forces; furthermore, also the third aspect of the attitudes' force was taken into consideration, at least in part. A more comprehensive view of the entire psychodynamics of a person requires that the same operational guidelines be followed in the present research as much as the tests used here will allow.

This will be done by assuming that: 1) the greater the central inconsistencies of vocationally dissonant needs-attitudes are, the greater the strength of the vulnerable part of the SI-II over its germinative part will be. 2) In turn, the greater the foregoing lack of balance is, the greater the degree of the unrealistically idealized SI-II of attitudes will be; i.e., the prevalence of central inconsistencies of dissonant and neutral variables as well as of conflicts of dissonant variables will produce and sustain in time an SI-II whose lack of objectivity and freedom will determine false expectations in the individual; and this lack of objectivity and freedom of the SI-II will be proportionate to the frequency and strength of the central inconsistencies. This theorizing is similar, at least in part, to the tenets and research findings of many authors; the reader may find them, for instance, in Atkinson (1957), Rotter (1954), McClelland (1951), Kelly (1955, 1963), Marlowe and Gergen (1969), Bradburn (1969), Secord and Backman (1974). 3) The foregoing false role expectations of the SI-II for attitudes will not be easily integrated (internalized, in Kelman's terms: cfr. the beginning of chapter 7) with the central inconsistencies, consistencies or with the conflicts existing in the psychodynamics of the individual because of the reasons previously discussed; therefore, discrepancies between these inconsistencies, consistencies, etc., and the SI-II's expectations for the homonymous attitudes will be a liability for the motivation of the vocationer.

In fact, a vicious circle will be established, which may gradually undermine the future commitment of the vocationer: a) the balance or imbalance between the central inconsistencies and consistencies will produce and sustain in time a more or less unrealistic SI-II of expectations of the individual about his future vocational roles; b) in turn, *these* unrealistic role expectations will present a great resistence to be *internalized*, to be personalized according to the objective system of vocational values chosen by the entering vocationer; c) there may follow a debilitating influence from the unrealistic attitudes of the SI-II upon the balance between central consistencies and inconsistencies, which will gradually undermine basic vocational attitudes and values.

The attentive reader can see that parts a and c of the vicious circle just described are a translation in operational terms of Propositions 4 and 5 of the theory, respectively (cfr. chapter 1). He can also see that part b of this vicious circle is directly related to the theorizing concerning internalizing vs. non-internalizing processes which were discussed throughout the previous formulation (Rulla, 1971) and which are considered in chapter 7

168

of the present book. Thus, one would expect that, for entering vocationers, the greater their inconsistencies of vocationally dissonant variables and the stronger their vulnerable part of the SI-II are, the weaker will be their capacity to internalize important vocational attitudes and values. Hence, the entering psychodynamics have potential which allows one to predict the future internalizing capacity of the vocationers for attitudes and/or instrumental values, and so to partially indicate *dispositions, trends* toward a more or less successful vocational commitment.

Note that here we are not implying that the bases of decisions to enter a vocation themselves become predictors of vocational effectiveness or perseverance. Dittes (1962, 1965) has called attention to the importance of distinguishing these two criteria from each other. As a matter of fact, in the previous chapters 5 to 7, we have tried to show that a decision to enter vocation is based on the self-ideal-in-situation (SI-II) with regard especially to vocational values and attitudes; now, we hypothesize that perseverance and effectiveness in religious life *in the final analysis* are based on the type, degree and number of aware or unaware central consistencies and inconsistencies of the actual-self with vocational attitudes and/or vocational values (Proposition 4 of the theory).

To sum up, there are three sets of elements which are distinct, even though not dynamically separated: 1) the conscious force to enter vocation, represented by the SI-II of pertinent values and, to a lesser degree, of attitudes; 2) the possible conscious or subconscious forces to enter coming from the self-conceptions of underlying vocational consistencies and/or inconsistencies and conflicts between the needs and attitudes; the attitudes may be related to homonymous or heteronymous needs; and 3) the more or less unrealistic SI-II of expectations of the individual about his future vocational roles; this unrealistic SI-II in the final analysis stems from the imbalance between the central inconsistencies and consistencies of needs vs. homonymous attitudes, on the one hand; the same unrealistic SI-II may influence vocational perseverance and effectiveness because it influences the capacity to internalize vocational attitudes and values, on the other hand. One can say that the elements considered under 1 and 2 allow an " assessment of "

169

(Prelinger and Zimet, 1964; Wiggins, 1973), i.e., a study of the entering psychodynamics with an emphasis on "understanding" its mechanism in the process of entrance; while the elements considered under 3 allow an "assessment for" (according to the same authors), i.e., a study of the entering psychodynamics with an emphasis on "predicting" its influence upon the future vocational perseverance and effectiveness. Chart 27 summarizes these conceptualizations.

CHART 27

THREE SETS OF ELEMENTS WHICH INFLUENCE
ENTRANCE, PERSEVERANCE AND EFFECTIVENESS

Assessment "of" entrance	1) SI-II of conscious values and attitudes 2) SI-II of attitudes *with* homonymous and/or heteronymous needs (self-conceptions)
Assessment "for" perseverance and effectiveness	3) SI-II *versus* central self-conceptions, i.e., inconsistencies and consistencies (predictable internalizing capacity)

The results discussed in chapters 5 to 7 are in line with the foregoing statements: they support the relevance for entrance of the conscious SI-II on the one hand, and the presence in a significant degree of its vulnerable and dissonant part as represented by central inconsistencies of vocationally dissonant variables and by conflicts of the same variables, on the other hand. Similarly, the findings of chapter 8 strongly suggest that this vulnerable part of the SI-II tends to persist after entrance.

On the basis of the discussion which has introduced the present chapter and of the findings of the previous chapters, the following research hypotheses may be formulated concerning the phenomenon of dropping out or not of vocation in its relation with the entering intrapsychic dynamics:

170

1) Values and attitudes relevant for vocation are a disposing factor to dropping out if they are only moderately present; they do not necessarily dispose toward perseverance if they are strongly present.

2) The predictable internalizing capacity which characterizes each entering vocationer tends to be lower in the future " dropouts " (DO) than in the " non-dropouts " (NDO).

3) The foregoing difference between DO and NDO for their predictable internalizing capacity is more present for the vulnerable part of the SI-II than for its germinative part.

4) The lower predictable internalizing capacity of DO in comparison with NDO is due, in decreasing order of importance, to the following structural patterns of self-conceptions: central inconsistencies of dissonant variables, central consistencies of dissonant variables, central inconsistencies of neutral variables, central consistencies of neutral variables, conflicts of dissonant and neutral variables.

5) Hypothesis 3 concerning the more relevant influence played by the vulnerable part of the SI-II over its germinative part in the process of dropping out is further supported when a comparison between these two parts is done in terms of frequencies of their components (inconsistencies, consistencies, etc.) in differentiating DO vs. NDO.

6) Hypothesis 4 concerning the decreasing importance in differentiating DO vs. NDO of the various structural patterns of self-conceptions is further supported when these patterns are compared in terms of frequencies of dissonant vs. frequencies of neutral variables.

7) The motivational weight is rather upon the values and to a lesser degree, upon the attitudes relevant to vocation for the process of entering into religious vocation; while it is rather upon the predictable internalizing capacity related to structural self-conceptions for the process of leaving it.

171

8) With the passing of time, people who will drop out earlier tend to show lower vocational values and attitudes than people who will drop out later; this should be true at least for vocational attitudes.

Before discussing the research, a few remarks are appropriate. The foregoing hypotheses may be applied both to perseverance and to effectiveness in vocation since they are based on the predictable capacity of individuals to internalize vocational attitudes and values. However, there is a difference between vocational perseverance and effectiveness. People may remain in religious life in spite of their poor capacity to internalize; as was seen in chapters 6 and 7, for some people both entering and remaining in religious life may be *also* the means to defend themselves against conflictual needs or to gratify some other needs. Still, the hypotheses contend that, in general, dropouts show lower capacity to internalize than do non-dropouts.

In this research, we are looking only for *trends*, i.e., for dispositions to the action of the spiritual and of the supernatural factors in relation to vocational perseverance and effectiveness. As such, our data do not fall *directly* under the influence of freedom and of spiritual dynamism. However, they speak of affective trends whose strength in disposing people to vocational perseverance and effectiveness may be considerable.

THE RESEARCH

Subjects

The subjects studied numbered 333. 191 of them were religious (96 men and 95 women), 40 seminarians, 52 and 50 males and females of lay Catholic colleges, respectively. The latter were the control groups. All these people were tested as they entered their training institutions. Further details concerning this sample are found on page 127. With regard to the matching of the experimental with the control groups, see page 71.

The interval of time between the entrance and the leaving or not of the vocational life varied from six to eight years for the religious, males and females. In this interval of time, 77 (81%) of the

172

female religious and 57 (59%) of the male religious had dropped out. 95% of the seminarians had left after four years; therefore, they were divided into DO and NDO according to their status two years after entrance; at this time, 21 (52.5%) of the entering 40 subjects had left.

Tests and Measurements

Values were studied by means of the General Goals of Life Inventory (GGLI). On the basis of content as well as of the results obtained in chapter 6 for the analyses of variance and/or the discriminant function analyses, it was decided to consider seven of the values of the GGLI as vocationally dissonant; the seven values correspond to the letters C, K, L, M, N, O, and P of Appendix B-2. The other values were considered as vocationally neutral, i.e., as less helpful in differentiating people who choose religious vocation from people who do not. Accordingly, a one-tail Wilcoxon test was used for the vocationally dissonant values and a two-tail test for the neutral variables (Siegel, 1956; Wallis and Roberts, 1956).

The attitudes studied in the present chapter numbered 12 and all were taken from the Modified Activities Index (MAI); they had been chosen because they were considered particularly relevant to religious vocation in terms of their content: Abasement, Adaptability (or Defendence), Aggression, Chastity, Exhibition, Harm Avoidance, Succorance, Mortification, Obedience, Piety, Poverty, Responsibility. The first seven variables correspond to the seven homonymous vocationally dissonant variables used in the assessment of the " predictable internalizing capacity. " The other attitudes come from the " religious scales " of the MAI.

All these attitudes were assessed on the basis of the means obtained by combining the means of the SI and the ones of the II.

Both the values and the attitudes used in this chapter were assessed as follows: 1) the data obtained in chapter 6 in comparing religious and seminarians vs. controls by means of analyses of variance and discriminant function analyses were used here, too; 2) comparisons among vocationers and of vocationers vs. controls were made also by means of the Wilcoxon test; for these Wilcoxon comparisons the data concerning the 333 subjects studied in the present chapter were used.

The predictable internalizing capacity of the 333 subjects considered in this chapter was assessed by obtaining: 1) the percentages over the total scores of each individual for his inconsistencies, consistencies and conflicts according to the structural approach described in chapter 3, section B; 2) similar percentages for the SI-II of each person; 3) the difference between the first and the second percentages for the fourteen variables used. These differences obtained for each person were then transformed into means of the fourteen variables for each group of the DO and NDO. Table 9.3 reports all these means for the five groups studied.

As had been noted in the introduction to this chapter, we were interested in obtaining *trends* of differences between DO and NDO concerning their predictable internalizing capacity. So such differences were computed by a test which fulfills this requirement: the Wilcoxon signed-rank test for matched samples. According to the theorizing and the findings discussed in the introduction to this chapter, a one-tail test was used, assuming that discrepancies between structural self-conceptions and SI-II were liabilities.

The fourteen variables (need-attitudes) used to assess the predictable internalizing capacity of each individual are described in Appendices B-3 and C-2. The reader can see for himself how deeply these " needs ", proposed by Murray (1938) and used in most of the best available tests, may influence, positively or negatively, the fruits of the Spirit mentioned by St. Paul in Galatians 5: 22-23: love, peace, patient endurance, kindness, generosity, faith, meekness, and chastity. This influence is particularly great if those needs-attitudes act under the force of central consistencies or inconsistencies.

Further details concerning the procedures of assessment used in this chapter are presented in Appendix C-10.

The Results

Hypothesis 1

The results are summarized in chart 28.

CHART 28

FINDINGS CONCERNING VALUES (GGLI) AND ATTITUDES (MAI) RELEVANT TO VOCATION RELATED TO THE PROCESS OF DROPPING OUT

Institutions	% of Dropouts after		ANALYSIS OF VARIANCE vs. Controls		WILCOXON vs. Controls		WILCOXON DO vs. NDO		WILCOXON for Values and Attitudes
	4 yrs.	6-8 yrs.	Values	Attitudes	Values	Attitudes	Values	Attitudes	
SEMINARIANS	95%	—	8 out of 21	0 out of 12	.04 for dissonant (3)	ns	ns for dissonant and neutral	ns	Male Rel. DO vs. Sems DO ns — Male Rel. NDO vs. Sems NDO ns
FEMALE RELIGIOUS	59%	81%	17 out of 21	6 out of 12 (1)	.02 for dissonant (3)	ns	ns for dissonant and neutral	ns	
MALE RELIGIOUS	47%	59%	15 out of 21	9 out of 12 (2)	.04 for dissonant (3)	ns	.01 for dissonant (4) ns for neutral	.02 NDO >DO (5)	

(1) 4 scales favorable to vocational commitment; 2 scales unfavorable.
(2) 7 scales favorable to vocational commitment; 2 scales unfavorable.
(3) Vocationers are lower in vocationally dissonant values.
(4) NDO are lower in vocationally dissonant values.
(5) NDO are higher in vocationally consonant attitudes.

In chapter 6, analyses of variance for values of the GGLI among seminarians, religious men and women, and controls of both sexes were made. The difference found between seminarians and their lay controls was less evident than the similar difference between religious men and women, and their controls: only 8 of the 21 values differentiate seminarians from their controls, while this difference is evident for 15 and 17 values for religious males and females, respectively. The content of these values gave a general picture characterizing vocationers as highly disciplined and selfless people committed to religious and altruistic concerns.

The contrast between seminarians vs. religious, males and females, is confirmed by the findings concerning the 12 scales of attitudes; on these scales, there is no difference between seminarians and controls, while religious women and men differ from their controls for six scales and for nine scales, respectively. For female Religious, 4 of the 6 scales which differentiate them from their controls are favorable to vocational commitment, while 2 scales are not; the same findings for male Religious are 7 favorable and 2 unfavorable scales.

When the comparison between vocationers (seminarians and religious of both sexes) and their controls concerning the values of the GGLI was made by means of the Wilcoxon test, all the three groups of vocationers were significantly different but only for the seven vocationally dissonant values: $p = .04$ for seminarians; $.02$ for female religious; $.04$ for male religious; the vocationers are lower in these values. No significant differences were present in the same comparisons when the neutral values were considered. Table 9.1 shows the means from which the foregoing computations were made. A Wilcoxon test comparison of vocationers vs. their controls for the 12 attitudes showed no significant differences. Table 9.2 presents the means of this assessment.

A Wilcoxon test comparison between DO and NDO gave the following results: no significant difference for dissonant values, nor for neutral values in the contrasts for seminarians and for female religious; male religious NDO are significantly lower ($p = .01$) than DO in vocationally dissonant values, while no differences are present for neutral values. Similar comparisons for attitudes showed no significant differences of NDO vs. DO for seminarians and female religious; male religious NDO were higher ($p = .02$) than DO in vocationally consonant attitudes.

Finally, a contrast by means of a two-tail Wilcoxon test of the seminarian DO vs. male religious DO as well as a similar contrast for NDO of both groups indicated no significant differences.

It should be emphasized that the rates of dropping out were

176

notably different for the three groups of vocationers: 4 years after entrance, 95% of the seminarians, 59% of the religious females, and 47% of the religious males had withdrawn.

All the foregoing findings suggest the following remarks: 1) values play an important role in the initial, conscious decision to enter a vocational commitment; in fact, vocationers differ from their controls in the values tapped by the GGLI when they are assessed by the analysis of variance. Furthermore, all the three groups of vocationers significantly differ from their controls for the vocationally dissonant values on the Wilcoxon test. A similar role is played by the attitudes which are relevant to vocation. However, the impact of attitudes is much lower; this is in agreement with the usually lower dynamic force exerted by attitudes in comparison with values. 2) The degree to which values are present at entrance is indicative of future perseverance in the vocational commitment; in fact, on the basis of the more statistically demanding analyses of variance, one can say that the 21 values of the GGLI differentiated the entering seminarians from their controls in a much lower degree than they did for religious, women and men; now, after 4 years of vocational training, the rates of dropping out were 95% for seminarians, 59% for religious women, and 47% for religious men. As for the entering process, so also for dropping out, attitudes have a lower influence than values. Thus, the first part of hypothesis 1 seems to be supported: values and, to a lesser degree, attitudes are a disposing factor of dropping out if they are only moderately present. As it was discussed in chapter 6, perhaps seminarians never really " entered " into a vocational setting.

3) The findings seem to support the second part of the hypothesis, also. At entrance, values were strongly present for religious of both sexes. Still, 6-8 years after their entrance, 81% of the women and 59% of the men had left. Thus, it would seem that when values are strongly present, they are not necessarily factors disposing toward perseverance. The same can be said for attitudes, but to a much lesser degree.

4) Our data do not support the opinion that people who will leave vocation have higher values; this was never true in the six comparisons between DO and NDO of the three groups studied, seminarians, religious women and men, for the vocationally dissonant or neutral values. Actually, for male religious the data indicate the opposite trend, at least for vocationally dissonant values. The same trend was present for the attitudes.

Hypothesis 2

The means used for the Wilcoxon one-tail computations concerning this hypothesis as well as hypotheses 3 and 4 are on Table 9.3. Chart 29 shows the findings relevant to hypothesis 2.

CHART 29

RESULTS RELEVANT TO THE PREDICTABLE INTERNALIZING CAPACITY CHARACTERIZING FUTURE DO AND NDO (WILCOXON TEST)

Institutions	DO% after		vs. Controls	DO vs. NDO	vs. Males	
	4 yrs.	6-8 yrs.			DO vs. DO	NDO vs. NDO
Seminarians	95%	—	ns	ns	ns	.05 (Sems<)*
Female Religious	59%	81%	ns (.08)	.01 (DO < NDO)*	—	—
Male Religious	47%	59%	ns	.05 (DO < NDO)*	—	—

* < = lower in predictable internalizing capacity.

According to the rates of dropping out shown by the three groups of vocationers, one would expect that the difference between DO and NDO for their predictable internalizing capacity would be quite different among these three groups. More precisely, one would expect no significant difference for the seminarians since in a span of four years 95% of them withdrew, while such a difference could be expected for religious women and men for whom the rates of withdrawal after 6-8 years were 81% and 59% respectively. The results correspond to these expectations: no significant difference between seminarian DO and NDO; female religious DO and male religious DO show a predictable internalizing capacity which is lower than the one of their NDO counterparts at the following levels of significance: .01 for women, .05 for men.

178

If comparisons across the two groups of male vocationers (religious and seminarians) are made by contrasting the DO and the NDO among themselves, the results further confirm the previous findings. Let us remember that 52.5% of the seminarians had left after two years of training, and 95% after four years, while after 6-8 years of training 59% of the male religious had dropped out. Thus, one would expect that, when seminarian DO are compared with male religious DO, no significant difference would be present, while a difference should be present for the groups of NDO: seminarian NDO should have lower predictable internalizing capacity since in a two-year span almost all will withdraw. The findings are in this line: no significant difference between the DO, while seminarian NDO are significantly lower at $p = .05$. A two-tail Wilcoxon test was used.

Finally, one should expect no difference concerning the predictable internalizing capacity when vocationers are compared with their lay controls. In general, there are not two different calls nor a " privileged status " with regard to apostolic zeal for the kingdom of God. This aim can be reached in every profession or situation of life. The results show no significant differences between the three groups of vocationers and their controls.

However, a *trend* is shown by religious females: they tend to have a lower predictable internalizing capacity than their controls ($p = .08$). A further analysis indicated that this trend is related to the DO rather than the NDO. The latter are not significantly different from the controls, while the DO are at $p < .007$, the religious having lower predictable internalizing capacity. Note that here we do not speak of personal holiness but only of the *disposition* toward apostolic effectiveness, and this, within the limitation of our measurements.

To sum up: the hypothesis is well supported because the psychodynamics of future DO always show a predictable internalizing capacity lower than the one of the NDO.

Hypothesis 3

The hypothesis was tested by contrasting DO vs. NDO in terms of the vulnerable part vs. the germinative part of their SI-II. Let us recall that the vulnerable part is made by the inconsistencies of dissonant and neutral variables as well as by the conflicts of the dissonant variables; the germinative part includes the consistencies of both types of variables and the conflicts of neutral variables.

The results are shown on chart 30 and they speak for themselves.

179

CHART 30
PREDICTABLE INTERNALIZING CAPACITY: VULNERABLE VS. GERMINATIVE PARTS OF THE SI-II OF *DO* VS. *NDO* (WILCOXON TEST)

Groups	Contrasts	Vulnerable	Germinative
Seminarians	Vocationers vs. Controls		
	DO vs. Controls		
	NDO vs. Controls		
	DO vs. NDO		
Female Religious	Vocationers vs. Controls	.03 Voc. —	
	DO vs. Controls	.02 DO —	
	NDO vs. Controls		
	DO vs. NDO	.04 DO —	.02 DO —
Male Religious	Vocationers vs. Controls		
	DO vs. Controls		
	NDO vs. Controls		
	DO vs. NDO	.04 DO —	
Male Religious vs. Seminarians	DO vs. DO		
	NDO vs. NDO	.06 Sem. —	

N.B. Blank spaces represent non-significant differences.
    — = lower predictable internalizing capacity

Differences significant at .05 or below are found in 4 cells of the vulnerable part vs. 1 difference found in the cells of the germinative part. There was only one difference at the .06 level and this was in the vulnerable part. Thus the hypothesis in supported.

The findings of chart 30 indicate the same trends already seen in hypothesis 2 and therefore they may be interpreted in the light of the discussion presented there. The only result which perhaps needs a brief comment is the significantly lower capacity to internalize which is predictable from the germinative part for the DO of religious females in comparison with their NDO. The fact that female religious DO present a predictable internalizing capacity which is lower both for the germinative and the vulnerable parts of the SI-II helps one to understand why women left at a higher percentage than men: 81% vs. 59% after 6-8 years. Note that male religious DO are lower only in the vulnerable part.

Interestingly enough, the data concerning hypothesis 2 and 3 are in line with the ones obtained in chapter 7 for the Index of Vocational Maturity. In chapter 7, the vulnerable part of the SI-II appeared to prevail over its germinative part. Here, in hypotheses 2 and 3, the same prevalence is present for the predictable internalizing capacity. Thus, there seems to be a support for the assumptions made in the introduction to this chapter: the prevalence of the vulnerable part of the SI-II over its germinative part produces and sustains in time a more or less unrealistic SI-II of expectations of the individual about his future vocational roles, and, in turn, these unrealistic role expectations will affect his internalizing capacity and so his vocational commitment.

Hypothesis 4

Which ones of the structural patterns of self-conceptions are more relevant for lowering the predictable internalizing capacity of DO in comparison with NDO? It is hypothesized that the patterns which are central, i.e., particularly important for the self-concept, are more relevant, especially if they are—by definition—unconscious and have vocationally dissonant components; so, the inconsistencies of dissonant variables are expected to be the more important factors in the process of withdrawal, followed by the other structural patterns, central consistencies, etc., indicated in the formulation of the hypothesis. Note that, because of the small number of variables which showed central consistencies, the Wilcoxon statistics for these structures had to combine dissonant and neutral variables.

The results are presented in chart 31. They confirm the hypothesis for religious males and females: all the significant data are in the expected direction. For these two groups of religious, the findings also suggest why women dropped out at a higher percentage than men: the internalizing capacity of female DO was lower than

181

Chart 31

PREDICTABLE INTERNALIZING CAPACITY: DECREASING IMPORTANCE
OF STRUCTURAL SELF-CONCEPTIONS (WILCOXON TEST)

Predictable Internalizing Capacity related to:	Seminarians (N = 40) 95% DO after 4 yrs.		Female Religious (N = 95) 59% DO after 4 yrs. 81% DO after 6-8 yrs.		Male Religious (N = 96) 47% DO after 4 yrs. 59% DO after 6-8 yrs.	
	Direction	Significance	Direction	Significance	Direction	Significance
Inconsistencies of Dissonant Variables	DO < NDO	.34	DO < NDO	**.04**	DO < NDO	**.04**
Consistencies of Dissonant and Neutral Variables	DO > NDO	.34	DO < NDO	**.01**	DO < NDO	**.10**
Inconsistencies of Neutral Variables	DO > NDO	.28	DO > NDO	.34	DO < NDO	.50
Conflicts of Dissonant Variables	DO > NDO	**.05**	DO < NDO	.13	DO < NDO	.22
Conflicts of Neutral Variables	DO > NDO	.47	DO < NDO	.40	DO > NDO	.28

N.B. < = lower in predictable internalizing capacity.
> = higher in predictable internalizing capacity.
Boldface numbers are the relevant ones for making a difference.

the one of their NDO in both the inconsistencies of dissonant variables and the consistencies.

The findings for seminarians may be interpreted in the light of the hard fact that 95% of them withdrew after 4 years of training, while after the same span of time, the figures for religious are 59% for women and 47% for men. As was already discussed in hypotheses 2 and 3, seminarian NDO did not differ from their DO in predictable internalizing capacity; in fact, almost all the NDO became DO after two years. This trend of the NDO to withdraw is indicated by the result for the conflicts of dissonant variables.

Hypothesis 5

The relative influence of the person's germinative and vulnerable SI-II in relation to dropping out was also assessed by analyzing and contrasting the different frequencies of inconsistencies, defensive consistencies, conflicts, and consistencies for the DO and NDO groups. This hypothesis answers the following questions: Are the vocationers who drop out different from those who persevere in the number and, therefore, percentage of central inconsistencies, defensive consistencies, conflicts, and consistencies? Is the difference more evident in the vulnerable SI-II or in the germinative SI-II?

Chart 32 shows the variables that significantly differentiate the groups along the dimension of dropping out when they are subdivided according to their structural qualities of inconsistencies, defensive consistencies, conflicts, and consistencies. In other words, the presence of abasement in the upper left cell of chart 32 indicates that male religious DO and NDO differ significantly in frequencies for the inconsistency of abasement. Table 9.4 lists the frequencies and percentages for all the variables involved in the contrasts for DO, for religious, and for seminarians; the frequencies and percentages for male and female controls are listed in Table 7.3.

Chart 33 is a further summary of the data listing the frequencies and percentages over all dimensions of the 75 variables contributing to the differentiation among the groups.

Keeping in mind that inconsistencies, defensive consistencies, and conflicts for dissonant variables constitute the vulnerable aspect of the SI-II, and that consistencies and conflicts for neutral variables constitute the germinative aspect of the SI-II, chart 33 indicates that 77.33% of the variables significantly differentiating the groups in terms of dropping out appear as inconsistencies, defensive consistencies, and conflicts for vocationally dissonant variables (the

183

CHART 32

VARIABLES SIGNIFICANTLY DIFFERENTIATING GROUPS OF DROPOUTS

Relevant Contrasts	Inconsistencies and Defensive Consistencies	Conflicts for Dissonant Variables	Conflicts for Neutral Variables	Consistencies
Male Religious DO and NDO	Abasement —* Succorance —	Abasement ++ Succorance + Aggression +		Exhibition —
Female Religious DO and NDO	Affiliation ++ Achievement +			
Seminarian DO and NDO	Dominance +			Aggression —
Male Rel. DO and Controls	Harm Avoidance — Affiliation ++ Counteraction +++ Chastity + Understanding —	Defendence ++ Succorance +	Affiliation — Counteraction — Dominance +	Harm Avoidance + Chastity —
Male Rel. NDO and Controls	Abasement + Dominance — Harm Avoidance — Counteraction ++ Chastity + Understanding —	Abasement — Defendence + Aggression — Succorance +	Counteraction —	

Group				Order
Female Rel. DO and Controls	Defendence −, Succorance −, Nurturance +, Affiliation +	Defendence +, Aggression +, Succorance +		−
Female Rel. NDO and Controls	Defendence −, Succorance −, Counteraction +	Defendence +, Aggression +		
Seminarian DO and Controls	Harm Avoidance −, Dominance +, Succorance +++, Chastity ++			
Seminarian NDO and Controls	Counteraction +, Order −	Aggression +	Affiliation −, Counteraction −	
Male Rel. DO and Sem. DO	Dominance −, Succorance −	Succorance +		Succorance −
Male Rel. NDO and Sem. NDO	Dominance −, Order ++, Chastity ++		Order −	Succorance −
Male Rel. DO and Female Rel. DO	Aggression +, Achievement −, Dominance −, Understanding −	Harm Avoidance +	Achievement +	Exhibition −, Harm Avoidance +
Male Rel. NDO and Female Rel. NDO	Aggression +, Dominance −			

* − 1st group lower than 2nd group.
  + 1st group higher than 2nd group.

CHART 33

PERCENTAGES AND FREQUENCIES OF
VARIABLES SIGNIFICANTLY DIFFERENTIATING GROUPS OF DROPOUTS
(Variables N = 75)

Relevant Contrasts	Inconsistencies and Defensive Consistencies %	f	Conflicts for Dissonant Variables %	f	Conflicts for Neutral Variables %	f	Consistencies %	f	Totals %	f
Male Religious DO and NDO	2.67	(2)	4.00	(3)	—	—	1.33	(1)	8.00	(6)
Female Religious DO and NDO	2.67	(2)	—	—	—	—	—	—	2.67	(2)
Seminarian DO and NDO	1.33	(1)	—	—	—	—	1.33	(1)	2.67	(2)
Male Rel. DO and Controls	6.67	(5)	2.67	(2)	4.00	(3)	2.67	(2)	16.00	(12)
Male Rel. NDO and Controls	9.33	(7)	5.33	(4)	1.33	(1)	—	—	16.00	(12)
Female Rel. DO and Controls	5.33	(4)	4.00	(3)	—	—	1.33	(1)	10.67	(8)
Female Rel. NDO and Controls	4.00	(3)	2.67	(2)	—	—	—	—	6.67	(5)
Seminarian DO and Controls	5.33	(4)	—	—	—	—	—	—	5.33	(4)
Seminarian NDO and Controls	2.67	(2)	1.33	(1)	2.67	(2)	—	—	6.67	(5)
Male Rel. DO and Seminarian DO	2.67	(2)	1.33	(1)	—	—	1.33	(1)	5.33	(4)
Male Rel. NDO and Seminarian NDO	4.00	(3)	—	—	1.33	(1)	1.33	(1)	6.67	(5)
Male Rel. DO and Female Rel. DO	5.33	(4)	1.33	(1)	1.33	(1)	2.67	(2)	10.67	(8)
Male Rel. NDO and Female Rel. NDO	2.67	(2)	—	—	—	—	—	—	2.67	(2)
	54.67	(41)	22.67	(17)	10.67	(8)	12.00	(9)	100.00	(75)
	77.33	(58)			22.67	(17)				

vulnerable SI-II), whereas 22.67% of the variables significantly differentiating the groups appear as consistencies or conflicts for neutral variables (the germinative SI-II).

A test for the differences between proportions applied to these results yielded a highly significant Z score with a p < .001. The groups contrasted along the DO-NDO dimensions appear to be differentiated more in terms of the vulnerable aspect of the SI-II than in terms of the germinative aspect of the SI-II, and so hypothesis 5 seems to be supported.

Hypothesis 6

This hypothesis was tested by comparing the number of vocationally dissonant with vocationally neutral variables that significantly contribute to the differentiation of the groups in terms of dropping out. Each of these variables, as previously discussed, represents a significant difference in terms of the frequency of the inconsistencies, conflicts, defensive consistencies, and consistencies for that variable found in the various groups contrasted along the DO dimension.

Chart 34 shows the breakdown of the variables that significantly contribute to this differentiation along the DO dimension into the vocationally neutral and vocationally dissonant.

There are 36 (48%) dissonant and 22 (29%) neutral variables corresponding to the vulnerable aspects of the SI-II (cfr. chart 34), and 8 (10.66%) dissonant and 9 (12%) neutral variables corresponding to the germinative aspect of the SI-II.

Tests of significance between these proportions revealed that: 1) the percentage of dissonant variables (59%) when the germinative and vulnerable aspects of the SI-II are considered together is not significantly higher than that of the neutral variables (41%), Z = = 1.52, p < .13. 2) The germinative and the vulnerable aspects of the SI-II differ significantly in terms of both the dissonant and neutral variables, the dissonant and neutral variables of the vulnerable aspect of the SI-II being the more important in differentiating the groups. The test of differences for the dissonant variables yielded a Z = 5.47, p < .001; for the neutral variables, Z = 2.57, p < .01. 3) The percentage of dissonant variables found in the vulnerable aspect of the SI-II is higher than the percentage of neutral variables in a measure very close to significance. The test of significance yielded a Z = 1.90, p < .06. 4) No significant difference was found within the germinative SI-II between the dissonant and neutral variables.

187

Chart 34

FREQUENCIES OF VOCATIONALLY DISSONANT AND NEUTRAL VARIABLES DIFFERENTIATING GROUPS OF DROPOUTS

Contrasts	Inconsistencies		Defensive Consistencies		Conflicts		Consistencies		Totals
	DV*	NV	DV	NV	DV	NV	DV	NV	
Male Religious DO and NDO	2	0	0	0	3	0	1	0	6
Female Religious DO and NDO	0	2	0	0	0	0	0	0	2
Seminarian DO and NDO	0	1	0	0	0	0	1	0	2
Male Rel. DO and Controls	1	0	1	3	2	3	2	0	12
Male Rel. NDO and Controls	2	1	2	2	4	1	0	0	12
Female Rel. DO and Controls	2	2	0	0	3	0	0	1	8
Female Rel. NDO and Controls	2	0	0	1	2	0	0	0	5
Seminarian DO and Controls	1	0	2	1	0	0	0	0	4
Seminarian NDO and Controls	0	0	0	2	1	2	0	0	5
Male Rel. DO and Seminarian DO	0	0	1	1	1	0	1	0	4
Male Rel. NDO and Seminarian NDO	0	1	1	1	0	1	1	0	5
Male Rel. DO and Female Rel. DO	1	0	0	3	1	1	2	0	8
Male Rel. NDO and Female Rel. NDO	1	0	0	1	0	0	0	0	2
Totals	12	7	7	15	17	8	8	1	75

* DV = Dissonant Variables.
  NV = Neutral Variables.

In summary, the results for the two last hypotheses indicate that using the frequencies of the inconsistencies, defensive consistencies, conflicts, and consistencies that significantly differentiate the groups along the DO dimension, the vulnerable aspect of the SI-II is more important in differentiating the groups than the germinative SI-II, and that the dissonant variables tend to be more important than the neutral variables—this being particularly true for the vulnerable aspect of the SI-II.

Hypothesis 7

The investigation made throughout chapters 5 to 8 as well as throughout the first six hypotheses of the present chapter have enucleated two sets of forces which may influence both the entrance and the leaving of vocation: the conscious force exerted by values and, to a lesser degree, by attitudes, on the one hand; the conscious or subconscious impact coming from the balance/imbalance between the central consistencies and inconsistencies which needs have in their relationship with attitudes and/or with values, on the other hand.

Now we ask the following question: which one of these two sets of forces seems to prevail in the entrance process and which one in the process of dropping out? Hypothesis 7 indicates that, for the entrance into vocation, values and, to a lesser degree, attitudes have a motivational weight greater than the balance/imbalance between the central consistencies and inconsistencies, while, for the leaving of vocation, the opposite is true.

The subjects studied for this hypothesis were the same considered in chapter 7 for the assessment of the Index of Vocational Maturity and in the present chapter for the first six hypotheses. Let us recall that the Index of Vocational Maturity indicated the degree of internalization shown by each vocationer when he decided to enter a vocational setting; this degree of internalization stemmed especially from the balance/imbalance of his consistencies/inconsistencies.

Our findings point to the following facts:

A) For the decision to enter the vocational setting, values and, to a lesser degree, attitudes differentiate the three groups of vocationers (seminarians, religious males and females) from their lay controls, while the balance/imbalance of consistencies/inconsistencies as expressed by the Index of Vocational Maturity does not. Chart 35 offers the findings which back the foregoing statement. The results concerning the Index of Vocational

189

Maturity were discussed in chapter 7; the other results of chart 35 are considered in hypothesis 1 of the present chapter.

B) *Vice versa*, for the process of leaving vocation, values and attitudes do not tend to differentiate dropouts vs. non-dropouts, while the balance/imbalance of consistencies/inconsistencies as expressed by the Predictable Internalizing Capacity shown by the entering psychodynamics tends to do so. Chart 36 presents the data which back this statement.

The findings of chart 36 need some brief explanation and comment. The data concerning the difference between dropouts and non-dropouts for values, and attitudes were discussed in hypothesis 1 of the present chapter: while there is no significant difference between DO and NDO of seminarians and female religious, male DO show higher vocationally dissonant values and lower vocationally consonant attitudes than NDO. However, when DO and NDO are contrasted with the lay controls, *both* DO and NDO tend to have lower vocationally dissonant values and higher vocationally consonant attitudes than the lay controls. Thus, at entrance, both DO and NDO proclaimed attitudes and especially the more motivationally powerful values, which differentiated them from lay people; but, in

CHART 35

ENTRANCE INTO VOCATION:
Influence of Values (GGLI) and of Vocationally Relevant Attitudes (MAI) vs.
Influence of Balance/Imbalance of Consistencies/Inconsistencies
as Expressed by the Index of Vocational Maturity (IVM)

Institutions	Values ANOVA* and Wilcoxon	Attitudes		Balance/Imbalance of Consistencies/Inconsistencies in the IVM
		ANOVA	Wilcoxon	
Seminarians vs. Lay	Sems > Lay**			
Female Religious vs. Lay	Rel. > Lay**	Rel. > Lay (4 vs. 2)***		
Male Religious vs. Lay	Rel. > Lay**	Rel. > Lay (7 vs. 2)***		

N.B. Blank spaces indicate no statistically significant differences.
> = greater than.
* ANOVA = Analysis of Variance.
** Analysis of Variance for 21 values and Wilcoxon for 7 dissonant values of the GGLI: cfr. chart 28.
*** Cfr. chart 28.

190

time, NDO acted more according to the initial differentiating proclamation, while the DO acted against such a differentiating proclamation. Why? Among the many possible factors influencing this
opposite behavior, the findings concerning the intrapsychic dynamics
indicate that people who drop out present a lower predictable internalizing capacity, which may lead to their leaving.

The results of chart 36 regarding the predictable internalizing
capacity and its relationships to central consistencies and central
vocational inconsistencies were discussed in hypotheses 2 and 4.
A special comment should be made concerning the fact that seminarian NDO showed lower predictable internalizing capacity than
religious NDO. In fact, as chart 37 shows, this difference is not
matched by differences regarding values and attitudes. Now, 95%
of the seminarians dropped out after 4 years of training while 59%
of male religious after 6-8 years. Thus, again, it would seem that,
among the intrapsychic forces present at entrance, the balance/
imbalance between central consistencies and inconsistencies is a
more influential factor for dropping out than the proclaimed values
and attitudes.

If charts 35 and 36 are juxtaposed, one can have a visual representation of the prevalence of values and attitudes for the process

CHART 36

LEAVING VOCATION:

Influences of Values and Vocationally Relevant Attitudes vs.
Influence of Central Consistencies (CC) and Central Dissonant Inconsistencies (CDI);
and of the Predictable Internalizing Capacity (PIC)

Institutions	Values	Attitudes	PIC as related to: CC	CDI	PIC	% DO after 4 yrs.	% DO after 6-8 yrs.
Seminarians DO vs. NDO					.05 NDO ⁄ NDO Sems ＼ Male Rel.*	95%	
Female Religious DO vs. NDO			.01 DO < NDO	.04 DO < NDO	.01 DO < NDO	59%	81%
Male Religious DO vs. NDO	.01 DO > NDO for dissonant BUT DO < Controls (.05) NDO < Controls (.04)	.02 DO < NDO for consonant BUT DO > Controls i (.06) NDO > Controls (.04)	.10 DO < NDO	.04 DO < NDO	.05 DO < NDO	47%	59%

N.B. Blank spaces indicate no statistically significant differences.
  < = less than.
  > = greater than.
  * See chart 37.

191

CHART 37

LEAVING VOCATION:

Influence of Values and Vocationally Relevant Attitudes
versus Predictable Internalizing Capacity (PIC)
for Seminarians and Male Religious
(Wilcoxon Test)

	Values Dissonant Neutral		Atti-tudes	Predictable Internalizing Capacity
DO vs. DO	ns	ns	ns	ns
NDO vs. NDO	ns	ns	ns	.05 NDO Sems < NDO Religious

N.B. ns = no statistically significant difference
      < = lower than

of entering vocation versus the prevalence of the balance/imbalance
of central consistencies/inconsistencies for the process of leaving it:
as the reader can see, the significant data are increasingly on the left
for chart 35 (entering process), while they are increasingly on the
right for chart 36 (leaving process).

The foregoing discussion does not imply that the values and,
to a lesser degree, the attitudes proclaimed at entrance have no
influence upon future dropping out. In this regard, the findings
considered in hypothesis 1 for seminarians vs. religious women and
men, suggest that values act together with the balance/imbalance
of central self-conceptions. However, the latter seem to be more
powerful in influencing the withdrawal from vocation.

A further support for hypothesis 7 is offered by comparisons
in terms of frequencies of the various structural patterns of self-
conceptions at entrance and for dropping out.

Structural patterns of self-conceptions constitute what we have
called the germinative aspect of the SI-II (consistencies for both
neutral and dissonant variables, conflicts for neutral variables) and
the vulnerable aspect of the SI-II (inconsistencies and defensive
consistencies for both neutral and dissonant variables and conflicts
for dissonant variables) (see chapter 7).

The relevance as well as the prevalence of the vulnerable aspect
of the SI-II over the germinative aspect has been already discussed
both in chapters 6 and 7 and in this chapter.

If the germinative aspect of the SI-II is the main pivot on which the decision to enter is based, the vulnerable aspect appears of greater importance especially when perseverance in vocation is concerned. Accordingly, one would expect the patterns of self-conceptions corresponding to the vulnerable aspect of the SI-II to make a greater psychodynamic contribution when the phenomenon of perseverance is considered in contrast to the entering process. Different proportions of frequencies for the structural patterns corresponding to the vulnerable and the germinative SI-II of the self should be expected.

Chart 38 (summarizing charts 16 and 34) shows the comparison of the contributions made by the structural patterns of self-conceptions taken as vulnerable SI-II and germinative SI-II (for dissonant and neutral variables) at entrance and for dropping out.

CHART 38

SUMMARY OF PERCENTAGES (AND FREQUENCIES)
OF DISSONANT AND NEUTRAL VARIABLES
DIFFERENTIATING GROUPS
AT ENTRANCE AND FOR DROPPING OUT

	Vulnerable SI-II		Germinative SI-II	
Dissonant Variables	At Entrance* 34%	(22)	At Entrance 12.5%	(8)
	Dropping Out** 48%	(36)	Dropping Out 11%	(8)
Neutral Variables	At Entrance 28%	(18)	At Entrance 25%	(16)
	Dropping Out 29%	(22)	Dropping Out 12%	(9)

* Total N of Variables = 64 (cfr. Chart 16)
** Total N of Variables = 75 (cfr. Chart 34)

A) The vulnerable aspect of the SI-II has greater weight in differentiating the groups for dropping out than for entering when the vocationally dissonant variables are considered. The test of differences between the two proportions (34% and 48%) yielded a $Z = 1.67$, $p < .05$.

B) When considering the contribution of the vulnerable SI-II as expressed by the neutral variables, there is no significant difference between the groups considered for the process of dropping out versus the process of entering.

193

C) When considering the contribution of the germinative SI-II as expressed by the dissonant variables, there is no significant difference between the groups for dropping out and for entering. This finding is in line with the data previously discussed concerning the relatively limited power for predicting perseverance of the vocationers based only on their values and attitudes at entrance.

D) There is a significant difference between the contribution made by the germinative SI-II for neutral variables in differentiating the groups in the analysis made for entering and for dropping out. The germinative SI-II expressed by vocationally neutral variables is significantly more helpful in characterizing vocationers at entrance than in differentiating vocationers for perseverance: $Z = 1.98$, $p < .02$. This finding also indirectly confirms the data of both chapters 5 and 6 as well as hypotheses 1 and 6 of this chapter.

In discussing the first seven hypotheses of the present chapter, differences of percentages in dropping out for various groups of vocationers have been frequently considered. Tests for difference between proportions were computed for the contrasts used in this chapter; the results for these differences were always significant, as the following data indicate: 1) the contrast between the 95% withdrawals of seminarians versus the 59% of female religious after 4 years of training is significant at $p < .001$ ($Z = 4.16$); 2) the similar contrast of 95% seminarians versus the 47% of male religious is significant at $p < .001$ ($Z = 5.23$); 3) finally, the contrast between the 59% of male religious versus the 81% of female religious after 6-8 years of training is significant at $p < .002$ ($Z = 3.32$).

Hypothesis 8

The findings of the previous hypotheses have indicated that the process of dropping out is related to the measurement of the Predictable Internalizing Capacity as proposed in this book: future dropouts, already in their psychodynamics present at entrance, show a lower capacity to internalize vocational values and attitudes than non-dropouts. But, do they really internalize less over time? One way to test this fact is to compare early dropouts vs. late dropouts: at entrance, the former should not show lower vocational values and attitudes than the latter, while this becomes true with the passing of time; or, since the attitudes possess less psychodynamic strength than values, this difference between early and later dropouts should be true at least for attitudes. As proposition 5 of the theory suggests (cfr. chapter 1), the lowering of the attitudes in general precedes the one of the values.

194

To test this hypothesis, an appropriate analysis of the data available at present in our longitudinal study was made.

Data obtained in the second testing administered two years after the first testing revealed that people who drop out early—that is, sometime after the second testing—are not significantly different in values from people who will drop out later—that is, after the third testing administered in the fourth year of life in the religious settings.

However, people who drop out *early* have lower vocational attitudes than people who will drop out *later*. This is true for both male and female subjects. Furthermore, the data of the second testing indicated that when values and attitudes are considered together there exists a strongly significant trend for both male and female early dropouts to show a lower level of vocational values and attitudes than is the case for late dropouts.

On the contrary, the foregoing differences between early and late dropouts were not present at entrance both for values and for attitudes.

The results are shown in chart 39. They concern the seven vocationally dissonant values and the twelve vocational attitudes considered for hypothesis 7. The data from which the foregoing findings are taken are in Tables 9.5, 9.6, 9.7, and 9.8. A one-tail Wilcoxon's test was used.

A contrast by means of a two-tail Wilcoxon's test of the early vs. the late dropout for the vocationally neutral values yielded no significant differences of trend for both male and female; this was true at entrance and after two years of vocational training.

Thus, the hypothesis was supported. The unconscious central inconsistencies, which are the most powerful factors in lowering the predictable capacity to internalize vocational attitudes and values (cfr. the results especially of hypotheses 3 and 4), over time seem to lower the level of these attitudes and values and thus dispose toward dropping out. This inference is based both on the findings and on the theoretical considerations discussed at the beginning of this chapter.

CHART 39

THE DIRECTION AND SIGNIFICANCE OF THE DIFFERENCES IN ATTITUDES AND VALUES OF MALE AND FEMALE RELIGIOUS AS MEASURED BY THE FIRST AND THE SECOND TESTINGS (Wilcoxon Test)

EARLY vs LATE DROPPING OUT:

Male

(EDO* : N = 25)
(LDO** : N = 9)

	Values	Attitudes	Dissonant Values Relevant Attitudes	Values	Attitudes	Dissonant Values Relevant Attitudes
First Testing	NS ***	NS	NS			
Second Testing	NS	EDO <LDO Z = 2.63 p < .004	EDO <LDO Z = 2.76 p < .003			

Female

(EDO : N = 32)
(LDO : N = 17)

	Values	Attitudes	Dissonant Values Relevant Attitudes
First Testing	NS	NS	NS
Second Testing	NS	EDO <LDO Z = 1.69 p < .05	EDO <LDO Z = 1.97 p < .02

* EDO = Early Dropouts.
** LDO = Late Dropouts.
*** NS = No significant difference between early and late Dropouts.

SUMMARY OF FINDINGS AND CONSIDERATIONS

1) The striking phenomenon of withdrawals from priestly and religious vocation, which has beset vocational institutions during the past decade, can be the result of at least five sets of elements: a) supernatural factors and the person's cooperation with them; b) personality characteristics of the individuals; c) pressures coming from the group or the kind of community in which the person lives; d) factors related to the norms, constitutions and structures of the vocational institutions; and e) pressures emerging from the historical socio-cultural milieu in general and, more specifically, from the structural functioning of the Church.

The present chapter considered only the influence of the second set of factors; more precisely, it analyzed the relation which the intrapsychic dynamics present in vocationers at their entrance into a vocational setting may have upon their future dropping out. Furthermore, within the limitations of the intrapsychic dynamics and of our procedures, it tried to answer the following questions: what are the elements of these entering psychodynamics which seem to *prevail* in the process of entering a vocational setting? What are the elements which seem to *prevail* in the process of leaving the vocational setting?

2) Some possible answers to the foregoing questions were sought in the framework of the structural approach to the study of vocation followed in this book and described in chapters 1 and 2. Since this structural approach is somehow trans-situational and transtemporal, it allows one to overcome, at least in part, a crucial difficulty in the evaluation of vocational issues: the differences in such an evaluation which may exist between the people officially responsible for the vocational institutions and their members; these differences are particularly felt in

197

times, like the present ones, in which values and institutional structures are called into question.

More specifically, with regard to the issue of predicting the future perseverance and effectiveness of entering vocationers, this structural approach is supposed to have built in itself the elements for assessing the " predictable internalizing capacity " of these vocationers: in the psychodynamics present in individuals as they enter the vocational setting, there are elements which indicate their predictable capacity *to internalize* vocational values and attitudes and thus their *dispositions*, their *trends* to persevere and to be effective in vocation. The reader is strongly advised to consult the introductions to chapter 7 and to the present chapter, where many pertinent concepts and distinctions are discussed.

3) The subjects studied in this chapter represented the following population: 288 vocationers of which there were 107 male religious, 136 female religious, and 45 seminarians; they were the entire groups entering their own institutions. These vocationers were properly matched with lay Catholic college students: 124 girls and 126 boys, which represented 70% of the freshmen randomly selected and invited to freely participate in the project. Therefore, a total population of 538 subjects coming from the Midwest, East and West of the USA was considered. All of them were tested as they entered their institutions.

The time-consuming nature of the projective test (TAT and ISB) scoring necessitated the choice of random sub-samples from both the religious and the lay groups. These sub-samples were as follows: 96 male religious, 95 female religious, and 40 seminarians, for a total of 231 entering vocationers. They were the same subjects studied in chapter 7 for the Index of Vocational Maturity. The similar sub-samples for lay controls totaled 102, 52 males and 50 females. Thus, a total sub-sample of 333 subjects was studied.

95% of the seminarians left the vocational setting after 4 years of training; therefore, they were divided into " dropouts " (DO) and " non-dropouts " (NDO) according to their status 2 years after entrance; at this time, 21 (52.5%) of the entering forty subjects had left. The similar data for male and female religious are: 47% and 59% drop out after 4 years of training, 59% and 81% drop out after 6-8 years of training, respectively. Thus, totals of 155 dropouts and of 76 non-dropouts were studied; they are *random* sub-samples of 193 DO and 95 NDO. All these people entered the vocational institution in the summer of 1965, 1966, and 1967. The check concerning their withdrawal was done in the summer of 1973.

Further details concerning the foregoing subjects are found in this chapter as well as in chapters 5 to 7.

4) Eight hypotheses were formulated and, in general, they were well supported by the results.

First of all, the findings suggest that values and, to a lesser degree, attitudes play an important role in the initial, conscious decision to enter a vocational commitment. They differentiate vocationers from non-vocationers quite well.

5) Values and, to a lesser degree, attitudes are a disposing factor of dropping out if they are only *moderately* present. However, when values are *strongly* present at entrance, they are not necessarily factors disposing toward perseverance. The same can be said, at least in part, for attitudes. Seminarians are the case in point for the first alternative: 95% of them left after 4 years; for the second alternative, the religious men and women, may be quoted; they presented very high vocational ideals at entrance and still left in the porportion of 59% and 81% after 6-8 years, respectively.

Our data do not support the opinion that people who will leave vocation have higher values or attitudes at entrance. Actually, at least for male religious, the opposite trend was true.

6) All these results suggest that forces other than the ideals consciously proclaimed at entrance for the SI-II of values and attitudes may exert their influence not only upon entrance, but also upon perseverance or effectiveness in religious life. Chapters 5 to 7 have already shown the presence of subconscious forces in a great number of entering vocationers; these forces indicate ego-defensive and/or utilitarian functions exerted by the proclaimed values and attitudes of the SI-II. Chapter 8 has strongly suggested that these conflictual and subconscious

forces tend to persist after entrance. The following results, further confirm the persistance of these forces by pointing to their possible influence upon the future vocational perseverance.

7) Perhaps the most interesting findings concern the origin and the perpetuation of a vicious circle in the psychodynamics of many of the entering vocationers: when and to the extent to which this psychodynamics is characterized by a prevalence of the vulnerable, conflictual part of the SI-II over its germinative part, the person produces and sustains in time a more or less unrealistic SI-II of expectations about his future vocational roles; in turn, with a feedback effect, these unrealistic role expectations will affect his capacity to internalize vocational values and attitudes and thus will have a debilitating influence upon the balance between the vulnerable and the germinative parts of his SI-II; thus, the vicious circle may gradually undermine the future commitment of the vocationer. The most important structural components of the person which start and sustain this vicious circle seem to be his central, unconscious inconsistencies of vocationally dissonant variables, like aggression, exhibition, etc. It would seem that if the psychodynamics of a person is characterized by unconscious inconsistencies, he will continue to react to these central inconsistencies with ego-defensive or utilitarian attitudes, which in turn would sustain unrealistic role expectations (cfr. Chart 42).

Chart 27 and the related discussion explain the vicious circle. Charts 29, 30 and 31 present the findings which back the possible existence and influence of this vicious circle. To substantiate the foregoing reasoning, the results of hypotheses 2, 3 and 4 show that the psychodynamics of future DO always has a predictable internalizing capacity lower than the one of the NDO (cfr. hypothesis 2); this difference between DO and NDO for their predictable internalizing capacity is more present for the vulnerable part of the SI-II than for its germinative part (hypothesis 3), and it is related especially to central, unconscious inconsistencies of vocationally dissonant variables (hypothesis 4).

8) Hypotheses 3 and 4 are further supported by the findings concerning hypotheses 5 and 6. Charts 32 and 33 and the

related discussion indicate the *frequencies* and *percentages* of the inconsistencies, conflicts and consistencies which contribute to the differentiation among the various groups of vocationers and controls in terms of dropping out: DO and NDO are differentiated more in terms of the vulnerable than in terms of the germinative aspect of their SI-II, i.e., more in terms of central inconsistencies than of central consistencies; they also tend to be differentiated more in terms of vocationally dissonant than of vocationally neutral variables.

9) Since the processes considered under 7 and 8 affect the capacity to internalize vocational values and attitudes, they may affect not only perseverance but also vocational effectiveness (cfr. chapter 1 for definition). As was discussed in the introduction to the present chapter, such an influence upon effectiveness does not mean an influence upon the subjective holiness of the person.

10) Why does the lower predictable capacity to internalize vocational values and attitudes lead to dropping out of vocation? One answer could be that, when vocational values and attitudes cannot be internalized, the vocational commitment is gradually undermined.

A second answer may be that a lower predictable internalizing capacity as considered here implies greater contradictions concerning the role expectations versus self-conceptions (cfr. chart 27). To the extent that the person perceives a discrepancy between self-conceptions and his role expectations, he experiences a state of *self*-dissatisfaction; and this self-dissatisfaction will be greater the more the discrepancy implicates self-conceptions which are central, i.e., particularly important for one's self-concept. Note that it is possible for the individual to be responsive to an inconsistency without being aware of it; such lack of awareness may be unawareness of the existence of the inconsistency itself, or unawareness of any associated stress or unawareness of the inconsistency-resolving activity (Tannenbaum, 1967, 1968; Brock, 1968; McGuire, 1960; Cohen, Greenbaum and Mansson, 1963; etc.). In such cases the subject may either change his own attitudes or distort his perception of the reference group or institution. Brock and Blackwood

(Brock, 1965; Brock and Blackwood, 1962) have shown that the second alternative is a strong tendency and this, we can add, especially if the person has to defend central self-conceptions. Thus, he gradually will feel isolated, alienated from his reference group or vocational institutions.

Perhaps it is in this perspective that one can explain, at least in part, the sense of loneliness found by Greeley (1972, and NORC, 1971) among American priests as an important factor for leaving vocation. In the same line are the findings of Potvin and Suziedelis (1969) among American seminarians; according to the results of their research " withdrawal... is more strongly related to subjective views of the seminary and the priesthood than it is to objective factors such as seminary quality " (p. 126).

11) Throughout chapters 5 through 8 as well as throughout the present chapter, two sets of forces which may influence both the entrance and the leaving of vocation have been enucleated: the conscious force exerted by values and, in lesser degree, by attitudes on the one hand; the conscious or subconscious impact coming from the balance/imbalance between the central consistencies and inconsistencies which needs have in their relationship with attitudes and/or with values, on the other hand. Which one of these two sets of forces seems to prevail in the entrance process and which one in the process of dropping out?

The findings, based on the psychodynamics present at entrance, and discussed in hypothesis 7, indicate that, for the entrance into vocation, values and, to a lesser degree, attitudes have a motivational weight greater than the balance/imbalance between the central consistencies and inconsistencies as expressed by the Index of Vocational Maturity, while, for the leaving of vocation, the opposite is true: values and, to a lesser degree, attitudes do not tend to differentiate dropouts from nondropouts, while the balance/imbalance of consistencies/inconsistencies as expressed by the predictable internalizing capacity shown by the entering psychodynamics tends to do so. The reader may have a visual representation of these processes by looking at the juxtaposed charts 35 and 36: for the entering process (chart 35) the significant data are increasingly on the left of the chart, i.e., toward the values, while for the process of leaving (chart 36) they are increasingly on the right, i.e., toward the predictable internalizing capacity.

Further support for this view is obtained by comparing the various groups in terms of frequencies of the various structural patterns of self-conceptions: inconsistencies, consistencies, etc. When the contribution of these patterns for the process of entering is compared with their contribution for the process of leaving vocation, it appears that, as expected: the germinative SI-II expressed by consistencies, etc., of vocationally neutral variables is significantly more helpful in characterizing vocationers at entrance than in differentiating them for perseverance (right lower cell in chart 38); vice versa, the vulnerable SI-II expressed by inconsistencies, etc., of vocationally dissonant variables makes a greater psychodynamic contribution when the phenomenon of perseverance is considered in contrast to the entering process (left upper cell in chart 38).

12) At entrance, future dropouts show a predictable capacity to internalize vocational values and attitudes which is lower than the one of future non-dropouts. As a consequence, if a testing is done two years after entrance, people who drop out early, e.g., between the second and the fourth year of their religious life, should present vocational attitudes and values which are lower than the ones of people who drop out after the fourth year. This should be truer for attitudes than for values, because the first have less motivational strength than the second. The results of hypothesis 8 support the foregoing statements. Furthermore, they show that the same differences between early and late dropouts were not present at entrance (cfr. Chart 39).

All these findings indicate that chronologically the difference between dropouts and non-dropouts is present at first for the Predictable Internalizing Capacity and its most important factors: the *subconscious* inconsistencies of dissonant variables. With the passing of time, dropouts become lower than non-dropouts also for vocational attitudes and later on for values (proposition 5 of the theory).

Of course, the present findings should be confirmed by further research.

Note that, as was discussed in point 5, values and attitudes play their role in both processes of entering and of leaving.

13) The results presented in point 11 indicate that some tenets of general social psychology are valid for entering vocationers also: a) values may be less central, less influential than self-conceptions upon one's motivation (Rokeach, 1973, who quotes other authors); b) it is easier to change behavior than attitudes that matter (see discussion of pertinent literature in Freedman, Carlsmith, and Sears, 1974). The gradual process of leaving vocation may be seen in the light of these tenets and findings. In the same framework, one can understand the trend of the vulnerable SI-II to persist after entrance (cfr. chapter 8) as well as its debilitating influence upon vocational effectiveness.

14) The results found throughout this book and, in particular, the ones shown in charts 35 and 36 seem to offer good support for the basic elements of the five " propositions " of the theory presented in chapter 1 of this book: the conscious SI-II of values and, to a lesser degree, of attitudes is the psychological force which disposes an individual to enter a religious vocation (propositions 1, 2 and 3); this SI-II will remain the psychological pivot of the future life in vocation provided it is not to a great degree the expression of central, unconscious inconsistencies between needs and vocational attitudes and/or values; if these inconsistencies prevail over the central consistencies, then vocational perseverance and effectiveness may be affected (proposition 4); initially there is a lowering of vocational attitudes, which may undermine basic vocational values (proposition 5).

15) The findings of this book seem to clearly indicate that what many authors and researchers in the field of social psychology in general and of depth psychology in particular have repeatedly stated and found, is also valid for religious vocationers: self-reports alone are an unreliable source of understanding the motivation of a person. Our data show that the values and attitudes consciously proclaimed at entrance into vocation are quite at variance with the psychodynamics which

the Index of Vocational Maturity indicates, (e.g., chart 35); furthermore, these values and attitudes are quite at variance with the predictable internalizing capacity and with the vocational perseverance of the entering vocationers (e.g., chart 36).

16) Our investigation studied entering vocationers who had not yet been exposed to a prolonged and direct influence by the vocational institution. Thus, the more or less unrealistic role expectations of the SI-II, which were found among many of these vocationers, were not the consequence of institutional-situational determinants but rather elaborations of the individuals. They entered with unrealistic expectations which could undermine their capacity to internalize vocational values and attitudes and lead many of them to withdraw.

While these individual dispositions cannot be attributed to the vocational institution, the latter has the responsibility of helping vocationers to develop their internalizing capacity during the years of their vocational formation. After all, this internalizing capacity may affect not only perseverance but also vocational effectiveness. Unfortunately, it does not seem that vocational institutions take into serious consideration what our data suggest: that centrally inconsistent and subconscious self-conceptions are individual *dispositions* which may exert an influence upon perseverance and effectiveness that is greater than the one of conscious vocational values and attitudes. Institutional reforms which do not help the vocationers to overcome these debilitating subconscious self-conceptions overlook a vital aspect of the formation problem.

17) Our results should not be interpreted in the sense that *all* the people who drop out are more psychologically inconsistent than people who do not drop out.

Actually, the opposite may be true: psychologically consistent people do not necessarily always stay in. Here two possibilities can be considered: 1) some DO may be individuals who entered vocation without really knowing what it entailed; however, their decision was not prompted by the conflictual wishful thinking and by the projections on the institution described for the inconsistent people, but rather by a lack of objective knowledge of it; by acquiring the latter, they may decide that vocational commitment is not what they were looking for; 2) *some* people may have chosen the vocation while still inconsistent and because of the conflictual needs present in them; later on, they got rid of their subconscious conflicts and became aware of not really having a vocation; their departure was a mature, objective decision.

" The psychological improvement of these people can be the result either of some professional help through psychotherapy or of the solution of their subconscious conflict, which is *possible* if such conflicts are preconscious rather than unconscious; in fact, the self-analysis, which takes place through a serious, repeated examination of conscience or meditation, *may* lead to the described psychological improvement; also, when the conflicts are starting to become conscious, the positive influence of a favorable environment can be quite helpful (cfr. Appendix C-8 of this book). However, experience teaches that usually such an improvement of *preconscious* conflicts is a rather slow process which takes many years of trial and error that do not favor full vocational effectiveness and that could be avoided if properly handled " (Rulla, 1971, p. 158).

Anyway, the present findings indicate greater inconsistencies among drop outs than among non-dropouts at entrance; in fact, the difference between these two groups is present especially for the vulnerable part of their psychodynamics and, in this part, dropouts show more inconsistencies than non-dropouts. Furthermore, the convergent results of Chapter 8 point to the strong trend these initial inconsistencies have to persist. Finally, hypothesis 8 shows a change in attitudes and in vocationally dissonant values which occurs more rapidly in early than in late drop outs.

In the light of the results discussed in this book, one would say that, with the qualifications made at the beginning of this Chapter 9, the right question to be asked concerning the drop outs is not why they leave, but rather what are the expectations, especially the subconscious ones, which influence their decision to enter: the *entire* psychodynamics of the person who enters *may* affect very much the decision of the person who leaves.

206

PART III

EPILOGUE

CHAPTER 10

IMPLICATIONS OF THE FINDINGS

The theory formulated in Part I of this book is not bound in a special way to any school of psychology ; rather it tries to select what seems best from various psychological and psychosocial models. Consequently, the experimental results of Part II are interpreted according to an eclectic frame of reference, which aims at a better understanding of processes related to religious experience and vocation.

The present Part III intends to offer some general considerations. They do not in every instance follow inevitably from our research results; however, they are not inconsistent with those results. The convergence of the findings presented in Part II as well as the structural approach adopted in the research (cfr. chapter 2) encourage us to suggest some generalizations, hoping that they are not merely impressionistic, but rather emerging from the interplay among the sets of the findings.

Some of the issues considered here were already partially discussed elsewhere (Rulla, 1971); reference to this source will be made when necessary. Other issues are more related to the results of the present book. Needless to say, we do not intend to offer an exhaustive, comprehensive discussion of these problems. Our aim is very limited: to present some questions as springboards rather than to offer solutions.

1. *Internalizing vocational motivation: inconsistencies or psychopathology?*

The theory and the findings suggest that personalities of vocationers should be considered according to vocational psychodynamics which are not necessarily related to the psychopathological dynamics of psychiatric taxonomy.

Any psycho-social conceptualization about the social status requires that its core be explicitly identified. This is true also for priestly or religious vocation. Now, with regard to religious vocation, *one* of the aspects of its core is the capacity which each vocationer has to internalize religious values and attitudes (cfr. chapters 7 and 9).

The theory and the findings discussed in this book allow one to see the entering vocationers according to the perspective of a continuum which presents 14 possible patterns or types when the intrapsychic dynamics of the individuals is considered, and 56 possible types when intra- and inter-personal dynamics are assessed together (cfr. chapter 3, C).

The 14 intrapsychic types present two characteristics: a) they are based on a typology of variables (e.g., abasement, aggression, etc.) more than of persons; in fact, they focus upon the central *vocational* consistencies and inconsistencies of each individual; note that the changing influence of the environment is also taken into consideration in this intrapsychic perspective because the consistencies/inconsistencies are assessed also according to the perception each individual has of his environment. b) This perspective of consistencies and/or inconsistencies salient in each individual points to the interaction among the various parts of his self, rather than to the behaviors according to which each individual may be described; therefore, it is a perspective that stresses behavior as the end result of *processes*, of interaction among systems of the self, rather than behavior as a set of descriptive patterns.

There follow several practical implications. First of all, the presented *psychodynamic* typology is not a typology of traits or of symptoms; in fact, it cuts across the normal or less normal traits as well as across the symptoms of the heterogeneous behaviors described by psychiatric psychopathology. This does not exclude the possibility that in *some* cases the inconsistent vocational psychodynamics may have its roots in the psychopathology of underlying neuroses, personality disorders, borderline cases, etc. However, people may be vocationally inconsistent because of psychodynamics which do not depend on or do not manifestly appear as psychiatric psychopathology. Consequently, vocationers can be seen according to a vocational perspective which is different from the one of psychopathology. Actually, they should be seen *also* according to this different, psycho-social perspective, because it touches a core aspect of vocation: the capacity to internalize religious values and attitudes; at least, the five values proper to any religious experience (cfr. chapter 1) and 14 attitudes-needs widely accepted by scholars as significantly, even though not exhaustively, representing human motivation (cfr. chapter 3 and Appendix C-1).

Another set of practical implications can be stressed. A particular kind of external behavior of vocationers does not necessarily stem from a corresponding kind of underlying psychodynamics; that is, similar external behaviors can be motivated by different psychodynamics and, vice versa, different external behaviors can be motivated by similar psychodynamics. As has been discussed in the previous publication of 1971 (e.g., pp. 152-160), these possibilities create delicate problems of evaluation for superiors about the suitability of their subjects for religious vocation, the possibility of helping and improving them, the appropriateness of allowing the stress of specific apostolic activities, etc. More will be said later on in this regard.

The *possible* separation of vocational psychodynamics from psychopathology should be distinguished from another relevant issue, which we now take up: the relationship between spiritual growth and psychological growth. If we consider entrance, perseverance, and growth in religious vocation as a socialization process, the issue to be now discussed is a common topic in the depth psychology literature; it suffices to mention Hartmann's and Erikson's ego-psychology formulations concerning the links between developmental stages and processes of social adaptation.

2. Spiritual and psychological growth: their interdependence and convergence.

The literature concerning this issue has notably increased during the past recent years. Many valuable contributions could be quoted. However, few of these contributions have called the attention to the relevance of the subconscious motivation in this regard; and, perhaps, none has offered some research support.

When speaking of spiritual growth or sanctification, one should distinguish it from the presentation of the means of sanctification. The latter may be called apostolic effectiveness and described as the visible manifestation and/or the social communication of the values of Christ. In turn, apostolic effectiveness should be distinguished from apostolic efficiency; as it was discussed elsewhere (1971), efficiency focuses upon means, effectiveness is concerned with the ends, i.e., the terminal values of union with God and imitation of Christ. Thus, for instance, to be an " efficient " teacher or administrator does not necessarily mean to be " effective " as a religious or a priest. Of course, this does not exclude the fact that efficiency has its importance as a means to foster the desired effectiveness.

Another distinction is pertinent here: the one between subjective and objective holiness or spiritual growth. Subjective holiness is related to the use a person makes of the possibilities, of all the supernatural and spiritual " talents " God has given to him personally. Objective holiness depends upon the availability to the action of God which a person de facto has.

What influence may the subconscious factors present in psychological growth have upon apostolic effectiveness, upon subjective and upon objective holiness? The elements in these interdependencies are extremely complex and we can bring only a few fore-glimpses.

First of all, it can be stated that subjective holiness does not depend on one's psychological growth or degree of developmental maturity. Holiness, that is, the presence of sanctifying grace and infused virtues in their cooperation with the human will, does not depend " intrinsically " on the psychological

212

dispositions of the individual, provided his freedom is not completely eliminated; in fact, God alone can sanctify souls who do not refuse His fully gratuitous action. Therefore, provided a minimum of freedom in the individual is present, the sanctifying action of God may grow by means of the sacraments and acts of supernatural virtues, regardless of the psycho-social elements influencing the individual.

In its essence, perfection has no relationship with quantity, and its possibility of growth in each individual is primarily related to the utilization of the possibilities which are given to each individual man; therefore, it is related neither primarily nor comparatively to the possibility and realizations of another man (Rahner, 1964).

While the subconscious psycho-social elements of the developmental or affective maturity do not exert an influence upon subjective holiness, because they do not touch the sanctifying action of God as well as the *conscious* and *free correspondence* of man to this action, they do affect both the objective holiness and the apostolic effectiveness; the first indirectly or extrinsically, the second directly or intrinsically.

In fact, these subconscious psycho-social elements may affect the *subconscious and unfree availability* of the person to the action of God and thus, in the limits of their influence, they condition objective holiness. In other words, given an equal supernatural action of grace, those elements may limit the margin of freedom within which the person may correspond t o God's action. God may overcome these subconscious limitations of the person, but this " sanating " influence of God does not seem to be a common, frequent event; actually, it seems to be more an exception than a rule.

Two elements seem to confirm this conclusion. First of all, the several, convergent findings of this book (cfr. especially chapters 7 to 9) indicate the interdependence between the developmental maturity and the vocational maturity; the relationship of the vocational maturity and, indirectly, of the developmental maturity with the predictable capacity of the individuals to internalize vocational values and attitudes; the greater influence of the unconscious over the preconscious or conscious factors for the capacity to internalize; the trends of the subconscious factors to persist, etc. All these results suggest that God respects the freedom of man and his personality.

Secondly, a logical consideration seems to be appropriate: as Einstein said, God is not capricious; so it is difficult to believe that God does not *usually* follow the natural psychodynamic laws which He Himself has made operative in a person.

What we have just said for the interdependence between spiritual and psychological elements with regard to objective holiness, is even truer for apostolic effectiveness.

As was discussed at length in the publication of 1971, other things being equal, priests or religious would be more " effective " if they would not have shortcomings stemming from subconscious inconsistencies of aggression, of dependency, etc. As instruments in the hands of God, they would be more fitting both for the goals for which they work and for the aims of Him, Who uses them.

Again, the findings of the present book are in this line; it is enough to recall the ones concerning the influence of subconscious inconsistencies upon the predictable capacity to internalize vocational values and attitudes. If a person has serious difficulty to internalize the self-transcendent values of religious commitment, he will be hampered " ...to free himself from those obstacles which might draw him away from the fervor of charity and the perfection of divine worship " (Vatican Council II, *Lumen Gentium*, no. 44). His basic attitudes tend to follow personal needs rather than self-transcendent ideals. His capacities to objectively listen to and to transmit the " word of God ", His messages through Scripture, liturgy, institutions and the deep meaning of reality will be notably jeopardized. He will have difficulty to transcend himself, to lose himself in the unselfish surrender of love.

These possible negative influences of subconscious psychological elements upon objective holiness and apostolic effectiveness suggest a corollary.

One of the ideals of St. Ignatius' spirituality has been expressed in the formula of Father Nadal: to be a contemplative in action. Without going into the historical-exegetical interpretation of this formula, one may say that its core message is well expressed by Ignatius' oft-reiterated phrase of " finding God in all things " as well as by his other statement " ...loving

214

God in all creatures and all of them in Him, in conformity with His holy and divine will " (The Constitutions of the Society of Jesus, no. 288; translated by G. E. Ganss, 1970).

As we have just seen, it will be rather difficult for a person with poor capacity to internalize self-transcendent ideals, to be a contemplative in action according to the foregoing Ignatian perspectives. Interestingly enough, the Ignatian statement " loving God in all creatures and all of them in Him " is the conclusion of number 288 of the " Constitutions " in which Ignatius practically already presented the quadruplex distinction of compliance, of non-internalizing identification, of internalizing identification, and of internalization, which modern social psychology has suggested (cfr. introduction to chapter 7): " ...they should always aim at serving and pleasing the Divine Goodness for its own sake and because of the incomparable love and benefits with which God has anticipated us, rather than for fear of punishments or hope of rewards, although they ought to draw help also from them. Further, they should often be exhorted to seek God our Lord in all things, stripping off from themselves the love of creatures to the extent that this is possible, in order to turn their love upon the Creator of them, by loving Him in all creatures and all of them in Him, in conformity with His holy and divine will ".

These statements call to mind the analogous ones which C. S. Lewis (1955) wrote about what God had taught him during his conversion: " The commands were inexorable, but they were backed by no ' sanctions '. God was to be obeyed simply because he was God. Long since, through the gods of Asgard, and later through the notion of the Absolute, He had taught me how a thing can be revered not for what it can do to us but for what it is in itself " (p. 185).

Spiritual growth is not dichotomous, but continuous with psychological growth; they are convergent processes strictly interdependent.

3. " The discernment of spirits ": some new perspectives.

The preceding two issues have indicated that the vocational intrapsychic dynamics is both different from psychopathology, even though not necessarily so, and the result of two interdependent and convergent sets of forces, spiritual and psychological.

The present third issue intends to bring a limited contribution by a further analysis of these forces by considering some of the possible interactions among them. The " Rules for the Discernment of Spirits " proposed by St. Ignatius in the first and second weeks of his " Spiritual Exercises " will be taken as a frame of reference for this analysis. It is assumed that the reader is familiar with the Spiritual Exercises of Saint Ignatius.

God aims at bringing back to Himself in a transforming union His creatures, men. But, what are the means God uses to direct human beings to Himself? According to Buckley (1973), three different and complex answers have been historically given to this question. Schematically, they may be presented as follows: 1) through preternatural influences of personalities or realities: saints, devils, angels; in the terminology of Ignatius, " good spirit " and " evil spirit; " 2) through human processes of intellection or of imagination; 3) through human attractions of affectivity. Seldom one of these three factors predominates to the total exclusion of the other two. Ignatius in his " Discernment of Spirits " has offered a unique coordination of all the foregoing three critical factors of religious experience. Note that in the Ignatian schematization evil spirit in the first week of the Spiritual Exercises appears to be what it is, while in the second week it is disguised under seeming good.

Two recent contributions have introduced new possible perspectives according to which the Ignatian outline can be interpreted. The first contribution comes from depth psychology. As authors like Beirnaert (1954) and Meissner (1964) have pointed out, the religious conducts which Ignatius attributed to the influence of the good or evil spirit may be the consequence, at least in part, of unconscious motivations. It is interesting to note that Ignatius himself had already realized that other psychological determinants than the preternatural " good spirit " could be at work in " consolation " (cfr. Spiritual Exercises, no. 336, eighth rule of the second week).

Particularly important is the second contribution by a theologian (Buckley, 1973), which has the merit of offering a structural approach. According to this author, the Ignatian schematization offers a structural matrix of causalities, of vectors in the discernment of "spirits". This basic matrix is presented in the first week (rules 1 to 4 and second part of rule 5) and reformulated in the second week (rules 1 to 4) of the Spiritual Exercises.

The relevant aspect of Buckley's presentation is the *two-way* causal interaction which exists among the three factors of religious experience described by Ignatius: preternatural influences of good and evil spirits, "thoughts" or "ideals" of human intellection or imagination, and human affectivity. These three vectors *causally* can move either downward, i.e., from good or evil spirit to "thoughts" and to affectivity, or upward; in the latter case (cfr. chart 40), affectivity can spontaneously generate commensurate thoughts: "the thoughts that spring from consolation (*que salen de la consolación*) are contrary to the thoughts which spring from desolation (*que salen de la desolación*)" (Spiritual Exercises, 317). These thoughts almost mechanically place one under the influence of the evil spirit: "as the good spirit guides and counsels us in consolation, so in desolation the evil spirit guides and counsels. Following the counsels of this latter spirit, one can never find the correct way to a right decision" (Spiritual Exercises, 318).

The foregoing two contributions convergently stress an important fact: the factor "affectivity" has a causal influence in the structure proposed by Ignatius which is greater than the one usually attributed to it by the writers who considered the Ignatian "rules for the discernment of spirits".

But there is more. We would like to add a few considerations which, perhaps, help toward a further understanding of Ignatius' causal schematization.

In the *first week* of the Spiritual Exercises affectivity is qualified by the moral worth of the attraction, i.e., by the obvious terms of its direction; this affectivity exists in the two states of "consolation" or of "desolation": it is consolation if the person is drawn toward God; it is desolation when he is drawn toward evil. Note that consolation and desolation do not identify necessarily with pleasure and pain; thus, "consolation is any interior movement of human sensibility — irrespective of the cause — whose direction is God, whether that movement be one of exuberant emotion or quiet peace, whether its presence is experientially pleasant or not " (Buckley, 1973, p. 29).

However, " affectivity " plays a basically different role in the two types of men which Ignatius considers in the first or in the second week of his Spiritual Exercises (cfr. Annotations 9 and 10): the man of the first week is drawn " strongly and openly " toward obvious evil; the man of the second week generously looks for the will of God. Furthermore, the " consolation " of the first man is the sign of the " good spirit ", while the consolation of the second man is ambiguous, equivocal.

In fact, in the *second week* Ignatius considers two kinds of consolation: 1) the consolation without cause (*consolación sin causa*), which is from God, " without any previous perception or knowledge of any object from which such consolation might come to the soul through its own acts of understanding and will " (Spiritual Exercises, 330) *; this consolation is not characterized by its suddeness nor by its engulfing qualities, but rather by the absence of any preceding intentionality proportional to the drawing of affectivity into God (Rahner, 1964); 2) the consolation with cause (*consolación con causa*), present when there is some preceding cause.

Now, the apparent good, which the man of the second week looks for, is really genuine and thus draws to God only when the feelings of peace and tranquility which he enjoyed at the beginning *will persist* over time, i.e. when the consolation of this man has an historical persistence throughout his past-present-future (Spiritual Exercises, 333 of the second week and 177 of the third time of election; also 336 of the second week).

These distinctions and considerations of Ignatius may be seen according to the theory and the findings presented in the present book.

The man of the first week, strongly pulled toward obvious evil, hopefully should not be frequent among the people entering the priestly or religious vocation. We said hopefully, because — irrespective of the spiritual or psychological origin of their poor dispositions — in the mind of Ignatius, these people

---

* Note that for Ignatius " soul " means the person, the self (Ganss· 1970, footnote 10, pp. 77-78).

will have little or no chance to make a proper discernment of spirits, unless these dispositions are changed.

In this regard, many texts could be quoted from the Directories for the Spiritual Exercises which St. Ignatius gave to Father Victoria. The reader can find them in "Directoria Exercitiorum Spiritualium " (1955). For instance, listing the conditions to be found — or not — in the person who is to be invited to the Exercises, we read that the subject "should be able to decide about his person" (*que pueda determinar de su persona*), and "should not be so attached to things that it would be difficult to lead him to set himself in a position of balance in front of God or even more he should be in some way worried (*angustiado*) by the desire to know what he should do with himself **and** be doubtful (*ambiguo*) " (p. 90).

Later on, speaking of the first week, we read that for " ...those who enter the Spiritual Exercises with some designs and intentions (*disegnos y intentos*), it is very useful to diligently take care that they untie themselves from this imperfection, because it is a moth which corrodes the precious fabric of true vocation, and it does not allow one in any way to know truth (*y no dexa conocer por ninguna manera la verdad*); and the person, who is known to be very obstinate (*muy pertinaz*) in this before entering the Exercises should not be incited to make them nor be admitted to them until he has not become maturer (*más maduro*) by means of frequent confessions " or of spiritual conversations (Directoria Exercitiorum Spiritualium, 1955, pp. 99-100). How can the foregoing " designs and intentions " which prevent the knowledge of truth be overcome when their psychological source is unconscious? Since 1954, Beirnaert has called attention to this important point, but — it would seem — without too much success. Ignatius gave the advice proper to the knowledge of his time, that is, when the possible deep psychological causalities were unknown.

However, the interest of our research has been rather for the man of the second week, that is, for vocationers who have good values and generously look for the will of God. But Ignatius cautions that their good disposition, their " consolation " or " affectivity " may be genuinely or only deceptively oriented toward God. These good people are not so much tempted by the obvious evil, but by the obvious good; however, this latter

219

is far more destructive than the former, precisely because its true nature is temporarily disguised and may overtly appear only later on in the life of the subject, i.e., when it is more difficult for him to reconsider vocational commitments previously taken.

In the framowork followed in the present book, the genuine affectivity described by Ignatius as having the characteristics of historical consistency throughout the past-present-future of the person, may be translated in terms of internalizing psychodynamics. In fact, the more internalizing people can be seen as the subjects with genuine consolation, that is, as the persons drawn toward God and self-transcendence. These " internalizers " are more consistent persons than the " non-internalizers " (the reader is urged to review the concepts discussed in Chapters 7 and 9); therefore they enjoy the persistent, underlying peace and tranquility which Ignatius presents as a sign of genuine consolation, of right inclination for God and His greater glory. Their psychological consistency disposes to their historical consistency of peace and tranquility throughout their past-present-future. This historical consistency is not present for the " non-internalizers ", i.e., for the people characterized by greater vocational inconsistencies; thus, the " consolation " felt by these people is not genuine but deceptive.

In addition to a persistent peace and tranquility, the " internalizers " or consistent people present nine other aspects of their personality which may be helpful for discerning a genuine " consolation " from a deceptive one (cfr. the 1971 publication, pp. 145-149). Of course these people feel a tension of renunciation but they do not have a tension of frustration; in fact, as the just-mentioned nine aspects of personality indicate, their vocational performance is not affected. Actually, their tension of renunciation can be useful for the growth of their personality and of their vocational commitment (cfr. 1971, pp. 143-145).

Chart 40 diagrammatically represents the view exposed here concerning the basic structural matrix of causalities, of vectors *only* for the *upward* interaction in " The Discernement of Spirits ". The downward causalities have been described in the text. The last column recalls the psychodynamic elements of the theory (cfr. Chapter 1 and chart 1) which may be seen as related to the causal matrix.

220

CHART 40

STRUCTURAL MATRIX OF UPWARD CAUSALITIES IN "THE DISCERNMENT OF SPIRITS"

Evil Spirit	Good Spirit		Preternatural Influences	Self- or non self-transcendent ideals (values and attitudes)
"Thoughts" or "ideals"	"Thoughts" or "ideals"		Processes of intellection or of imagination	Consistencies or inconsistencies of needs with vocational attitudes and/or values
Desolation	Consolation	without cause → (from God; however, in time, unconscious factors may interfere too) * with cause → − internalizing or genuine − non-internalizing or deceptive	Processes of affectivity	
				Consistencies dispose to self-transcendence, to self-fulfillment, and to effectiveness, and thus they foster persistent, underlying "peace and tranquility"

* Spiritual Exercises, n. 336.

A look at the Chart may help one to see the prudence and the skill of Ignatius in qualifying the appropriateness and the *usefulness* of the Spiritual Exercises not only for the man of the first week, but also for that of the second week: in spite of the good intentions which the man of the second week has, his internalizing or non-internalizing psychodynamics is a crucial factor to make the discernment of spirits profitable for him. And the same can be said for the three " occasions " or " times " of election discussed in nn. 175-177 of the Spiritual Exercises; in fact, the first " occasion " of election may correspond psychologically to the " consolation without cause " of the discernment of spirits, while the second and third " occasions " are parallel to the discernment of spirits related to consolation-desolation or to the " consolation with cause ".

What does St. Ignatius tell us in terms of depth psychology? First of all, that people with a non-internalizing psychodynamics, i.e. the men of the first week strongly and openly drawn toward evil as well as the men of the second week drawn toward the seeming good, cannot make a useful discernment of spirits or a profitable election. In spite of the absence of psychopathology, the subconscious inconsistencies of these men seriously undermine their decisional efforts. Of course, as it was discussed at length in the 1971 publication (pp. 186-190), these subconscious inconsistencies may affect the *growth* of the vocational commitment, but do not affect its *existence*. However, to give to these people the rules of discernment of spirits of the first and/or of the second week without disentangling their subconscious inconsistencies, is dangerous (cfr. e.g., Spiritual Exercises, Annotation 9). Why? Because it implies treating psychodynamically inconsistent people as if they were consistent. But this is harmful to these individuals. In fact, their inconsistent psychodynamics will prevent a proper internalization of vocational values and instead will perpetuate the processes of non-internalizing identification which—we have seen—lead to false expectations. Thus, these people will be prevented from understanding the proper implications and applications of these rules to their person.

In the long run, these people will come out more subconsciously self-deceived and disoriented than properly enlightened and guided. This is particularly true for the individuals who present a deceptive consolation of seemingly good intentions: their initial joyful commitment to the renunciations implied in Christian life in time will become a source of disturbing frustrations originated by their false expectations concerning this life. A mature, long-lasting commitment is possible only if the person has developed a sufficiently consistent psychodynamics capable of internalizing vocational values and attitudes. A proper help, also in the realm of depth psychology, should be offered to these people to make their discernment of spirits or their election in the Spiritual Exercises a profitable one.

The many convergent findings of the present book show that the foregoing cautions of Ignatius are valid and pertinent also for vocationers. Also for them, one should ask if without a proper discernment of spirits and a proper election, the Spiritual Exercises are profitable. Among the findings which are relevant to these issues, let us recall the high percentage of poor internalizers (60-80%), also among people who did not show signs of apparent psychopathology; the lack of significant change shown by the vocationers after four years of formation which included the Spiritual Exercises of St. Ignatius; the high frequency of transferences in religious life, that is, the frequent presence of resistances to change; the great rate of dropping out, which is in relation to the poor predictable capacity to internalize vocational values and attitudes; the prevalent influence of the vulnerable part of the self which, also, leads to dropping out and which makes a proper discernment and election difficult since it is characterized by *unconscious* forces; the two facts that self-conceptions show greater motivational strength than the accepted values and that people may more easily change behavior than attitudes that matter; the lack of face-value credibility of the ideals proclaimed by the entering vocationers. All these results call to mind St. Augustine's statement: " For it is one thing to see the land of peace from a wooded ridge... and another to tread the road that leads to it " (Confessions, VII, 21).

To some extent there is a parallelism between the man of the first week of the Spiritual Exercises, and the one of the second week on the one hand, and our findings, on the other hand.

In fact, analogous to the man of the first week, we found that vocationers with rather poor religious values need to be helped to grow precisely in this area of personality in order to be able to seriously consider a vocational commitment. Our sample of seminarians correspond to this situation, at least in the sense that their ascetical ideals were not as high as the ones of religious males and females. The first step is to be able to appreciate the appeal of religious values as Ignatius says.

Our sample of religious males and females corresponds to the man of the second week: they proclaimed high religious values, but beneath this proclamation, for many of them there existed a poor capacity to live according to these proclaimed values, as was indicated by the contrast between DO and NDO for the predictable internalizing capacity. The spiritual quest of individuals with low predictable internalizing capacity may be easily undermined with the passing of time: historical consistency or stability is undermined by psychological inconsistency.

Thus, an understanding of this psychological inconsistency may become another sign for the discernment of spirit, as is the historical consistency suggested by Ignatius. The predictable internalizing capacity indicates the possibility of historical consistency; the subconscious perspective complements the conscious one.

On the basis of the foregoing findings as well as of our observations of several hundreds of additional vocationers, we believe that 60 to 80% of entering vocationers present in different degrees one of the following two possibilities: either—like our seminarians—they did not acquire to a high degree the proper religious values, or—like a substantial majority of our religious males and females—they do not have a sufficient capacity to internalize these values. The helps offered by the traditional spirituality will make up for the first type of deficiency, but will not usually and significantly touch the second type which has its roots in subconscious layers of personality. A proper discernment of these two types of vocationers and corresponding helps are part of a sound program of formation.

Of course, God can supply for all these deficiencies. However, it seems that in these areas too, He *usually* respects the human personality and builds on this personality. It should be clear that we do not intend to diminish in any way neither the possibility for grace to influence the inner recesses of the unconscious, nor the imperative need to offer supernatural and spiritual helps. As we have said previously, subjective sanctification does not intrinsically depend on psychological dispositions, and the growth in the spiritual and psychological dimensions are interdependent. However, precisely because of this interdependence, *both* dimensions should be taken into serious account. Ignatius reminds us that the discernment of spirits is profitable for people who have a good degree of maturity and freedom and that the Spiritual Exercises are intended for this kind of people. In turn, contemporary depth psychology calls attention to the fact that maturity and freedom of human decisions toward a greater good may be really affected by *subconscious* non-internalizing "affectivity".

As Buckley (1973) says: "only when affectivity is ordered can it in turn become the clue to the direction in which one should go within the myriad good options which surround one's life" (p. 35). However, as the many convergent results of this book show, such an ordered, internalizing affectivity is a condition which is extremely hard to meet; therefore it would be very rarely prudent to take *felt* affectivity as the sole criterion for important decisions unless a discernment of its subconscious and noninternalizing elements has been properly made.

Without a doubt, conversion or spiritual progress is not so much a matter of doing differently, as of being different; and this being different is the result of a long, slow process of becoming different.

The findings and considerations concerning the individual's discernment prompt some comments about community discernment. First of all, if 60-80% of the vocationers, even after four years of formation, present the many signs of difficulties in the discernment shown by the results of this book, it is unrealistic to believe that the same difficulties will disappear in a community discernment. After all, the findings of Kennedy and Heckler (1971) and of Baars and Terruwe (1971) indicate analogous difficulties for "formed" priests and religious.

Secondly, as discussed at some length in the 1971 publication, group participation in making decisions should not be judged with the attitude of a wholesale condemnation or deification. Rather, as the pertinent literature shows, it is important to consider the mediating conditions, that is, the properties of individuals and of situations which shape the effectiveness of community discernment. Here it suffices to mention two points.

For deliberations concerning structural changes of a vocational institution, a vicious circle may easily develop: "... the internalizing psychodynamics prevailing in a religious Order may determine the potentials for internalization inherent in a structural change promoted by its representatives as individuals or as group (or cliques), for instance in the general chapter; in turn, the effectiveness of this change is contingent on the psychodynamics predominant among the members and the groups. The crucial variable in the vicious circle is the internalizing psychodynamics of individuals and of groups. The one prevailing in the Order will influence both the establishing and the implementation of institutional changes " (Rulla, 1971, p. 335). In such a case, the communal discernment concerning ideals *may* become a factor of entrenched immobility rather than of innovative growth.

For decisions concerning persons, one can recall the interesting, recent findings of the research by Lieberman, Yalom and Miles (1973) on " encounter groups ". Judgments were asked about the changes in personality which had been noticed in the participants to group encounters six months after the ending of this educational experience. The evaluations were obtained from different kinds of judges: each participant, his co-participants, the leaders, the social networks, i.e., the friends and relatives of the participants. Benefit, viewed from these different perspectives of the sets of judges, was found to be unrelated to one another; and friends and relatives saw change in as many participants as controls who did not participate in the encounter groups.

Community discernment is more a point of arrival than of departure, more an end, an ideal, a sign of achieved maturity than a means to it. In general, a long, in-depth background work with individuals should be done to prepare them for it.

4. *The functions of psychology in the vocational training.*

Perhaps the most important implications which emerge from our findings are, the ones related to the issue of the contributions of psychology to the vocational training.

226

At least the following five functions seem to be relevant; they are listed here:

1) and 2) — a *pedagogical* function as distinguished from a *psychotherapeutic* one: the contribution of psychology should be oriented especially toward the pedagogical function of fostering the individuals' capacity to internalize vocational values and attitudes rather than toward solving problems of overt or covert psychopathology.

3) — a *preventive* function as opposed to a reparative one; our results indicate that already when individuals enter the vocational settings, it is possible to detect the difficulties which each individual will have in the future to internalize vocational values and attitudes. Why do we wait many years and allow these difficulties to grow and to generate stressful situations which often cannot be handled anymore? Would it not be more charitable to offer an *early* help which could lower the rate of onset of these frustrations? Of course, this help should take into consideration the limitations of both the individuals and the institutions.

4) — an *integrative* function as substantially different from one which implies a dichotomy; here we are referring to the strict interdependence and convergence which exists between the spiritual and psychological growth. The discussion presented in the foregoing points 2.) and 3.) of this chapter has underlined the fallacy of a program of training which allows a dichotomy between spiritual and psychological growth.

5) — a *selective* function of screening of candidates before they enter vocation.

Let's elaborate briefly on some aspects of the foregoing five functions.

The training, the formation of young vocationers should avoid a dichotomy between spiritual and psychological growth. The consensus on this point is increasing among the people responsible for such a formation.

However, while an agreement for reaching this end of an integration between spirituality and psychology exists, inconsistently there remains the trend to keep a rather sharp separation between the means to reach this end: the spiritual and the psychological helps are offered to the vocationers as f the spiritual and the psychological dimensions of man were completely separate. Actually, sometimes one of these two dimensions is inappropriately accentuated almost to the exclusion of the other. Thus, for instance, a point of view common among religious educators holds that psychology should serve especially or only the two functions of screening candidates and of treating people who present psychopathological problems.

On the basis of the findings of this book, we believe that these diagnostic-predictive and psychotherapeutic functions are relevant, but less salient than the pedagogical function of helping the individuals to increase their capacity to internalize vocational values and attitudes through a gradual growth in their developmental and vocational maturities. As spiritual direction should not aim primarily at solving difficulties, but at a progressive education in the discernment of spirits, thus, the contribution of psychology should not be primarily diagnostic or therapeutic, but pedagogical.

Similarly, we believe that the means offered in formation should *continuously* integrate the interdependent spiritual and psychological growth. And these means should take into serious account the *subconscious* factors which — according to our findings — may notably affect the capacity to internalize values and attitudes as well as the capacity of a proper discernment of spirits and election.

Here again, St. Ignatius had some interesting foresights. When advising how to counteract the influence of the " evil spirit ", he uses three images: the angry woman, the false lover, the commander of an army (Spiritual Exercises, 325, 326, 327). These three images point to the three means to be used: strength and determination which originates from union with God; openness with a confessor or spiritual director, which implies interpersonal guidance and points to a need for a preventive, early intervention; persistent and perceptive *self-knowledge* which is also related to a good *self-mastery*; the parallel between this last point and the relevance of an objective and free self-ideal-in-situation shown by our findings seems to be quite great.

A program of formation which intends to be effective should offer means to grow in all these three dimensions. This would not seem to be the case at present in the settings of vocational training. A systematic discussion of this topic is beyond the purpose of the present book. Some considerations have been offered in the 1971 publication (e.g., pages 130-131, 145-149, 214-224, and 322-363). They discuss the insufficiency of the helps offered at present by the vocational institutions; furthermore, they offer suggestions specifically geared to the aim of increasing the capacity of the vocationers to internalize vocational values and attitudes. Among the issues discussed there, one can mention: *two new kinds of educators*; behavioral signs which may be indicative of underlying consistent or inconsistent psychodynamics; basic characteristics of the experiences which should be offered to people in formation; some principles which may be helpful in the institutionalization of the changes; systems of leadership and types of structure of vocational organizations, which may foster the capacity of members to internalize values and attitudes; the limitations of the type of experience linked with the encounter groups or with group dynamics for inducing a real growth in the personality of the participants.

With regard to this last topic, a recent review of the pertinent literature (Reddy and Lansky, 1974) has shown that " there is a dearth of carefully designed and executed research, a plethora of anecdotal and exhortative-descriptive pieces " (p. 477). Croghan (1974) too stresses the " need for a scientific investigation of the effects of the growth group experience. Lieberman, Yalom and Miles have filled this need with their 1973 work, *Encounter Groups: First Facts* " (p. 443). This recent, extensive research with normal college students brings a further support to the considerations formulated by the first author of the present book in his 1971 publication. In their final chapter, Lieberman, Yalom and Miles discuss the confusion of liking with learning which can derive from the experience of group dynamics. Here are some of their statements: " Leaders (of encounter groups) value spontaneity, expressiveness, openness and self-disclosure and work from theoretical propositions from which they derive that these are the mechanisms *par excellence* which can induce learning or growth in the participants. The findings presented in their Chapter 12 clearly suggest that the expressions of strong positive or negative feeling, a great amount of self-disclosure in and of itself and the experience of intense emotional events are not mechanisms

229

that uniquely maximize member learning. They are, however, vivid, intense experiences in participants' minds, and thus the leaders whose techniques are oriented toward producing them come to believe that they are ' right on '. Perhaps both members and leaders have contributed to the construction of an elaborate mythology which specifies that where there is stimulation (or expressivity, or self-disclosure) there also will be learning: a mythology for which there is evidence, not of learning, but of involvement, of liking what is happening " (pp. 451-452).

More specifically related to the content of the present book are the research conclusions which Lieberman, Yalom and Miles offer concerning who would learn and who would falter in educational experiences like the encounter groups: " What a person enters with tells us something about what kind of experience he will have in an encounter group " (p. 334). The real differences among the High Learners, Moderate Changers, Negative Changers, Casualties, and Dropouts from encounter groups were " ...not in their experiences in the groups but in what they were like when they entered, and how they anticipated the experience before they got started in it " (p. 334). Our findings of Chapter 9 are in complete concordance with these results of the foregoing authors. In the same line are their data concerning the changes resulting from the encounter group experience: " ...one third of those who participated in the groups benefited from them, a little over one-third remained unchanged, and the remainder experienced some form of negative outcome; dropping out of the group for psychological reasons, making negative changes, or experiencing psychological decompensation " (p. 129). These percentages are very similar to the ones found in our research and in similar investigations among religious and priests (cfr. Chapters 7 and 8): between 60-80% of these people show signs of psychological underdevelopment which can seriously affect their improvement.

Throughout this book, the relevance of *subconscious* factors for growth in vocation has been stressed and supported by many convergent results. This relevance may be diagrammatically represented by Chart 41, which reproduces the Johari window, the brain-child of Joseph Luft (Jo) and Harrington (Hari).

CHART 41

THE JOHARI WINDOW

	Known to Self	Not Known to Self
Know to Others	Public Self	Blind Self
Not Known to Others	Hidden Self	Unknown or Undeveloped Potential

In Chart 41, one's public self is that part known both to oneself and to others; the hidden self represents what is known to oneself but not to others; the blind self is a part known to others but not to oneself; and one's undeveloped potential is unknown both to others and to oneself.

The results presented in this book indicate that the " unknown ", subconscious area of the self related to central vocational inconsistencies is present in at least 2/3 of the vocationers. Furthermore, the same results show that these subconscious factors have a significant, negative influence which prevents internalization of vocational values and attitudes. Now, the help usually offered in vocational institutions in this area of unconscious processes is not proportionate to the nature of the problem. As discussed in the 1971 publication (pp. 216-219), two new categories of educators and appropriate centers of training for them are an impelling need. Charity toward the vocationers and the greater glory of God ask this.

These two new categories of educators should be able to perceive the existence of (first type of educator) and to handle (second type of educator) the following four kinds of vocational difficulties which seem to be the most common:

1) problems of a " spiritual " nature: e.g. doubts of faith, of morals, etc.;

2) problems resulting from the usual developmental difficulties; these should be significantly solved by the time the individual has reached a chronological age of about 27 years, provided a proper existential experience has been possible for him;

231

3) the subconscious vocational inconsistencies which do not give signs of and are not directly related to psychopathology; these inconsistencies have been the topic of the findings of the present book;

4) the difficulties coming from the psychopathological dynamics of psychiatric taxonomy.

Note that the first two kinds of vocational difficulties may be independent of, i.e., not related to the problems described under 4) and especially under 3). If this is the case, the first two sets of problems usually do not present serious difficulty in being handled. Supernatural means, time, experience, proper help by spiritual directors, counselors, superiors, etc. will gradually improve the situation.

However, the case is quite different if the " spiritual " and " developmental " difficulties are in reality the *expression* of subconscious vocational inconsistencies or of psychopathology. Let us emphasize that the cases of subconscious vocational inconsistencies without signs of psychopathology are usually considered as " normal " by superiors. Still, on the one hand, as the results of the present book show, they are highly frequent. On the other hand, for these subconscious vocational inconsistencies, existential experience, time, counselors, group dynamics, spiritual directors, etc. will not be helpful or not meaningfully so, especially if unconscious or deeply preconscious problems are not properly handled. New types of educators are necessary for these subconscious difficulties.

Note that, after all, the function of these new types of educators is no different from the one exerted by the present " spiritual advisors " or directors or formators, except in the following crucial aspect: to the helps offered to a person for his conscious life, the new educators would *add and integrate* the helps necessary to disentangle the negative effects of his subconscious life. Thus meditation, examination of conscience, etc. would more easily reach the subconscious roots of attitudes and habits which jeopardize the apostolic effectiveness and the growth in *objective* holiness of the person. Furthermore, these new educators would have solved for themselves the third or fourth kinds of the above-mentioned problems of vocation; therefore they would avoid the deleterious influence coming from the subconscious projection of their own unsolved vocational difficulties onto the group or some of its members.

The high frequency of inhibiting *subconscious inconsistencies* presented by the entering vocationers is the most relevant reason for helping them *also* in this aspect of their vocational growth. In fact, a person is free only if his motivational affirmations are consistent with the structures of his self (Weigel, 1960); man is free when his choices are the product of full awareness of his operative needs and actual constraints. If these needs and constraints are buried in the unconscious, they engender irrationalities which remain invulnerable behind masks of rationality. Our data repeatedly confirm this fact. Now, the removal of these masks allows men to know what they truly want and what they can truly have; this truth does not make men free, but makes freedom *possible* (Kaplan, 1957). After all, truth is the root of freedom. In turn, freedom — or lack of it — may affect one's being disposed to supernatural grace.

*5. The growth in vocational commitment: experiencing roles or internalizing values?**

One of the most intriguing problems of social psychology in general (cfr., e.g., Zigler and Child, 1969; Secord and Backman, 1974) and of vocational commitment in particular, concerns the various factors which influence the behavior of an individual in his growth. If we limit our considerations just to the two sets of individual and situational determinants of behavior, two difficult questions arise: What is the relative importance of the person's assigned *and conceived* roles as a member of a group in comparison with his internal and entire psychodynamics? What is the relevance of the experiencing of roles in comparison with the internalizing of vocational values and attitudes?

Our purpose here is not to answer exhaustively these extremely complex questions. We will only offer first, some speculative considerations; then the findings of our research relevant to these considerations will be recalled; finally some practical suggestions will be presented for problems concerning

---

* We would like to thank B. Kiely, S. J. for his very valuable contribution to this section.

spiritual life, professional-occupational involvement of priests and religious, and planning of programs of training for vocational growth.

If there is some common definition of role of which we speak, it is that role is the set of prescriptions defining what the behavior of a group member should be (Thomas, 1968). Some roles are not chosen, e.g. being a man or a woman, infant, adult, or old. But some roles *are chosen*, e.g. professional and vocational roles. Such a choice implies values, in the general sense defined by Rokeach (1968): enduring abstract ideals about ideal modes of conduct and ideal end-states of existence.

One can in principle distinguish two possibilities: either the role *itself* is chosen as a kind of ideal end-state, or else the role is chosen for the sake of values beyond itself. In the former case one can speak of role-orientation, and in the latter case of value-orientation.

If role-orientation in this sense is in question, then there are no motives beyond the role for remaining in the role, or for working in the role. Perseverance and effectiveness appear to be conditioned by role-satisfaction. The gratification of the individual's needs found in the role becomes central.

Where value-orientation is in question, however, the main reason for choosing the role will not be the gratification which it offers, but the " ideal modes of conduct " which the role makes possible, and which serve to reach the " ideal end-states of existence ", i.e. the role-transcendent values on account of which the role is chosen. Any treatment of the priestly role which makes no explicit provision for such an orientation is basically inadequate.

Secondly, it must be conceded that any role whatsoever entails some renunciation of satisfactions. This is true in its own way of the priest's and religious' role. Hence a part of the matter of value-orientation is the question of whether the individual's values are so held as to permit that the necessary price be paid. On the other hand, when values are not clearly introduced into the discussion, vocational outcome (perseverance/dropping out) can only be conceived in terms of a " balance of payments " model, or of role-conflict; that is, of role-orientation.

234

In other words, by role-orientation we mean a way of using the role as an end in itself rather than using the role as a means to realize values which are both role-transcendent and self-transcendent.

Sullivan, Grant, and Grant (1957), writing in a context of social integration versus delinquency, distinguish seven theoretical stages of development. The fourth, fifth, sixth, and seventh stages imply different ways in which the individual relates to the roles he lives. In the fourth of these stages the individual is relying heavily on roles to provide a sense of identity and to protect him from insecurity and inadequacy. Relying so heavily on roles, he tends to identify with the role of the moment, to adhere to it rigidly, and to try to impose in authoritarian fashion his expectations on others so that their behaviour will be predictable.

At the fifth stage, the individual is capable of differentiating roles, both for himself and for others. He becomes capable within certain limits of tolerating variation in the behaviour of others. He may still be subject to uncertainty in his own case, wondering which of the roles he plays is more basic for his own identity.

At the sixth stage the individual is capable of distinguishing himself from the different social roles he adopts at different moments. There is a stronger sense of his own continuity and stability. This " makes possible the establishment of mature, long-term relationships and goals ".

At the seventh and final stage distinguished by Sullivan *et al.*, the individual becomes able " to comprehend focusing or integrating processes in himself or others ", and becomes capable of reaching some " perspective on previous modes of experiencing ".

> With this frame of reference he no longer seeks absolute realities, but sees a variety of ways of perceiving and integrating, some of which lead to more adequate expectations and hypotheses than others (p. 385).

These distinctions of Sullivan *et al.* remind one that the use made of roles is complex, and that the broad disjunction being used here (role-orientation versus value-orientation) is highly abstract. However, their analysis also serves to indicate

235

(indirectly) the need for a special distinction of this kind for the case of the role of the priestly or religious vocation. For such a vocation is a *total role* (cfr. Chapter 1 and Mönikes, 1973). If the individual is to take a distance from this total role, the kind of distance conceived by Sullivan *et al.* as part of growing maturity, this can hardly be done by seeing the " total role " as just one of " a variety of ways of perceiving and integrating ". Independence of such a total role can only be achieved by adherence to a clear system of values which transcend the enactment of the role. The distinction between value-orientation and role orientation thus retains a special validity for the case of such a total role.

Returning now to a consideration of the consequences to be expected when such a value-orientation is not effective in the individual's life, that is, when role-orientation prevails, it can be seen that because of the motivational forces implied, certains consequences in terms of perseverance and effectiveness in the role can be anticipated.

As to perseverance, this is threatened by the prevalence of non-internalizing identification and compliance (in Kelman's terms, with the application to vocation: cfr. Chapter 7, p. 115 ff.) over internalization or internalizing identification, as ways in which the role is interpreted and sustained. Behaviour maintained on account of compliance or of non-internalizing identification *is dependent on* the persistence of external factors; reward and punishment for the case of compliance, a satisfying self-defining relationship with another or others (including a profession, a vocation) for the case of non-internalizing identification. Note that to the extent to which the *part* of the self gratified by the role relationship cannot be integrated with objective vocational values, to the same extent this role relationship will lead to compliance or at least away from internalization (non-internalizing identification). Perseverance, being thus conditional, is precarious.

The behaviour of a person maintained on account of internalization depends on the worth of a value (e.g. imitation of Christ) for its own sake, rather than for the person's sake. To the extent that a role relationship with others gratifies a *part* of the self that may be integrated with objective vocational values, to that extent the identifying relation will lead toward

236

internalization of vocational values and attitudes (internalizing identification).

Kelman (1961) tested his ideas in a context of induced opinion-change. In general, conditions inducing role-orientation produced identification, while value-orientation conditions led to internalization. While the situations examined in Kelman's research are somewhat remote from that of a priestly or religious vocation, the validation of his ideas in the one situation suggests that they may be valid also in the other.

With respect to effectiveness in the chosen role, it must be obvious that anyone who is going to intervene actively in changing himself or in changing any situation in which he intervenes must hold some ideals which differ from his own present reality or from that of the actual situation, so that between the ideal and the reality there prevails a certain tension, as between the poles of a battery. This statement is necessarily true unless one takes the reality as already ideal, or else takes as one's ideal the search for gratification and the avoidance of frustration.

Lacking such ideals, a person must be in a profound sense passive. He will operate in terms of compliance and non-internalizing identification. His behaviour is dictated by reward and punishment or by the expectations of others whom he seeks to please and with whom he seeks to relate in a way gratifying to himself. He is at the mercy of outside factors, and lacks the basis for an active intervention towards changing either himself or a situation in the direction of some ideal. Further, the more his conduct is passive, i.e., reactive rather than active with respect to frustrations and satisfactions, the more subconscious factors may be expected to expand their influence in his life.

Thus, insofar as one is role-oriented in the sense explained, the more perseverance and effectiveness are undermined.

It is also to be expected that insofar as role-orientation prevails, time spent in a role by no means guarantees growth in the direction of value-orientation. What counts is not time, but the way in which the role is " used ". If it is used passively in the sense explained here, growth in vocational commitment is not to be expected. Whether such passivity, lived over a period of time, will produce a deterioration of the person as distinct from a merely static condition, is a further question which at this point remains open, but which will be considered shortly.

In more technical language:

> ...the priestly character (i.e. values) should specify the activities (the experiencing of roles) and not vice versa... In fact the activities of the professional role enactment are supposed to enhance the corresponding vocational attitude-value system and thus to determine a personal internalization of such a system (a basic factor for vocational effectiveness) as well as the genuine personal self-fulfilment coming from *internal* consistency among values-attitudes-needs (as opposed to the pseudo-self-fulfilment coming *only* from *external* gratifications of compliance or non-internalizing identification). Therefore professional role-enactment is a means to the end of internal consistency and not an end in itself; to make it an end is to create two ends in the individual's personality which may be in opposition and thus split his identity, a fact quite probable in people with subconscious central inconsistencies. As a means, role enactment should be subordinated to vocational internal consistency if vocational effectiveness and self-fulfilment are to be obtained. Now if this consistency is disturbed by subconscious vocational inconsistencies of personality, role enactment of functions may not lead to internalization of vocational attitudes (and values); *in such a case*, the functional enactment of a profession may gratify, fulfill the individuals because of the external incentive of compliance or of non-internalizing identification, but not because of interior consistency; this may explain why especially vocationally inconsistent people like professional gratification and look for it: as a role orientation rather than a value orientation, it gives gratification without asking for consistency; however, it does not help toward vocational equilibrium and growth (Rulla, 1971, pp. 211-212).

The previous section was speculative and considered the inadequacies of role-orientation, whether as model for research on the priestly and religious vocation or as a way of actually interpreting and living this vocation.

The results of the research presented in this book are in line with the foregoing consideration.

238

First of all, in the vocational commitment there is initially a conscious emphasis on values and appropriate attitudes which the individual professes and desires to realize (hypothesis 1 of Chapter 9). Such a conscious emphasis differentiates all three groups of vocationers (seminarians, female and male religious) from their lay controls. While this may not seem surprising, it goes to confirm an earlier assertion made above: to omit any explicit consideration of personal role-transcendent ideals is to approach the question of vocation with a systematic oversight.

On the other hand, the fact that such a conscious emphasis on values and attitudes does not guarantee perseverance, as seen by the majority of all three groups of vocationers having left within 4-8 years, has another implication that may also seem obvious but which is important. Insofar as the traditional kind of seminary or religious formation seemed to operate on the assumption that values initially professed plus time spent in role-enactment was sufficient provision for the vocation to be " grown into ", it is seen to be inadequate.

The factors which principally serve to differentiate Drop outs from Non Dropouts (hypotheses 2 to 7 of Chapter 9) are not accessible via self-reports alone: central subconscious inconsistencies and consistencies are very relevant elements. This indicates that to rely solely on self-reports constitutes a serious systematic limitation in the investigation of vocational outcome; self-reports based on questionnaires readily permit a defensive style of answering.

Verification of the eighth hypotheses of Chapter 9 shows a trend towards the undermining of vocational attitudes and towards an increase in vocationally dissonant values prior to the actual moment of leaving the vocation. Seeing this as a manifestation of the vulnerability of the ideals proclaimed, recalling that this vulnerability is rooted mainly in vocationally dissonant subconscious needs, and taking it that the individual will feel frustrated when these needs are not being satisfied, support is found for the idea of the *vicious circle* already mentioned in Chapter 9 (cfr. p. 200). This vicious circle is diagrammed in Chart 42.

CHART 42

THE VICIOUS CIRCLE OF MANY ENTERING VOCATIONERS

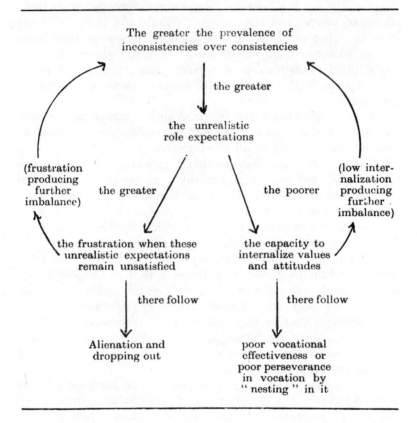

The findings of hypothesis 8 (an actual change in attitudes and vocationally dissonant values, occurring more rapidly in early drop outs) indicates movement rather than a static balance-of-forces; such movement can be interpreted in terms of such a vicious circle.

Translating this scheme into the terms of value-orientation versus role-orientation, as these terms were used in the initial discussion: insofar as frustrations/satisfactions experienced in the role become functionally significant, or, in other words, insofar as the individual is in effect using the role in the search for gratification of needs dissonant with vocational values rather than as a means to realizing and internalizing role-transcendent values, his perseverance in the vocation is being undermined. Further, the findings would suggest that by the time that role-satisfaction has reached on the conscious level the status of a rival purpose with respect to value-orientation, the process intervening between entry and dropping out has already reached a late stage.

The findings relevant to hypothesis 8 also suggest that the vulnerability of the ideals proclaimed and the unrealistic role-expectations to which this leads, also undermines effectiveness in the vocation as time passes; that is, that the changing attitudes and the change in vocationally dissonant values which seem to take place more rapidly in early drop-outs is undermining their effectiveness as well as predisposing to dropping out.

The implications of the findings relevant to the first hypothesis of Chapter 9 for the kind of role-enactment that seems to have been used by the traditional kind of seminary or religious formation have been pointed out. In view of the findings related to the other seven hypotheses of Chapter 9, and the vicious circle which they indicate, there arise implications regarding a different kind of role-enactment which seems in some cases at least to have replaced the older kind. One recalls Greeley's comments on the desperate search for " relevance " in which some seminaries seem to be engaged, in a rather aimless way (Greeley, 1972, p. 31). There may be at present an attempt being made to provide role-gratification as if this would solve basic problems relating to effectiveness and perseverance; while role-gratification, if it enters into the kind of vicious circle just described, cannot really solve any of the basic problems, but at most provide a temporary relief.

In other words, one could say that before Vatican Council II the growth in vocational commitment was seen especially as a process of internalization of vocational values and attitudes without proper concerns for the useful contribution coming from the *free* experiencing of roles. Vice versa, after Vatican Council II, the focus may be upon experiencing of roles without

241

proper concerns for the *necessary* internalization of vocational values and attitudes.

Our findings, emerging from numerous and different vocational settings, convergently indicate that *both* experiencing of roles and internalization of values should be given proper consideration; however, the *possibility* of internalizing values and attitudes resulting from the conscious and subconscious intrapsychic dynamics is a necessary *pre*requisite for making the experiencing of roles profitable. To expect growth in vocational commitment only or especially by these role-experiences may lead to stressful frustrations for the individuals and to painful failures in their vocational growth. In fact, roles may be an expression of vocationally inconsistent needs rather than of vocational values. The psychodynamics of individuals should be adequately free and thus capable of internalizing vocational values and attitudes *before* the experiencing of roles has a positive influence upon the growth in vocational commitment. Otherwise, such role-experiencing may easily have a negative, destructive influence.

Interestingly enough, in the last presentation of his extensive research and theorizing concerning moral development, Kohlberg (1973) suggests similar considerations: role taking opportunities lead only to conventional morality, while the movement from the conventional to the mature principled morality is one which must be considered as a matter of personal choice and is a *free choice of a self.*

Some practical suggestions follow. First of all, should our *spiritual life* be directed rather by an interior focus of prayer or of meditation *or* by an exterior involvement in social activities and relationships? Should our spirituality be characterized by the *role*-experiences of active life with people and for people or by the *role*-experiences related to interiority?

To *overly* stress one type of role over the other would mean overlooking two important facts: first, that roles as such have an highly ambivalent power; according to the way they are used, roles may lead toward or away from internalization; secondly, it would mean to overlook the determining influence of the psychodynamics of each individual on this ambivalence. If the prevailing psychodynamics of a person is one of central vocational inconsistencies, either the roles of the "interior" life or the roles of the "exterior" life will be subconsciously used not so much as a means to actualize and to internalize the spiritual values of a genuine self-ideal, but rather as a means to gratify or to defend oneself against conflictual needs (cfr. Chapter 6 and 7).

On the one hand, for the "interior" roles, chastity may become a means of narcissistic self-centeredness, poverty and penance a source of masochistic dependency, obedience the occasion to develop a conforming symbiosis. On the other hand, for the "exterior" roles, to be with people and for people may become for a person either a means of giving in order to get, or of being continuously and masochistically a sacrificed victim, or of fighting for social justice in all sorts of activities subconsciously moved by deep feelings of personal abasement or by strong needs of rebellion against authority.

The primacy of supernatural means should not be diminished. The relevance of charity for men should be upheld. However, the crucial issue is not the prevalence of one oves the other; rather the freedom, the objectivity of the idealr (values and attitudes) each individual has in both.

What has been said about spirituality can be applied to *two other recent trends in vocational life:* first, for people who have been in vocation for some time (e.g. people in temporary vows or theology students), the trend to overstress involvement in professional or academic roles before a sufficient help for the growth in vocational commitment has been offered; secondly, the trend to train, to form *entering* vocationers by engaging them immediately and prevailingly in role-experiences of external apostolic activities. Again, for both situations, the prevailing psychodynamics of each individual is a crucial factor determining the internalization or lack of internalization of vocational values by means of the various roles the individual enacts.

If, as the several findings quoted in Chapters 7 and 8 indicate, from 60-80% of the vocationers may present central subconscious inconsistencies which tend to persist, a premature emphasis on role opportunities will tend to be rather destructive than constructive for vocational commitment. In fact, even though the conscious motivation of the individual is for a genuine commitment, the underlying subconscious orientation may not be integrating, i.e., not defining, informing and molding the roles the individual plays at different times according to that conscious motivation. His behavior in each one of these different roles may represent an important *part* of the individual and be regarded as such by him, but it will tend to be isolated from the *rest* of his value-system; actually — in extreme cases — this part " may be encapsulated and function almost like a foreign body within the person " (Kelman, 1961, p. 71).

In such cases, the experiencing of roles will not lead toward internalization of values. This outcome is highly probable if the institution does not provide the conditions, which help the members to overcome the vocational inconsistencies with which they entered. A discussion of these conditions is not possible here; the interested reader is referred to the 1971 publication, pp. 322-384.

However, let us recall that the vocational growth will be effectively helped if the role experiences fulfill at least the four following conditions: to be existential, integrating, proportionate, and supported. These four conditions are all necessary during the period of training of the priest or of the religious; later on, the level of " psychological " age, as distinguished from " chronological " age, reached by the individual will determine the extent to which each one of them will be needed and useful.

" *Existential experience* means that the young vocationer is offered the possibility *to test himself* in substantially different kinds of tasks, in various types of social situations which require personal initiative and decisions. In fact, if the individual has to develop an internal and internalized basis for self-evaluation and self-direction, he must have the experiences that confront him with his own self. These experiences should challenge as much as possible his real self, his abilities, values, underlying needs, should expose him to failure, to frustration, to a sense of loneliness. Only in this way does he have the ' possibility ' to know and to accept his real self into the depths of his personality; only so can he achieve the joy of being himself and thus have the joy of giving himself to others. The period of training is particularly favorable for this existential experience; the individual is not required to make any permanent commitment and thus the continuous opportunity to test himself in various spheres of activity does not make his failures catastrophic and does not catalyze his succ esses to premature commitments.

Integrating experience is required by the fact that m an is a differentiated existing unity... his psychic life inclu de s the three levels of psycho-physiological, psycho-social a nd s pi-ritual functions and potentialities. It is true that th ese th ree dimensions of the human psyche are inextricably mingl ed in every act of man; however, every human act may be in itiated independently in any one of the three levels. After th e initial inducement, the functions of the starting new level should be integ rated, should be adjusted to the other levels in ord er to hav e consistency and internalization with the unifying value-system. It follows that any member of vocational in-stitutions should be repeatedly confronted with the challenge to perform these integrating, adjusting endeavors. The thre e vows of poverty, chastity and obedience offer, among many other factors, the occasions inducing these challeng es of in-tegration. Thus the possibility to practice them s hould be offered to every member. Any success in this int egration process will mean a strengthening of the capacity of the self for internalization.

Proportionate experience is a very delicate aspect of the continuous learning process of religious members. The functio ns and potentialities of the self improve as they are performed with success in increasingly challenging situations. The issue is a delicate one because these situations should fulfill two requirements: on the one hand, they should be a step ahead of the develpment stage reached by the individual so that he may learn new patterns of integration; on the other hand, they should not be so difficult or anxiety-arousing that he is forced to make use of primitive, childish, immature defensive devices. It follows that the growth of the self is hampered both by authoritarian and by laissez-faire regimes of training. Authoritarian or overprotective systems do not give the func-tions and potentials of the self the chance for exercise; laissez-faire or permissive systems, through an excessive stimulation of needs, of impulses with consequent anxiety may put too heavy a strain upon the self, and lead him toward a regression to immature feelings and behavior. The relevance of these considerations is brought to the fore if two elements are re-called: 1) the differences in psychodynamic consistency pos-sible among members of vocational institutions (as indicated by the findings); to deal with all the members as if they had the same ' psychological ' age is both unrealistic and not according to charity; 2) the frequent possibility for some members to find other people inside or outside the vocational institution who will respond to and support unconsciously the shaky psychodynamics of the individual by positive or negative reciprocation, transferences of subconscious, conflictual patterns, whether these are dependent, submissive, passive-resistant or rebellious. Blocking of growth or regression to infantile patterns rather than new developmental learning will follow; non-internalizing identification or compliance rather than internalization of vocational values and attitudes will be the end result.

Supported experience is demanded by the need which every member has to develop objective and free ideals if internalization of vocational values and attitudes is to take place. Let us recall the vulnerability of these ideals especially because of subconscious factors " (Rulla, 1971, pp. 324-326).

The findings of the present book all converge to substantiate the foregoing vulnerability and its trend to persist especially because of the influence of *subconscious* factors.

" In spite of the fact that people are well intentioned about their vocational commitment and willing to question their previous cherished but less appropriate personal attitudes, it is gratuitous to assume (actually the opposite is proven), that all or even the majority of them has a high degree of self-awareness. They may be open in specific areas, but closed, frozen in others, in which the *readiness for learning* may be seriously jeopardized. In these aspects of their personality they may be subconsciously searching more for safety or gratification than for genuine growth. Actually these subconscious areas may be or may become *dominant* in the equilibrium of their total psychodynamics. It is true, people should be free to learn through trials and errors, free to be wrong; but they should also be free to be *not* wrong; that is, able to recognize, to accept errors and free to ' really ' change, free not to fall into the same mistakes. If this self-awareness and this freedom are not present, they should be helped; if they are not able to learn through experience, they should be supported. More precisely, help should be offered, and if this ' offering ' is not reaching its aims, people should be invited to reconsider their situation with regard to their commitment. To allow the perpetuation of an incapacity to learn through experience without offering the proper help, especially for the subconscious hindrances, is against charity toward the individual and the other members of the community " (Rulla, 1971, pp. 326-327).

Concerning the last statements, the reader is invited to recall what has been said in the present chapter when discussing the functions of psychology in vocational training. The importance of the pedagogical function emerges from these statements. We should not pretend that subjects become " perfect " prior to and without personal experience (as was assumed frequently in the past); but we should not betray our duty to *properly* help them personally in establishing new attitudes and values before throwing away their previous ones, in integrating new inner controls before loosening the longstanding ones of previous experiences, in taking important decisions before rejecting altogether the support of past identities. The accent here is on the individual person and on personal help to him. Great numbers and concomitant structured group formation of the past are unrealistic, i.e., not existential; but laissez-faire policy of the present is not existential either. The idea that to change structures and to give freedom in experiencing roles will automatically be followed by improvement of individuals is simply naive.

6. *Vocational development and the challenge of sexuality.* [1]

Several reasons can be indicated for focusing on the issue of celibacy, chastity, and the whole area of sexuality in priestly and religious life. The major focus and impact of our research was not directed to this area. However, a few considerations seem appropriate when confronting the data analyzed and presented in this work with a set of data obtained from the same subjects concerning their sexual behavior and attitudes. These data were collected by means of the depth-interview and partially from the Biographical Inventory. Such data are

---

[1] This section is being expanded on the basis of further empirical investigations which are in course.

analyzed in detail, but are reported here only indirectly and in summary form. They are available to professional people for further consultation upon request to the authors.

An analysis of the available data suggest the following considerations:

1) Weaknesses in chastity like masturbation, hetero- and homosexual manifestations are present in individuals with different personality traits and disorders. Our data are in line with the empirical findings and scientific tenets of the authorities in the field (cfr. e.g., review of pertinent literature in Schmidt, Meyer and Lucas, 1974; Emmerich, 1973): sex shows a great plasticity and ubiquitousness. Sex should not be seen only or especially as a biological, developmental instinct; rather it is a psychological need with a social direction or orientation. As such, it may be related to *many* different personality traits or disorders; i.e. *any* personality trait or disorder may use sexual manifestations as an outlet or as a defense. Thus, a serious approach to the problem of religious chastity should take into consideration the *entire* personality of the vocationer.

2) This conclusion that sexual identity and sexual weaknesses are related to the entire personality, emerges also from the results of other researches, and has interesting connections with the issue of perseverance.

Recent studies concerning ordained priests of the regular and secular clergy have indicated that the dissatisfactions of the clergy in the Western world arise from conflicts centered around institutional work roles and values; with differences of nuances and of perspectives, one can quote the following investigations: Greeley (1972) and NORC (1971) for the priests of the USA; Schmidtchen (1973) for the clergy of West Germany; Olabuenaga for the Spanish milieu (1970 and Pro Mundi Vita, 1971); Stryckman (1971) for the Quebec area; Schallert and Kelley (1970) for American priests who had left the active ministry.

According to these studies, the foregoing conflicts concerning institutional roles and values lead to a sense of self-dissatisfaction, of loneliness, of alienation and isolation from the vocational institutions. In turn, this sense of self-dissatisfaction leads to the desire to marry. In the nation-wide investigation by the National Opinion Research Center (NORC, 1971) for

248

the American priests, a desire to marry is the strongest pre-dictor of plans to leave the priesthood, and the principal reason for the desire to marry is loneliness (Greeley, 1972).

Our research did not consider ordained priests, but young vocationers, and studied their personality as soon as they entered their vocational settings; therefore, before they were exposed to the influence of the vocational institutions. Our data indicate that, at entrance, people who will leave vocation in a span of 6 to 8 years, already show personality characteristics which, in time, will develop in them a sense of alienation from the institution, a sense of loneliness, and concomitantly the desire to marry as the foregoing quoted studies suggested.

It is interesting that, future " dropouts " of vocation al-ready at entrance present a capacity to internalize vocational values and attitudes which is significantly lower than the one of people who remain in vocation. Thus, the roots of a future sense of alienation from the vocational institution, of a future sense of loneliness are already present at entrance and they are related to *dispositions* characterizing the entire personality.

3) According to our research data, the shortcomings of the *entering* personality produce and sustain in time false expec-tations concerning the roles which the individuals look forward to playing in their vocational life. Since these expectations are unrealistic, it is not surprising that frustrations can be felt in vocation and that these frustrations may seek some outlets in sexual phenomena. In this regard, a comparison between sexual weaknesses at entrance and after 4 years, revealed cer-tainly no hint toward an improvement. This result was true for male religious, female religious, and for seminarians.

The findings and considerations presented in the foregoing three points seem to confirm the conclusions reached in a recent publication by Emmerich (1973) after reviewing the pertinent research literature. He states: " A life-span framework thus alerts investigators to the likelihood that sex-role phenomena are subordinated to more fundamental organizing processes in personality development " (p. 144).

If a person wants to integrate his sexual identity and cha-racteristics, he should do it in the framework of the ideals of his entire personality (A. Van Kaam, 1970). However, our study indicates that these ideals which play an important role

249

for entering a vocation, are frequently undermined by short-comings which touch the entire personality.

4) Furthermore, our results indicate that some tenets of general social psychology are valid for entering vocationers also: a) the values a person proclaims may be less influential upon his motivation than what he considers central for his self-concept (Rokeach, 1973, who quotes other authors); b) it is easier to change behavior than attitudes that matter (see discussion of pertinent literature in Freedman, Carlsmith, and Sears, 1974).

In this regard, the case in point is the fact indicated by our findings: some people succeeded to overcome their sexual weakness during the first 1-2 years of vocational formation; later on, after only 4 years of vocational life, these weaknesses gradually reappeared and sometimes increased. The deep roots of these problems had not been sufficiently influenced by the formation.

5) Another consideration seems to be appropriate. As the research findings have indicated, the personality of entering vocationers already presents the elements which may lead to future shortcomings in the vocational commitment in general and in the handling of sex phenomena, in particular. These shortcomings are mostly of a subconscious nature. Thus, in the light of the foregoing findings, merely an institutional, role, or behavioral approach would not seem to offer the *most* helpful intervention toward integration in the area of sexual identity.

Here the results obtained by NORC (1971) on the marital adjustment of priests who left the ministry are important in suggesting that the mere change of status — in this case from celibate to married — is no guarantee that the individual will find, because of changed circumstances, the resources to resolve his personality shortcomings.

In the sociological investigation mentioned above on the Catholic Priests in the United States, Greeley and his associates (NORC, 1971), by means of a questionnaire, have requested the opinion of priests who have resigned from the ministry. They obtained 873 responses on several issues including information about marital relationships. Such information constitutes a measure of " marriage adjustment " (Bradburn, 1969; Orden and Bradburn, 1968, 1969) articulated in three indices:

the Index of Marital Tension, the Index of Marital Sociability, and the Index of Marital Companionship. By combining the first index with the other two taken together, a Marriage Adjustment Balance Scale was obtained, expressive of a level of marital satisfaction. Chart 43 reports these findings according to year of resignation from the ministry in comparison with the scores obtained by a sample of college-educated males.

CHART 43

MARITAL ADJUSTMENT BALANCE SCALE SCORES
OF RESIGNED PRIESTS AND COLLEGE-EDUCATED MALES

Resigned priest (by year of resignation)	Mean Scores
1970	6.9
1969	6.6
1968	6.2
1967	5.8
1966	4.9
1964-65	5.0
TOTAL	6.1
College-educated males (by age): *	
26-35	5.5
36-45	5.4
46-55	6.4

* Data from NORC Happiness Study, 1963.

The over-all mean score on the Marriage Adjustment Balance Scale for all resignees is higher than that of American college-educated males between 26 and 45. However, for priests, with the passing of time, this high level of marriage adjustment progressively decreased to a point lower than that of college-educated males. " Whatever the explanation, former Roman Catholic priests do seem to experience greater tensions in marriage than the typical college-educated American male, and these tensions increase as the resignation date recedes into the past (NORC, 1971, p. 298).

Somewhat in the same line of reasoning, our data have shown that for both boys and girls, the experience of steady dating *before* entering the vocational institutions has no influence upon the degree of developmental and vocational maturity. Advantages and disadvantages of dating have been discussed by different authors and researches (Kobler, Rizzo, and Doyle, 1967; Mietto, 1968; Vergote, 1968;' Godin, 1975). More information is needed to reach definite conclusions, but perhaps we can advance the hypothesis that the experience of steady dating before entering vocation may well offer useful opportunities for acquisition of social roles and skills in the area of interpersonal competence and in the area of sexual identity *when* the only problems are those of normal developmental growth. However, the situation is different when the individuals have *central* inconsistencies coming from unconscious conflictual needs. The usefulness or harmfulness of the role-opportunities, like the ones offered for sex-identity in the experiences of dating, should be carefully considered. The reader is referred for this discussion to the previous topic of this Chapter, keeping in mind that data of several researches indicate that conflictual needs are present in 60-80% of vocationers (cfr. Chapters 7 and 8).

After all, friendship between a man and a woman is different in many aspects from the one between two persons of the same sex. Providence has disposed a complementarity of roles which entails complementarity of needs: therefore role-enactment in heterosexual *interaction* puts into motion *new* powerful forces. Now, if a person presents subconscious central inconsistencies, the vicious circle described in Chart 42 may become operative and thus seriously undermine the vocational commitment. As already said, it is the prevailing psychodynamics which will make the relationship constructive or destructive.

6) The " Guide to Formation to Priestly Celibacy " (S. Congregation of Education, 1974) quoting Paul VI (Encyclical " Sacerdotalis Caelibatus ", Acta Apostolica Sedis, 1967, 59, p. 682) states that " every candidate for the priesthood must know himself thoroughly, his physical, psychological, moral, religious and emotional dispositions, so that he can answer the call of God with a creative, responsible and considered decision " (n. 50).

252

Speaking of the training in celibacy, the Guide also indicates that "while the motives for choosing celibacy are particularly personal to each candidate, through his developing relationships with God and others, these motives are *subject to a process of growth*. It is *here* that attention should be paid more than in trying to evaluate the initial motivation" (*ibid.*, n. 48, underlining ours).

In the light of these statements, the question arises concerning what is being done concretely toward the goal outlined above, keeping in mind the presence of the subconscious inconsistent components in the personalities of people in vocational training. As the data of this research have convergently indicated, these subconscious components are frequently present and do affect the capacity to grow.

Again, we are reminded at this point of the previously discussed functions of psychology, particularly of the pedagogical one, but also of the suggestions concerning *new* types of educators. Their contribution appears to be strongly needed if an "enlightened direction" is to be offered which "can notably facilitate the overcoming of this kind of crisis" (developmental and personality imbalances in the area of sexual identity) and "securely assure the integral development of the pesonality of the young" (*ibid.*, n. 36).

Of course, this does not intend to diminish the importance of taking into consideration also the spiritual, supernatural factors. However, "unum facere et aliud non omittere". Spiritual and psychological elements of the vocationers are not dichotomous as we have emphasized earlier, but strictly interdependent and convergent for the final purpose to "form that perfect man who is Christ come to full stature" (*Ephesians*, 4: 13).

7. *Why have so many people left vocation after Vatican Council II?*

Leaving aside the influence deriving from the new policy of the Church for dispensation, a tentative answer to this question would require a long discussion which cannot be made here. The interested reader may find some pertinent considerations in the 1971 book, e.g. on pp. 194-212, 137-140, and

— indirectly — on pp. 266-321. These considerations discuss the influences coming from the changes in the Church after Vatican Council II as well as the ones emerging from the impact of the socio-cultural factors of our time. All these influences explain the phenomenon of massive dropping out in terms of social forces external to the organism. But, what about the influence of internal psychodynamics?

The findings of the present book suggest that the intrapsychic dynamics which disposes to dropping out has not changed after Vatican Council II: people were and are undermined in their vocational commitment by central, subconscious vocational inconsistencies (cfr. Chapter 9). Our approach to the influence of intrapsychic factors is a structural one and as such, prescinds from the norms which characterize a vocational group or institution as well as from the ones proper to a particular socio-cultural milieu or historical period (cfr. Chapter 2). Thus, our approach is somehow transituational, transtemporal.

Apart from the influence of supernatural or spiritual factors, people leave more because their subconscious vocational inconsistencies more frequently and more deeply may affect their commitment. Why more frequently and more deeply? Referring the reader to the above quoted discussion of the 1971 publication for more comprehensive considerations, here we will answer by schematically pointing out three sets of possible influences.

a) As our data indicate, about 2/3 of the vocationers present central inconsistencies, i.e., a rather shaky psychodynamics in which *subconscious* needs are inconsistent, i.e. dissonant with the objective vocational values of imitation of Christ or union with God and of the three evangelical counsels. However, as explained on p. 10, inconsistent people may be distinguished as psychologically inconsistent (PsI) or as socially inconsistent (SoI): the former have attitudes which are consonant with the objective vocational values, while the latter have attitudes which are consonant with the needs of the individual. Thus, psychologically inconsistent people may be called " uniformists " since they are socially adjusted to the vocational institution, but psychologically maladjusted because of their vocationally dissonant attitudes; socially inconsistent people may be called " rebels " because they are both socially *and* psychologically maladjusted. Thus the vocational perseverance and effectiveness of the " rebels " is worse than the ones of the " uniformists "; as a consequence, defections or poor vocational effectiveness are greater among the " rebels " (cfr. Appendix C-8).

Now, before Vatican Council II, the type of leadership prevailing in vocational institutions was somehow oriented toward forced compliance to the norms of the institution. After Vatican Council II the prevailing orientation in leadership is not toward such forced compliance; structures are not fixed and rigid; actually, sometimes, they are almost non-existent. The first, rigid orientation tends to favor the development of " uniformists "; the second, permissive orientation leads rather to the emergence of " rebels ".

In fact, both uniformists and rebels have unconscious needs which are dissonant with objective vocational values. But " when dissonance is present, in addition to trying to reduce it, the person will actively avoid situations and information which would likely increase the dissonance " (Festinger, 1957, p. 3).

Now: " 1) when the environment is somewhat oriented toward forced compliance of attitudes and of not-directly vocational values, the religious vocationer cannot avoid many of such dissonant situations and information; however, he can reduce his inner dissonance between his subconscious needs and vocational values by accepting the attitudes and the not directly vocational values and by warding off the latter dissonance by means of the mechanisms of defense: such vocational inconsistency is the one previously described as psychological inconsistency of the " uniformist ". 2) The situation is different when the rather forced compliance environment about attitudes and not directly vocational values is not present, but subconscious needs conflicting with vocational values are present in the individual; in fact, in such a case, especially if the general atmosphere of the environment is toward indiscriminate freedom, the individual or part of the peers in the institution can try to reduce the dissonance by favoring *new* situations and information, i.e., by choosing attitudes which are consonant with the subconscious needs but are dissonant with the vocational values and again by warding off such dissonance by means of mechanisms of defense: this vocational inconsistency is the

one we have called the social inconsistency of the 'rebels' "
(Rulla, 1971, p. 139).

Needless to say, here we are not stating that, because
central social inconsistencies are vocationally worse than psychological inconsistencies, we should go back to the "holy
uniformity" ideas and methods which we have seen in the past.
Just the opposite. Both social and psychological inconsistencies
are compromises rather than genuine coping with the underlying persistent conflicts between vocational values and subconscious inconsistent needs; both are detrimental to healthy
personality growth and real internalization of vocational values
and attitudes (cfr. findings of Chapter 9). We do not remedy
a mistake by making another one.

However, the point may be made that the rigid, fixed
structures of the pre-Vatican II situation were offering some
help to the shaky psychodynamics of the *inconsistent* people
and keeping them in, with the defensiveness of the "uniformists". Still, this was a very artificial help as has been shown
by the massive dropping out of the post-Vatican II period; it
was enough that the crutches of the structures more or less
compliantly accepted were taken out and the inconsistent psychodynamics of the individual fell apart, leading to his defection.

b) In the 1971 book (pp. 195-199) some considerations have
been presented concerning the changes brought out by Vatican
Council II for the ideas, for the functions and for the structures
related to priestly and religious vocation. In the same publication (pp. 293-321) the influence of recent theological and socio-
cultural patterns upon leadership in the Church was discussed
(e.g., the questioning of belief in prior knowledge or of any
normative standard, the uncertainty about previous frames of
reference).

What are the possible effect of all these changes upon the
individuals' psychodynamics? For the purpose of our discussion
we can limit ourself to mention one among many others: the
functional relation among the three significant operative forces
of psychodynamics — values, attitudes, and needs (conscious
and subconscious) — has been changed. In fact, values have
diminished or, better, *may be* more easily lessened in power;
attitudes are less subject to the influence of institutional structures which have been more or less loosened; the needs of the

256

individuals, conscious and especially subconscious remain the same. Thus, the functional relation among values, attitudes and needs, tends toward less strength for the two first elements, and a " relatively " greater influence of the last ones especially in the inconsistent people. There follows a greater influence of the *subconscious* elements in the psychodynamics of inconsistent people. Such a greater subconscious influence is felt also in creating one's ideals which hence may more easily become less objective and free, may more frequently be *pseudo-values*. The greater relative strength of subconscious needs makes them more influential than values upon the attitudes; as a consequence, the attitudes will tend to coincide with the needs rather than with the values. Concretely this means that social inconsistencies become more frequent than psychological inconsistencies; and since social inconsistencies are worse than psychological inconsistencies for both vocational perseverance and effectiveness, more frequent defections and vocational maladjustment are the consequences. Note that the relationship between values and subconscious factors may become a two-way street: decrease in spiritual life makes possible greater negative influence of subconscious elements, and vice versa, increase in subconscious factors may affect spiritual life.

c) As was previously mentioned (cfr. p. 241), before Vatican Council II the growth in vocational commitment was seen especially as a process of internalization of vocational values and attitudes without proper concerns for the useful contribution coming from the *free* experiencing of roles. Vice versa, after Vatican Council II, the focus is upon experiencing of roles without proper concerns for the *necessary* internalization of vocational values and attitudes.

However, as discussed in part 5) of this Chapter, role-enactment may not lead to internalization of vocational values and attitudes. This is true at least for the centrally inconsistent people. Actually, for them the role orientation may be in opposition with the value orientation and role enactment may initiate the vicious circle described in Chart 42. As a consequence, people may drop out.

All the three sets of factors described point to the relevance of the intrapsychic dynamics in the process of dropping out *when* such psychodynamics is centrally inconsistent. Social forces external to the individual's personality may have a strong negative influence on this process. However, it would seem that people who are vocationally consistent have the strength both to stand this influence and to overcome it by creatively, constructively acting upon these social forces; while people undermined by central inconsistencies more easily fail in their vocational endeavors. After all, man may and in fact does " code " all the social messages he receives; among these one can include the messages from spiritual sources like readings, conferences, constitutions of religious institutions, etc. The findings of our Chapters 5 to 9 are all indicative of this.

The same three sets of factors point also to a situation which has appeared in vocational institutions after Vatican Council II: there is a gap between the healthy ideas of personal freedom, responsibility, initiative proposed by Vatican Council II on the one hand, and the capacity of individuals to implement them on the other hand. To give greater personal freedom does not automatically make people free; to give responsibility does not necessarily make people responsible; to foster initiative does not inevitably lead to a mature use of it.

Before Vatican Council II, institutional structures offered some help to the shaky psychodynamics of the *inconsistent* people. It was a precarious help, because it fostered more compliance or non-internalizing identification than genuine internalization of vocational values and attitudes. Now that, after Vatican Council II, the precarious help of structures is not present, some new help should be offered to increase the internalizing capacity of individuals.

" If we want, and we should (in order not to perpetuate previous mistakes), to implement the new ideas of Vatican Council II about personal freedom, responsibility, initiative, functions, etc., *then we should have more mature subjects, and educators who can help them to become so*. To implement the ideas without having prepared the subjects and the educators will lead more to problems than to the solution of them, as the experience of recent years has shown. Freedom and responsibility are useful in a degree proportionate to the personality psychodynamics of each individual and, therefore, the psy-

258

chodynamics should be prepared to profit of this usefulness, otherwise more harm than help will result" (Rulla, 1971, p. 216).

8. *Are there psychological laws of priestly and religious vocations?*

Let us qualify the meaning of the proposed question. The findings of this book did not necessarily consider the whole man, especially his superior activites of the spiritual level.

Our results first of all tend to show some elements (needs, values and attitudes) and the "psychological" relations of consistency-inconsistency among them; secondly, they indicate how both the elements and their *structural* relations act as *dispositions* to the self-transcendent action of the spiritual and of the supernatural factors in the processes of vocational entrance, perseverance and effectiveness. (For "structural approach" see Chapter 2).

As such, many of our data do not fall *directly* under the influence of freedom and of spiritual dynamism. The French philosopher Ricoeur (1949) assigns to the foregoing dispositions the function of a "material cause" of human behavior: "Ce peut être le même potentiel affectif qui alimente la sexualité enfantine et la moralité de l'adulte. L'origine de la 'matière' affective et le *sens* de la 'forme' intentionelle posent deux problèmes radicalement différents. Il n'y a rien de scandaleux à ce que le psychanalyste retrouve à la racine de la série discontinue des valeurs parcourues par la conscience, depuis le vital jusqu'au sacré, l'unité d'une même matière affective..." (p. 380). It is the "affective charge" (potentiel affectif) of which Ricoeur speaks that may dispose the individual priest or religious in a different way and degree to the action of the spiritual and supernatural forces for his entrance, perseverance and effectiveness in his vocation.

It is with the foregoing connotations in mind that we speak of affective dispositions as psychological laws in vocation. In fact, as our findings indicate, the strength of these affective dispositions may be considerable. After all, supernatural grace builds on nature and brings it to completion (Thomas Aquinas: "Gratia perficit naturam").

In spite of the difference among individuals, the structural consistencies — inconsistencies are basic, *common* processes which dispose them to the action of self-transcendent and *objective* values. Seen in this perspective, the vocational " laws " found in our research point to the fallacies inherent in approaches to an understanding of and dealing with vocation which imply one of the following two views of man: the deterministic-pessimistic view of classical Freudian psychoanalysis (to be distinguished from " Ego-psychology ") and the subjectivistic-optimistic view of the self-fulfilment, self actualization model of man expressed by authors like C. Rogers, A. Maslow and some of the existentialists.

According to the first view, man is a product or effect of a chain of diverse causes. The human person is a phenomenon whose essence can be grasped as if it were a fully conditioned and *wholly* predictable thing among and like other things. Now, as our research confirms, it is true that we may try to predict the dynamics of the human psyche. But man is more than psyche: man is spirit and thus he has the chance of changing. Note that we admit the fact that man has " dispositions ", but — against the strictly deterministic view — we uphold that man may dispose of his dispositions (Frankl, 1949); i.e., man is not responsible for some of his dispositions, but he is responsible for the attitude he takes to do or not to do something in order to change them; e.g. to seek or not to seek help in fostering his vocational perseverance and effectiveness.

The concept " responsibility " leads us to another aspect concerning the view of man which is common to both the deterministic-pessimistic and to the subjectivistic-optimistic conceptions of man. As Frankl (1967, 1969) has shown, both Freudian psychoanalysis and the self-actualization models imply a subjectification of values, i.e., for both, values are not " objective " but a mere self-expression of the subject himself. But, this excludes self-transcendence as an inherent characteristic of the human person. In the words of Frankl: " If meanings and values were just something emerging from the subject himself — that is to say, if they were not something that stems from a sphere beyond man and above man — they would instantly lose their demand quality. They could no longer be a real challenge to man, they would never be able to summon him up, to call him forth. If that for the realization of which we are *responsible* is to keep its obligative quality, then it must be seen in its objective quality " (1967, p. 64 with footnote 4).

And the same holds for the concepts of " happiness " of psychoanalysis and of " peak-experiences " of Maslow; in fact, they are the same, irrespective of the experiences that cause them. But, " It is obvious that dealing with the uniform forms of experiences rather than with their different contents presupposes that the self-transcendent quality of human existence has been shut out " (Frankl, 1969, p. 39).

Both " happiness " and " self-actualization " point to fulfilment of the self, or self-actualization rather than to the fulfilment of self-transcendent values and meanings. But: " self-actualization is not man's ultimate destination. It is not even his primary intention. Self-actualization, if made an end in itself, contradicts the self-transcendent quality of human existence. Like happiness, self-actualization is an effect, the effect of meaning fulfilment. Only to the extent to which man fulfills a meaning out there in the world, does he fulfill himself. If he sets out to actualize himself rather than fulfill a meaning, self-actualization immediately loses its justification " (Frankl, 1969, p. 38).

With regard to the self-actualization model, it should be noted that this view of man has been fairly widely accepted in vocational institutions after Vatican Council II, but not necessarily because of any empirical substantiation. In the words of Berkowitz: " Basically... the self-actualization thesis is a romantic throwback to the eighteenth-century notion of the ' noble savage '. Based more on wishes of what man should be like than on actual hard fact... this growth-through-gratification doctrine has a dubious scientific and philosophic status, both as a motivational theory and as a formula for bringing up the young " (1969, p. 87).

The previously quoted findings of Lieberman, Yalom and Miles (1973), which consider the application of the self-actualization model to the experience of the " encounter groups ", are in line with the quotation from Berkowitz.

The inherent characteristic of man for self-transcendence rather than for self-actualization, self-fulfilment, is valid not only for priestly and religious vocations, but for any form of

261

Christian commitment. Such a vital characteristic has been proclaimed by Christ: " I tell you, unless a grain of wheat falls on the ground and dies, it remains just one grain. But if it dies, it yields a great harvest " (St. John's Gospel, 12, 24) and " Whoever gains his life will lose it, and whoever loses his life for my sake will gain it " (St. Matthew's Gospel, 10, 39).

Our results of Chapters 5 and 6 indicate that in the call to religious vocation, God seems to underline sef-transcendence rather than self-actualization.

9. Some concluding considerations.

The following general messages seem to emerge from the results and discussion of our study.

Every human life is a vocation, is a mission. Every mission is a person before being a work; a man must be before acting, he must be entirely himself with his humanity redeemed by Christ before offering himself for the work of the Kingdom. It is this priority in time of the person over his mission, over his work-roles, that is underscored by the findings of the present book.

A second message: vocation is usually begun with ideals which are seemingly evangelical, i.e. unselfishly self-transcendent. But, while these initial ideals develop genuinely and are Christianly germinative in some instances, in others they present already in themselves the roots not only of self-transcendence, but also of *prevailing* self-centeredness. In time, the person may identify more and more with the latter and make of himself and of his apostolic activities an absolute, which has no freedom to transcend itself in the gift of unselfish love. In these frequent instances, blocked in himself, in his needs, the vocationer consequently has to create his own expectations which meet his needs but which often are at variance with the evangelical message.

The self-detachment, the self-transcendence proclaimed by Christ as the royal road to the love of God and of neighbour is replaced by self-fulfilment. Accordingly, the person will feel more and more alienated, isolated; his vocational perseverance and/or effectiveness will gradually be undermined. The person will be prompted to try different roles; but this will hardly

262

change the foregoing absolute, which stands as a strong impediment to his freedom for vocational growth.

A third message: the presentation and the internalization of the vocational ideals offered by the traditional methods of spirituality should be complemented in most instances by an appropriate help offered by the methods of *depth*-psychology to uproot the self-centered elements which may seriously impair both a more mature election of and the growth in the self-transcendent commitment of Christian vocation.

After all, if the divine inspiration depends on God, the way of receiving and implementing it depends also on the *whole* man; as Laplace (1972) says, a decision is as valuable as the man who takes it. The empirical findings of this book say the same, and point to an important distinction: perceiving the appeal coming from a set of values is different from the capacity to internalize it. A proper help to vocationers should offer spiritual food, but should also assure an adequate capacity to assimilate it. Actually, there should be some proportion between the spiritual values offered and the capacity the person has to assimilate, to internalize them; otherwise, the ideals proposed will become sources more of frustration than of growth. And, as we have repeatedly seen, depth psychology has a lot to contribute to increase such a capacity to assimilate, to internalize the proposed ideals. Any dichotomy between spiritual and in-depth psychological help is most likely to be more harmful than helpful.

This is particularly true now, after Vatican II, if the healthy principles of individual responsibility and initiative proposed by the Council are to be implemented: there should be a proportion between these ideals and the capacity to actualize them. But, as our very recent findings concerning vocationers of 1974 confirm, the man, the vocationer of post-Vatican II is still the same fragile vessel as the one of pre-Vatican II; also for him, chronological age does not necessarily coincide with psychological age; also for him, having opportunity for experiences does not necessarily mean learning and growth; at least this seems to be true for 60-80% of the vocationers. Individual responsibility, freedom and initiative are a challenge which the vocationer of post-Vatican II has to meet without the crutches of rigid insitutional structures. It is our serious

263

duty to replace these precarious supports from without by more mature personality structures from within.

From this follows the fourth message: the need for new educators. Two new types of educators were previously described in this chapter and—at greater length—in the 1971 publication. Here we would like only to explain what we hope could be somehow " new " in them.

First of all, these educators should be able to perceive the deep, underlying psychodynamics of the vocationers and help them to avoid the " tunnel syndrome ". An example will indicate what is meant by this expression. Recently a superior stated that the formation program of his religious community was very good at the novitiate level; people would come out of the novitiate with promising signs of real growth. But then, he added, " our program does not seem to function when individuals are in their college studies or in their first experiences of the apostolate ". As had happened before Vatican II, so now, after Vatican II, in all good faith, vocationers go through the first years of their religious life and formation almost as one would go through a tunnel: many aspects of their personality *seem* to have changed; but, in fact, they were only covered-up. Unfortunately, especially when deeply subconscious inconsistencies are present, later on reality will catch-up with these persons. In such cases—which, also in the words of the foregoing superior seem to be quite frequent—it is not the later, but especially the earlier program of formation that did not function because it did not touch the depths of the personality. The findings of this book indicate that this is what seems to happen.

Secondly, these educators should be able to avoid projecting some of their unsolved personality problems upon their vocationers and/or falling into some fo the inordinate demands which the latter subconsciously might make. In both instances, charity is not served. These educators should have worked out their own " tunnel syndrome ". They should be able to love unselfishly, to give without getting.

This leads to the fifth message: as previously discussed, the integration of spiritual and psychological helps should offer especially the pedagogical support, as distinguished from the ones of psychotherapy and screening; i.e., this integration should aim at fostering the growth of vocationers in their capacity to internalize vocational values and attitudes, rather than at solving problems of overt or covert psychopathology (which however, should not be overlooked).

As was seen in Chapter 9, this capacity is related to structural rather than to content properties of the personality of the individuals. Therefore it transcends the content of the system of values (excluding the basic five indicated in Chapter 1) and especially of attitudes proposed in different vocational situations. Thus, it helps the educators to overcome a dilemma in which they frequently find themselves: to side with the institution or with the subjects, with the " establishment " or with the " reformers ".

What is at stake in the pedagogical help is the combined effort o everyone involved—subjects, representatives of the institution, and educators—to search for truth and for the growth in the capacity to live it. And this effort should be made not only by the educators, but also and especially by the interested subjects *and* the legitimate representatives of the institution. The educators, paradoxically, should be at the service of neither one of the other two interested parties, *and* of both. The educators should serve neither one, or one, or both the parties according to whether they ask to be helped to grow in their capacity to internalize the basic vocational ideals *they* profess. After all, the obligation for this personal growth is valid for the educators, for the superiors, and the other members of the community.

Of course, many may resist the dismantling of the false expectations they may have created; thus the new educators may be disliked by both, the right and the left wings, even though the opposite may be true. Anyway, the new educators should be ready to pay the price asked by self-transcendent love: to profess in themselves and to help the others to " ...profess the truth in love " and thus to " ...grow to the full maturity of Christ the head " (Ephesians, 4, 15).

APPENDIXES

A. TABLES

TABLE 3.1

RELIGIOUS, SEMINARIANS AND CONTROL GROUPS BY INSTITUTION AND SETTING

MALES

RELIGIOUS OR SEMINARIANS			LAY CONTROL	
Institution I		Institution II	Institution I	Institution II
Setting 1	Setting 2	Setting 3		
Group A	Group A	Group A	Group A	Group A
Group B	Group B	Group B		
Group C	Group C			
Group D				
Group E				

FEMALES

RELIGIOUS			LAY CONTROL	
Institution I		Institution II	Institution I	Institution II
Setting 1	Setting 2	Setting 3		
Group A	Group A	Group A	Group A	Group A
Group B	Group B	Group B		
Group C	Group C	Group C		
Group D		Group D		

TABLE 3.2

RANK ORDER CORRELATION COEFFICIENT FOR PB-SI, PB-II, SI-II OF THE MAI FOR THE RELIGIOUS GROUP (DFRHO = 50)

Variables	PB-SI	PB-II	SI-II
Sc 1	0.34 c	0.10	0.60 a
Sc 2	0.58 a	0.25	0.57 a
Sc 3	0.27 c	0.12	0.51 a
Sc 4	0.63 a	0.04	0.17
Sc 5	0.57 a	0.39 b	0.60 a
Sc 6	0.27 c	0.14	0.41 b
Sc 7	0.46 a	— 0.07	0.28 c
Sc 8	0.20	— 0.10	0.35 b
Sc 9	0.55 a	0.29 c	0.35 b
Sc 10	0.45 a	0.15	0.39 b
Sc 11	0.60 a	0.22	0.44 a
Sc 12	0.51 a	0.28 c	0.42 b
Sc 13	0.43 a	0.21	0.40 b
Sc 14	0.41 b	0.12	0.28 c
Sc 15	0.51 a	0.39 b	0.46 a
Sc 16	0.56 a	0.26	0.42 b
Sc 17	0.58 a	0.07	0.46 a
Sc 18	0.43 a	0.07	0.35 b
Sc 19	0.52 a	0.30 c	0.55 a
Sc 20	0.34 b	0.38 b	0.55 a
Sc 21	0.48 a	0.43 a	0.78 a
Sc 22	0.51 a	0.02	0.29 c
Sc 23	0.37 b	0.25	0.43 a
Sc 24	0.48 a	0.20	0.52 a
Sc 25	0.56 a	0.35 b	0.52 a
Sc 26	0.62 a	0.24	0.36 b
Sc 27	0.22	0.13	0.54 a
Sc 29	0.39 b	0.02	0.34 b
Sc 30	0.52 a	0.14	0.25
Sc 31	0.41 b	0.08	0.54 a
Sc 32	0.50 a	0.50 a	0.25
Sc 33	0.59 a	0.66 a	0.50 a
Sc 34	0.03	0.10	0.46 a
Sc 36	0.27 c	0.31 c	0.24
Sc 37	0.01	0.28 c	0.40 b

Levels of significance: a = .001
                        b = .01
                        c = .05

Taken from: Rulla, L. M. (S. J.) Psychological Significance of Religious Vocation. Unpublished Doctoral Dissertation. The University of Chicago, 1967.

TABLE 3.3

RANK ORDER CORRELATION COEFFICIENT FOR PB-SI, PB-IJ,
SI-II OF THE MAI FOR LAY GROUP (DFRHO = 46)

Variables	PB-SI	PB-II	SI-II
Sc 1	0.42 b	0.30 c	0.56 a
Sc 2	0.64 a	0.35 c	0.65 a
Sc 3	0.53 a	0.10	0.42 b
Sc 4	0.62 a	0.18	0.39 b
Sc 5	0.53 a	0.35 c	0.50 a
Sc 6	0.54 a	0.24	0.21
Sc 7	0.43 b	0.08	0.42 b
Sc 8	0.51 a	0.13	0.37 b
Sc 9	0.52 a	0.35 c	0.54 a
Sc 10	0.61 a	0.15	0.39 b
Sc 11	0.68 a	0.28 c	0.37 b
Sc 12	0.71 a	0.46 a	0.49 a
Sc 13	0.44 b	0.21	0.06
Sc 14	0.50 a	— 0.14	0.17
Sc 15	0.61 a	0.20	0.44 b
Sc 16	0.60 a	0.13	0.31 c
Sc 17	0.52 a	0.37 b	0.53 a
Sc 18	0.36 b	— 0.06	0.26
Sc 19	0.58 a	0.13	0.33 c
Sc 20	0.48 a	0.06	0.18
Sc 21	0.28 c	0.15	0.62 a
Sc 22	0.59 a	0.39 b	0.33 c
Sc 23	0.57 a	0.18	0.46 a
Sc 24	0.61 a	0.47 a	0.41 b
Sc 25	0.65 a	0.52 a	0.65 a
Sc 26	0.66 a	0.46 a	0.57 a
Sc 27	0.51 a	0.31 c	0.57 a
Sc 29	0.43 b	0.22	0.36 b
Sc 30	0.71 a	0.38 b	0.47 a
Sc 31	0.37 b	— 0.14	0.27
Sc 32	0.23	0.25	0.21
Sc 33	0.27	0.12	0.32 c
Sc 34	— 0.03	0.05	0.31 c
Sc 36	0.28 c	0.29 c	0.22
Sc 37	0.04	0.28 c	0.51 a

Levels of significance: a = .001
b = .01
c = .05

Taken from: Rulla, L. M. (S. J.) Psychological Significance of Religious
Vocation. Unpublished Doctoral Dissertation. The University of Chicago, 1967.

TABLE 3.4

PEARSON PRODUCT MOMENT CORRELATIONS BETWEEN
PB-SI, PB-II, SI-II OF THE MAI FOR THE RELIGIOUS GROUP
(DFR = 50)

Variables	PB-SI	PB-II	SI-II
Sc 1	0.24	— 0.02	0.61 a
Sc 2	0.57 a	0.24	0.54 a
Sc 3	0.26	0.08	0.46 a
Sc 4	0.62 a	0.03	0.15
Sc 5	0.65 a	0.38 b	0.55 a
Sc 6	0.28 c	0.20	0.39 b
Sc 7	0.47 a	— 0.09	0.17
Sc 8	0.25	— 0.10	0.26 c
Sc 9	0.49 a	.0.18	0.32 c
Sc 10	0.48 a	0.15	0.38 b
Sc 11	0.57 a	0.15	0.37 b
Sc 12	0.55 a	0.26	0.36 b
Sc 13	0.35 b	0.24	0.44 a
Sc 14	0.42 b	0.13	0.32 c
Sc 15	0.54 a	0.21	0.25
Sc 16	0.62 a	0.31 c	0.45 a
Sc 17	0.54 a	0.04	0.38 b
Sc 18	0.44 a	0.02	0.27 c
Sc 19	0.48 a	0.19	0.46 a
Sc 20	0.41 b	0.34 b	0.52 a
Sc 21	0.22	0.10	0.72 a
Sc 22	0.51 a	— 0.009	— 0.27 c
Sc 23	0.33 c	0.13	0.26 c
Sc 24	0.52 a	0.22	0.51 a
Sc 25	0.61 a	0.32 c	0.52 a
Sc 26	0.61 a	0.10	0.32 c
Sc 27	0.20	— 0.10	0.41 b
Sc 29	0.26	— 0.04	0.45 a
Sc 30	0.54 a	0.06	0.19
Sc 31	0.38 b	0.05	0.59 a
Sc 32	0.49 a	0.49 a	0.20
Sc 33	0.56 a	0.67 a	0.50 a
Sc 34	0.06	0.08	0.46 a
Sc 36	0.25	0.29 c	0.19
Sc 37	— 0.05	0.20	0.32 c

Levels of significance: a = .001
b = .01
c = .05

Taken from: Rulla, L. M. (S. J.) Psychological Significance of Religious Vocation. Unpublished Doctoral Dissertation. The University of Chicago, 1967.

TABLE 3.5

PEARSON PRODUCT MOMENT CORRELATIONS BETWEEN PB-SI, PB-II, SI-II OF THE MAI FOR THE LAY GROUP (DFR = 46)

Variables	PB-SI	PB-II	SI-II
Sc 1	0.42 b	0.31 c	0.56 a
Sc 2	0.66 a	0.29 c	0.58 a
Sc 3	0.49 a	0.02	0.44 b
Sc 4	0.59 a	0.12	0.36 b
Sc 5	0.55 a	0.31 c	0.55 a
Sc 6	0.52 a	0.17	0.16
Sc 7	0.40 b	0.07	0.43 b
Sc 8	0.54 a	0.19	0.35 c
Sc 9	0.46 a	0.40 b	0.52 a
Sc 10	0.65 a	0.14	0.39 b
Sc 11	0.68 a	0.30 c	0.33 c
Sc 12	0.70 a	0.30 c	0.38 b
Sc 13	0.48 a	0.21	0.14
Sc 14	0.55 a	— 0.18	0.11
Sc 15	0.61 a	0.19	0.44 b
Sc 16	0.60 a	0.09	0.28
Sc 17	0.53 a	0.42 b	0.57 a
Sc 18	0.27 c	— 0.16	0.34 c
Sc 19	0.54 a	0.16	0.27
Sc 20	0.45 a	0.02	0.25
Sc 21	0.21	0.12	0.64 a
Sc 22	0.60 a	0.36 b	0.35 b
Sc 23	0.52 a	0.07	0.40 b
Sc 24	0.63 a	0.46 a	0.40 b
Sc 25	0.62 a	0.60 a	0.68 a
Sc 26	0.67 a	0.48 a	0.61 a
Sc 27	0.48 a	0.18	0.33 c
Sc 29	0.40 b	0.24	0.42 b
Sc 30	0.67 a	0.37 b	0.43 b
Sc 31	0.38 b	— 0.20	0.24
Sc 32	0.19	0.22	0.18
Sc 33	0.22	0.05	0.25
Sc 34	— 0.09	0.03	0.22
Sc 36	0.30 c	0.30 c	0.21
Sc 37	0.03	0.28 c	0.49 a

Levels of significance: a = .001
b = .01
c = .05

Taken from: Rulla, L. M. (S. J.) Psychological Significance of Religious Vocation. Unpublished Doctoral Dissertation. The University of Chicago, 1967.

TABLE 3.6

LIST(ING) OF ITEMS WITH DISCRIMINATIVE POWER (R = 0.25 OR MORE) BETWEEN THE RELIGIOUS AND LAY GROUPS FOR THE PB, SI, AND II OF THE MAI

Variables	N	r	N	r	N	r	N	r	N	r	N	r	N	r	N	r	N	r	N	r
Sc 1 SI			36	—.29	71	—.41	106	—.44			177	—.26	212	—.36	246	—.48			303	—.42
Sc 1 II			36	—.41	71	—.48							212	—.31						
Sc 3 PB	3	.25	38	—.28	73	.25	108	—.26												
Sc 3 SI	3	—.28													248	—.30				
Sc 3 II	3	—.41	38	—.58	73	—.29	108	—.57	144	—.41	179	—.43	214	—.28	248	—.29	277	—.46	305	—.47
Sc 5 PB	5	.37																		
Sc 5 II	5	.31																		
Sc 6 PB			42	.29							183	.26			251	.42				
Sc 6 SI					77	.29											280	.26		
Sc 7 II	8	—.27			78	—.38			149	—.34			219	—.39	252	—.45				
Sc 8 PB					79	.25														
Sc 9 SI	10	—.48					115	—.26			186	—.29			254	—.26	283	—.37		
Sc 9 II							115	—.33	151	—.33			226	—.42			283	—.38		
Sc 13 II							120	—.53			191	—.50			258	—.31	286	—.27		
Sc 15 SI					87	.28	122	.25											317	.28
Sc 15 II					87	.31	122	.27	158	.32					260	—.34				
Sc 16 SI	19	.28									194	.32								
Sc 16 II			54	.39			124	.28					230	—.36	261	—.26	289	—.28		
Sc 17 II									161	.33										
Sc 19 SI																	292	.30		
Sc 20 SI	25	—.70	58	—.50	93	—.28	128	—.60	164	—.31	198	—.50			265	—.50	293	—.45		
Sc 20 II			60	—.29			130	—.30	164	—.44	200	—.30	236	—.37	266	—.27	294	—.51	322	—.46
Sc 21 PB	25	—.46	60	—.38	95	—.43	130	—.38	166	—.70	200	—.47			266	—.42	294	—.38	323	—.52
Sc 21 SI									166	—.46									323	—.43
Sc 21 II	25	—.56	60	—.53	95	—.48	130	—.62	166	—.68	200	—.52			266	—.46	294	—.52	323	—.55

TABLE 3.6 (continued)

Variables	N	r	N	r	N	r	N	r	N	r	N	r	N	r	N	r
Sc 22 II	61	—.36	131	—.44	201	—.46	267	—.50	295	—.30						
Sc 26 PB	31	.33	101	.42	271	.26										
II	31	.44	136	.42	172	.43	206	.32	242	.32	271	.38	299	.38	328	.34
Sc 27 SI	32	.28														
Sc 29 PB	33	—.35	103	—.30	174	—.28	273	—.30	301	—.32	331	—.31				
SI	68	—.37	139	—.36	209	—.31										
II	33	—.54	103	—.37	174	—.39	273	—.44	301	—.54	331	—.28				
Sc 30 II	69	.46	140	.28	210	—.30	274	.54								
Sc 31 II	41	—.40	76	—.48	111	—.64	138	—.52	147	—.42	208	—.50	272	—.82		
Sc 32 SI	182	—.28														
II	182	—.86	205	—.62	217	.59	229	—.51	241	—.58						
Sc 33 SI	18	—.28	53	—.29	88	—.35	123	—.26								
II	88	—.44														
Sc 34 II	24	—.40	74	—.43	129	—.30	165	—.36								
Sc 36 PB	35	—.38	141	—.30	211	—.35										
SI	105	—.33	141	—.26												
Sc 37 PB	5	—.45	115	—.26	151	—.28										
II	5	—.59	50	—.25	110	—.36	115	—.35	151	—.29	250	—.28	254	—.33	283	—.43

N.B. The first number in each column corresponds to the item numner. The second number corresponds to its r value.

Taken from: Rulla, L. M. (S.J.) Psychological Significance of Religious Vocation. Unpublished Doctoral Dissertation. The University of Chicago, 1967.

TABLE 3.7

NUMBER AND PERCENTAGE OF ITEM/TOTAL CORRELATIONS FALLING AT VARIOUS SIGNIFICANT LEVELS FOR THE MAI-PB, MAI-SI, AND MAI-II VERSIONS OF THE MAI (N = 100)

	MAI-PB		MAI-SI		MAI-II	
	Original scales	Religious scales	Original scales	Religious scales	Original scales	Religious scales
.005	292 (97%)	53 (95%)	293 (98%)	52 (93%)	284 (95%)	54 (96%)
.01	2 (.7)	1 (2)	0 (0)	0 (0)	1 (.3)	0 (0)
.05	5 (2)	1 (2)	2 (.7)	2 (4)	7 (2)	2 (4)
n.s.	1 (.3)	1 (2)	5 (2)	2 (4)	8 (3)	0 (0)

Note: Corrected point biserial r's were computed. The total number of items for each version of the MAI was 332.

Taken from: Maddi, S. R. and L. M. Rulla, (S. J.) Personality and the Catholic Religious Vocation, I: Self and Conflict in Female Entrants. *Journal of Personality*, Vol. 40, No. 1, March, 1972.

TABLE 5.1

MODIFIED GENERAL GOALS OF LIFE INVENTORY
Entering Religious Females — N = 39

Variables	Correlations PB-II	Correlations SI-II
A. Serving God, Doing His Will	0	0
B. Achieving Immortality in Heaven	.223	.688**
C. Self-discipline, Overcoming Irrational and Sensuous Desires	.279	.369*
D. Self Sacrifice for a Better World	—.015	.537**
E. Doing My Duty	.793**	.793**
F. Peace of Mind, Contentment, Stillness of Spirit.	—.150	.639**
G. Serving My Community	0	0
H. Having Fine Relations with Others	—.039	1.000**
I. Self-development, Becoming a Real, Genuine Person	—.047	0
J. Finding My Place in Life and Accepting It	.254	.793**
K. Living for the Pleasures of the Moment		
L. Getting as Many Deep and Lasting Pleasures Out of Life as I Can	.580**	.729**
M. Promoting the Most Deep and Lasting Pleasures For the Greatest Number of People	—.159	.688**
N. Making a Place for Myself, Getting Ahead	.372*	.706**
O. Power, Control Over People and Things	0	1.000**
P. Security, Protecting My Way of Life Against Adverse Changes	.174	.685**
Q. Accepting What Circumstances Bring	.250	.880**
R. Doing the Best I Can for Myself and Mine	.620**	.846**
S. Survival, Continued Existence	.351*	.429**
T. Coping With Life's Problems as They Come	—.089	-.038
U. Developing My Mind, Intellectual Endeavor	—.005	.606**

Level of Significance: * = .05.
                        ** = .01.
                       *** = .001.

TABLE 5.2

MODIFIED GENERAL GOALS OF LIFE INVENTORY
Entering Lay Females — N=84

Variables	Correlations PB-II	Correlations SI-II
A. Serving God, Doing His Will	.234*	.702**
B. Achieving Immortality in Heaven	.491**	.644**
C. Self-discipline, Overcoming Irrational and Sensuous Desires	.293*	.481**
D. Self Sacrifice for a Better World	.102	.559**
E. Doing My Duty	.467**	.471**
F. Peace of Mind, Contentment, Stillness of Spirit.	.273*	.587**
G. Serving My Community	.210	.266*
H. Having Fine Relations with Others	.296*	.550**
I. Self-development, Becoming a Real, Genuine Person	.194	.618*
J. Finding My Place in Life and Accepting It	.378**	.653**
K. Living for the Pleasures of the Moment	.204	.588**
L. Getting as Many Deep and Lasting Pleasures Out of Life as I Can	.126	.436**
M. Promoting the Most Deep and Lasting Pleasures For the Greatest Number of People	.069	.278*
N. Making a Place for Myself, Getting Ahead	.346**	.643**
O. Power, Control Over People and Things	.191*	.313**
P. Security, Protecting My Way of Life Against Adverse Changes	.258*	.436**
Q. Accepting What Circumstances Bring	.036	.335**
R. Doing the Best I Can for Myself and Mine	.442**	.703**
S. Survival, Continued Existence	.474**	.670**
T. Coping With Life's Problems as They Come	—.065	.424**
U. Developing My Mind, Intellectual Endeavor	—.042	—.021

Level of Significance: * = .05.
** = .01.
*** = .001.

TABLE 5.3

MODIFIED ACTIVITIES INDEX
Entering Religious Females — N = 297

Variables	Correlations PB-II	Correlations SI-II
1. Abasement-Assurance	—.042	.460**
2. Achievement	.184**	.571**
3. Adaptability-Defensiveness	—.142*	.493**
4. Affiliation	.092	.289**
5. Aggression-Blame Avoidance	.178**	.447**
6. Change-Sameness	.142*	.347**
7. Conjunctivity-Disjunctivity	—.014	.241**
8. Counteraction	—.024	.505**
9. Deference-Restiveness	.076	.489**
10. Dominance-Tolerance	.176**	.432**
11. Ego Achievement	.261**	.562**
12. Emotionality-Placidity	.218**	.461**
13. Energy-Passivity	.006	.458**
14. Exhibitionism-Inferiority Avoidance	.043	.333**
15. Fantasied Achievements	.140*	.317**
16. Harm Avoidance-Risktaking	.128*	.423**
17. Humanities, Social Science	.089	.395**
18. Impulsiveness-Deliberation	.102	.380**
19. Narcissism	.165**	.305**
20. Nurturance	.184**	.313**
21. Objectivity-Projectivity	.294**	.725**
22. Order-Disorder	.037	.431**
23. Play-Work	—.031	.305**
24. Practicalness-Impracticalness	.244**	.434**
25. Reflectiveness	.346**	.526**
26. Science	.069	.312**
27. Sensuality-Puritanism	.035	.354**
28. Sexuality-Prudishness		
29. Supplication-Autonomy	.235**	.354**
30. Understanding	.060	.424**
31. Chastity	.093	.545**
32. Observance of rules	.083	.466**
33. Piety	.111	.512**
34. Mortification	—.117	.291**
35. Love of Vocation	—.108	.526**
36. Responsibility to work and study	—.004	.452**
37. Obedience	.207**	.500**

Level of Significance: * = .05.
                        ** = .01.
                       *** = .001.

TABLE 5.4

MODIFIED ACTIVITIES INDEX
Entering Lay Females — N=136

Variables	Correlations PB-II	Correlations SI-II
1. Abasement-Assurance	.045	.531**
2. Achievement	.222**	.615**
3. Adaptability-Defensiveness	.156	.549**
4. Affiliation	.019	.424**
5. Aggression-Blame Avoidance	.169**	.494**
6. Change-Sameness	.187*	.577**
7. Conjunctivity-Disjunctivity	.057	.503**
8. Counteraction	—.016	.430**
9. Deference-Restiveness	.153	.542**
10. Dominance-Tolerance	.166	.470**
11. Ego Achievement	.256**	.571**
12. Emotionality-Placidity	.071	.472**
13. Energy-Passivity	.010	.417**
14. Exhibitionism-Inferiority Avoidance	.141	.413**
15. Fantasied Achievements	.209*	.419**
16. Harm Avoidance-Risktaking	.119	.556**
17. Humanities, Social Science	.248**	.475**
18. Impulsiveness-Deliberation	.144	.385**
19. Narcissism	.164	.462**
20. Nurturance	.277*	.513**
21. Objectivity-Projectivity	.183*	.660**
22. Order-Disorder	.267**	.589**
23. Play-Work	.059	.468**
24. Practicalnees-Impracticalness	.215*	.373**
25. Reflectiveness	.221	.543**
26. Science	.308**	.303**
27. Sensuality-Puritanism	.028	.388**
28. Sexuality-Prudishness		
29. Supplication-Autonomy	.303**	.569**
30. Understanding	.280**	.551**
31. Chastity	.224**	.553**
32. Observance of rules	.192*	.642**
33. Piety	.173*	.283**
34. Mortification	.130	.372**
35. Love of Vocation	.134	.445**
36. Responsibility to work and study	.213	.377**
37. Obedience	.095	.461**

Level of Significance: * = .05.
                       ** = .01.
                      *** = .001.

TABLE 5.5

MODIFIED GENERAL GOALS OF LIFE INVENTORY
Entering Religious Males — N=54

	Variables	Correlations PB-II	Correlations SI-II
A.	Serving God, Doing His Will	0	0
B.	Achieving Immortality in Heaven	0	0
C.	Self-discipline, Overcoming Irrational and Sensuous Desires	0	0
D.	Self Sacrifice for a Better World	.257	1.000**
E.	Doing My Duty	0	0
F.	Peace of Mind, Contentment, Stillness of Spirit.	.073	.388**
G.	Serving My Community	—.058	0
H.	Having Fine Relations with Others	.070	.476**
I.	Self-development, Becoming a Real, Genuine Person	0	0
J.	Finding My Place in Life and Accepting It	.431**	.633**
K.	Living for the Pleasures of the Moment	.099	0
L.	Getting as Many Deep and Lasting Pleasures Out of Life as I Can	.016	.257
M.	Promoting the Most Deep and Lasting Pleasures For the Greatest Number of People	.283*	.650**
N.	Making a Place for Myself, Getting Ahead	.224	.279*
O.	Power, Control Over People and Things	.107	.401**
P.	Security, Protecting My Way of Life Against Adverse Changes	.240	.538**
Q.	Accepting What Circumstances Bring	.400**	.566**
R.	Doing the Best I Can for Myself and Mine	.281*	.666**
S.	Survival, Continued Existence	.506**	.902**
T.	Coping With Life's Problems as They Come	.201	.566**
U.	Developing My Mind, Intellectual Endeavor	—.077	.275*

Level of Significance: * = .05.
** = .01.
*** = .001.

TABLE 5.6

MODIFIED GENERAL GOALS OF LIFE INVENTORY
Entering Lay Males — N=56

Variables	Correlations PB-II	Correlations SI-II
A. Serving God, Doing His Will	.200	—.045
B. Achieving Immortality in Heaven	.178	.512**
C. Self-discipline, Overcoming Irrational and Sensuous Desires	.206	.373*
D. Self Sacrifice for a Better World	.167	.427**
E. Doing My Duty	.195	.241
F. Peace of Mind, Contentment, Stillness of Spirit.		
G. Serving My Community	.317*	.282
H. Having Fine Relations with Others	.365**	.127
I. Self-development, Becoming a Real, Genuine Person	—.217	.380*
J. Finding My Place in Life and Accepting It	.304*	.471**
K. Living for the Pleasures of the Moment	.189	.560**
L. Getting as Many Deep and Lasting Pleasures Out of Life as I Can	.297*	.441**
M. Promoting the Most Deep and Lasting Pleasures For the Greatest Number of People	.279	.511**
N. Making a Place for Myself, Getting Ahead	.050	.414**
O. Power, Control Over People and Things	.360*	.452**
P. Security, Protecting My Way of Life Against Adverse Changes	.371**	.374**
Q. Accepting What Circumstances Bring	.213	.578**
R. Doing the Best I Can for Myself and Mine	.511**	.700**
S. Survival, Continued Existence	.296	.423**
T. Coping With Life's Problems as They Come	.246	.509**
U. Developing My Mind, Intellectual Endeavor	—.084	.563**

Level of Significance: * = .05.
                   ** = .01.
                   *** = .001.

TABLE 5.7

MODIFIES ACTIVITIES INDEX
Entering Religious Males — N=140

Variables	Correlations PB-II	Correlations SI-II
1. Abasement-Assurance	.042	.633**
2. Achievement	.334**	.609**
3. Adaptability-Defensiveness	—.123	.493**
4. Affiliation	.146	.368**
5. Aggression-Blame Avoidance	.360**	.518**
6. Change-Sameness	.245**	.385**
7. Conjunctivity-Disjunctivity	—.080	.108
8. Counteraction	—.022	.460**
9. Deference-Restiveness	.110	.483**
10. Dominance-Tolerance	.083	.468**
11. Ego Achievement	.227**	.506**
12. Emotionality-Placidity	.204*	.510**
13. Energy-Passivity	.102	.370**
14. Exhibitionism-Inferiority Avoidance	.171*	.377**
15. Fantasied Achievements	.222**	.383**
16. Harm Avoidance-Risktaking	.133	.475**
17. Humanities, Social Science	—.121	.223
18. Impulsiveness-Deliberation	.111	.155
19. Narcissism	.214*	.567**
20. Nurturance	.407**	.374*
21. Objectivity-Projectivity	.352**	.773**
22. Order-Disorder	.067	.192
23. Play-Work	.062	.192
24. Practicalness-Impracticalness	.291**	.473**
25. Reflectiveness	.347**	.522**
26. Science	.207*	.449**
27. Sensuality-Puritanism	.003	.394**
28. Sexuality-Prudishness		
29. Supplication-Autonomy	.296**	.550**
30. Understanding	.008	.304**
31. Chastity	.087	.576**
32. Observance of rules	—.072	.145
33. Piety	.109	.578**
34. Mortification	.098	.477**
35. Love of Vocation	.192*	.560**
36. Responsibility to work and study	.234**	.538**
37. Obedience	.398**	.643**

Level of Significance: * = .05.
** = .01.
*** = .001.

TABLE 5.8

MODIFIED ACTIVITIES INDEX
Entering Lay Males — N=107

Variables	Correlations PB-II	Correlations SI-II
1. Abasement-Assurance	.273**	.524**
2. Achievement	.180	.469**
3. Adaptability-Defensiveness	.077	.445**
4. Affiliation	.193*	.313**
5. Aggression-Blame Avoidance	.212*	.388**
6. Change-Sameness	.119	.273**
7. Conjunctivity-Disjunctivity	.174	.394**
8. Counteraction	.202*	.470**
9. Deference-Restiveness	.198*	.400**
10. Dominance-Tolerance	.191*	.436**
11. Ego Achievement	.177	.315**
12. Emotionality-Placidity	.232*	.288**
13. Energy-Passivity	.091	.329**
14. Exhibitionism-Inferiority Avoidance	—.062	.195*
15. Fantasied Achievements	.207*	.429**
16. Harm Avoidance-Risktaking	.027	.177
17. Humanities, Social Science	.266**	.517**
18. Impulsiveness-Deliberation	—.057	.319**
19. Narcissism	.144	.352**
20. Nurturance	.139	.403**
21. Objectivity-Projectivity	.205*	.608**
22. Order-Disorder	.157	.283**
23. Play-Work	.128	.345**
24. Practicalness-Impracticalness	.222*	.455**
25. Reflectiveness	.470**	.641**
26. Science	.346**	.491**
27. Sensuality-Puritanism	.121	.260**
28. Sexuality-Prudishness		
29. Supplication-Autonomy	.321**	.435**
30. Understanding	.355**	.529**
31. Chastity	.081	.949**
32. Observance of rules	.047	.407**
33. Piety	.024	.199*
34. Mortification	.276**	.374**
35. Love of Vocation	.221*	.413**
36. Responsibility to work and study	.032	.357**
37. Obedience	.332	.557**

Level of Significance: * = .05.
                               * = .01.
                             *** = .001.

TABLE 6.1

MEAN COMPARISONS OF RELIGIOUS FEMALE (N=283) AND
LAY (N=136) GROUPS ON THE
GENERAL GOALS OF LIFE INVENTORY

Goals	Religious	Lay	F-ratio	p. value & rank
A. Serving God, Doing His Will	18.10	15.06	117.26	.001 (2)
B. Achieving Immortality in Heaven	12.35	10.93	11.75	.001 (6)
C. Self-discipline, Overcoming Irrational and Sensuous Desires	10.95	10.28	7.96	.005 (9)
D. Self Sacrifice for a Better World	12.63	10.42	46.17	.001 (14)
E. Doing My Duty	11.40	9.79	23.12	.001 (19)
F. Peace of Mind, Contentment, Stillness of Spirit	11.86	12.50	3.66	.05 (12)
G. Serving My Community	13.78	9.82	106.95	.001 (1)
H. Having Fine Relations with Others	11.79	12.63	10.51	.001 (18)
I. Self-Development, Becoming a Real, Genuine Person	15.71	15.64	3.84	.05 (15)
J. Finding My Place in Life and Accepting It	12.04	9.43	33.29	.001 (4)
K. Living for the Pleasure of the Moment	2.90	3.08	2.41	ns (3)
L. Getting as Many Deep and Lasting Pleasures Out of Life as I Can	6.30	8.88	88.34	.001 (10)
M. Promoting the Most Deep and Lasting Pleasures for the Greatest Number of People	12.18	12.80	1.15	ns (16)
N. Making a Place for Myself, Getting Ahead	4.05	6.04	78.97	.001 (7)
O. Power, Control Over People and Things	1.47	1.69	5.64	.01 (12)
P. Security, Protecting My Way of Life Against Adverse Changes	4.99	6.72	12.27	.001 (17)
Q. Accepting What Circumstances Bring	10.93	9.37	14.79	.001 (5)
R. Doing the Best I can for Myself and Mine	9.32	10.00	4.98	.02 (20)
S. Survival, Continued Existence	3.17	3.25	1.46	ns (13)
T. Coping with Life's Problems as They Come	12.30	12.22	0.62	ns (8)
U. Developing My Mind, Intellectual Endeavor	10.56	12.24	21.85	.001 (21)

Note: A multivariate analysis of variance yielded a highly significant overall
F-ratio. The rank order of each variable's weighting on the discriminant function defined by all the variables is indicated in parentheses.

TABLE 6.2

MEAN COMPARISONS OF RELIGIOUS FEMALE (N = 283) AND LAY (N = 136) GROUPS ON THE MODIFIED ACTIVITIES INDEX

VARIABLES	Present Behavior				Self-Ideal				Institutional-Ideal			
	Rel.	Lay	F	p value and rank	Rel.	Lay	F	p value and rank	Rel.	Lay	F	p value and rank
Abasement	5.12	5.33	11.59	.001 (5)	5.72	5.24	11.79	.001 (8)	5.28	3.51	69.78	.001 (4)
Achievement	4.86	4.82	2.36	ns (25)	5.49	6.20	2.69	ns (11)	4.59	5.36	16.52	.001 (6)
Adaptability	4.99	6.22	7.78	.006 (6)	7.05	6.92	1.44	ns (26)	7.26	5.55	35.70	.001 (19)
Affiliation	5.44	5.93	1.64	ns (20)	5.46	5.30	0.81	ns (9)	2.98	2.68	0.07	ns (15)
Aggression	3.14	2.77	3.45	ns (2)	1.77	2.01	0.01	ns (3)	0.67	1.14	2.74	ns (24)
Change	4.29	6.02	67.05	.001 (1)	3.41	3.86	3.44	.06 (19)	2.25	1.50	23.28	.001 (21)
Planfulness	4.84	4.55	12.04	.001 (24)	7.14	7.02	0.01	ns (20)	7.42	7.12	2.75	ns (29)
Counteraction	4.80	5.62	2.85	ns (11)	7.02	7.29	1.63	ns (16)	6.46	6.54	1.07	ns (11)
Deference	7.71	7.70	0.08	ns (17)	7.40	6.58	13.89	.001 (2)	6.92	6.32	16.82	.001 (25)
Dominance	3.43	3.75	0.10	ns (3)	3.30	3.56	4.69	.03 (4)	2.07	2.40	13.73	.001 (9)
Ego Achievement	2.23	2.36	0.77	ns (14)	4.71	4.67	0.01	ns (13)	3.94	4.32	5.39	.02 (26)
Emotionality	5.36	6.07	11.85	.001 (9)	3.30	3.30	1.16	ns (10)	1.44	1.06	5.17	.02 (23)
Energy	6.11	6.04	6.11	.01 (15)	5.63	6.02	0.21	ns (29)	4.25	3.43	14.14	.001 (12)
Exhibition	2.93	2.67	0.01	ns (27)	3.09	2.74	1.14	ns (28)	1.67	1.82	2.54	ns (27)
Fantasied Achievement	2.32	2.89	1.67	ns (21)	1.52	2.11	9.87	.001 (7)	0.94	1.40	15.08	.001 (11)
Harm Avoidance	5.63	5.21	0.51	ns (22)	3.58	3.01	0.70	ns (24)	3.42	2.70	40.12	.001 (16)

TABLE 6.2 (continued)

VARIABLES	PRESENT BEHAVIOR				SELF-IDEAL				INSTITUTIONAL-IDEAL			
	Rel.	Lay	F	p value and rank	Rel.	Lay	F	p value and rank	Rel.	Lay	F	p value and rank
Humanities and Social Sciences	4.91	5.48	1.60	ns (18)	6.56	6.94	0.72	ns (12)	5.13	7.52	60.51	.001 (7)
Impulsiveness	5.14	5.56	0.92	ns (16)	3.12	3.61	2.10	ns (27)	1.38	1.40	2.24	ns (14)
Narcissism	4.33	4.88	10.16	.001 (10)	2.26	2.53	5.29	.02 (5)	0.95	0.78	0.20	ns (20)
Nurturance	6.36	7.06	4.46	.04 (12)	7.32	7.17	1.85	ns (15)	6.04	4.83	27.31	.001 (28)
Objectivity	8.57	9.12	3.45	.06 (28)	6.91	6.84	0.01	ns (23)	6.53	5.68	0.75	ns (10)
Order	5.02	4.14	22.46	.001 (4)	6.32	6.12	0.25	ns (21)	6.18	3.46	99.39	.001 (1)
Play	5.11	4.64	0.01	ns (19)	2.67	2.80	0.36	ns (22)	1.01	1.18	0.01	ns (18)
Practicalness	3.47	3.72	5.09	.02 (13)	4.67	4.62	2.07	ns (6)	3.34	3.31	2.49	ns (13)
Reflectiveness	5.38	6.55	5.10	.02 (26)	5.15	5.46	0.44	ns (25)	3.70	4.79	5.09	.02 (22)
Natural Science	2.37	2.47	3.71	.05 (23)	2.94	2.84	0.28	ns (17)	1.38	4.69	94.54	.001 (3)
Sensuality	4.38	4.92	10.19	.001 (8)	2.45	2.24	0.01	ns (18)	0.61	0.59	0.14	ns (8)
Succorance	6.64	6.20	3.04	ns (7)	5.92	4.94	0.70	.001 (1)	4.99	3.24	69.36	.001 (2)
Understanding	4.36	5.19	0.06	ns (29)	5.21	5.70	0.02	ns (14)	3.72	5.64	46.30	.001 (5)

Note: Multivariate analyses of variance were performed on the Present Behavior, Self-Ideal, and Institutional-Ideal forms of the test separately, with a highly-significant overall F-ratio in each case. Discriminant function analysis was also performed for each form separately. The rank order of each variable's weighting on this function is indicated in parentheses.

TABLE 6.3

MEAN COMPARISONS OF RELIGIOUS FEMALE (N = 283) AND LAY (N = 136) GROUPS ON SCALES CONCERNING RELIGIOUS LIFE (FROM THE MODIFIED ACTIVITIES INDEX)

VARIABLES	PRESENT BEHAVIOR				SELF-IDEAL				INSTITUTIONAL-IDEAL			
	Rel.	Lay	F	p value and rank	Rel.	Lay	F	p value and rank	Rel.	Lay	F	p value and rank
Chastity	5.47	5.13	3.11	ns (4)	4.55	3.85	6.27	.01 (4)	4.91	2.06	138.97	.001 (3)
Mortification	1.48	1.54	1.16	ns (6)	1.41	1.39	2.11	ns (5)	1.54	0.68	40.07	.001 (5)
Obedience	7.13	7.16	0.47	ns (5)	6.97	5.30	23.91	.001 (3)	7.64	5.74	55.40	.001 (4)
Piety	2.25	1.76	32.36	.001 (1)	2.98	2.16	48.90	.001 (1)	3.46	3.00	10.46	.001 (6)
Poverty	4.95	4.43	6.60	.01 (3)	4.92	3.78	13.76	.001 (6)	6.01	3.44	127.77	.001 (2)
Responsibility	4.65	5.19	5.85	.01 (2)	4.64	4.90	2.69	ns (2)	4.42	5.15	24.71	.001 (1)

Note: Multivariate analyses of variance were performed on the Present Behavior, Self-Ideal, and Institutional-Ideal forms of the test separately, with a highly-significant overall F ratio in each case. The rank order of each variable's weighting on a discriminant function defined by the variables in each form separately is indicated in parentheses.

TABLE 6.4

MEAN COMPARISONS OF RELIGIOUS FEMALE (N=126)
AND LAY (N=48) GROUPS
ON THE ROTTER INCOMPLETE SENTENCES BLANK

Variables	Rel.	Lay	F-ratio	p values and rank	
Needs					
Abasement	3.60	4.47	45.86	.001	(2)
Achievement	1.62	1.46	56.95	.001	(28)
Acquirement	1.62	1.47	124.00	.001	(14)
Adaptability	3.42	4.82	144.96	.001	(1)
Affiliation	2.13	1.83	7.42	.007	(7)
Aggression	2.65	2.65	0.17	ns	(31)
Autonomy	2.04	2.23	10.63	.001	(5)
Change	1.66	1.53	21.37	.001	(34)
Counteraction	1.56	0.92	202.65	.001	(4)
Deference	1.63	1.49	85.86	.001	(24)
Dominance	1.69	1.64	5.35	.02	(33)
Emotionality	1.69	1.75	1.63	ns	(3)
Exhibition	1.73	1.57	22.43	.001	(27)
Harm Avoidance	1.67	1.62	4.67	.03	(10)
Nurturance	1.84	1.68	13.78	.001	(17)
Order	1.66	1.48	49.27	.001	(41)
Play	1.83	1.75	3.30	ns	(29)
Recognition	1.80	1.79	0.01	ns	(25)
Sex	1.94	1.82	3.60	ns	(38)
Succorance	3.36	3.42	0.06	ns	(35)
Understanding	1.82	1.75	3.50	.06	(22)
Emotional Styles					
Anxiety, overt	2.23	2.10	4.46	.03	(15)
Anxiety, covert	2.90	3.37	49.81	.001	(16)
Depression, overt	2.09	1.90	7.27	.007	(39)
Depression, covert	2.93	3.90	101.70	.001	(12)
Paranoid thinking	1.64	1.47	76.60	.001	(37)
Guilt, overt	1.89	1.67	34.14	.001	(36)
Guilt, covert	2.14	1.92	11.07	.001	(20)
Defenses					
Compensation	1.74	1.58	21.61	.001	(40)
Denial	1.83	1.93	1.34	ns	(6)
Displacement	2.32	2.65	26.02	.001	(11)
Identification	2.07	2.09	0.02	ns	(32)
Intellectualization	2.13	2.61	85.67	.001	(8)
Isolation	1.69	1.49	42.47	001	(30)
Parentification	1.62	1.46	149.76	.001	(26)
Projection, supplm.	2.10	1.86	23.86	.001	(21)
Projection, complm.	1.80	2.14	41.23	.001	(13)
Reaction Formation	2.32	2.21	3.46	.06	(18)
Regression	2.69	3.08	14.23	.001	(9)
Repression	3.09	3.04	0.11	ns	(23)
Undoing	1.63	1.47	102.08	.001	(19)

Note: For each subject, scores on variables were translated into percentages of total score. Hence, the entries in this table are mean percentages. A multivariate analysis of variance yielded a highly significant overall F-ratio. The rank order of each variable's weighting on the discriminant function defined by all the variables is indicated in parentheses.

TABLE 6.5
MEAN COMPARISONS OF RELIGIOUS FEMALE (N=126)
AND LAY (N=48) GROUPS
ON THE THEMATIC APPERCEPTION TEST

Variables	Rel.	Lay	F.ratio	p values and rank	
Needs					
Abasement	2.42	2.61	25.65	.001	(32)
Achievement	1.56	1.45	15.34	.001	(16)
Acquirement	1.56	1.56	21.48	.001	(28)
Adaptability	2.70	2.71	0.01	ns	(30)
Affiliation	1.53	1.42	2.92	ns	(42)
Aggression	2.36	2.36	0.01	ns	(12)
Autonomy	2.44	2.59	12.50	.001	(31)
Change	2.01	1.99	0.07	ns	(21)
Counteraction	1.68	1.48	10.23	.001	(9)
Deference	1.67	1.61	3.77	.05	(24)
Dominance	2.62	2.71	7.96	.005	(14)
Emotionality	2.09	2.17	11.56	.001	(39)
Exhibition	1.77	1.63	16.20	.001	(15)
Harm Avoidance	1.86	1.92	3.42	.06	(34)
Nurturance	1.88	1.74	13.84	.001	(1)
Order	1.69	1.58	17.04	.001	(11)
Play	1.85	1.86	0.15	ns	(33)
Recognition	1.92	1.88	3.15	ns	(18)
Sex	1.85	1.78	1.97	ns	(17)
Succorance	2.46	2.57	13.05	.001	(35)
Understanding	1.65	1.61	2.93	ns	(22)
Emotional Styles					
Anxiety, overt	2.05	2.20	17.90	.001	(27)
Anxiety, covert	2.05	1.96	3.25	ns	(23)
Depression, overt	2.05	2.11	1.95	ns	(3)
Depression, covert	2.13	2.02	9.62	.002	(4)
Paranoid thinking	1.56	1.51	8.93	.003	(40)
Guilt, overt	1.62	1.55	16.87	.001	(19)
Guilt, covert	1.82	1.71	11.31	.001	(7)
Defenses					
Compensation	1.92	1.67	28.76	.001	(2)
Denial	2.13	2.15	0.22	ns	(10)
Displacement	2.53	2.61	5.92	.01	(20)
Identification	2.34	2.27	3.98	.04	(26)
Intellectualization	2.14	2.35	28.42	.001	(38)
Isolation	1.64	1.57	11.10	.001	(8)
Parentification	1.57	1.51	20.14	.001	(29)
Projection, supplm.	2.00	1.99	0.05	ns	(25)
Projection, complm.	2.36	2.58	36.87	.001	(36)
Reaction Formation	2.13	2.03	8.66	.003	(6)
Regression	2.52	2.52	0.03	ns	(5)
Repression	2.77	2.76	0.45	ns	(37)
Undoing	1.61	1.53	17.21	.001	(13)

Note: For each subject, scores on variables were translated into percentages of total score. Hence, the entries in this table are mean percentages. A multivariate analysis of variance yielded a highly significant overall F-ratio. The rank order of each variable's weighting on the discriminant function defined by all the variables is indicated in parentheses.

TABLE 6.6

MEAN COMPARISONS OF RELIGIOUS FEMALE (N=126)
AND LAY (N=48) GROUPS ON CONFLICTS

Conflicts	Tests	Rel.	Lay	F-ratio	p value and rank	
Trust vs. Mistrust	TAT	1.95	2.19	23.07	.001	(2)
	Rotter	1.70	1.58	19.14	.001	(7)
Autonomy vs. Shame	TAT	2.58	2.77	15.83	.001	(4)
	Rotter	1.77	1.64	67.56	.001	(8)
Initiative vs. Guilt	TAT	1.94	1.78	12.86	.001	(6)
	Rotter	1.77	1.58	94.27	.001	(2)
Industry vs. Inferiority	TAT	2.57	2.72	13.50	.001	(7)
	Rotter	1.82	1.64	109.49	.001	(4)
Identity vs. Role Diffusion	TAT	2.26	2.63	59.17	.001	(1)
	Rotter	1.81	1.64	145.31	.001	(3)
Intimacy vs. Isolation	TAT	2.31	2.53	33.84	.001	(3)
	Rotter	1.63	1.79	80.31	.001	(6)
Generativity vs. Stagnation	TAT	1.82	1.75	1.83	ns	(8)
	Rotter	1.76	1.56	66.06	.001	(5)
Integrity vs. Despair	TAT	1.61	1.57	1.78	ns	(5)
	Rotter	1.63	1.46	159.71	.001	(1)

Note: For each subject, scores on variables were translated into percentages
of total score. Hence, the entries in this table are mean percentages.
A multivariate analysis of variance was performed on each test separately and yielded highly significant F-ratios. The rank order of
each variable's weighting on the discriminant function defined by
all the variables on that test is indicated in parentheses.

TABLE 6.7

MEAN COMPARISON OF SEMINARIAN (N=47)
AND LAY (N=64) GROUPS ON THE
GENERAL GOALS OF LIFE INVENTORY

Goals	Sems	Lay	F-ratio	p value & rank
A. Serving God, Doing His Will	17.38	13.43	16.01	.001 (18)
B. Achieving Immortality in Heaven	13.27	12.21	1.10	ns (12)
C. Self-discipline, Overcoming Irrational and Sensuous Desires	12.06	11.49	0.45	ns (7)
D. Self Sacrifice for a Better World	12.74	10.41	5.95	.01 (4)
E. Doing My Duty	10.38	10.35	0.01	ns (5)
F. Peace of Mind, Contentment, Stillness of Spirit	10.95	12.23	1.62	ns (2)
G. Serving My Community	12.70	10.24	7.82	.006 (16)
H. Having Fine Relations with Others	13.02	11.86	2.27	ns (19)
I. Self-Development, Becoming a Real, Genuine Person	15.08	14.21	2.32	ns (20)
J. Finding My Place in Life and Accepting It	11.04	10.23	0.84	ns (11)
K. Living for the Pleasure of the Moment	2.31	3.58	3.01	ns (10)
L. Getting as Many Deep and Lasting Pleasures Out of Life as I Can	6.76	7.98	1.92	ns (14)
M. Promoting the Most Deep and Lasting Pleasures for the Greatest Number of People	12.38	11.09	1.99	ns (3)
N. Making a Place for Myself, Getting Ahead	5.80	9.72	22.53	.0001 (1)
O. Power, Control Over People and Things	2.72	4.40	4.75	.03 (13)
P. Security, Protecting My Way of Life Against Adverse Changes	6.00	8.40	9.67	.002 (6)
Q. Accepting What Circumstances Bring	10.36	9.26	1.76	ns (17)
R. Doing the Best I can for Myself and Mine	9.12	9.47	0.19	ns (15)
S. Survival, Continued Existence	4.06	4.58	0.78	ns (21)
T. Coping with Life's Problems as They Come	10.46	11.89	3.63	.05 (9)
U. Developing My Mind, Intellectual Endeavor	10.68	12.38	4.61	.03 (8)

Note: A multivariate analysis of variance yielded a highly significant overall F-ratio. The rank order of each variable's weighting on the discriminant function defined by all the variables is indicated in parentheses.

TABLE 6.8

MEAN COMPARISONS OF SEMINARIAN (N = 45) AND LAY (N = 64) GROUPS ON THE MODIFIED ACTIVITIES INDEX

VARIABLES	PRESENT BEHAVIOR				SELF-IDEAL				INSTITUTIONAL-IDEAL			
	Sems	Lay	F	p value and rank	Sems	Lay	F	p value and rank	Sems	Lay	F	p value and rank
Abasement	5.19	4.75	1.92	ns (12)	5.45	5.00	1.84	ns (16)	4.06	3.81	0.48	ns (24)
Achievement	5.34	5.17	0.17	ns (5)	5.91	6.26	0.67	ns (24)	4.89	5.78	3.86	.05 (18)
Adaptability	6.13	4.89	10.44	.001 (7)	6.84	6.17	3.28	ns (17)	5.84	5.06	3.42	ns (21)
Affiliation	6.21	6.04	0.16	ns (24)	6.41	6.26	0.09	ns (18)	3.60	3.43	0.16	ns (26)
Aggression	2.76	4.23	10.64	.001 (18)	2.02	2.54	1.71	ns (29)	0.60	1.01	4.13	.04 (19)
Change	5.54	5.51	0.01	ns (26)	3.76	3.67	0.05	ns (28)	1.89	1.42	2.77	ns (10)
Planfulness	5.13	4.40	2.16	ns (25)	7.30	7.25	0.02	ns (19)	6.82	7.31	1.31	ns (16)
Counteraction	6.00	6.06	0.02	ns (6)	7.04	7.50	1.25	ns (3)	5.84	6.82	3.97	.04 (4)
Deference	7.67	7.06	3.03	ns (22)	7.04	6.31	3.63	.05 (6)	6.43	5.81	2.16	ns (5)
Dominance	3.23	3.98	2.78	ns (3)	3.91	4.45	1.62	ns (9)	2.11	2.48	0.85	ns (15)
Ego Achievement	3.28	2.78	1.04	ns (11)	5.47	5.10	0.63	ns (15)	4.56	4.87	0.59	ns (23)
Emotionality	4.34	4.48	0.14	ns (16)	3.47	3.37	0.09	ns (22)	1.36	1.39	0.01	ns (28)
Energy	5.91	6.06	0.18	ns (17)	5.78	5.60	0.22	ns (7)	3.86	3.76	0.07	ns (3)
Exhibition	3.56	3.34	0.24	ns (4)	3.78	3.57	0.31	ns (5)	1.73	2.45	5.74	.01 (11)
Fantasied Achievement	3.41	4.07	2.49	ns (21)	2.43	3.34	5.46	.02 (2)	1.26	1.59	2.02	ns (21)
Harm Avoidance	5.30	4.21	7.21	.008 (9)	3.63	3.17	1.54	ns (20)	1.91	2.25	0.90	ns (6)

TABLE 6.8 (*continued*)

VARIABLES	PRESENT BEHAVIOR				SELF-IDEAL				INSTITUTIONAL-IDEAL			
	Sems	Lay	F	p value and rank	Sems	Lay	F	p value and rank	Sems	Lay	F	p value and rank
Humanities and Social Sciences	4.89	4.39	0.99	ns (29)	5.26	5.34	0.03	ns (27)	4.69	6.65	13.35	.001 (14)
Impulsiveness	4.73	5.34	1.92	ns (20)	3.15	3.64	1.67	ns (23)	1.17	1.23	0.05	ns (13)
Narcissism	3.84	4.68	3.64	.05 (27)	2.58	2.84	0.40	ns (21)	0.78	1.04	1.24	ns (29)
Nurturance	6.13	5.37	3.08	ns (10)	7.15	6.53	1.91	ns (11)	5.95	4.64	7.53	.007 (8)
Objectivity	9.00	8.85	0.29	ns (23)	6.84	7.03	0.13	ns (25)	5.26	4.60	1.17	ns (20)
Order	4.67	3.98	1.52	ns (14)	5.69	6.06	0.47	ns (10)	3.71	3.79	0.02	ns (22)
Play	4.39	5.96	13.30	.001 (1)	3.34	3.48	0.12	ns (26)	1.28	0.98	1.18	ns (12)
Practicalness	3.23	3.60	0.96	ns (28)	4.56	5.79	7.51	.007 (4)	3.18	4.10	4.85	.02 (9)
Reflectiveness	5.56	5.43	0.08	ns (8)	5.28	4.93	0.63	ns (1)	3.73	4.12	0.91	ns (2)
Natural Science	2.86	3.84	4.43	.03 (2)	3.15	4.95	9.70	.002 (12)	2.39	5.96	45.73	.0001 (1)
Sensuality	3.67	4.15	1.99	ns (13)	2.06	2.51	1.46	ns (8)	0.36	0.48	0.57	ns (25)
Succorance	5.89	5.48	1.59	ns (19)	5.69	5.07	3.24	ns (14)	4.93	3.73	13.82	.001 (2)
Understanding	4.71	4.78	0.02	ns (15)	5.17	5.70	1.59	ns (13)	3.60	5.64	18.54	.0001 (11)

Note: Multivariate analyses of variance were performed on the Present Behavior, Self-Ideal, and Institutional-Ideal forms of the test separately, with a highly-significant overall F-ratio in each case. Discriminant function analysis was also performed for each form separately. The rank order of each variable's weighting on this function is indicated in parentheses.

TABLE 6.9

MEAN COMPARISONS OF SEMINARIAN (N = 45) AND LAY (N = 64) GROUPS ON SCALES CONCERNING RELIGIOUS LIFE (FROM THE MODIFIED ACTIVITIES INDEX)

VARIABLES	Present Behavior				Self-Ideal				Institutional-Ideal			
	Sems	Lay	F	p value and rank	Sems	Lay	F	p value and rank	Sems	Lay	F	p value and rank
Chastity	6.32	5.65	2.55	ns (4)	4.32	5.32	0.50	ns (6)	2.47	2.70	0.03	ns (5)
Mortification	1.69	1.45	1.55	ns (3)	1.62	1.39	1.98	ns (2)	1.36	0.90	7.55	.007 (6)
Obedience	7.56	6.07	12.58	.001 (1)	5.84	5.15	2.47	ns (3)	5.50	5.12	0.83	ns (4)
Piety	2.28	1.43	11.93	.001 (5)	2.56	2.03	4.55	.03 (4)	3.02	3.01	0.01	ns (1)
Poverty	5.41	4.56	8.61	.004 (6)	3.82	4.10	0.61	ns (5)	3.45	3.20	0.43	ns (2)
Responsability	5.21	4.92	1.91	ns (2)	4.93	4.76	0.56	ns (1)	4.36	4.59	0.53	ns (3)

Note: Multivariate analyses of variance were performed on the Present Behavior, Self-Ideal, and Institutional-Ideal forms of the test separately, with a highly-significant overall F ratio in each case. The rank order of each variable's weighting on the discriminant function defined by the variables in each form separately is indicated in parentheses.

TABLE 6.10

MEAN COMPARISONS OF SEMINARIAN (N=45)
AND LAY (N=64) GROUPS
ON THE ROTTER INCOMPLETE SENTENCES BLANK

Variables	Sems	Lay	F-ratio	p values and rank	
Needs					
Abasement	4.09	3.55	17.31	.0001	(24)
Achievement	1.39	1.44	2.44	ns	(8)
Acquirement	1.42	1.51	5.47	.02	(37)
Adaptability	4.51	4.15	7.11	.008	(25)
Affiliation	2.04	1.98	0.30	ns	(34)
Aggression	2.61	2.45	2.66	ns	(27)
Autonomy	2.23	2.21	0.02	ns	(36)
Change	1.53	1.55	0.44	ns	(29)
Counteraction	0.88	0.53	16.87	.0001	(6)
Deference	1.42	1.46	1.49	ns	(15)
Dominance	2.56	2.81	3.89	.05	(4)
Emotionality	1.64	1.63	0.10	ns	(18)
Exhibition	1.52	1.58	2.24	ns	(9)
Harm Avoidance	1.63	2.09	52.40	.0001	(3)
Nurturance	1.68	1.67	0.02	ns	(30)
Order	1.51	1.53	0.10	ns	(41)
Play	1.77	1.92	4.17	.04	(2)
Recognition	1.84	1.97	4.01	.04	(31)
Sex	1.67	1.75	1.19	ns	(5)
Succorance	2.59	2.59	0.01	ns	(1)
Understanding	1.56	1.58	0.20	ns	(38)
Emotional Styles					
Anxiety, overt	2.20	2.30	1.89	ns	(35)
Anxiety, covert	3.12	3.16	0.11	ns	(19)
Depression, overt	2.00	2.05	0.32	ns	(14)
Depression, covert	3.60	3.26	8.78	.003	(17)
Paranoid thinking	1.46	1.50	1.22	ns	(20)
Guilt, overt	1.66	1.73	1.73	ns	(12)
Guilt, covert	1.88	1.87	0.04	ns	(39)
Defenses					
Compensation	1.56	1.57	0.07	ns	(33)
Denial	2.06	2.05	0.02	ns	(23)
Displacement	2.95	2.97	0.02	ns	(13)
Identification	2.21	2.20	0.01	ns	(21)
Intellectualization	2.80	2.73	0.48	ns	(28)
Isolation	1.50	1.55	0.94	ns	(32)
Parentification	1.41	1.45	2.56	ns	(7)
Projection, supplm.	1.80	1.90	3.34	ns	(40)
Projection, complm.	2.11	2.35	8.80	.003	(26)
Reaction Formation	2.16	2.07	1.40	ns	(11)
Regression	2.73	2.62	1.24	ns	(16)
Repression	4.59	4.33	3.25	ns	(10)
Undoing	1.41	1.48	4.48	.03	(22)

Note: For each subject, scores on variables were translated into percentages of total score. Hence, the entries in this table are mean percentages. A multivariate analysis of variance yielded a highly significant overall F-ratio. The rank order of each variable's weighting on the discriminant function defined by all the variables is indicated in parentheses.

TABLE 6.11

MEAN COMPARISONS OF SEMINARIAN (N=45)
AND LAY (N=64) GROUPS
ON THE THEMATIC APPERCEPTION TEST

Variables	Sems	Lay	F-ratio	p values and rank	
Needs					
Abasement	2.62	2.49	13.32	.001	(25)
Achievement	1.52	1.54	0.27	ns	(28)
Acquirement	1.62	1.70	5.86	.02	(23)
Adaptability	2.64	2.50	18.70	.0001	(16)
Affiliation	1.63	1.64	0.01	ns	(20)
Aggression	2.32	2.23	5.09	.03	(31)
Autonomy	2.44	2.26	19.60	.0001	(18)
Change	2.13	1.99	6.76	.01	(39)
Counteraction	1.61	1.43	5.16	.02	(38)
Deference	1.55	1.59	1.51	ns	(6)
Dominance	2.65	2.48	28.38	.0001	(22)
Emotionality	2.05	1.98	2.46	ns	(12)
Exhibition	1.58	1.70	11.19	.001	(40)
Harm Avoidance	1.95	2.12	11.84	.001	(7)
Nurturance	1.86	1.85	0.01	ns	(36)
Order	1.86	1.79	1.78	ns	(21)
Play	1.76	1.92	13.88	.001	(24)
Recognition	1.81	1.86	1.52	ns	(15)
Sex	1.64	1.76	12.70	.001	(13)
Succorance	1.96	2.23	33.09	.0001	(9)
Understanding	1.57	1.63	1.65	ns	(29)
Emotional Styles					
Anxiety, overt	2.14	2.15	0.05	ns	(2)
Anxiety, covert	2.03	1.93	4.09	.04	(5)
Depression, overt	2.16	2.15	0.02	ns	(11)
Depression, covert	2.00	1.91	2.72	ns	(4)
Paranoid thinking	1.56	1.72	17.55	.0001	(17)
Guilt, overt	1.56	1.64	6.34	.01	(33)
Guilt, covert	1.83	1.76	3.88	.05	(34)
Defenses					
Compensation	1.85	1.85	0.01	ns	(19)
Denial	2.23	2.23	0.01	ns	(32)
Displacement	2.60	2.50	6.68	.01	(37)
Identification	2.10	2.09	0.01	ns	(41)
Intellectualization	2.34	2.34	0.02	ns	(30)
Isolation	1.67	1.80	5.37	.02	(14)
Parentification	1.53	1.57	2.46	ns	(3)
Projection, supplm.	1.98	2.07	4.62	.03	(26)
Projection, complm.	2.44	2.45	0.12	ns	(8)
Reaction Formation	2.09	2.05	0.34	ns	(10)
Regression	2.40	2.39	0.13	ns	(27)
Repression	2.73	2.53	44.59	.0001	(1)
Undoing	1.59	1.66	4.42	.03	(35)

Note: For each subject, scores on variables were translated into percentages of total score. Hence, the entries in this table are mean
percentages. A multivariate analysis of variance yielded a highly
significant overall F-ratio. The rank order of each variable's
weighting on the discriminant function defined by all the variables is indicated in parentheses.

TABLE 6.12

MEAN COMPARISONS OF SEMINARIAN (N=45) AND LAY (N=64) GROUPS ON CONFLICTS

Conflicts	Tests	Sems	Lay	F-ratio	p value and rank	
Trust vs. Mistrust	TAT	2.29	2.38	4.10	.04	(2)
	Rotter	1.51	1.57	3.70	.05	(4)
Autonomy vs. Shame	TAT	2.61	2.48	12.35	.001	(1)
	Rotter	1.59	1.58	0.05	ns	(7)
Initiative vs. Guilt	TAT	1.83	1.88	1.77	ns	(5)
	Rotter	1.50	1.55	2.45	ns	(5)
Industry vs. Inferiority	TAT	2.65	2.53	10.34	.001	(7)
	Rotter	1.56	1.58	0.43	ns	(8)
Identity vs. Role Diffusion	TAT	2.59	2.50	5.70	.01	(6)
	Rotter	1.59	1.58	0.08	ns	(3)
Intimacy vs. Isolation	TAT	2.51	2.46	1.37	ns	(3)
	Rotter	1.57	1.58	0.39	ns	(2)
Generativity vs. Stagnation	TAT	1.82	1.94	5.68	.01	(4)
	Rotter	1.47	1.47	0.01	ns	(6)
Integrity vs. Despair	TAT	1.70	1.79	3.16	ns	(8)
	Rotter	1.44	1.48	1.49	ns	(1)

Note: For each subject, scores on variables were translated into percentages of total score. Hence, the entries in this table are mean percentages. A multivariate analysis of variance was performed on each test separately and yielded highly significant F-ratios. The rank order of each variable's weighting on the discriminant function defined by all the variables on that test is indicated in parentheses.

TABLE 6.13

MEAN COMPARISONS OF MALE RELIGIOUS (N=135)
AND LAY (N=105) GROUPS ON THE
GENERAL GOALS OF LIFE INVENTORY

Goals	Religious	Lay	F-ratio	p value & rank
A. Serving God, Doing His Will	18.93	12.88	137.11	.0001 (2)
B. Achieving Immortality in Heaven	14.82	11.70	22.16	.0001 (9)
C. Self-discipline, Overcoming Irrational and Sensuous Desires	12.65	11.33	7.31	.007 (15)
D. Self Sacrifice for a Better World	14.70	10.38	63.87	.0001 (12)
E. Doing My Duty	12.63	10.29	20.71	.0001 (16)
F. Peace of Mind, Contentment, Stillness of Spirit	12.80	12.32	0.81	ns (14)
G. Serving My Community	12.92	9.70	35.48	.0001 (20)
H. Having Fine Relations with Others	11.65	11.86	0.22	ns (6)
I. Self-Development, Becoming a Real, Genuine Person	14.29	14.56	0.53	ns (17)
J. Finding My Place in Life and Accepting It	10.32	10.12	0.14	ns (7)
K. Living for the Pleasure of the Moment	1.75	3.67	28.87	.0001 (18)
L. Getting as Many Deep and Lasting Pleasures Out of Life as I Can	6.30	8.31	14.52	.001 (13)
M. Promoting the Most Deep and Lasting Pleasures for the Greatest Number of People	11.94	11.20	1.74	ns (10)
N. Making a Place for Myself, Getting Ahead	4.25	9.33	122.59	.0001 (1)
O. Power, Control Over People and Things	2.85	4.61	14.48	.001 (21)
P. Security, Protecting My Way of Life Against Adverse Changes	5.31	8.68	50.58	.0001 (3)
Q. Accepting What Circumstances Bring	8.93	8.73	0.18	ns (8)
R. Doing the Best I can for Myself and Mine	7.30	9.71	20.73	.0001 (5)
S. Survival, Continued Existence	3.39	4.79	14.29	.001 (19)
T. Coping with Life's Problems as They Come	10.79	11.78	5.63	.01 (11)
U. Developing My Mind, Intellectual Endeavor	10.59	13.00	24.32	.0001 (7)

Note: A multivariate analysis of variance yielded a highly significant overall
F-ratio. The rank order of each variable's weighting on the discriminant function defined by all the variables is indicated in parentheses.

TABLE 6.14

MEAN COMPARISONS OF MALE RELIGIOUS (N = 135) AND LAY (N = 105) GROUPS ON THE MODIFIED ACTIVITIES INDEX

VARIABLES	PRESENT BEHAVIOR				SELF-IDEAL				INSTITUTIONAL-IDEAL			
	Rel.	Lay	F	p value and rank	Rel.	Lay	F	p value and rank	Rel.	Lay	F	p value and rank
Abasement	4.89	4.71	0.02	ns (16)	6.22	4.89	29.60	.0001 (5)	6.02	3.66	11.76	.0001 (4)
Achievement	5.44	5.72	0.34	ns (21)	6.37	6.71	0.12	ns (15)	5.79	6.00	40.24	ns (9)
Adaptability	5.00	5.13	2.54	ns (3)	7.79	6.35	34.14	.0001 (17)	8.88	5.20	19.42	.0001 (16)
Affiliation	5.97	5.99	0.09	ns (25)	5.62	6.15	3.83	ns (10)	2.89	3.42	6.30	.01 (6)
Aggression	3.66	4.30	0.34	ns (13)	2.33	2.83	1.14	ns (27)	0.85	1.16	1.06	ns (19)
Change	4.42	5.66	31.07	.0001 (1)	3.15	4.05	12.92	.001 (7)	1.96	1.48	5.87	.01 (24)
Planfulness	4.80	4.71	0.01	ns (27)	7.21	7.03	0.23	ns (21)	8.06	7.28	17.74	.0001 (21)
Counteraction	5.78	6.46	3.40	ns (17)	7.83	7.63	2.73	ns (11)	7.62	7.00	14.11	.001 (10)
Deference	7.25	6.97	0.09	ns (14)	7.36	6.31	14.15	.001 (20)	7.55	5.88	53.25	.0001 (13)
Dominance	4.58	4.47	2.58	ns (8)	4.91	4.84	1.62	ns (19)	3.08	2.84	3.64	.05 (17)
Ego Achievement	3.45	3.15	0.69	ns (24)	6.32	5.32	11.51	.001 (28)	5.28	4.93	3.59	.05 (15)
Emotionality	4.45	4.40	0.06	ns (29)	2.80	3.40	6.91	.008 (25)	1.32	1.28	0.01	ns (14)
Energy	6.10	6.39	0.42	ns (19)	6.31	6.02	2.56	ns (4)	5.64	3.79	65.29	.0001 (2)
Exhibition	3.43	3.46	0.03	ns (26)	3.46	3.58	0.51	ns (9)	1.89	2.27	1.68	ns (11)
Fantasied Achievement	4.00	4.56	0.49	ns (10)	2.15	3.66	22.16	.0001 (13)	1.22	1.73	7.48	.006 (18)
Harm Avoidance	4.76	4.16	0.91	ns (28)	2.63	3.36	11.91	.001 (8)	2.96	2.20	14.42	.001 (29)

TABLE 6.14 (continued)

VARIABLES	PRESENT BEHAVIOR				SELF-IDEAL				INSTITUTIONAL-IDEAL			
	Rel.	Lay	F	p value and rank	Rel.	Lay	F	p value and rank	Rel.	Lay	F	p value and rank
Humanities and Social Sciences	5.72	4.95	6.37	.01 (4)	7.07	5.79	22.77	.0001 (2)	5.22	6.91	10.48	.001 (27)
Impulsiveness	4.77	5.21	1.57	ns (22)	2.82	3.50	6.13	.01 (14)	1.04	1.20	1.08	ns (25)
Narcissism	3.73	4.52	4.73	.03 (15)	1.32	2.76	25.32	.0001 (24)	0.44	0.91	11.59	.001 (23)
Nurturance	6.34	5.62	4.17	.04 (7)	8.02	6.52	26.16	.0001 (3)	7.77	4.58	112.88	.0001 (3)
Objectivity	9.33	8.86	9.79	.002 (12)	8.17	7.03	18.18	.0001 (16)	8.08	4.75	100.71	.0001 (5)
Order	3.45	4.23	7.21	.007 (5)	4.68	5.90	11.52	.001 (6)	5.07	3.71	18.28	.0001 (26)
Play	4.81	5.40	0.94	ns (18)	2.74	3.35	20.32	.0001 (23)	0.64	1.00	10.47	.001 (20)
Practicalness	2.86	3.78	9.27	.002 (11)	4.42	5.39	6.41	.01 (18)	3.10	4.02	5.22	.02 (7)
Reflectiveness	6.27	5.97	2.46	ns (9)	5.68	5.48	0.96	ns (22)	4.39	4.44	0.46	ns (22)
Natural Science	2.71	4.23	13.84	.001 (2)	3.45	5.12	8.76	.003 (1)	1.58	5.88	116.42	.0001 (1)
Sensuality	3.61	4.24	4.12	.04 (20)	1.68	2.56	11.61	.001 (29)	0.27	0.55	6.78	.009 (28)
Succorance	6.62	5.74	16.99	.0001 (6)	6.22	5.29	14.67	.001 (26)	6.31	3.97	98.82	.0001 (8)
Understanding	5.45	5.49	0.45	ns (23)	6.28	6.17	2.70	ns (12)	4.94	5.95	1.30	ns (12)

Note: Multivariate analyses of variance were performed on the Present Behavior, Self-Ideal, and Institutional-Ideal forms of the test separately, with a highly-significant overall F-ratio in each case. Discriminant function analysis was also performed for each form separately. The rank order of each variable's weighting on this function is indicated in parentheses.

TABLE 6.15

MEAN COMPARISONS OF MALE RELIGIOUS (N = 135) AND LAY (N = 105) GROUPS ON SCALES CONCERNING RELIGIOUS LIFE (FROM THE MODIFIED ACTIVITIES INDEX)

VARIABLES	Present Behavior				Self-Ideal				Institutional-Ideal			
	Rel.	Lay	F	p value and rank	Rel.	Lay	F	p value and rank	Rel.	Lay	F	p value and rank
Chastity	6.74	5.82	9.96	.001 (1)	5.11	5.08	0.21	ns (6)	5.82	2.38	4.12	.0001 (4)
Mortification	1.77	1.51	2.26	ns (2)	1.91	1.47	8.74	.003 (3)	2.39	0.90	95.80	.0001 (2)
Obedience	6.41	5.81	0.05	ns (5)	5.94	5.20	3.92	.04 (5)	7.07	5.36	46.00	.0001 (6)
Piety	1.93	1.54	1.23	ns (6)	2.90	2.01	23.81	.0001 (2)	3.80	3.05	26.33	.0001 (5)
Poverty	5.30	4.59	4.08	.04 (3)	5.26	4.05	28.67	.0001 (1)	7.41	3.13	336.03	.0001 (1)
Responsibility	5.08	4.99	0.03	ns (4)	5.41	4.89	13.62	.0003 (4)	5.45	4.83	20.03	.0001 (3)

Note: Multivariate analyses of variance were performed on the Present Behavior, Self-Ideal, and Institutional-Ideal forms of the test separately, with a highly-significant overall F ratio in each case. The rank order of each variable's weighting on a discriminant function defined by the variables in each form separately is indicated in parentheses.

TABLE 6.16
MEAN COMPARISONS OF MALE RELIGIOUS (N = 82)
AND LAY (N = 64) GROUPS
ON THE ROTTER INCOMPLETE SENTENCES BLANK

Variables	Rel.	Lay	F-ratio	p values and rank	
Needs					
Abasement	3.58	3.55	4.40	.03	(30)
Achievement	1.42	1.44	1.59	ns	(13)
Acquirement	1.40	1.51	16.07	.0001	(2)
Adaptability	4.37	4.15	0.01	ns	(11)
Affiliation	2.01	1.98	0.23	ns	(38)
Aggression	2.59	2.45	3.62	.05	(26)
Autonomy	2.22	2.21	0.01	ns	(29)
Change	1.53	1.55	6.49	.01	(31)
Counteraction	0.72	0.53	11.12	.001	(16)
Deference	1.40	1.46	5.01	.02	(8)
Dominance	2.75	2.81	1.96	ns	(6)
Emotionality	1.57	1.63	0.62	ns	(25)
Exhibition	1.53	1.58	3.10	ns	(22)
Harm Avoidance	1.81	2.09	47.41	.0001	(1)
Nurturance	1.82	1.67	3.52	ns	(17)
Order	1.55	1.53	0.05	ns	(32)
Play	1.78	1.92	7.12	.008	(7)
Recognition	1.96	1.97	.098	ns	(18)
Sex	1.56	1.75	6.73	.01	(3)
Succorance	2.69	2.59	0.39	ns	(5)
Understanding	1.62	1.58	0.59	ns	(10)
Emotional Styles					
Anxiety, overt	2.13	2.30	5.47	.02	(39)
Anxiety, covert	3.42	3.16	3.12	ns	(41)
Depression, overt	1.85	2.05	5.47	.02	(24)
Depression, covert	3.29	3.26	2.31	ns	(9)
Paranoid thinking	1.44	1.50	3.60	.05	(4)
Guilt, overt	1.76	1.73	0.04	ns	(27)
Guilt, covert	1.97	1.87	1.99	ns	(34)
Defenses					
Compensation	1.53	1.57	0.74	ns	(33)
Denial	2.01	2.06	0.36	ns	(28)
Displacement	3.08	2.97	0.42	ns	(19)
Identification	2.28	2.20	0.48	ns	(15)
Intellectualization	3.03	2.73	6.11	.01	(35)
Isolation	1.44	1.55	6.52	.01	(20)
Parentification	1.39	1.45	6.85	.009	(14)
Projection, supplm.	1.90	1.90	0.51	ns	(36)
Projection, complm.	2.33	2.35	2.64	ns	(12)
Reaction Formation	2.27	2.07	6.59	.01	(23)
Regression	2.30	2.62	5.25	.02	(40)
Repression	4.71	4.33	8.67	.003	(21)
Undoing	1.42	1.48	6.87	.009	(37)

Note: For each subject, scores on variables were translated into percentages of total score. Hence, the entries in this table are mean percentages. A multivariate analysis of variance yielded a highly significant overall F-ratio. The rank order of each variable's weighting on the discriminant function defined by all the variables is indicated in parentheses.

303

Table 6.17
MEAN COMPARISONS OF MALE RELIGIOUS (N=82)
AND LAY (N=64) GROUPS
ON THE THEMATIC APPERCEPTION TEST

Variables	Rel.	Lay	F-ratio	p values and rank	
Needs					
Abasement	2.57	2.49	15.23	.001	(26)
Achievement	1.52	1.54	0.44	ns	(18)
Acquirement	1.57	1.70	20.97	.0001	(6)
Adaptability	2.60	2.50	23.04	.001	(32)
Affiliation	1.52	1.64	1.49	ns	(13)
Aggression	2.34	2.23	8.58	.003	(41)
Autonomy	2.32	2.26	9.44	.002	(39)
Change	1.97	1.99	0.73	ns	(38)
Counteraction	1.47	1.43	1.92	ns	(34)
Deference	1.50	1.59	10.14	.001	(21)
Dominance	2.57	2.48	22.47	.0001	(27)
Emotionality	2.10	1.98	6.75	.01	(8)
Exhibition	1.62	1.70	10.91	.001	(31)
Harm Avoidance	2.05	2.12	8.05	.005	(5)
Nurturance	1.83	1.85	0.14	ns	(17)
Order	1.75	1.79	0.01	ns	(9)
Play	1.90	1.92	4.42	.03	(30)
Recognition	1.85	1.86	0.62	ns	(35)
Sex	1.69	1.76	9.85	.002	(15)
Succorance	2.20	2.23	8.73	.003	(10)
Understanding	1.60	1.63	1.34	ns	(40)
Emotional Styles					
Anxiety, overt	2.20	2.15	0.67	ns	(2)
Anxiety, covert	1.88	1.93	0.01	ns	(1)
Depression, overt	2.16	2.15	0.03	ns	(23)
Depression, covert	1.92	1.91	0.58	ns	(35)
Paranoid thinking	1.66	1.72	7.75	.006	(19)
Guilt, overt	1.55	1.64	11.77	.001	(37)
Guilt, covert	1.75	1.83	7.69	.006	(14)
Defenses					
Compensation	1.80	1.85	0.55	ns	(33)
Denial	2.25	2.23	0.09	ns	(20)
Displacement	2.60	2.50	12.58	.001	(22)
Identification	2.15	2.09	0.10	ns	(24)
Intellectualization	2.43	2.34	2.23	ns	(11)
Isolation	1.68	1.80	8.40	.004	(7)
Parentification	1.50	1.57	8.97	.003	(3)
Projection, supplm.	2.14	2.07	0.24	ns	(27)
Projection, complm.	2.53	2.45	2.16	ns	(12)
Reaction Formation	2.05	2.05	0.05	ns	(16)
Regression	2.42	2.39	0.52	ns	(28)
Repression	2.63	2.53	35.38	.0001	(4)
Undoing	1.57	1.66	10.48	.001	(36)

Note: For each subject, scores on variables were translated into percentages of total score. Hence, the entries in this table are mean percentages. A multivariate analysis of variance yielded a highly significant overall F-ratio. The rank order of each variable's weighting on the discriminant function defined by all the variables is indicated in parentheses.

TABLE 6.18

MEAN COMPARISONS OF MALE RELIGIOUS (N=82) AND LAY (N=64) GROUPS ON CONFLICTS

Conflicts	Tests	Rel.	Lay	F-ratio	p value and rank	
Trust vs. Mistrust	TAT	2.42	2.38	0.02	ns	(2)
	Rotter	1.52	1.57	6.37	.01	(6)
Autonomy vs. Shame	TAT	2.57	2.48	16.28	.0001	(1)
	Rotter	1.54	1.58	1.19	ns	(7)
Initiative vs. Guilt	TAT	1.83	1.88	2.71	ns	(5)
	Rotter	1.52	1.55	2.72	ns	(8)
Industry vs. Inferiority	TAT	2.61	2.53	11.70	.001	(7)
	Rotter	1.55	1.58	2.42	ns	(2)
Identity vs. Role Diffusion	TAT	2.59	2.50	10.98	.001	(8)
	Rotter	1.54	1.58	1.07	ns	(4)
Intimacy vs. Isolation	TAT	2.53	2.46	4.67	.03	(4)
	Rotter	1.55	1.58	2.42	ns	(5)
Generativity vs. Stagnation	TAT	1.84	1.94	7.21	.008	(3)
	Rotter	1.47	1.47	0.01	ns	(3)
Integrity vs. Despair	TAT	1.72	1.79	3.63	.05	(6)
	Rotter	1.41	1.48	6.67	.01	(1)

Note: For each subject, scores on variables were translated into percentages of total score. Hence, the entries in this table are mean percentages. A multivariate analysis of variance was performed on each test separately and yielded highly significant F-ratios. The rank order of each variable's weighting on the discriminant function defined by all the variables on that test is indicated in parentheses.

TABLE 7.1

DATA MATCHED FOR THE COMPARISON BETWEEN THE INDEX OF VOCATIONAL MATURITY (IVM) AND THE INDEX OF DEVELOPMENTAL MATURITY (IDM)

Case No.	IVM	IDM	Case No.	IVM	IDM	Case No.	IVM	IDM
1	.86	III	31	—.11	I	61	—.42	II
2	.86	III	32	—.12	III	62	—.42	II
3	.79	III	33	—.12	II	63	—.44	II
4	.76	II	34	—.13	II	64	—.48	II
5	.64	I	35	—.14	II	65	—.48	I
6	.44	I	36	—.15	I	66	—.51	II
7	.29	III	37	—.20	II	67	—.54	II
8	.25	II	38	—.21	II	68	—.60	II
9	.25	III	39	—.21	II	69	—.62	I
10	.23	II	40	—.22	II	70	—.62	II
11	.22	III	41	—.22	II	71	—.68	II
12	.22	II	42	—.22	II	72	—.68	I
13	.20	III	43	—.24	II	73	—.69	II
14	.19	III	44	—.24	II	74	—.69	I
15	.18	III	45	—.26	II	75	—.70	I
16	.16	III	46	—.26	II	76	—.71	I
17	.16	III	47	—.27	II	77	—.73	I
18	.12	II	48	—.30	II	78	—.74	I
19	.10	III	49	—.32	II	79	—.74	II
20	.09	III	50	—.32	II	80	—.77	I
21	.06	III	51	—.33	II	81	—.77	III
22	.03	III	52	—.33	II	82	—.78	II
23	—.02	II	53	—.33	II	83	—.80	I
24	—.03	I	54	—.34	II	84	—.81	II
25	—.04	II	55	—.35	II	85	—.84	II
26	—.07	I	56	—.36	II	86	—.87	I
27	—.08	II	57	—.39	II	87	—.91	I
28	—.069	IV	58	—.41	III	88	—.94	I
29	—.10	II	59	—.41	II	89	—1.03	I
30	—.10	III	60	—.41	II	90	—1.35	I
						91	—1.40	I

TABLE 7.2

COMPARISON OF THE INDEX OF VOCATIONAL MATURITY
WITH THE INDEX OF DEVELOPMENTAL MATURITY
(N=91; p < .0001)

Degree of
Vocational Maturity

		Low	High	
Degree of Developmental Maturity	High	FN .055 (5)	VP .165 (15)	BR= .220
	Low	VN .703 (64)	FP .077 (7)	1-BR= .780

1-SR= .758   SR= .242

BR = Base Rate
SR = Selection Ratio
FN = False negative: 5 subjects
VP = Valid positive: 15 subjects
VN = Valid negative: 64 subjects
FP = False positive: 7 subjects

(According to Wiggins, 1973, pp. 240-257.)

N. B. The criterion standard was obtained from the percentages of
degrees III and IV (« high » degrees) of Developmental Maturity
present in the sample of 91 subjects. This criterion standard
was 22% (BR). The cut off of the « predictor » (SR) for the
degrees of Vocational Maturity was set at score O of Table 7.1,
which corresponds to 24% of the sample of 91 subjects. Scores
.01 and higher are considered as « high » degrees of vocational
maturity; scores —.01 and lower as « low » degrees.

TABLE 7.3

GROUP PERCENTAGES (FREQUENCIES) OF INCONSISTENCIES, CONFLICTS, CONSISTENCIES AND STATISTICAL SIGNIFICANCE OF THEIR DIFFERENCES

VARIABLES	Male Religious N=96 %	Male Religious N	Female Religious N=95 %	Female Religious N	Seminarians N=40 %	Seminarians N	Male Controls N=52 %	Male Controls N	Female Controls N=50 %	Female Controls N	R.Males vs. R.Fem.	R.Males vs. M.Cont.	R.Fem. vs. F.Cont.	R.Males vs. Sems.	Sems. vs. M.Cont.
INCONSISTENCIES															
Dissonant:															
Abasement	75	(72)	74	(70)	75	(30)	63	(33)	82	(41)	ns*	.07	ns	ns	ns
Aggression	56	(54)	57	(54)	52	(21)	52	(27)	66	(32)	ns	ns	ns	ns	ns
Chastity	2	(2)	8	(8)	—	(0)	4	(2)	2	(1)	ns	ns	ns	ns	ns
Defendence	65	(62)	58	(55)	80	(32)	73	(38)	82	(41)	ns	ns	.003	.04	ns
Exhibition	1	(1)	2	(2)	—	(0)	6	(3)	—	(0)	ns	ns	ns	ns	ns
Harm-Avoidance	13	(13)	7	(7)	10	(4)	31	(16)	8	(4)	ns	.004	ns	ns	.008
Succorance	37	(36)	41	(39)	35	(14)	46	(24)	64	(32)	ns	ns	.004	ns	ns
Neutral:															
Achievement	—	(0)	—	(0)	—	(0)	—	(0)	—	(0)	ns	ns	ns	ns	ns
Affiliation	11	(11)	16	(15)	5	(2)	10	(5)	—	(0)	ns	ns	.001	ns	ns
Counteraction	1	(1)	6	(6)	2	(1)	2	(1)	2	(1)	ns	ns	ns	ns	ns
Dominance	62	(60)	76	(72)	87	(35)	77	(40)	78	(39)	.02	.03	ns	.002	ns
Nurturance	7	(7)	9	(9)	—	(0)	6	(3)	—	(0)	ns	ns	.02	ns	ns
Order	5	(5)	—	(0)	—	(0)	6	(3)	—	(0)	ns	ns	ns	ns	ns
Understanding	1	(1)	3	(3)	—	(00)	—	(0)	—	(0)	.002	ns	ns	ns	ns
CONFLICTS															
Dissonant:															
Abasement	21	(20)	19	(18)	22	(9)	29	(15)	14	(7)	ns	ns	ns	ns	ns
Aggression	18	(17)	17	(16)	7	(3)	25	(13)	2	(1)	ns	ns	.004	.05	.01
Chastity	6	(6)	20	(19)	12	(5)	13	(7)	26	(13)	.002	ns	ns	ns	ns

Defendence	35	(34)	37	(35)	20	(8)	19	(10)	18	(9)	ns	.09	.02	.04	.05
Exhibition	18	(17)	7	(7)	17	(7)	10	(5)	10	(5)	.01	ns	ns	ns	ns
Harm-Avoidance	29	(28)	54	(51)	40	(16)	25	(13)	50	(25)	.0002	ns	ns	ns	.06
Succorance	55	(53)	54	(51)	35	(14)	25	(13)	32	(16)	ns	.0002	.01	.02	ns
Neutral:															
Achievement	31	(30)	14	(13)	32	(13)	27	(14)	20	(10)	.002	ns	ns	ns	ns
Affiliation	28	(27)	30	(29)	30	(12)	44	(23)	26	(13)	ns	.04	ns	ns	ns
Counteraction	33	(32)	26	(25)	30	(12)	54	(28)	40	(20)	ns	.01	.04	ns	.02
Dominance	18	(17)	16	(15)	6	(2)	17	(9)	6	(3)	ns	ns	.04	.02	.05
Nurturance	36	(35)	26	(25)	37	(15)	21	(11)	38	(19)	.07	.04	.07	ns	.04
Order	12	(12)	19	(18)	22	(9)	13	(7)	12	(6)	ns	ns	ns	.01	ns
Understanding	24	(23)	12	(11)	25	(10)	17	(9)	12	(6)	.02	ns	ns	ns	ns
DEFENSIVE CONSISTENCIES															
Dissonant:															
Abasement	—	(0)	2	(2)	—	(0)	—	(0)	—	(0)	ns	ns	ns	ns	ns
Aggression	1	(1)	1	(1)	—	(0)	2	(1)	—	(0)	ns	ns	ns	ns	ns
Chastity	23	(22)	9	(9)	10	(4)	—	(0)	2	(1)	.004	.009	ns	.04	ns
Deference	—	(0)	5	(5)	—	(0)	—	(0)	—	(0)	ns	ns	ns	ns	ns
Exhibition	2	(2)	1	(1)	—	(0)	4	(2)	—	(0)	ns	ns	ns	ns	ns
Harm-Avoidance	4	(4)	3	(3)	5	(2)	6	(3)	6	(3)	ns	ns	ns	ns	ns
Succorance	5	(5)	—	(0)	7	(3)	2	(1)	—	(0)	ns	ns	ns	ns	ns

TABLE 7.3 (continued)
GROUP PERCENTAGES (FREQUENCIES) OF INCONSISTENCIES, CONFLICTS, CONSISTENCIES AND STATISTICAL SIGNIFICANCE OF THEIR DIFFERENCES

VARIABLES	Male Religious N=96		Female Religious N=95		Semi-narians N=40		Male Controls N=52		Female Controls N=50		R.Males vs. R.Fem.	R.Males vs. M.Cont.	R.Fem. vs. F.Cont.	R.Males vs. Sems.	Sems. vs. M.Cont.
Neutral:															
Achievement	59	(57)	77	(73)	57	(23)	69	(36)	76	(38)	.004	ns	ns	ns	ns
Affiliation	54	(52)	46	(44)	40	(16)	40	(21)	56	(28)	ns	.05	ns	.07	ns
Counteraction	68	(65)	64	(61)	65	(26)	44	(23)	58	(29)	ns	.002	ns	ns	.02
Dominance	11	(11)	50	(48)	17	(7)	6	(3)	66	(33)	.0001	ns	.03	ns	.05
Nurturance	47	(45)	44	(42)	45	(18)	52	(27)	46	(23)	ns	ns	ns	ns	ns
Order	76	(73)	65	(62)	57	(23)	75	(39)	76	(38)	.05	ns	ns	.01	.03
Understanding	55	(53)	72	(68)	65	(26)	75	(39)	64	(32)	.007	.009	ns	ns	ns
CONSISTEN-CIES															
Dissonant:															
Abasement	—	(0)	3	(3)	—	(0)	2	(1)	—	(0)	ns	ns	ns	ns	ns
Aggression	10	(10)	18	(17)	20	(8)	17	(9)	26	(13)	.06	ns	ns	ns	ns
Chastity	62	(60)	47	(45)	70	(28)	77	(40)	58	(29)	.02	.03	ns	ns	ns
Defendence	—	(0)	1	(1)	—	(0)	1	(1)	—	(0)	ns	ns	ns	ns	ns
Exhibition	75	(72)	85	(81)	80	(32)	77	(40)	90	(45)	.04	ns	ns	ns	ns
Harm-Avoidance	47	(44)	24	(23)	47	(19)	31	(16)	24	(12)	.0003	.02	ns	ns	.06
Succorance	—	(0)	2	(2)	12	(5)	8	(4)	2	(1)	ns	ns	ns	.001	ns
Neutral:															
Achievement	—		—		—		—		—		ns	ns	ns	ns	ns
Affiliation	—		—		—		—		—		ns	ns	ns	ns	ns
Counteraction	—		—		—		—		—		ns	ns	ns	ns	ns
Dominance	—		—		—		—		—		ns	ns	ns	ns	ns
Nurturance	—		—		—		—		—		ns	ns	ns	ns	ns
Order	16	(15)	6	(6)	15	(6)	15	(8)	24	(12)	.01	ns	.0007	.01	ns
Understanding	—		—		—		—		—		ns	ns	ns	ns	ns

ns = not significant.

TABLE 9.1

MEAN SCORES OF VALUES (GGLI) FOR SEMINARIANS, RELIGIOUS DROPOUTS AND NON-DROPOUTS, AND CONTROLS

VARIABLES	Seminarians DO (N=21)	Seminarians NDO (N=19)	Male Religious DO (N=57)	Male Religious NDO (N=39)	Female Religious DO (N=77)	Female Religious NDO (N=18)	Male Controls (N=52)	Female Controls (N=50)
Dissonant:								
1. Self-discipline; overcoming my irrational and sensuous desires	11.81	13.00	12.05	12.57	11.94	11.11	11.61	10.36
2. Living for the pleasure of the moment	2.90	1.26	1.63	1.28	1.84	1.41	3.77	3.30
3. Getting as many deep and lasting pleasures out of life as I can	6.48	6.89	7.29	5.89	4.85	5.52	7.69	8.76
4. Promoting the most deep and lasting pleasures for the greatest number of people	11.85	12.26	12.37	12.34	12.47	12.41	10.98	13.16
5. Making a place for myself; getting ahead	5.90	6.15	4.25	3.71	3.57	3.47	9.52	5.84
6. Power; control over people and things	2.57	3.31	3.24	1.42	1.35	.94	4.62	1.00
7. Security; protecting my way of life against adverse changes	7.28	5.15	5.24	4.76	5.28	4.47	8.58	6.90
Neutral:								
8. Serving God; doing God's Will	17.33	18.00	18.89	18.81	19.10	18.82	13.63	13.88
9. Achieving personal immortality in heaven	13.95	13.21	14.41	14.34	13.48	13.11	12.71	9.28
10. Self-sacrifice for the sake of a better world	12.04	13.42	14.41	15.60	14.71	14.52	10.33	10.20
11. Doing my duty	10.47	10.47	12.31	13.00	11.50	12.88	10.38	8.20
12. Peace of mind, contentment, stillness of spirit	12.09	8.78	12.65	12.15	12.21	11.82	11.85	12.46
13. Serving the community of which I am a part	11.47	13.36	12.79	14.26	13.58	14.82	10.15	10.40
14. Having fine relations with others	12.85	12.94	12.68	11.76	11.55	10.70	12.00	13.22
15. Self-development, becoming a real, genuine person	15.42	14.47	14.12	15.68	14.70	15.82	14.11	16.64
16. Finding my place in life and accepting it	10.19	11.78	10.01	9.73	12.15	12.41	10.15	9.84
17. Being able to «take it»; brave and uncomplaining acceptance of what circumstances bring	10.19	10.00	8.48	8.81	10.85	10.35	9.69	8.82
18. Realizing I cannot change the bad features of the world and doing the best I can for myself and those dear to me	9.28	9.36	7.50	8.07	8.97	8.00	9.23	10.38
19. Survival; continued existence	4.90	3.21	3.34	3.34	3.48	2.94	4.54	3.05
20. Handling the specific problems of life as they arise	10.00	11.15	11.03	10.42	11.66	11.76	11.83	11.76
21. Developing my mind so that I am knowledgeable and effective in intellectual endeavor	10.14	11.47	10.43	10.39	10.07	11.52	12.10	11.72

TABLE 9.2

MEAN SCORES OF VOCATIONALLY RELEVANT ATTITUDES (MAI SI-II)

Attitudes	SEMINARIANS		FEMALE RELIGIOUS		MALE RELIGIOUS		FEMALE CONTROLS	MALE CONTROLS
	DO (N=21)	NDO (N=19)	DO (N=77)	NDO (N=18)	DO (N=57)	NDO (N=39)	(N=50)	(N=52)
Abasement	4.76	4.87	5.65	5.94	6.32	6.34	5.06	4.27
Adaptability (Defendence)	6.59	6.10	7.11	7.78	7.98	8.38	7.04	5.43
Aggression	1.35	1.34	1.12	1.41	1.45	1.64	1.09	1.86
Chastity	3.78	3.08	4.65	5.22	5.30	5.85	3.01	2.82
Exhibition	2.90	2.63	2.43	2.83	2.85	2.22	2.79	2.97
Harm Avoidance	3.55	2.21	3.99	3.44	3.00	2.94	3.51	2.84
Succorance	5.69	4.86	5.75	5.77	6.42	6.04	4.05	4.24
Mortification	1.60	1.32	1.30	1.92	2.15	2.15	1.08	1.11
Obedience	5.76	5.44	7.54	6.80	6.44	7.05	6.28	4.85
Piety	2.90	2.58	3.27	3.17	3.57	3.48	2.30	2.52
Poverty	4.00	3.26	5.50	5.75	6.44	6.63	4.30	3.58
Responsibility	4.93	4.32	4.80	5.06	5.23	5.44	5.10	4.53

TABLE 9.3

MEAN SCORES OF THE PREDICTABLE INTERNALIZING CAPACITY
FOR DROPOUTS (DO) AND NON-DROPOUTS (NDO)

VARIABLES	SEMINARIANS		FEMALE RELIGIOUS		MALE RELIGIOUS		MALE CONTROLS (N=52)	FEMALE CONTROLS (N=50)
	DO (N=21)	NDO (N=19)	DO (N=77)	NDO (N=18)	DO (N=57)	NDO (N=39)		
INCONSISTENCIES:								
Abasement	7.38	5.14	6.61	4.46	3.21	2.32	4.24	6.68
Aggression	7.00	5.00	7.61	7.90	6.50	4.08	3.77	4.93
Chastity	3.33	3.00	3.08	2.25	3.40	3.75	1.50	3.50
Defendence	.66	7.43	5.06	3.10	4.92	5.58	5.52	7.14
Exhibition	—	—	3.50	—	7.00	—	5.33	—
Harm Avoidance	3.50	8.00	4.60	5.33	1.75	1.50	1.75	3.66
Succorance	5.44	2.20	8.29	5.17	3.89	2.32	3.25	3.65
Achievement	3.91	3.81	3.82	3.20	3.26	3.54	3.11	—
Affiliation	2.77	5.11	4.88	5.18	4.03	3.40	3.28	—
Counteraction	7.00	9.76	6.70	7.23	11.72	11.65	10.45	5.67
Dominance	5.55	4.27	7.54	8.00	3.71	4.52	3.63	7.34
Nurturance	4.36	4.85	6.60	4.80	4.36	5.43	5.17	5.30
Order	5.35	4.10	4.36	5.30	4.20	3.13	3.45	4.95
Understanding	4.06	4.72	3.29	4.09	3.94	3.33	4.71	5.37
CONFLICTS:								
Abasement	2.40	3.50	6.07	5.00	3.06	2.67	3.07	3.71
Aggression	1.00	1.00	5.50	1.67	3.60	2.33	4.23	1.00
Chastity	1.66	7.50	2.53	3.00	4.43	2.00	2.71	2.61
Defendence	3.00	4.66	5.93	4.87	3.82	5.69	3.10	6.33
Exhibition	3.20	4.00	3.50	4.00	3.08	4.20	4.80	3.80
Harm Avoidance	3.50	3.87	4.51	4.08	2.61	2.25	2.07	3.80

Table 9.3 (continued)

| VARIABLES | SEMINARIANS | | FEMALE RELIGIOUS | | MALE RELIGIOUS | | MALE CONTROLS | FEMALE CONTROLS |
	DO (N=21)	NDO (N=19)	DO (N=77)	NDO (N=18)	DO (N=57)	NDO (N=39)	(N=52)	(N=50)
Succorance	5.00	4.57	4.86	4.80	4.35	3.00	3.85	3.43
Achievement	3.83	2.57	4.50	3.50	3.88	3.69	3.21	4.60
Affiliation	3.50	6.75	3.12	3.50	3.16	3.17	3.82	4.92
Counteraction	7.14	4.00	4.45	6.67	3.12	6.33	8.36	3.30
Dominance	—	1.00	4.75	3.67	3.20	3.57	3.83	3.33
Nurturance	7.71	9.12	5.48	3.00	6.17	4.91	5.90	6.84
Order	4.33	5.16	4.50	6.00	3.78	4.67	4.00	5.66
Understanding	5.00	3.85	4.62	4.00	4.92	4.64	2.88	6.50
CONSISTENCIES:								
Abasement	—	—	5.50	—	3.17	—	5.00	—
Aggression	1.50	1.33	2.33	2.40	3.17	1.33	1.78	2.38
Chastity	4.84	2.66	3.60	3.30	3.72	3.28	3.60	4.90
Defendence	—	—	5.00	—	—	—	6.00	—
Exhibition	6.25	8.22	6.75	6.43	7.15	7.14	5.65	7.88
Harm Avoidance	4.12	8.44	4.65	4.33	4.37	3.64	4.81	3.41
Succorance	4.00	4.66	9.00	2.00	—	3.50	3.50	2.00
Achievement	—	—	—	—	—	—	—	—
Affiliation	—	—	—	—	—	—	—	—
Counteraction	—	—	—	—	—	—	—	—
Dominance	—	—	—	—	—	—	—	—
Nurturance	—	—	—	—	—	—	—	—
Order	2.33	3.66	5.20	0.00	4.14	2.87	3.00	5.25
Understanding	—	—	—	—	5.00	—	—	—

TABLE 9.4

GROUP PERCENTAGES (FREQUENCIES) OF INCONSISTENCIES, CONFLICTS, AND CONSISTENCIES FOR DROPOUTS AND NONDROPOUTS

VARIABLES	Seminarians DO (N=21) %	f	NDO (N=19) %	f	Female Religious DO (N=77) %	f	NDO (N=18) %	f	Male Religious DO (N=57) %	f	NDO (N=39) %	f
INCONSISTENCIES												
Dissonant:												
Abasement	76	(16)	74	(14)	71	(55)	83	(15)	67	(38)	87	(34)
Aggression	48	(10)	58	(11)	57	(44)	56	(10)	53	(30)	62	(24)
Chastity	—	(0)	—	(0)	9	(7)	6	(1)	—	(0)	—	(0)
Defendence	76	(16)	84	(16)	57	(44)	61	(11)	63	(36)	67	(26)
Exhibition	—	(0)	—	(0)	3	(2)	—	(0)	—	(0)	—	(0)
Harm Avoidance	10	(2)	11	(2)	5	(4)	17	(3)	14	(8)	13	(5)
Succorance	43	(9)	26	(5)	42	(32)	39	(7)	33	(19)	43	(17)
Neutral:												
Achievement	—	(0)	—	(0)	—	(0)	—	(0)	—	(0)	—	(0)
Affiliation	—	(0)	11	(2)	19	(15)	—	(0)	12	(7)	10	(4)
Counteraction	—	(0)	5	(1)	8	(6)	—	(0)	—	(0)	—	(0)
Dominance	86	(18)	89	(17)	80	(60)	67	(12)	67	(38)	56	(22)
Nurturance	—	(0)	5	(1)	12	(9)	—	(0)	5	(3)	10	(4)
Order	—	(0)	5	(1)	—	(0)	—	(0)	7	(4)	3	(1)
Understanding	—		—	(0)	3	(2)	6	(1)	—	(0)	—	(0)
CONFLICTS												
Dissonant:												
Abasement	24	(5)	21	(4)	19	(15)	17	(3)	30	(17)	8	(3)
Aggression	10	(2)	5	(1)	17	(13)	17	(3)	23	(13)	10	(4)
Chastity	14	(3)	11	(2)	21	(16)	17	(3)	9	(5)	3	(1)
Defendence	24	(5)	16	(3)	35	(27)	44	(8)	37	(21)	33	(13)

Table 9.4 (continued)

VARIABLES	Seminarians DO (N=21) %	f	Seminarians NDO (N=19) %	f	Female Religious DO (N=77) %	f	Female Religious NDO (N=18) %	f	Male Religious DO (N=57) %	f	Male Religious NDO (N=39) %	f
Exhibition	24	(5)	11	(2)	8	(6)	6	(1)	21	(12)	13	(5)
Harm Avoidance	38	(8)	42	(8)	52	(40)	61	(11)	23	(13)	38	(15)
Succorance	33	(7)	37	(7)	53	(41)	56	(10)	63	(36)	44	(17)
Neutral:												
Achievement	29	(6)	37	(7)	12	(9)	22	(4)	28	(16)	36	(14)
Affiliation	38	(8)	21	(4)	32	(25)	22	(4)	26	(15)	31	(12)
Counteraction	33	(7)	26	(5)	29	(22)	17	(3)	33	(19)	33	(13)
Dominance	5	(1)	5	(1)	16	(12)	17	(3)	17	(10)	18	(7)
Nurturance	33	(7)	42	(8)	29	(22)	17	(3)	42	(24)	28	(11)
Order	14	(3)	32	(6)	19	(15)	17	(3)	16	(9)	8	(3)
Understanding	14	(3)	37	(7)	10	(8)	17	(3)	19	(12)	28	(11)
DEFENSIVE CONSISTENCIES												
Dissonant:												
Abasement	—	(0)	—	(0)	3	(2)	—	(0)	—	(0)	—	(0)
Aggression	—	(0)	—	(0)	1	(1)	—	(0)	—	(0)	3	(1)
Chastity	14	(3)	5	(1)	0	(7)	11	(2)	18	(10)	31	(12)
Defendence	—	(0)	—	(0)	6	(5)	—	(0)	—	(0)	—	(0)
Exhibition	—	(0)	—	(0)	1	(1)	—	(0)	—	(0)	—	(0)
Harm Avoidance	5	(1)	5	(1)	3	(2)	6	(1)	4	(2)	5	(2)
Succorance	14	(3)	—	(0)	—	(0)	6	(1)	—	(0)	13	(5)
Neutral:												
Achievement	57	(12)	58	(11)	81	(62)	61	(11)	61	(35)	56	(22)
Affiliation	43	(9)	37	(7)	43	(33)	61	(11)	58	(33)	49	(19)

TABLE 9.4 (continued)

Counteraction	62 (13)	68 (13)	61 (47)	78 (14)	68 (39)	67 (26)
Dominance	29 (6)	5 (1)	52 (40)	44 (8)	10 (6)	13 (5)
Nurturance	52 (11)	37 (7)	42 (32)	56 (10)	47 (27)	46 (18)
Order	67 (14)	47 (9)	68 (52)	56 (10)	77 (44)	74 (29)
Understanding	71 (15)	58 (11)	73 (56)	67 (12)	56 (32)	54 (21)
CONSISTENCIES						
Dissonant:						
Abasement	— (0)	— (0)	4 (3)	— (0)	— (0)	— (0)
Aggression	10 (2)	32 (6)	16 (12)	28 (5)	7 (4)	15 (6)
Chastity	62 (13)	79 (15)	48 (37)	56 (10)	61 (35)	64 (25)
Defendence	— (0)	— (0)	1 (1)	— (0)	— (0)	— (0)
Exhibition	71 (15)	89 (17)	87 (67)	78 (0)	67 (38)	87 (34)
Harm Avoidance	48 (10)	47 (9)	26 (20)	17 (14)	53 (30)	36 (14)
Succorance	10 (2)	16 (3)	1 (1)	6 (3)	— (0)	— (0)
Neutral:						
Achievement	— (0)	— (0)	— (0)	— (0)	— (0)	— (0)
Affiliation	— (0)	— (0)	— (0)	— (0)	— (0)	— (0)
Counteraction	— (0)	— (0)	— (0)	— (0)	— (0)	— (0)
Dominance	— (0)	— (0)	— (0)	— (0)	— (0)	— (0)
Nurturance	— (0)	— (0)	— (0)	— (0)	— (0)	— (0)
Order	14 (3)	16 (3)	1 (5)	6 (1)	14 (8)	18 (7)
Understanding	— (0)	— (0)	— (0)	— (0)	— (0)	— (0)

TABLE 9.5
MEAN SCORES OF VALUES (GGLI) FOR EARLY AND LATE DROPOUT RELIGIOUS MALES AND FEMALES
Second Testing

VALUES	MALE RELIGIOUS Early Dropouts (N=25)	MALE RELIGIOUS Late Dropouts (N=9)	FEMALE RELIGIOUS Early Dropouts (N=32)	FEMALE RELIGIOUS Late Dropouts (N=17)
Dissonant:				
1. Self-discipline; overcoming my irrational and sensuous desires	9.84	11.56	11.53	12.88
2. Living for the pleasure of the moment	2.04	.89	3.22	3.59
3. Getting as many deep and lasting pleasures out of life as I can	6.68	5.78	4.60	4.88
4. Promoting the most deep and lasting pleasures for the greatest number of people	12.88	13.33	12.44	11.12
5. Making a place for myself; getting ahead	3.48	3.33	4.28	3.53
6. Power; control over people and things	2.48	2.89	1.44	1.41
7. Security; protecting my way of life against adverse changes	4.16	4.67	3.87	3.71
Neutral:				
8. Serving God; doing God's Will	18.16	20.00	18.94	19.35
9. Achieving personal immortality in heaven	11.28	17.44	11.12	12.18
10. Self-sacrifice for the sake of a better world	15.68	16.77	15.25	13.35
11. Doing my duty	13.44	13.33	10.56	10.65
12. Peace of mind, contentment, stillness of spirit	8.52	10.11	11.19	10.82
13. Serving the community of which I am a part	16.60	15.88	16.03	16.53
14. Having fine relations with others	12.10	11.77	13.66	12.47
15. Self-development, becoming a real, genuine person,	14.48	12.11	15.37	15.12
16. Finding my place in life and accepting it	10.56	12.11	11.09	11.47
17. Being able to « take it »; brave and uncomplaining acceptance of what circumstances bring	7.64	6.44	10.19	10.29
18. Realizing I cannot change the bad features of the world and doing the best I can for myself and those dear to me	7.64	7.33	9.16	8.41
19. Survival; continued existence	3.48	2.88	2.75	3.53
20. Handling the specific problems of life as they arise	10.76	11.22	13.56	13.94
21. Developing my mind so that I am knowledgeable and effective in intellectual endeavor	10.32	10.11	9.78	10.53

TABLE 9.6

MEAN SCORES OF VOCATIONALLY RELEVANT ATTITUDES (MAI-SI-II) FOR EARLY AND LATE DROPOUT RELIGIOUS MALES AND FEMALES

Second Testing

ATTITUDES	MALE RELIGIOUS		FEMALE RELIGIOUS	
	Early Dropouts (N = 25)	Late Dropouts (N = 9)	Early Dropouts (N = 32)	Late Dropouts (N = 17)
Abasement	6.36	5.61	5.30	5.35
Adaptability (Defendence)	8.12	8.72	7.42	8.03
Aggression	1.72	.94	1.03	1.23
Chastity	5.76	7.11	5.36	5.29
Exhibition	2.58	1.89	2.31	2.02
Harm Avoidance	2.42	2.78	3.95	3.82
Succorance	5.48	5.39	4.87	5.03
Mortification	2.54	3.33	1.43	1.32
Obedience	5.80	8.00	6.33	6.94
Piety	3.14	3.61	2.78	3.20
Poverty	6.50	7.55	5.73	6.05
Responsibility	5.86	5.67	5.12	5.53

TABLE 9.7
MEAN SCORES OF VALUES (GGLI) FOR EARLY AND LATE DROPOUT RELIGIOUS MALES AND FEMALES

First Testing

VALUES	Male Religious Early Dropouts (N=25)	Male Religious Late Dropouts (N=9)	Female Religious Early Dropouts (N=32)	Female Religious Late Dropouts (N=17)
Dissonant:				
1. Self-discipline; overcoming my irrational and sensuous desires	12.76	10.50	12.00	12.35
2. Living for the pleasure of the moment	1.64	1.44	2.00	2.29
3. Getting as many deep and lasting pleasures out of life as I can	7.64	4.89	4.59	4.82
4. Promoting the most deep and lasting pleasures for the greatest number of people	11.72	12.44	12.47	12.23
5. Making a place for myself; getting ahead	3.96	3.22	3.28	3.71
6. Power; control over people and things	3.08	3.00	.91	1.47
7. Security; protecting my way of life against adverse changes	4.68	6.11	4.65	4.82
Neutral:				
8. Serving God; doing God's Will	18.92	19.11	18.97	18.76
9. Achieving personal immortality in heaven	15.64	14.89	14.00	13.18
10. Self-sacrifice for the sake of a better world	13.84	15.56	14.68	14.47
11. Doing my duty	13.40	11.78	11.37	12.59
12. Peace of mind, contentment, stillness of spirit	12.48	13.78	11.81	11.82
13. Serving the community of which I am a part	13.16	12.11	13.44	13.41
14. Having fine relations with others	13.00	12.00	12.31	10.94
15. Self-development, becoming a real, genuine person,	14.32	13.89	14.53	15.00
16. Finding my place in life and accepting it	9.92	10.22	12.91	11.35
17. Being able to «take it»; brave and uncomplaining acceptance of what circumstances bring	8.64	9.00	11.59	10.53
18. Realizing I cannot change the bad features of the world and doing the best I can for myself and those dear to me	6.96	4.22	9.12	8.29
19. Survival; continued existence	3.04	4.11	3.47	3.76
20. Handling the specific problems of life as they arise	10.68	11.88	11.69	12.65
21. Developing my mind so that I am knowledgeable and effective in intellectual endeavor	10.36	12.44	9.06	11.29

TABLE 9.8

MEAN SCORES OF VOCATIONALLY RELEVANT ATTITUDES (MAI SI-II) FOR EARLY AND LATE DROPOUT RELIGIOUS MALES AND FEMALES

First Testing

ATTITUDES	MALE RELIGIOUS		FEMALE RELIGIOUS	
	Early Dropouts (N = 25)	Late Dropouts (N = 9)	Early Dropouts (N = 32)	Late Dropouts (N = 17)
Abasement	6.34	5.83	5.59	5.62
Adaptability (Defendence)	8.28	7.27	6.96	7.38
Aggression	.96	1.00	1.18	1.00
Chastity	5.04	5.72	4.57	4.38
Exhibition	2.70	2.89	2.45	2.26
Harm Avoidance	2.42	3.27	3.81	3.76
Succorance	6.44	6.89	5.86	5.18
Mortification	1.92	2.16	1.15	1.35
Obedience	6.24	7.83	7.42	7.29
Piety	3.54	3.94	3.19	3.53
Poverty	6.42	6.50	5.40	5.38
Responsibility	5.36	5.28	4.65	4.29

B. INSTRUMENTS

MODIFIED ACTIVITIES INDEX

Directions

This booklet contains a number of brief statements describing many different kinds of activities. You are asked to address yourself to each of the statements in three different ways.

Before beginning, print the information called for at the top of the special answer sheet: your name, the date, your age and sex, etc. Then read each statement and answer it in each of the three ways before going on to the next statement, following this procedure until you have finished all the statements.

The first way in which you should address yourself to a statement is to determine whether it is *true* or *false* as a description of your present behavior and activities, that is, of you as you actually are at this point in your life.

The second way in which you should address yourself to a statement is to determine whether it is *consistent with, inconsistent with,* or *irrelevant to* the ideals you hold for yourself.

The third way in which you should address yourself to a statement is to determine whether it is *consistent with, inconsistent with,* or *irrelevant to* the ideals of the educational institution in which you are functioning at present.

Recognize that in the first judgment you are not to consider what you would like to be, or what you ought to be if you take the institution's point of view, but rather what you are at this point in your life. In the second judgment, do not consider what you currently are, or what the institution would like you to be, but rather what the ideals are that you hold for yourself. In the third judgment, do not consider what you are, or what you would like to be, but rather what the ideals of the institution are for people like you. In making the second and third judgments, if you do not have a definite impression that a statement is positively expressive of or contrary to either an institution or a personal ideal, then you should answer *irrelevant*.

1. Taking the blame for something done by someone I like.
2. Setting difficult goals for myself.
3. Concealing a failure or humiliation from others.
4. Having other people let me alone.
5. Getting what is coming to me even if I have to fight for it.
6. Preferring not to think about the defects of a friend.
7. Being quite changeable in my likes and dislikes.
8. Scheduling time for work and play during the day.
9. Working twice as hard at a problem when it looks as if I don't know the answer.
10. Seeing someone make fun of a person who has been foolish.
11. Persuading a group to do something my way.
12. Having a nice room.
13. Being someone who crusades to improve the community.
14. Listening to music that makes me feel very sad.
15. Taking up a very active outdoor sport.
16. Keeping in the background when I'm with a group of wild, fun-loving, noisy people.
17. Toughening myself, going without an overcoat, seeing how long I can go without food or sleep, etc.
18. Giving exact time to spiritual duties.
19. Diving off the tower or high board at a pool.
20. Learning about the causes of some of our social and political problems.
21. Doing something crazy occasionally, just for the fun of it.
22. Imagining what I would do if I could live my life over again.
23. Feeding a stray dog or cat.
24. Eating only what is necessary.
25. Taking special precautions on Friday, the 13th.
26. Washing and polishing things like a car, silverware, or furniture.
27. Making my work go faster by thinking of the fun I can have after it's done.
28. Being good at typewriting, knitting, carpentry, or other practical skills.
29. Understanding myself better.
30. Feeling fulfilled in my present state of life.
31. Learning how to prepare slides of plant and animal tissue, and making my own studies with a microscope.
32. Holding something very soft and warm against my skin.
33. Belonging to a close group that expects me to bring my problems to them.
34. Concentrating intently on a problem.
35. Studying hard in order to gain self-fulfillment.
36. Suffering for a good cause or for someone I love.

326

37. Working for someone who will accept nothing less than the best that's in me.
38. Defending myself against criticism or blame.
39. Going to the park or beach with a crowd.
40. Shocking narrow minded people by saying and doing things of which they disapprove.
41. Having persistent thoughts about someone and feeling uncomfortable when he is not there.
42. Getting up and going to bed at the same time each day.
43. Planning a reading program for myself.
44. Returning to a task which I have previously failed.
45. Doing what most people tell me to do, to the best of my ability.
46. Having other people depend on me for ideas or opinions.
47. Keeping books overdue from the library.
48. Being an important social figure in a time of crisis.
49. Crying at a funeral, wedding, graduation, or similar ceremony.
50. Exerting myself to the utmost for something unusually important or enjoyable.
51. Wearing clothes that will attract a lot of attention.
52. Working until I'm exhausted, to see how much I can take.
53. Liking to spend time in private prayer.
54. Being careful to wear a raincoat and rubbers when it rains.
55. Studying the music of particular composers, such as Bach, Beethoven, etc.
56. Acting impulsively just to blow off steam.
57. Thinking about ways of changing my name to make it sound striking or different.
58. Discussing with younger people what they like to do and how they feel about things.
59. Making myself comfortable in my activities.
60. Waiting for a falling star, white horse, or some other sign of success before I make an important decision.
61. Keeping my bureau drawers, desk, etc., in perfect order.
62. Spending most of my extra money on pleasure.
63. Learning how to repair such things as the radio, sewing machine, or car.
64. Thinking about different kinds of unusual behavior, like insanity, drug addiction, crime, etc.
65. Reading and talking about the progress of my institution.
66. Studying wind conditions and changes in atmospheric pressure in order to better understand and predict the weather.
67. Eating after going to bed.
68. Working for someone who always tells me exactly what to do and how to do it.

69. Finding the meaning of unusual or rarely used words.
70. Commitment to studying something that may never be put to practical use.
71. Being polite or humble no matter what happens.
72. Setting higher standards for myself than anyone else would, and working hard to achieve them.
73. Admitting when I'm in the wrong.
74. Leading an active social life.
75. Doing something that might provoke criticism.
76. Disliking the exclusive company of friends.
77. Rearranging the furniture in the place where I live.
78. Putting off something I don't feel like doing, even though I know it has to be done.
79. Having to struggle hard for something I want.
70. Listening to a successful person tell about his experience.
81. Getting my friends to do what I want to do.
82. Keeping a commonly used appliance for your personal use.
83. Taking an active part in social and political reform.
84. Avoiding excitement or emotional tension.
85. Staying up all night when I'm doing something that interests me.
86. Speaking at a club or group meeting.
87. Imagining myself president of the United States.
88. Being casual in taking points for meditation.
89. Crossing streets only at the corner and with the light.
90. Listening to TV or radio programs about political and social problems.
91. Being in a situation that requires quick decision and action.
92. Pausing to look at myself in a mirror each time I pass one.
93. Helping to collect money for poor people.
94. Reading for entertainment whenever I have a chance.
95. Paying no attention to omens, signs, and other forms of superstition.
96. Keeping an accurate record of the money I spend.
97. Dropping out of a crowd that spends most of its time playing around or having parties.
98. Helping to direct a fund drive for the Red Cross, Community Chest, or other organizations.
99. Imagining life on other planets.
100. Defending my institution when criticized.
101. Reading articles which tell about new scientific developments, discoveries, or inventions.
102. Chewing on pencils, rubber bands, or paper clips.
103. Being a lone wolf, free of family and friends.

104. Spending my time thinking about and discussing complex problems.
105. Applying oneself conscientiously to studies.
106. Trying to figure out how I was to blame after getting into an argument with someone.
107. Competing with others for a prize or goal.
108. Being ready with an excuse or explanation when criticized.
109. Meeting a lot of people.
110. Arguing with an instructor or superior.
111. Desiring to embrace a friend.
112. Being generally consistent and unchanging in my behavior.
113. Going to a party where all the activities are planned.
114. Doing a job under pressure.
115. Going along with a decision made by a supervisor or leader rather than starting an argument.
116. Organizing groups to vote in a certain way in elections.
117. Using without permission small tools not in common use.
118. Living a life which is adventurous and dramatic.
119. Having someone for a friend who is very emotional.
120. Sleeping long hours every night in order to have lots of rest.
121. Playing music, dancing, or acting in a play before a large group.
122. Thinking about what I could do that would make me famous.
123. Reading books that have little to do with prayer and meditation.
124. Riding a fast and steep roller coaster.
125. Comparing the problems and conditions of today with those of various times in the past.
126. Doing whatever I'm in the mood to do.
127. Daydreaming about what I would do if I could live my life any way I wanted.
128. Comforting someone who is feeling low.
129. Sleeping as much as possible when it is permitted.
130. Avoiding things that might bring bad luck.
131. Arranging my clothes neatly before going to bed.
132. Getting as much fun as I can out of life, even if it means sometimes neglecting more serious things.
133. Learning how to make such things as furniture or clothing myself.
134. Trying to figure out why the people I know behave the way they do.
135. Envying friends who get married.
136. Doing experiments in physics, chemistry or biology in order to test a theory.
137. Sleeping in a very soft bed.
138. Seeing love stories in the movies.

139. Having someone help me out when I'm in trouble.
140. Working crossword puzzles, figuring out moves in checkers or chess, playing anagrams or scrabble, etc.
141. Studying hard in order to gain recognition.
142. Admitting defeat.
143. Taking examinations.
144. Being corrected when I'm doing something the wrong way.
145. Belonging to a social club.
146. Teasing someone who is too conceited.
147. Being impressed by the physical attractiveness of people.
148. Moving to a new neighborhood or city, living in a different country, etc.
149. Finishing something I've begun, even if it is no longer enjoyable.
150. Staying away from activities which I don't do well.
151. Following directions.
152. Being able to hypnotize people.
153. Keeping small gifts that have been given to you.
154. Playing an active part in community affairs.
155. Going on an emotional binge.
156. Walking instead of riding whenever I can.
157. Doing something that will create a stir.
158. Thinking about winning recognition and acclaim as a brilliant public figure.
159. Liking meetings, discussions, or readings about the apostleship of prayer.
160. Standing on the roof of a tall building.
161. Studying different types of government, such as the American, English, Russian, German, etc.
162. Doing things on the spur of the moment.
163. Having lots of time to take care of my hair, hands, face, clothing, etc.
164. Having people come to me with their problems.
165. Doing small, self-imposed penances.
166. Being especially careful the rest of the day if a black cat should cross my path.
167. Recopying notes or memoranda to make them neat.
168. Finishing some work even though it means missing a party or dance.
169. Working with mechanical appliances, household equipment, tools, electrical apparatus, etc.
170. Thinking about what the end of the world might be like.
171. Feeling sorry when members of the institution have small setbacks.
172. Studying the stars and planets and learning to identify them.

173. Listening to the rain fall on the roof, or the wind blow through the trees.
174. Knowing an older person who likes to give me guidance and direction.
175. Being a philosopher, scientist, or professor.
176. Indulging in studies that have not been assigned.
177. Having people laugh at my mistakes.
178. Working on tasks so difficult I can hardly do them.
179. Keeping my failures and mistakes to myself.
180. Going to parties where I'm expected to mix with the whole crowd.
181. Annoying people I don't like, just to see what they will do.
182. Eating between meals without permission.
183. Leading a well-ordered life with regular hours and an established routine.
184. Planning ahead so that I know every step of a project before I get to it.
185. Avoiding something at which I have once failed.
186. Turning over the leadership of a group to someone who is better for the job than I.
187. Being an official or leader.
188. Desiring to participate in parties.
189. Actively supporting a movement to correct a social evil.
190. Letting loose and having a good cry sometimes.
191. Taking frequent rest periods when working on any project.
192. Imagining situations in which I am a great hero.
193. Envying friends who have successful social lives.
194. Driving fast.
195. Talking about music, theater or other art forms, with people who are interested in them.
196. Controlling my emotions rather than expressing myself impulsively.
197. Catching a reflection of myself in a mirror or window.
198. Lending my things to other people.
199. Not keeping up with your study program.
200. Carrying a good luck charm like a rabbit's foot or a four-leaf clover.
201. Making my bed and putting things away every day before I leave the house.
202. Going to a party or dance with a lively crowd.
203. Managing a store or business enterprise.
204. Seeking to explain the behavior of people who are emotionally disturbed.
205. Not taking care of clothes.

206. Going to scientific exhibits.
207. Chewing or popping gum.
208. Reading novels and magazine stories about love.
209. Having others offer their opinions when I have to make a decision.
210. Losing myself in a hard thought.
211. Being concerned with keeping study notes.
212. Accepting criticism without talking back.
213. Doing something very difficult in order to prove I can do it.
214. Pointing out someone else's mistakes when they point out mine.
215. Having lots of friends who come to stay with us for several days during the year.
216. Playing practical jokes.
217. Talking when you feel like it.
218. Doing things a different way every time I do them.
219. Keeping to a regular schedule, even if this sometimes means working when I don't really feel like it.
220. Quitting a project that seems too difficult for me.
221. Listening to older persons tell about how they did things when they were young.
222. Organizing a protest meeting.
223. Disliking public discussions about school matters.
224. Getting my friends to change their social, political, or religious beliefs.
225. Yelling with excitement at a ball game, horse race, or other public event.
226. Having something to do every minute of the day.
227. Speaking before a large group.
228. Imagining how it would feel to be famous.
229. Not following too closely the schedule for your personal activities.
230. Playing rough games in which someone might get hurt.
231. Finding out how different languages have developed, changed, and influenced one another.
232. Letting my reasoning be guided by my feelings.
233. Dressing carefully, being sure that the colors match and the various details are exactly right.
234. Taking care of youngsters.
235. To engage in personal investigation of topics covered in your studies.
236. Having a close friend who ignores or makes fun of supersitious beliefs.
237. Shining my shoes and brushing my clothes every day.

332

238. Giving up whatever I'm doing rather than miss a party or other opportunity for a good time.
239. Fixing light sockets, making curtains, painting things, etc., around the house.
240. Reading stories that try to show what people really think and feel inside themselves.
241. Loosely following the schedule for common activities.
242. Collecting data and attempting to arrive at general laws about the physical universe.
243. Sketching or painting.
244. Having people fuss over me when I'm sick.
245. Engaging in mental activity.
246. Making a fuss when I they seem to be taking advantage of me.
247. Choosing difficult tasks in preference to easy ones.
248. Apologizing when I've done something wrong.
249. Going to the park or beach only at times when no one else is likely to be there.
250. Questioning the decisions of people who are supposed to be authorities.
251. Eating my meals at the same hour each day.
252. Doing things according to my mood, without following any plan.
253. Doing something over again, just to get it right.
254. Disregarding a supervisor's directions when they seem foolish.
255. Talking some one into doing something I think ought to be done.
256. Trying to improve my community by persuading others to do certain things.
257. Being with people who seem always to be calm, unstirred, or placid.
258. Giving all of my energy to whatever I happen to be doing.
259. Being the center of attention at a party.
260. Setting myself tasks to strengthen my mind, body, and will power.
261. Skiing on steep slopes, climbing high mountains, or exploring narrow underground caves.
262. Learning more about the work of different painters and sculptors.
263. Speaking or acting spontaneously.
264. Imagining the kind of life I would have if I were born at a different time in a different place.
265. Talking over personal problems with someone who is feeling unhappy.
266. Going ahead with something important even though I've just accidentally walked under a ladder, broken a mirror, etc.
267. Keeping my room in perfect order.
268. Being with people who are always joking, laughing, and out for a good time.

269. Being treasurer or business manager for a club or organization.
270. Imagining what it will be like when rocket ships carry people through space.
271. Reading scientific theories about the origin of the earth and other planets.
272. Eating so much I can't take another bite.
273. Receiving advice from others.
274. Solving puzzles that involve numbers or figures.
275. Taking the part of a servant or waiter in a play.
276. Sacrificing everything else in order to achieve something outstanding.
277. Having my mistakes pointed out to me.
278. Going on a vacation to a place where there are lots of people.
279. Fighting for something I want, rather than trying to get it by asking.
280. Avoiding any kind of routine or regularity.
281. Organizing my work in order to use time efficiently.
282. Avoiding something because I'm not sure I'll be successful at it.
283. Carrying out orders from others with snap and enthusiasm.
284. Directing other people's work.
285. Seeing sad or melodramatic movies.
286. Avoiding things that require intense concentration.
287. Telling jokes or doing tricks to entertain others at a large gathering.
288. Pretending I am a famous movie star.
289. Swimming in rough, deep water.
290. Studying the development of English or American literature.
291. Being guided by my heart rather than by my head.
292. Making my handwriting decorative or unusual.
293. Taking care of someone who is ill.
294. Finding out which days are lucky for me, so I can hold off important things to do until then.
295. Having a special place for everything and seeing that each thing is in its place.
296. Doing something serious with my leisure time instead of just playing around with the crowd.
297. Learning how to raise attractive and healthy plants, flowers, vegetables, etc.
298. Thinking about the meaning of eternity.
299. Reading about how mathematics is used in developing scientific theories, such as explanations of how the planets move around the sun.
300. Walking along a dark street in the rain.
301. Having people talk to me about some personal problem of mine.

302. Following through in the development of a theory, even though it has no practical applications.
303. Telling other about the mistakes I have made and the sins I have committed.
304. Picking out some hard task for myself and doing it.
305. Concealing my mistakes from others whenever possible.
306. Inviting a lot of people home for a snack or party.
307. Proving that an instructor or superior is wrong.
308. Staying in the same circle of friends all the time.
309. Striving for precision and clarity in my speech and writing.
310. Giving up on a problem rather than doing it in a way that may be wrong.
311. Having friends who are superior to me in ability.
312. Influencing or controlling the actions of others.
313. Converting or changing the views of others.
314. Being unrestrained and open about my feelings and emotions.
315. Doing things that are fun but require lots of physical exertion.
316. Doing things which will attract attention to me.
317. Thinking about how to become the most important person.
318. Being extremely careful about sports involving some danger like sailing, hunting, or camping.
319. Reading editorials or feature articles on major social issues.
320. Making up my mind slowly, after considerable deliberation.
321. Trying out different ways of writing my name, to make it look unusual.
322. Providing companionship and personal care for a very old helpless person.
323. Going to a fortune-teller, palm reader or astrologer for advice on something important.
324. Keeping a calendar or notebook of the things I have done or plan to do.
325. Limiting my pleasures so that I can spend all of my time usefully.
326. Being efficient and successful in practical affairs.
327. Concentrating so hard on a work of art or music that I don't know what's going on around me.
328. Studying rock formations and learning how they developed.
329. Reading in the bathtub.
330. Reading about the love affairs of movie stars and other famous people.
331. Being with someone who always tries to be sympathetic and understanding.
332. Working out solutions to complicated problems, even though the answers may have no apparent, immediate usefulness.

MAI: MODIFIED ACTIVITIES INDEX

Scales, Symbols and Number of Their Constitutive Items

Symbols		Scales	No. of Items
Sc	1	Abasement	10
Sc	2	Achievement	10
Sc	3	Humility (as opposed to defendance and in-favoidance), Adaptability	10
Sc	4	Affiliation	10
Sc	5	Aggression	10
Sc	6	Change, novelty	10
Sc	7	Conjunctivity, planfulness	10
Sc	8	Counteraction	10
Sc	9	Deference	10
Sc	10	Dominance	10
Sc	11	Ego Achievement, striving for social action	9
Sc	12	Emotional Expressiveness	10
Sc	13	Energy, effort	10
Sc	14	Exhibition	9
Sc	15	Fantasied Achievement	10
Sc	16	Harm Avoidance	10
Sc	17	Humanities and Social Science	10
Sc	18	Impulsiveness	10
Sc	19	Narcissism	10
Sc	20	Nurturance	10
Sc	21	Not Superstitious	10
Sc	22	Order	10
Sc	23	Pleasure Seeking, Play	10
Sc	24	Practicalness	10
Sc	25	Reflectiveness	10
Sc	26	Science	10
Sc	27	Sensuality, sentience	10
Sc	29	Supplication, succorance	10
Sc	30	Understanding	10
Sc	31	Chastity	11
Sc	32	Conscientiousness in observance of rules (poverty)	10
Sc	33	Piety	5
Sc	34	Mortification	6
Sc	36	Responsability to Studies and Work	9
Sc	37	Obedience	10

MODIFIED ACTIVITIES INDEX

Scale 1 — Self-Depreciation-Self-Confidence (10 items)

1 –*L Taking the blame for something done by someone I like.

36 – L Suffering for a good cause or for someone I love.

71 – L Being polite or humble no matter what happens.

106 – L Trying to figure out how I was to blame after getting into an argument with someone.

142 – L Admitting defeat.

177 – L Having people laugh at my mistakes.

212 – L Accepting criticism without talking back.

246 – D Making a fuss when someone seems to be taking advantage of me.

275 – L Taking the part of a servant or a waiter in a play.

303 – L Telling others about the mistakes I have made and the sins I have committed.

Scale 2 — Relaxing-*Sriving for success* through personal effort (10 items)

2 – L Setting difficult goals for myself.

37 – L Working for someone who will accept nothing less than the best that is in me.

72 – L Setting higher standards for myself than anyone else would and working hard to achieve them.

107 – L Competing with others for a prize or a goal.

143 – L Taking examinations.

178 – L Working on tasks so difficult I can hardly do them.

213 – L Doing something very difficult in order to prove I can do it.

247 – L Choosing difficult tasks in preference to easy ones.

276 – L Sacrificing everything in order to achieve something outstanding.

304 – L Picking out some hard task for myself and doing it.

---

* *N.B.* – " L " corresponds to " true " for PB and corresponds to " consistent " for SI and II.

" D " corresponds to " false " for PB and corresponds to " inconsistent " for SI and II.

Scale 3 — Pride-*Humility* (10 items)

3 – D Concealing a failure or humiliation from others.
33 – D Defending myself against criticism or blame.
73 – L Admitting when I am in the wrong.
108 – D Being ready with an excuse or explanation when criticized.
144 – L Being corrected when I am doing something the wrong way.
179 – D Keeping my failures and mistakes to myself.
214 – D Pointing out someone elses mistakes when they point out mine.
248 – L Apologizing when I have done something wrong.
277 – L Having my mistakes pointed out to me.
305 – D Concealing my mistakes from others whenever possible.

Scale 4 — Aloofness-*Sociability* (10 items)

4 – D Having other people let me alone.
39 – L Going to the park or beach with a crowd.
74 – L Leading an active social life.
109 – L Meeting a lot of people.
145 – L Belonging to a social club.
188 – L Going to parties where I am expected to mix with the whole crowd.
215 – L Having a lot of friends who come to stay with us for several days during the year.
249 – D Going to the park or beach only at times when no one else is likely to be there.
278 – L Going on a vacation to a place where there are a lot of people.
306 – L Inviting a lot of people home for a snack or a par'y.

Scale 5 — *Quarrelsome*-Adaptable (I.S.S.) (10 items)
(*N.B.* – I.S.S. = Inverted score scale, i.e., Highest = quarrelsome; Lower = adaptable)

5 – L Getting what is coming to me even if I have to fight for it.
40 – L Shocking narrow minded people by saying and doing things of which they disapprove.
75 – L Doing something that might provoke criticism.
110 – L Arguing with an instructor or superior.
146 – L Teasing someone who is too conceited.
181 – L Annoying people I don't like, just to see what they will do.
216 – L Playing practical jokes.
250 – L Questioning the decision of people who are supposed to be authorities.
279 – L Fighting for something I want, rather than trying to get it by asking.

307 – L Proving that an instructor or superior is wrong.

Scale 6 — Changeability of Behavior-Sameness of Behavior (I.S.S.)
(10 items)

7 – L Being quite changeable in my likes and dislikes.
42 – D Getting up and going to bed at the same time each day.
77 – L Rearranging furniture in the place where I live.
112 – D Being generally consistent and unchanging in my behavior.
148 – L Moving to a new neighborhood or city, living in a different country, etc.
183 – D Leading a well ordered life with regular hours and an established routine.
218 – D Doing things a different way every time I do them.
251 – D Eating my meals at the same hour each day.
280 – L Avoiding any kind of routine or regularity.
308 – D Staying in the same circle of friends at all times.

Scale 7 — Planfulness-Spontaneity (I.S.S.) (10 items)

8 – L Scheduling time for work and play during the day.
43 – L Planning a reading program for myself.
78 – D Putting off something I don't feel like doing, even though I know it has to be done.
113 – L Going to a party where all the activities are planned.
149 – L Finishing something I've begun, even if it is no longer enjoyable.
184 – L Planning ahead so that I know every step of a project before I get to it.
219 – L Keeping to a regular schedule, even if this sometimes means working when I don't really feel like it.
252 – D Doing things according to my mood, without following any plan.
281 – L Organizing my work in order to use time efficiently.
309 – L Striving for precision and clarity in my speech and writing.

Scale 8 — Withdrawal after Failure-*Restriving after Failure*
(10 items)

9 – L Working twice as hard at a problem when it looks like I don't know the answer.
44 – L Returning to a task which I have previously failed.
79 – L Having to struggle hard for something I want.
114 – L Doing a job under pressure.
150 – D Staying away from activities which I don't do well.
185 – D Avoiding something at which I have once failed.
220 – D Quitting a project that seems too difficult for me.

339

253 – L Doing something over again, just to get it right.
282 – D Avoiding something because I'm not sure I'll be successful at it.
310 – D Giving up on a problem rather than doing it in a way that may be wrong.

Scale 9 — *Rebelliousness-Deference* (10 items)
10 – D Seeing someone make fun of a person who deserves it.
45 – L Doing what most people tell me to do, to the best of my ability.
80 – L Listening to a successful person tell about his experiences.
115 – L Going along with a decision made by a supervisor or leader rather than start an argument.
151 – L Following directions.
186 – L Turning over the leadership of a group to someone who is better qualified than I.
221 – L Listening to older persons tell about how they did things when they were young.
254 – D Disregarding a supervisor's directions when they seem foolish.
283 – L Carrying out orders from others with snap and enthusiasm.
311 – L Having friends who are superior to me in ability.

Scale 10 — *Dominance*-Lack of Dominance (I.S.S.) (10 items)
11 – L Persuading a group to do something my way.
46 – L Having other people depend on me for ideas or opinions.
81 – L Getting my friend to do what I want to do.
116 – L Organizing groups to vote a certain way in elections.
152 – L Being able to hypnotize people.
187 – L Being an official or a leader.
222 – L Organizing a protest meeting.
255 – L Talking someone into doing something I think ought to be done.
284 – L Directing other people's work.
312 – L Influencing or controlling the actions of others.

Scale 11 — Lack of Social Concern-*Striving for Social Action* (9 items)
13 – L Being someone who crusades to improve the community.
48 – L Being an important figure in time of crisis.
83 – L Taking an active part in social and political reform.
113 – L Living a life which is adventurous and dramatic.
154 – L Playing an active part in community affairs.

340

189 - L Actively supporting a movement to correct a social evil.
244 - L Getting my friends to change their social, political or religious beliefs.
256 - L Trying to improve my community by persuading others to do certain things.
251 - Deleted.
313 - L Converting or changing the views of others.

Scale 12 — Emotional Expressiveness-Emotional Restraint (I.S.S.) (10 items)
14 - L Listening to music that makes me very sad.
49 - L Crying at a funeral, wedding, graduation or similar ceremonies.
84 - D Avoiding excitement or emotional tension.
119 - L Having someone for a friend who is very emotional.
155 - L Going on an emotional binge.
190 - L Letting loose—having a good cry sometimes.
225 - L Yelling with excitement at a ball game, horse race or other public event.
257 - D Being with people who seem always to be calm, unstirred or placid.
285 - L Seeing sad or melodramatic movies.
314 - L Being unrestrained and open about my feelings and emotions.

Scale 13 — Inertia-Effort (10 items)
15 - L Taking up a very active outdoor sport.
50 - L Exerting myself to the utmost for something unusually important or enjoyable.
85 - L Staying up all night when I'm doing something that interests me.
120 - D Sleeping long hours every night in order to have lots of rest.
156 - L Walking instead of riding whenever I can.
191 - D Taking frequent rest periods when working on a project.
226 - L Having something to do every minute of the day.
258 - L Giving all my energy to whatever I happen to be doing.
286 - D Avoiding things that require intense concentration.
315 - L Doing things that are fun but require lots of physical exertion.

Scale 14 — Exhibitionism-Modesty (I.S.S.) (9 items)
16 - D Keeping in the background when I'm with a group of wild, funloving, noisy people.
51 - L Wearing clothes that will attract a lot of attention.

86 - L Speaking at a club or group meeting.
121 - L Playing music, dancing, or acting in a play before a large group.
157 - L Doing something that will create a stir.
164 -   Deleted.
227 - L Speaking before a large group.
259 - L Being the center of attention at a party.
287 - L Telling jokes or doing tricks to entertain others at a large gathering.
316 - L Doing things which will attract others to me.

Scale 15 — Fantasied Achievement (10 items)
17 - L Toughening myself, going without an overcoat, seeing how long I can go without food or sleep, etc.
· 52 - L Working until I am exhausted, to see how much I can take.
87 - L Imagining myself President of the United States.
122 - L Thinking about what I could do that would make me famous.
158 - L Thinking about winning recognition and acclaim as a brilliant public figure.
192 - L Imagining situations in which I am a great hero.
228 - L Imagining how it would feel to be rich and famous.
260 - L Setting myself tasks to strengthen my mind, body and will power.
288 - L Pretending that I'm a famous movie star.
317 - L Thinking about how to become the richest and cleverest financial genius in the world.

Scale 16 — Risk Avoidance-Risk Taking (I.S.S.) (10 items)
19 - D Diving off the tower or high board at a pool.
54 - L Being careful to wear a raincoat and rubbers when it rains.
89 - L Crossing streets only at the corner and with the light.
124 - D Riding a fast and steep roller coaster.
160 - D Standing on the roof of a tall building.
194 - D Driving fast.
230 - D Playing rough games in which someone might get hurt.
261 - D Skiing on steep slopes, climbing high mountains or exploring narrow underground caves.
289 - D Swimming in rough, deep water.
318 - L Being extremely careful about sports that involve some danger like sailing, hunting and camping.

Scale 17 — Humanities-Social Science (10 items)
20 - L Learning about the causes of some of our social and political problems.

342

55 – L Studying the music of particular composers, such as Bach, Beethoven, etc.

90 – L Listening to T.V. or radio programs about political and social problems.

125 – L Comparing the problems and conditions of today with those of various times in the past.

161 – L Studying different types of government, such as American, English, Russian, German, etc.

195 – L Talking about music, theatre or other art forms with people who are interested in them.

231 – L Finding out how different languages have developed, changed and influenced one another.

262 – L Learning more about the works of different painters and sculptors.

Scale 18 — Impulsiveness-Deliberation (I.S.S.) (10 items)

21 – L Doing something crazy occasionally, just for the fun of it.

56 – L Acting impulsively just to blow off steam.

91 – L Being in a situation that requires quick decision and action.

126 – L Doing whatever I'm in the mood to do.

162 – L Doing things on the spur of the moment.

196 – D Controlling my emotions rather than expressing myself impulsively.

232 – L Letting my reasoning be guided by my feelings.

263 – L Speaking or acting spontaneously.

291 – L Being guided by my heart rather than by my head.

320 – D Making up my mind slowly, after considerable deliberation.

Scale 19 — Narcissism (10 items)

22 – L Imaginig what I could do if I could live my life over again.

57 – L Thinking about ways to change my name to make it sound striking or different.

92 – L Pausing to look at myself in a mirror each time I pass one.

127 – L Daydreaming about what I would do if I could live my life any way I wanted.

163 – L Having lots of time to take care of my hair, hands, face, clothing, etc.

197 – L Catching a reflection of myself in a mirror or window.

233 – L Dressing carefully, being sure that the colors match and the various details are exactly right.

264 – L Imagining the kind of life I would have if I were born at a different time in a different place.

292 – L Making my handwriting decorative or unusual.

321 - L Trying out different ways to write my name, to make it look unusual.

Scale 20 — Indifference-Helping Others (10 items)
23 - L Feeding a stray dog or cat.
53 - L Discussing with younger people what they like to do and how they feel about things.
93 - L Helping to collect money for poor people.
128 - L Comforting someone who is feeling low.
164 - L Having people come to me with their problems.
198 - L Lending my things to other people.
234 - L Taking care of youngsters.
265 - L Talking over personal problems with someone, who is feeling unhappy.
293 - L Taking care of someone who is ill.
322 - L Providing companionship and personal care for a very old helpless person.

Scale 21 — Superstitious-Not Superstitious (10 items)
25 - D Taking special precautions on Friday the 13th.
60 - D Waiting for a falling star, white horse or some other sign of success before I make an important decision.
95 - L Paying no attention to omens, signs and other forms of superstition.
130 - D Avoiding things that might bring bad luck.
166 - D Being especially careful the rest of the day if a black cat should cross my path.
200 - D Carrying a good luck charm like a rabbit's foot or a four-leaf clover.
236 - L Having a close friend who ignores or makes fun of superstitious beliefs.
266 - L Going ahead with something important even though I've just accidently walked under a ladder, broken a mirror, etc.
294 - D Finding out which days are lucky for me, so I can hold off important things to do until then.
323 - D Going to a fortune teller, palm reader or astrologer for advice on something important.

Scale 22 — Disorganized-Orderly (10 items)
26 - L Washing and polishing things like a car, silverware or furniture.
61 - L Keeping my bureau drawers, desk, etc. in perfect order.
96 - L Keeping an accurate record of the money I spend.
131 - L Arranging my clothes neatly before I go to bed.
167 - L Recopying notes or memoranda to make them neat.

344

201 – L Making my bed, and putting things away every day before I leave the house.

237 – L Shining my shoes and brushing my clothes every day.

267 – L Keeping my room in perfect order.

295 – L Having a special place for everything and seeing that each thing is in its place.

324 – L Keeping a calendar or notebook of the things I have done or plan to do.

Scale 23 — Pleasure-Seeking-*Purposefulness* (I.S.S.) (10 items)

27 – L Making my work go faster by thinking of the fun I can have when its done.

62 – L Spending most of my extra money on pleasure.

97 – D Dropping out of a crowd that spends most of its time playing around or having parties.

132 – L Getting as much fun out of life as I can, even if it means sometimes neglecting more serious things.

168 – D Finishing some work even though it means missing a party or dance.

202 – L Going to a party or a dance with a lively crowd.

233 – L Giving up whatever I'm doing rather than miss a party or other opportunity for a good time.

268 – L Being with people who are always joking, laughing and out for a good time.

296 – D Doing something serious with my leisure time instead of just playing around with the crowd.

325 – D Limiting my pleasure so that I can spend all of my time usefully.

Scale 24 — *Practicalness*-Impracticalness (I.S.S.) (10 items)

28 – L Being good at typewriting, knitting, carpentry or other practical skills.

63 – L Learning how to repair such things as the radio, sewing machine or car.

98 – L Helping to direct a fund drive for the Red Cross, Community Chest, or other organization.

133 – L Learning how to make such things as furniture or clothing myself.

169 – L Working with mechanical appliances, household equipment, tools, electrical apparatus, etc.

203 – L Managing a store or business enterprise.

239 – L Fixing light sockets, making curtains, painting things, etc. around the house.

269 – L Being treasurer or business manager for a club or organization.

297 – L Learning how to raise healthy flowers, plants, vegetables, etc.
326 – L Being efficient and successful in practical affairs.

Scale 25 — Reflectiveness (10 items)
29 – L Understanding myself better.
64 – L Thinking about different kinds of unusual behavior, like
insanity, drug addiction, crime, etc.
99 – L Imagining life on other planets.
134 – L Trying to figure out why the people I know behave the
way they do.
170 – L Thinking about what the end of the world might be like.
204 – L Seeking to explain the behavior of people who are emotionally disturbed.
270 – L Imagining what it will be like when rocket ships carry
people through space.
298 – L Thinking about the meaning of eternity.
327 – L Concentrating so hard on a work of art or music that I
don't know what's going on around me.

Scale 26 — Science (10 items)
31 – L Learning how to prepare slides of plant and animal tissues
and making my own studies with a microscope.
66 – L Studying wind conditions and changes in atmospheric
pressure in order to better understand and predict the
weather.
101 – L Reading articles which tell about new scientific develp-
ments, discoveries or inventions.
136 – L Doing experiments in physics, chemistry or biology in
order to test a theory.
172 – L Studying the stars and planets and learning to identify
them.
206 – L Going to scientific exhibits.
242 – L Collecting data and attempting to arrive at general laws
about the physical universe.
271 – L Reading scientific theories about the origin of the earth
and other planets.
299 – L Reading about how mathematics is used in developing
scientific theories such as explanations of how the planets
move around the sun.
328 – L Studying rock formations and learning how they developed.

Scale 27 — Sensuality-Puritanism (I.S.S.) (10 items)
32 – L Holding something very soft and warm against my skin.
67 – L Eating after going to bed.

346

102 – L Chewing on pencils, rubber bands or paper clips.
137 – L Sleeping in a very soft bed.
173 – L Listening to the rain fall on the roof, or the wind blow through the trees.
207 – L Chewing or popping gum.
243 – L Sketching or painting.
272 – L Eating so much I can't take another bite.
300 – L Walking along a dark street in the rain.
329 – L Reading in the bathtub.

Scale 29 — Psychological Dependency-Psychological Autonomy (I.S.S.) (10 items)
 33 – L Belonging to a close group that expects me to bring my problems to them.
 63 – L Working for someone who is always telling me what to do and how to do it.
103 – L Being a lone wolf, free of family and friends.
139 – L Having someone help me out when I'm in trouble.
174 – L Knowing an older person who likes to give me guidance and direction.
209 – L Having others offer their opinions when I have to make a decision.
244 – L Having people fuss over me when I am sick.
273 – L Receiving advice from others.
301 – L Having people talk to me about some personal problem of mine.
331 – L Being with someone who always tries to be sympathetic and understanding.

Scale 30 — Understanding (10 items)
 34 – L Concentrating intently on a problem.
 69 – L Finding the meaning of unusual or rarely used words.
104 – L Spending my time thinking about and discussing complex problems.
140 – L Working crossword puzzles, figuring out moves in checkers or chess, playing anagrams or scrabble, etc.
175 – L Being a philosopher, scientist or professor.
210 – L Losing myself in hard thought.
245 – L Engaging in mental activity.
274 – L Solving puzzles that involve numbers or figures.
302 – L Following through in the development of a theory, even though it has no practical application.
332 – L Working out solutions to complicated problems, even though the answers may have no apparent, immediate usefulness.

347

Scale 31 — Chastity (11 items)
> N.B. - Partly from scales 27 and 28.
> High scores = good chastity.

  6 – D Preferring not to think about the defects of a friend.
 32 – D Holding something very soft and warm against my skin (Scale 27).
 41 – D Having persistent thoughts about someone and feeling uncomfortable when he is not around.
 76 – L Disliking the exclusive company of friends.
111 – D Desiring to embrace a friend.
135 – D Envying friends who get married.
138 – D Seeing love stories in the movies (Scale 28).
147 – D Being impressed by the physical attractiveness of people.
208 – D Reading novels and magazine stories about love (Scale 28).
272 – D Eating so much I can't take another bite (Scale 27).
330 – D Reading about the love affairs of movie stars and other famous people (Scale 28).

Scale 32 — Observance of rules (10 items)
> High Score = good observance.
> Seven items are about poverty.

 12 – D Having a nice room (poverty).
 47 – D Keeping books overdue from the library (poverty).
 82 – D Keeping a commonly used appliance for your personal use (poverty).
117 – D Using without permission small tools not in common use (poverty).
153 – D Keeping a small gift that has been given to you (poverty).
182 – D Eating between meals without permission (poverty).
205 – D Not taking care fo clothes (poverty).
217 – D Talking when you feel like it.
229 – D Not following too closely the schedule for your personal activities.
241 – D Loosely following the schedule for common activities.

Scale 33 — Piety (Five items) (High score = good piety)
 18 – L Giving exact time to spiritual duties.
 53 – L Liking to spend time in private prayers.
 88 – D Being casual in taking points for meditations.
123 – D Reading books that have little to do with prayers and meditation.
159 – L Liking meetings, discussions or readings about the apostleship of prayer.

348

Scale 34 — Mortification (Six items) (High score = great mortification)

24 – L Eating only what is necessary.
59 – D Making myself comfortable in my activities.
94 – D Reading for entertainment whenever I have a chance.
129 – D Sleeping as much as possible when it is permitted.
165 – L Doing small self-imposed penances.
188 – D Desiring to participate in parties.

Scale 36 — Lack of Responsibility to studies and work-*Responsibility to studies and work* (9 items) (High score = great responsibility)

35 – D Studying hard in order to gain self-fulfillment.
70 – L Commitment to studying something that may never be put to practical use.
105 – L Applying oneself conscientiously to studies.
141 – D Studying hard in order to gain recognition.
176 – D Indulging in studies that have not been assigned.
199 – D Not keeping up with your study program.
211 – L Being concerned with keeping study notes.
223 – D Disliking public discussions about school matters.
235 – L To engage in personal investigation of topics covered in your studies.

Scale 37 — Obedience (10 items) (From scales 5 and 9) (High score = Good obedience)

5 – D Getting what is coming to me even if I have to fight for it (Scale 5).
40 – D Shocking narrow minded people by saying and doing things of which they disapproved (5).
75 – D Doing something that might provoke criticism (5).
110 – D Arguing with an instructor or superior (5).
115 – L Going along with a decision made by a supervisor or leader rather than starting an argument (9).
151 – L Following directions (9).
250 – D Questioning the decision of people who are supposed to be authorities (5).
254 – D Disregarding a supervisor's directions when they seem foolish (9).
283 – L Carrying out orders from others with snap and enthusiasm (9).
307 – D Proving that an instructor or superior is wrong (5).

Appendix B–2

MODIFIED GENERAL GOALS OF LIFE INVENTORY

This inventory consists of a number of statements which express what some persons have considered the main goals of life. You are asked to address yourself to each of the statements in three different ways.

The first way is to determine whether the statement is *True* or *False* in regard to your present behavior, that is, if this goal is usually operative at this point in your life. The code for this is PB.

The second way is to address yourself to the statement to determine whether it is *consistent with, inconsistent with*, or *irrelevant to* the ideal you hold for yourself. The code for this is SI (Self Ideal)-CON-INC-IR.

The third way is to address yourself to the statement to determine whether it is *consistent with, inconsistent with*, or *irrelevant to* the ideals of the educational institution in which you are functioning at present. The code for this is II (Institutional Ideal)-CON-INC-IR.

Recognize that in the first judgment you are not to consider what you would like to be, or what you ought to be if you take the institution's point of view, but rather what you are at this point in your life. In the second judgment, do not consider what you currently are, or what the institution would like you to be, but rather what the ideals are that you hold for yourself. In the third judgment, do not consider what you are, or what you would like to be, but rather what the ideals of the institution are for people like you. In making the second and third judgments, if you do not have a definite impression that a statement is positively expressive of or contrary to either an institution or a personal ideal, then you should answer *irrelevant*.

General Goals of Life

A. Serving God, doing God's will.
B. Achieving personal immortality in heaven.
C. Self-discipline . . . overcoming my irrational and sensuous desires.
D. Self-sacrifice for the sake of a better world.
E. Doing my duty.

F. Peace of mind, contentment, stillness of spirit.
G. Serving the community of which I am a part.
H. Having fine relations with other people.
I. Self-development ... becoming a real, genuine person.
J. Finding my place in life and accepting it.
K. Living for the pleasure of the moment.
L. Getting as many deep and lasting pleasures out of life as I can.
M. Promoting the most deep and lasting pleasures for the greatest number of people.
N. Making a place for myself; getting ahead.
O. Power; control over people and things.
P. Security ... protecting my way of life against adverse changes.
Q. Being able to " take it ": brave and uncomplaining acceptance of what circumstances bring.
R. Realizing that I cannot change the bad features of the world and doing the best I can for myself and those dear to me.
S. Survival, continued existence.
T. Handling the specific problems of life as they arise.
U. Developing my mind so that I am knowledgeable and effective in intellectual endeavor.

Appendix B–3

ROTTER AND THEMATIC APPERCEPTION TEST DEFINITIONS

Definitions of Emotions

Anxiety, Overt: public, unconcealed anguish, marked and continuous apprehension.

Anxiety, Covert: concealed anguish, marked and continuous apprehension of evil.

Sadness (Depression), Overt: Unconcealed inaccessibility to stimulation, low initiative, gloom.

Sadness (Depression), Covert: concealed inaccessibility to stimulation, low initiative, gloom, feeling of abandonment and frustration.

Pride: Paranoid thinking: lack of objectivity in the form of exaggerated ideation (Cameron, 1963).

Guilt, overt: unconcealed, manifest sorrow or anxiety for ethical or moral or psychological wrong performed. Expectation of retribution.

Guilt, covert: concealed, manifest anxiety or apprehension for ethical, moral or psychological wrong performed or vicariously performed in thought, with expectation of retribution.

ROTTER AND THEMATIC
APPERCEPTION TEST

Definitions of Needs
(Murray's)

Abasement: to submit passively to external force. To accept injury, blame, criticism, punishment. To surrender. To become resigned to fate. To admit inferiority, error, wrogdoing, or defeat. To confess and atone. To blame, belittle, or mutilate the self. To seek and enjoy pain, punishment, illness and misfortune.

Achievement: to accomplish something difficult. To master, manipulate, or organize physical objects, human beings, or ideas. To do this as rapidly and as independently as possible. To overcome obstacles and attain a high standard. To excel oneself. To rival and surpass others. To increase self-regard by the successful exercise of talent.

Acquirement: to gain possession and property, to get goods or money for himself.

Affiliation: to draw near and enjoyably cooperate or reciprocate with an allied other (another who resembles the subject or likes the subject). To please and win the affection of a cathected object. To adhere and remain loyal to a friend. (Two-way relationship. See succorance) Negative schizoid.

Aggression: to overcome opposition forcefully. To fight. To revenge an injury. To attack, injure or kill another. To oppose forcefully or punish another.

Autonomy: to get free, shake off restraint, break out of confinement. To resist coercion and restriction. To avoid or quit activities prescribed by domineering authorities. To be independent and free to act according to impulse. To be unattached, irresponsible. To defy convention.

Avoid Censure or Failure: defendence.—to defend the self against assault, criticism or blame. To conceal or justify a misdeed, failure or humiliation. To vindicate the ego. *Passive* conformity, or Infavoidance—to avoid humiliation. To quit embarrassing situations or to avoid conditions which may lead to belittlement: the scorn, derision, or indifference of others. To refrain from action because of the fear of failure.

Change (Novelty): to change, to alter his circumstances, environment, associations, activities, to avoid routine or sameness.

Knowledge (Curiosity): to know, to satisfy curiosity, to explore, to acquire information or knowledge.

Submission (Deference): to admire and support a superior. To praise, honor or eulogize. To yield eagerly to the influence of an allied other. To emulate an exemplar. To conform to custom. *Active* conformity.

Domination: to control one's human environment. To influence or direct the behavior of others by suggestion, seduction, persuasion, or command or enticement. To dissuade, restrain or prohibit.

Excitement: to be easily aroused, stimulated, excited or agitated.

Exhibition: to make an impression. To be seen and heard. To excite, amaze, fascinate, entertain, shock, intrigue, amuse or entice others.

Avoid Injury (Harm avoidance): to avoid pain, physical injury, illness and death. To escape from a dangerous situation. To take precautionary measures.

To Nurture (Nurturance): To give sympathy and gratify the needs of a helpless object: an infant or any object that is weak, disabled, tired, inexperienced, infirm, defeated, humiliated, lonely, dejected, sick, mentally confused. To assist an object in danger. To feed, help, support, console, protect, comfort, nurse, heal.

Organization (Order): to put things in order. To achieve cleanliness, arrangement, organization, balance, neatness, tidiness, and precision.

Playfulness (Play): to act for " fun " without further purpose. To like to laugh and make jokes. To seek enjoyable relaxation of stress. To participate in games, sports, dancing, drinking parties, cards. Daydreaming.

Recognition (Social Approval): to gain prestige, to win honors, to get praise and recognition.

Sexual Gratification: to form and further an erotic relationship. To have sexual intercourse.

Succ rance: to have one's needs gratified by the sympathetic aid of an allied object. To be nursed, supported, sustained, surrounded, protected, loved, advised, guided, indulged, forgiven, consoled. To always have a supporter. *One* way relationship.

Counteraction: to strive persistently to overcome difficult, frustrating or humiliating or embarassing experiences and failures versus avoidance or hasty withdrawal from task or situations that might result in such outcomes.

353

ROTTER AND THEMATIC
APPERCEPTION TEST

Conflict Descriptions
(Erikson, 1950, 1959)

1. Trust-mistrust:
   (a) A disposition to trust others, a capacity to receive from others and to depend on them.
   (b) The opposite.

2. Autonomy-shame, doubt:
   (a) Capacity to self assertion and self-expression, an ability to maintain self control without loss of self esteem;
   (b) lack of self-esteem reflected in shame, and lack of self confidence implied in self-doubt (Note: this version of autonomy is less rebellious and aggressive than on MAI scale 37, and the Murray TAT description).

3. Initiative-guilt:
   (a) Sense of responsibility, capability, and discipline—capacity to direct energies toward goals (ego);
   (b) harsh, rigid, moralistic, self-punishing superego (guilt superego). Sexual conflict.

4. Industry-inferiority:
   (a) Capacity to *maintain* the directed energies until the goal is achieved or the task completed;
   (b) fear of failure or inability to compete with others.

5. Identity-role diffusion:
   (a) Confident sense of ability to maintain inner sameness and continuity, and solidarity with a realistic system of values as embodied in social or cultural contexts;
   (b) uncertainty about self-image and no commitment to a system of values.

6. Intimacy-isolation:
   (a) Capacity to relate intimately and meaningfully with others in mutually satisfying and productive interactions;

(b) opposite of that as a failure to realize secure and mature self- acceptance. (Note: In contrast to 1, this implies both acceptance of self and other).

7. Generativity-stagnation:

(a) Concern with, and capacity for the utilization of productive capabilities for the welfare of others;

(b) the absence of expression of productive capabilities, or the use of such capabilities in a self-centered way.

8. Ego integrity-despair:

(a) Acceptance of oneself and all the aspects of life, and the integration of these elements into a stable pattern of living;

(b) lack of acceptance of oneself and one's life, associated with self- contempt and fear of death.

TAT Stories

Scorer's Sheet

	1	2	3	4	5	6	7	Rotter

Emotions

Anxiety
  overt
  covert

Sadness
  overt
  covert
  (Depression)

1 Pride

Guilt
  overt
  covert

Abasement
Achievement
2* Acquirement
Affiliation
Aggression
Autonomy
3 Avoid Censure
   or Failure
4* Change
   (Novelty)
5* Knowledge
   (Curiosity)
Submission
   (Deference)
Domination
Excitement
Exhibition
Avoid Injury
To Nurture

356

Organization
(Order) —— —— —— —— —— —— —— ——
Playfulness —— —— —— —— —— —— —— ——
6* Recognition
(Social Approval) —— —— —— —— —— —— —— ——
Sexual Gratification —— —— —— —— —— —— —— ——
Succorance —— —— —— —— —— —— —— ——
Counteraction —— —— —— —— —— —— —— ——

*= Not on Murray's List.
1   Pride: Paranoid thinking; lack of objectivity in the form of exaggerated ideation (Cameron, 1963).
2* Acquirement: to gain possessions and property, to get goods or money for himself.
3   Avoid censure or failure (defendance or infavoidance).
4* Change (Novelty): to change, to alter circumstances, environment, associations, or activities, to avoid routine or sameness.
5* Knowledge (Curiosity): to know, to satisfy curiosity, to explore, to acquire information or knowledge.
6* Recognition (Social Approval): to gain prestige, to win honors, to get praise and recognition.

TAT Stories

Scorers' Sheet

Defenses	1	2	3	4	5	6	7	Rotter
Compensation (in fantasy or action)	—	—	—	—	—	—	—	—
Denial (external)	—	—	—	—	—	—	—	—
Displacement (symbolization)	—	—	—	—	—	—	—	—
Identification	—	—	—	—	—	—	—	—
Intellectualization (rationalization)	—	—	—	—	—	—	—	—
Isolation	—	—	—	—	—	—	—	—
Parentification	—	—	—	—	—	—	—	—
Projection	—	—	—	—	—	—	—	—
Reaction Formation	—	—	—	—	—	—	—	—
Regression	—	—	—	—	—	—	—	—
Repression (suppression)	—	—	—	—	—	—	—	—
Undoing	—	—	—	—	—	—	—	—
Conflict by Erikson	—	—	—	—	—	—	—	—

358

Appendix B-4

BIOGRAPHICAL INVENTORY

1. Father's occupation:
   a. Type of work ....
   (e.g., salesman, teacher)
   b. Rank or title ....

3. Fathers' education:
   a. Grade School
   1 2 3 4 5 6 7 8
   b. High School   1 2 3 4
   c. College   1 2 3 4
   d. Graduate or Professional
   1 2 3 4

5. Father's income ....

7. Father's place of birth .....

9. If Father was born in U. S.,
   indicate how many genera-
   tions back from him one
   must go in order to find
   someone in his family who
   was born outside of U. S.
   .... Where was this
   ancestor(s) born? ....

11. Father's religion ....

13. Is Father a convert? ....

15. How religious is Father?
    a. more than most men .....
    b. average   .....
    c. less than most men ,....

17. Is Father still alive? (if no,
    then how long ago did he
    die?) ....

2. Mother's occupation:
   a. Type of work ....
   b. Rank or title ....

4. Mother's education:
   a. Grade School
   1 2 3 4 5 6 7 8
   b. High School   1 2 3 4
   c. College   1 2 3 4
   d. Graduate or Professional
   1 2 3 4

6. Mother's income ....

8. Mother's place of birth ....

10. If Mother was born in U. S.,
    indicate how many genera-
    tions back from her one must
    go in order to find someone in
    her family who was born out-
    side of U. S. ....
    Where was this ancestor(s)
    born? ....

12. Mother's religion ....

14. Is Mother a convert? ....

16. How religious is Mother?
    a. more than most women .....
    b. average   .....
    c. less than most women .....

18. Is Mother still alive? (if no,
    then how long ago did she
    die?) ....

19. Are mother and father still living together? (If no, please explain)
....
....

20. In what type of area did you grow up? Urban .... Rural ....
21. Ordinal number in family and number of children ....
    of .... children (e.g., if you are the 2nd oldest of 5 children:
    2nd of *5* children).
22. Circle the highest year in school completed prior to your entrance
    into the novitiate.

High School:	1 2 3 4
College:	1 2 3 4
Graduate Study:	1 2 3 4

23. If you have gone to school since entering the novitiate, kindly
    cross out the highest year in school you have completed to the
    present time (use the data above).
24. Describe the types of schools you have attended prior to entering
    the novitiate by checking the following items:

	Public	Catholic	Other (specify)	Boys & Girls	One Sex	Enrollment	
						Over 500	Under 500
Grade School							
High School							
College							

25. What grade average (approximately) did you usually get in high
    school? ....
26. In what high school activities did you participate?
    High School ....
    College ....
27. What student offices did you hold? ....
28. What did you major in, or what subjects did you like most?
    High School ....
    College ....
29. Describe any jobs you have held:
    Type of work   Length of time in weeks, months or years
    ....
    ....
    ....
30. Check the types of recreation you engage in most frequently:
    .... a. spectator sports   .... f. participator sports

.... b. movies

.... c. theater, concerts

.... d. museums, art gal-
leries

.... e. reading

k. other (please specify) ....

.... g. dancing (on stage),
acting

.... h. playing music

.... i. drawing or painting

.... j. dating

31. What did you most like to do with your time? ....

32. Did you date in high school or college? ....

33. Did you ever go steady? ....

34. Were you ever engaged? ....

35. Have you ever felt attracted to people of the opposite sex? ....

36. How many really close friends did you have before entering the religious life? ....

37. With how many other people did you feel friendly but not so close before entering the religious life? ....

38. How often did you tend to see your really close friends

.... every evening

.... 2 or 3 evenings a week

.... once a week

.... once every two weeks

.... less frequently

39. Did you find your relationships with people of your own age satisfactory? ....

40. Did you feel lonely very much? ....

41. Would you consider yourself as having b' en popular? ....

42. How old were you when you entered the novitiate? ....

43. What state did you grow up in? ....

44. Are there others in your family who have chosen the religious vocation? (If so, please specify the relationship to you) ....

....

45. How old were you when you first started thinking about entering? ....

46. Where were you, and what were you doing at the time? ....

....

47. When and under what circumstances did you make the definite decision to enter? ....

48. What were some of the reasons why you wanted to enter? Why this novitiate and not some other one? ....

....

49. What did your family think of your decision? ....

....

50. Check any people who were influential in your decision to enter the novitiate.

Lay persons .... Father .... Mother ....

Brother .... Sister .... Priest ....
Nun .... Scholastic teacher ....

51. Is life in the novitiate what you expected it to be? (explain)
....

52. Are your reasons for staying in religion any different from those
that led you to enter? (If yes, please explain.) ....
....

53. What recommendations or advice might you give to a young
person who was considering entering the religious vocation?
....

54. Can you conceive of any possible reasons that might cause you
to leave the religious vocation? ....
....

55. (The following five tasks pertain to your family life before entering the novitiate.)

First Task: Please circle the appropriate number in each of
the following rows, considering each row to refer to an aspect
of the way your mother was toward you.

Extreme   *Extreme*

Affectionate   0 1 2 3 4 5 6 7 8 9   Unaffectionate
Strict   0 1 2 3 4 5 6 7 8 9   Lenient
Trusting   0 1 2 3 4 5 6 7 8 9   Distrustful
Consistent   0 1 2 3 4 5 6 7 8 9   Inconsistent
Self-Preoccupied 0 1 2 3 4 5 6 7 8 9   Generous
Understanding   0 1 2 3 4 5 6 7 8 9   Unsympathetic
Punitive   0 1 2 3 4 5 6 7 8 9   Supportive
Critical   0 1 2 3 4 5 6 7 8 9   Forgiving
Envious   0 1 2 3 4 5 6 7 8 9   Appreciative
Open-Minded   0 1 2 3 4 5 6 7 8 9   Close-Minded
In Conflict   0 1 2 3 4 5 6 7 8 9   In Harmony
Independent   0 1 2 3 4 5 6 7 8 9   Dependent
Overpowering   0 1 2 3 4 5 6 7 8 9   Gentle
Pushy   0 1 2 3 4 5 6 7 8 9   Relaxed
Trustworthy   0 1 2 3 4 5 6 7 8 9   Untrustworthy

Second Task: Please circle the appropriate number in each
of the following rows, considering each row to refer to an aspect
of the way your father was toward you.

Extreme   *Extreme*

Affectionate   0 1 2 3 4 5 6 7 8 9   Unaffectionate
Strict   0 1 2 3 4 5 6 7 8 9   Lenient

362

Trusting	0 1 2 3 4 5 6 7 8 9	Distrustful
Consistent	0 1 2 3 4 5 6 7 8 9	Inconsistent
Self-Preoccupied	0 1 2 3 4 5 6 7 8 9	Generous
Understanding	0 1 2 3 4 5 6 7 8 9	Unsympathetic
Punitive	0 1 2 3 4 5 6 7 8 9	Supportive
Critical	0 1 2 3 4 5 6 7 8 9	Forgiving
Envious	0 1 2 3 4 5 6 7 8 9	Appreciative
Open-Minded	0 1 2 3 4 5 6 7 8 9	Close-Minded
In Conflict	0 1 2 3 4 5 6 7 8 9	In Harmony
Independent	0 1 2 3 4 5 6 7 8 9	Dependent
Overpowering	0 1 2 3 4 5 6 7 8 9	Gentle
Pushy	0 1 2 3 4 5 6 7 8 9	Relaxed
Trustworthy	0 1 2 3 4 5 6 7 8 9	Untrustworthy

Third Task: Please circle the appropriate number in each of the following rows, considering each row to refer to an aspect of the way your parents were toward each other.

Extreme / *Extreme*

Affectionate	0 1 2 3 4 5 6 7 8 9	Unaffectionate
Strict	0 1 2 3 4 5 6 7 8 9	Lenient
Trusting	0 1 2 3 4 5 6 7 8 9	Distrustful
Consistent	0 1 2 3 4 5 6 7 8 9	Inconsistent
Self-Preoccupied	0 1 2 3 4 5 6 7 8 9	Generous
Understanding	0 1 2 3 4 5 6 7 8 9	Unsympathetic
Punitive	0 1 2 3 4 5 6 7 8 9	Supportive
Critical	0 1 2 3 4 5 6 7 8 9	Forgiving
Envious	0 1 2 3 4 5 6 7 8 9	Appreciative
Open-Minded	0 1 2 3 4 5 6 7 8 9	Close-Minded
In Conflict	0 1 2 3 4 5 6 7 8 9	In Harmony
Independent	0 1 2 3 4 5 6 7 8 9	Dependent
Overpowering	0 1 2 3 4 5 6 7 8 9	Gentle
Pushy	0 1 2 3 4 5 6 7 8 9	Relaxed
Trustworthy	0 1 2 3 4 5 6 7 8 9	Untrustworthy

Fourth Task: Please circle the appropriate number in each of the following rows, considering each row to refer to an aspect of the way your brothers and sisters were toward you. (You may find it helpful to note the instructions for the fifth task, on the next page, before doing this task.)

Extreme / *Extreme*

Affectionate	0 1 2 3 4 5 6 7 8 9	Unaffectionate
Strict	0 1 2 3 4 5 6 7 8 9	Lenient
Trusting	0 1 2 3 4 5 6 7 8 9	Distrustful

Consistent	0 1 2 3 4 5 6 7 8 9	Inconsistent
Self-Preoccupied	0 1 2 3 4 5 6 7 8 9	Generous
Understanding	0 1 2 3 4 5 6 7 8 9	Unsympathetic
Punitive	0 1 2 3 4 5 6 7 8 9	Supportive
Critical	0 1 2 3 4 5 6 7 8 9	Forgiving
Envious	0 1 2 3 4 5 6 7 8 9	Appreciative
Open-Minded	0 1 2 3 4 5 6 7 8 9	Close-Minded
In Conflict	0 1 2 3 4 5 6 7 8 9	In Harmony
Independent	0 1 2 3 4 5 6 7 8 9	Dependent
Overpowering	0 1 2 3 4 5 6 7 8 9	Gentle
Pushy	0 1 2 3 4 5 6 7 8 9	Relaxed
Trustworthy	0 1 2 3 4 5 6 7 8 9	Untrustworthy

Fifth Task: Although you have already characterized the relationship of your brothers and sisters to you in the fourth task, it may be that one or two of your brothers or sisters has had a relationship to you that is different than that you had with the others. If this is so, please circle the appropriate number in each of the following rows, considering each row to refer to an aspect of the way the particular brother or sister was toward you.

Extreme		*Extreme*
Affectionate	0 1 2 3 4 5 6 7 8 9	Unaffectionate
Strict	0 1 2 3 4 5 6 7 8 9	Lenient
Trusting	0 1 2 3 4 5 6 7 8 9	Distrustful
Consistent	0 1 2 3 4 5 6 7 8 9	Inconsistent
Self-Preoccupied	0 1 2 3 4 5 6 7 8 9	Generous
Understanding	0 1 2 3 4 5 6 7 8 9	Unsympathetic
Punitive	0 1 2 3 4 5 6 7 8 9	Supportive
Critical	0 1 2 3 4 5 6 7 8 9	Forgiving
Envious	0 1 2 3 4 5 6 7 8 9	Appreciative
Open-Minded	0 1 2 3 4 5 6 7 8 9	Closed-Minded
In Conflict	0 1 2 3 4 5 6 7 8 9	In Harmony
Independent	0 1 2 3 4 5 6 7 8 9	Dependent
Overpowering	0 1 2 3 4 5 6 7 8 9	Gentle
Pushy	0 1 2 3 4 5 6 7 8 9	Relaxed
Trustworthy	0 1 2 3 4 5 6 7 8 9	Untrustworthy

56. Do you feel that some relative(s) of yours, other than those already referred to in question 55 (e.g., uncle, cousin, grandmother) was important in your development   Yes .... No ....

57. Any comments you wish to make will be gratefully received:

....

....

Appendix B-5

FAMILY DYNAMICS INTERVIEW

No Communication						Great Communication
Father	1	2	3	4	5	
Mother	1	2	3	4	5	
No Affection						Great Affection
Father	1	2	3	4	5	
Mother	1	2	3	4	5	
No Interactional Conflict						Great Interactional Conflict
Father	5	4	3	2	1	
Mother	5	4	3	2	1	
Usual Role	5	4	3	2	1	Role Reversal
No Parental Conflict	5	4	3	2	1	Great Parental Conflict

Psychopathology in Family:

Father ....

Mother ....

Siblings ....

Others ....

Personal Characteristics:

Insecurity	1	2	3
Rapport	1	2	3
Defensiveness	1	2	3

Appendix B-6

INTUITIVE ANALYSIS OF STRUCTURED TESTS
FOR THE DEPTH INTERVIEW

Subject ——————————————— Group ————————————

Test and Scales	Entrance	Second Testing	Third Testing
MMPI			
Lie			
Faking			
K.			
Hypochondriasis (HS-T)			
A. Depression (D)			
D 1. Subjective depression			
D 2. Psychomotor retardation			
D 3. Physical malfunction			
D 4. Mental dullness			
D 5. Brooding			
B. Hysteria (Hy)			
Hy 1. Denial of social anxiety			
Hy 2. Need for affection and reinforcement from others			
Hy 3. Lassitude and malaise			
Hy 4. Somatic complaints			
Hy 5. Inhibition of aggression			
C. Psychopathic deviate (Pd-T)			
Pd 1. Family discord			
Pd 2. Authority conflict			
Pd 3. Social imperturbability			
Pd 4. Social alienation			
Pd 5. Self alienation			
Masculinity-femininity			

D. Paranoia (Pa) —————————— ———— ——— ———
    Pa 1. Ideas of external influence — ——— ——— ——— ———
    Pa 2. Poignancy ———————— ——— ——— ———
    Pa 3. Moral virtue ————— ——— ——— ———
Psychaesthenia (Pt-T) —————————— ——— ——— ———
E. Schizophrenia (Sc-T) ——————— ——— ——— ———
    Sc 1a. Social alienation ——————— ——— ——— ———
    Sc 1b Emotional alienation ——— ——— ——— ———
    Sc 2a. Lack of ego mastery, cognitive ——— ——— ———
    Sc 2b. Lack of ego mastery, conative ——— ——— ———
    Sc 2c. Lack of ego mastery, defect
        of inhibition and control — ——— ——— ———
    Sc 3. Sensory-motor dissociation ——— ——— ———
F. Hypomania (Ma-T) ——————— ——— ——— ———
    Ma 1. Amorality ——————— ——— ——— ———
    Ma 2 Psychomotor acceleration — ——— ——— ———
    Ma 3. Imperturbability —————— ——— ——— ———
    Ma 4. Ego inflation ————— ——— ——— ———
Social introversion ————————— ——— ——— ———
Anxiety (A) —————————— ——— ——— ———
Repression (R) —————————— ——— ——— ———

Finney Scales (31)

Sc   1. Dependency ———————— ——— ——— ———
Sc   3. Repression of Dependency — ——— ——— ———
Sc   4. Basic Trust, Confidence, Opti-
      mism ———————— ——— ——— ———
Sc   5. Discouragements ————— ——— ——— ———
Sc   7. Anxiety ————————— ——— ——— ———
Sc   8. Bitterness ————————— ——— ——— ———
Sc   9. Demandingness ———————— ——— ——— ———
Sc 10. Order ————————— ——— ——— ———
Sc 12. Resisting being told what to do
      (with reservation) ————— ——— ——— ———
Sc 13. Amount of resentment and hos-
      tility (regardless of how shown
      or covered up) ————— ——— ——— ———
Sc 14. Blaming Self ———————— ——— ——— ———
Sc 16. Taking Things out on self (un-
      worthiness) ————— ——— ——— ———
Sc 17. Taking Things out on others
      (sadism) ————— ——— ——— ———
Sc 18. Reaction formation against ag-
      gression ————— ——— ——— ———

Sc 22. Controlingness & sadism ——

Sc 24. Impotence & frigidity (oversensitivity rather in a negative sense) ——————————————

Sc 25. Promiscuity ——————————

Sc 26. Doing things the hard way ——

Sc 27. Concern with what people think

Sc 28. Psychopathic manipulation ——

Sc 29. Guilt feelings (depression rather)

Sc 30. Conscience ————————

Sc 33. Feeling sorry for self (unworthiness) ——————————————

Sc 34. Dependent masochism, getting rejected ——————————

Sc 35. Behaving to get punished ——

Sc 36. Repression or hysterical character ——————————————

Sc 37. Denial (with reservation) ——

Sc 39. Reaction formation (with reservation) ——————————

Sc 40. Conversion ————————

Sc 42. Phobia and fear ——————

Sc 44. Worry & obsession ————

Other MMPI Scales

— from Dahlstrom & Welsh, 1972

Sc 19. Response bias ——————

Sc 51. Depression, obvious ————

Sc 56. Depression, subtle ————

Sc 58. Escapism ——————————

Sc 62. Ego strength ——————

Sc 68. Female masochism ————

Sc 70. General maladjustment ————

Sc 124. Positive malingering ————

Sc 142. Obvious paranoia ————

Sc 143. Subtle paranoia ————————

Sc 173. Social responsibility ————

Sc 175. Rigidity, female ————

Sc 176. Rigidity, male ————————

Sc 195. Social desirability ————

Sc 200. CS .... (No. 200 St-r Gough + 84 = CS) ——————————

Sc 203. Shyness factor.————————

368

Sc 205. Tolerance . ———————————— ———— ———— ————
Sc 209. Ulcer personality ———————— ———— ———— ————
          Neurotic Triad ——————— ———— ———— ————

— from Finney, J. C., 1966, b
Sc Ph Phobia, manifest content —— ———— ———— ————
Sc GU Guilt ———————————————— ———— ———— ————
Sc REB Rebelliousness, manifest con-
          tent ——————————————— ———— ———— ————
Sc SUB Submissiveness, manifest con-
          tent ——————————————— ———— ———— ————
Sc SO Socialization, reverse of delin-
          quency ————————— ———— ———— ————

— from Mac Andrew, C., 1965
Sc AL Alcoholism ———————————— ———— ———— ————
— from Fulkerson, S. C., 1958
Sc Aq Acquiescence ———— ——— | — ———— ———— ————

16 *PF of Cattell*

A.   Aloof-warm ———————————— ———— ————
B.   Dull-bright (concrete-abstract
       thinking)————————————— ———— ————
C.   Emotional-mature (ego strength) ——— ———— ————
E.   Submissive-dominant ———— ———— ————
F.   Glum-enthusiastic ———— ———— ————
G.   Casual-conscientious (superego) ——— ———— ————
H.   Timid-adventurous ——— ———— ————
I.   Tough-sensitive ——— ———— ————
L.   Trustful-suspecting ——— ———— ————
M.   Conventional-bohemian —— ———— ————
N.   Simple-sophisticated ——— ———— ————
O.   Confident-insecure——— ———— ————
Q 1. Conservative-experimenting — ——— ———— ————
Q 2. Dependent-self-sufficient —— ——— ———— ————
Q 3. Lax-controlled ———————— ———— ————
Q 4. Phlegmatic-tense ——————— ——— ———— ————

Second Order factors

1. Anxiety ——————————— ———— ———— ————
2. Introversion-extroversion ——— ———— ———— ————
3. Tenderminded emotionality-alert,
     poise ————————————— ———— ———— ————
4. Subduedness-independence .——— ———— ———— ————

MAI-PB

Sc 1. Self depreciation-self confidence (abasement) .——————— ——— ——— ———

Sc 2. Relaxing-striving for success through personal effort (achievement) ——————— ——— ——— ———

Sc 3. Pride-humility (defendance and infavoidance) ——————— ——— ——— ———

Sc 4 Aloofness-sociability (affiliation) ——— ——— ——— ———

Sc 5. Quarrelsome-adaptable ISS (aggression) ——————— ——— ——— ———

Sc 6. Changeability of behavior-sameness of behavior ISS (novelty) — ——— ——— ———

Sc 7. Planfulness-spontaneity ISS — ——— ——— ———

Sc 8. Withdrawal after failure-striving after failure (counteraction) — ——— ——— ———

Sc 9. Rebelliousness-deference (deference) ——————— ——— ——— ———

Sc 10. Dominance-lack of dominance ISS (dominance) ——————— ——— ——— ———

Sc 11. Lack of social concern-striving for social action ——————— ——— ——— ———

Sc 12. Emotional expressiveness-emotional restraint ISS ——————— ——— ——— ———

Sc 13. Inertia-effort ——————— ——— ——— ———

Sc 14. Exhibitionism-modesty ISS (exhibition) ——————— ——— ——— ———

Sc 15. Fantasied achievement —— ——— ——— ———

Sc 16. Risk avoidance-risk taking ISS (harm avoidance) ——————— ——— ——— ———

Sc 17. Humanities-social science ——— ——— ——— ———

Sc 18. Impulsiveness-deliberation ISS ——— ——— ———

Sc 19. Narcissism ISS ——————— ——— ——— ———

Sc 20. Indifference-helping others (nurturance) ——————— ——— ——— ———

Sc 21. Superstitious-not superstitious ——— ——— ———

Sc 22. Disorganized-orderly (order)—— ——— ——— ———

Sc 23. Pleasure seeking-purposefulness ISS (play) ——————— ——— ——— ———

Sc 24. Practicalness-impracticalness ISS ——— ——— ———

Sc 25. Reflectiveness ——————— ——— ——— ———

Sc 26. Science ——————— ——— ——— ———

Sc 27. Sensuality-Puritanism ISS (sentience) ——————— ——— ——— ———

370

Sc 29. Psychological dependency-psychological autonomy ISS (succorance) ———————— ——— ——— ———

Sc 30. Understanding ———————— ——— ——— ———

Sc 31. Chastity ———————— ——— ——— ———

Sc 32. Lack of consciousness in observance of rule-consciousness (poverty) ———————— ——— ——— ———

Sc 33. Piety ———————— ——— ——— ———

Sc 34. Mortification ———————— ——— ——— ———

Sc 35. Love for vocation ———————— ——— ——— ———

Sc 36. Lack of responsibility to studies and work-responsibility ——— ——— ——— ———

Sc 37. Obedience ———————— ——— ——— ———

Vassar

Social maturity ———————— ——— ——— ———

Impulse expression .———————— ——— ——— ———

Developmental status ———————— ——— ——— ———

Repression-suppression ———————— ——— ——— ———

Flexibility (C.P.I.) ———————— ——— ——— ———

Appendix B-7

DEPTH
INTERVIEW SUPPLEMENT

Interaction in the novitiate:

No Communication				Great Communication
Father master	1	2	3	
Assistant	1	2	3	
Peers	1	2	3	

Strict				Lenient (Autonomy)
Father master	1	2	3	
Assistant	1	2	3	
Peers	1	2	3	

Inconsistent				Consistent
Father master	1	2	3	
Assistant	1	2	3	
Peers	1	2	3	

Cold				Warm
Father master	1	2	3	
Assistant	1	2	3	
Peers	1	2	3	

In Conflict				In Harmony
Father master	1	2	3	
Assistant	1	2	3	
Peers	1	2	3	

Personality Variables

Guilt	1	2	3
Hostility (rage; uncooperativeness)	1	2	3
Tension	1	2	3
Pride	1	2	3
Depression	1	2	3
Affection	1	2	3

Appendix B-8

OUTLINE FOR DEPTH INTERVIEW

1. Skimming through family interview results plus most relevant information of the Biographical Inventory.
2. Interpretation of the most important data in the profile configurations of the MMPI for the three testing periods.
3. Checking of the data of the Intuitive Analysis for the three testing periods and clustering of them according to clinical and dynamic significance.
4. Questionnaire guided interview following the Depth Interview Supplement.
5. More unstructured depth interview about the conflictual aspects of the personality in order to discriminate the conscious from the subconscious elements of personality.
6. Inquiry about the psychogenesis of the main conflict.
7. Inquiry about sex life.
8. Final investigation about the degree of developmental maturity at the beginning, during the first two years of life in religious settings (or Novitiate), and during the third and fourth years.
9. Subject is asked if he has something to discuss, to object to, or to clarify.
10. Filling up of the items in " TAT stories " according to the result of the interview.
11. Ranking of the developmental stages or conflicts described by Erikson found in the interview.
12. Writing of a summary with psychopathological, dynamic and psychogenetic evaluations.

C. EXPLANATORY NOTES

Appendix C-1

THE NUMBER OF VARIABLES

There were 35 variables measured by each of the three sets of the MAI. The same number of variables was used to score the TAT and the Rotter ISB. Appendix B-1 shows the MAI scales and Appendix B-3, the scoring sheet.

All 35 variables were used in computing the percentages for all scores (pg. 43). The percentages obtained for the MAI-PB, MAI-SI, MAI-II, for the Rotter ISB, and for the TAT were, therefore, comparable.

The assessing procedures, explained in Chapter 3 " The Structural Approach ", were carried out using 14 variables selected from the 35 previously mentioned. 21 variables were not used. The eleven defenses and three of the emotions were scored on the projective techniques only and were not found in the MAI scales. 7 variables were not used because of a lack of satisfactory correspondence with the MAI scales.

The 14 variables were: Abasement, Achievement, Affiliation, Aggression, Chastity, Counteraction, Defendence, Dominance, Exhibition, Harm-avoidance, Nurturance, Order, Succorance, and Understanding.

Appendix C-2

THE DEFINITION OF TYPE
OF CONSISTENCY/INCONSISTENCY

The definition of type of consistency/inconsistency involved the decision concerning dissonance or neutrality of each of the 14 variables considered.

The content analysis of the definitions of variables used in scoring the TAT and Rotter ISB (Appendix B-3) and of the items constituting the MAI scales was made in the light of the 5 vocational

377

values indicated in Chapter 1 and in Chapter 3. Such analysis led to the following categorizations:

> *vocationally dissonant or non-neutral variables:* Abasement, Aggression, Chastity (the label for the measurement of heterosexual need gratification), Defendence, Exhibition, Harm avoidance, and Succorance.
>
> *vocationally less dissonant or more neutral variables:* Achievement, Affiliation, Counteraction, Dominance, Nurturance, Order, and Understanding.

This categorization had to be used for assessing types (see Chart 3, p. 39). The functional dissonance of the more neutral variables was assessed in the light of the total psychodynamics as characterized by the non-neutral variables. The rationale underlying this strategy was the psychodynamic unity of the person and the concept of centrality. Consistencies or inconsistencies on the seven vocationally dissonant variables were considered more central in comparison to the consistencies or inconsistencies on the other seven.

The following criteria were established to interpret the dissonance of the seven *more neutral* variables.

1. Whenever a vocationally neutral variable was present with an SI-II higher than the mean of all SI-II variables and a need in the actual-self (PB, LSR, LST) lower than the mean of all variables of the actual-self or vice versa (low SI-II and high need), this variable was considered vocationally *dissonant*. In this case, the discrepancy between attitude and need was higher than the mean of all need/attitude discrepancies for all variables. This vocationally neutral variable was considered to play a role of defense against another variable vocationally dissonant and inconsistent. This central inconsistency obviously had to be present. The defensive role could take the form of a conflict or the form of a defensive consistency. The reasons for this criterion was that the high discrepancy between the actual-self and the ideal-self was, in itself, an inconsistency, a polarization and should be considered psychodynamically a liability for the implementation of vocational values: it points out the presence of an ideal with no corresponding support in the actual self, be it in its more conscious (PB) or in its less conscious (LSR or LST) component/level.

In line with the theorizing regarding the prevailing influence of unconscious factors (chapter 1), when a high discrepancy was present between the ideal-self (SI-II) and the less conscious part of the actual-self (LST), even without the presence of such a discrepancy at the pre-conscious level (LSR), the first discrepancy (LST) was considered as decisive in assigning a character of dissonance to the neutral variable for the psychodynamics of the case at hand.

2. When neutral variables did not show a high discrepancy between the ideal-self (SI-II) and the actual-self (PB, LSR, LST) so that a consistency appeared to be present for that variable, the decision about the vocational dissonance of the variable had to be made entirely in the light of the dominant non-neutral functional inconsistencies. Throughout the entire study, this pattern and its related decision showed up rather infrequently. As an example, we may mention the case of an individual with a high consistency for nurturance (high need and high attitude) and a high central inconsistency for succorance. Given the basic unity of personal psychodynamics, it was assumed that his nurturance was affected by his strong inconsistency for succorance, and his nurturant quality was considered to fulfill a defensive, rather than a value expressive function. Consequently, nurturance was considered vocationally dissonant. Such dissonance should not lead us to conclude that the person was socially inconsistent on this variable, but should indicate that such a consistency, even though a consistency, was defensive rather than value expressive.

A defensive consistency is, therefore, a central consistency between the actual- and ideal-self that, due to the presence of a central inconsistency on a vocationally dissonant variable, fulfills a defensive function. Basically, the motivation is functionally dependent on another inconsistent aspect of the personality, like a role played in reference to another person or a group. However, it may acquire a motivational-autonomous function and lose its exclusive reference to a disturbing inconsistent motivation which counteracts as a defense. An example is the above-mentioned consistency for nurturance with a predominant inconsistency for succorance. During the depth interview the individual was genuinely convinced of the goodness of his nurturance and did not realize (as expected of a defense) the functionally defensive aspect of his nurturance. The same individual displayed an unconscious central inconsistency for affiliation with a preconscious consistency for affiliation. The defensive character of this affiliation was confirmed by the massive resistance found in the same depth interview to the understanding of the defensive function of his affiliation, an aspect which the rest of the interview strongly supported. In contrast, a psychological conscious consistency for knowledge was readily recognized as a defense by the subject during the interview, that is, that there was a lack of real interest for knowledge.

The variables vocationally less dissonant and more neutral were frequently found to be the ones fulfilling the function of defensive consistencies. These were the variables which would more easily manifest the vulnerability (non-objective and non-free character) of the SI-II (cfr. chapters 5 and 6). For instance, through the depth interview, one subject who had a very high SI-II for counteraction (restriving after failure) revealed information regarding his gastric ulcer condition.

Though more research is necessary in this area, one may be led to think of these vocationally non-dissonant variables as those which could possibly explain the perseverance of subjects whose lives display limited effectiveness. These variables are, indeed more socially acceptable to the group and appear less vocationally dissonant for the institution.

3. Vocationally non-neutral variables (abasement, aggression, chastity, defendence, exhibition, harm avoidance and succorance) were considered vocationally dissonant.

If they were present as consistencies, they could be *real* consistencies or *defensive* consistencies. They were considered defensive consistencies when two conditions were fulfilled: 1) the consistency was of a PsC type, and 2) the variable presenting this PsC was considered in combination with a central vocationally dissonant inconsistency. To give an example: the subject who is PsC for chastity because he has a low need for sexual gratification (LS) and a low attitude (SI-II) for chastity *and* who is socially inconsistent for succorance (needs *and* is afraid of people) may be seen as a person who passively accepts (does not strongly endorse) the ideal (SI-II) of chastity because of his inconsistent motivation in the area of succorance. Accordingly, his PsC is a functionally significant defensive consistency in light of his succorance.

The attentive reader will have noticed that for chastity (and the same applies to defendence) the definition of type of consistency/inconsistency requires a modification of chart 4. This is due to the fact that in the other variables (e.g., aggression, abasement, etc.) the MAI and the LS measure the same variable in the same direction. For chastity and defendence, the MAI measures chastity and humility (one side of the continuum) whereas, the Rotter ISB and the TAT measure the need for heterosexual gratification and pride, respectively (the other side of the same continuum).

The principles underlying the interpretation are the same and the psychodynamics are the same, but in reading chart 3 for chastity and defendence, the following should be observed:

— A high discrepancy between need and attitude *with* high need (LS) defines ——————————————— SoI
— A high discrepancy between need and attitude *with* low need (LS) defines ————————————————— SC

380

— A low discrepancy between need and attitude *with* high need (LS) defines —————————————— PsI

— A low discrepancy between need and attitude *with* low need (LS) defines ———————————————— PsC

The usual patterns are followed when defining conscious types of consistency/inconsistency because PB and SI-II measurements for chastity and humility are made in the same direction.

Following chart 3 and keeping in mind the lower contribution attributed to the different types of consistency/inconsistency as compared to level and degree, these coefficients were used:

for Social Consistency (SC) ——————————————— 1.50
Psychological Consistency (PsC) ———————————— .50
Psychological Inconsistency (PsI). ————————— .50
Social Inconsistency (SoI) ——————————————— 1.00

Appendix C-3

THE DEFINITION OF LEVEL
OF CONSISTENCY/INCONSISTENCY

The coefficients for level of consistency/inconsistency based on the assumption of the greater influence (chapter 1) of unconscious psychodynamics have been assigned as follows:

for Unconscious Consistency/Inconsistency, LST-(SI-II) — 3
Preconscious Consistency/Inconsistency, LSR-(SI-II) — 2
Conscious Consistency/Inconsistency, PB-(SI-II) ———— 1

Appendix C-4

THE DEFINITION OF DEGREE OF
INTRA-ACTUAL-SELF CONSISTENCY/INCONSISTENCY

The coefficients for the degree of intra-actual-self consistency/inconsistency were devised to measure quantitatively the degree of consistency/inconsistency resulting from the comparison of different substructures of the actual-self: the conscious (PB), preconscious (LSR), and unconscious (LST) in their relationship to the ideal-self (SI-II) (see chart 4).

381

This degree of intra-actual-self consistency/inconsistency is figuratively expressed by the ranking as found in chart 4 (p. 44). The ranking and the corresponding coefficients follow:

Degree	Rank	Components	Coefficient	
1	Conscious Consistency and			⎱Vocational
	Subconscious Inconsistency	2.00 + .99	2.99	⎰Inconsis-
2	Subconscious Inconsistency	2.00 + .66	2.66	tencies
3	Conscious Inconsistency and			
	Subconscious Inconsistency	.50 + .99	1.49	
4	Conscious Inconsistency	.50 + .66	1.16	Conflicts
5	Conscious Inconsistency and			
	Subconscious Consistency	.50 + .33	.83	
6	Conscious Consistency	2.00 + .33	2.33	
7	Subconscious Consistency	2.00 + .66	2.66	Vocational
8	Conscious Consistency and			Consis-
	Subconscious Consistency	2.00 + .99	2.99	tencies

Each coefficient assigned to each degree (1 to 8) is the result of two components: a) the first component — consistencies and inconsistencies are equated in terms of their psychodynamic weights and are given the coefficient 2; conflicts, as less psychodynamically important are given .50; and b) the second component — a weight was given to the intra-actual-self consistency/inconsistency proper, as it appears in the horizontal line of Chart 4. Fractions of 1 were used to assign a relative weight to patterns showing greater psychodynamic consistency or inconsistency. Notice that the above ranking consider conscious versus subconscious dimensions leaving aside the preconscious/unconscious distinction. The psychodynamics underlying the above rankings, as discussed in chapter 3, do not call for further differentiation or combinations.

However, in computing the weight for the psychodynamics for each individual's variables, the case was often presented where subconscious inconsistency or consistency appeared as central both at the preconscious and unconscious level. For degree 1, for instance, a conscious consistency for aggression could be accompanied by both, a preconscious *and* an unconscious inconsistency. In such a case, the pattern defined by the intra-actual-self degree was measured by using the sum of the two patterns, e.g., for degree 1, the pattern conscious consistency and preconscious inconsistency plus the pattern conscious consistency and unconscious inconsistency. The reader can see that such eventuality can occur for degrees 1, 2, 3, 5, 7, and 8.

382

This leads to a discussion of Appendix C-5. Each number in parenthesis is the result of the sum of three coefficients. The reader now has the elements to verify these coefficients for himself.

For example, the score of 6.99 for the SoI in the upper right cell of the table can be broken down as follows:

the coefficient for *level*	3	(unconscious)
the coefficient for *type*	1	(SoI)
the coefficient for intra-actual-self *degree*	2.99	(vocational
	———	inconsistency)
Sum $= 6.99$		

Appendix C-5

TYPOLOGY OF VOCATIONAL INCONSISTENCIES, CONFLICTS AND CONSISTENCIES AND CORRESPONDING COEFFICIENTS (In parenthesis)

Degree of Intra-Actual Self*	Vocational Inconsistencies			Number of Possible Types of Variable Patterns		Number of Possible Types of Individuals	
	Conscious	*Preconscious*	*Unconscious*	Ia	Ir	Ia	Ir
1	Consistency	PsI (5.49) SoI (5.99)	PsI (6.49) SoI (6.99)	4	16	4	16
2	—	PsI (5.16) SoI (5.66)	PsI (6.16) SoI (6.66)	4	16	4	16
		Conflicts					
	Conscious	*Preconscious*	*Unconscious*	Ia	Ir	Ia	Ir
3	Inconsistency	PsI (3.99) SoI (4.49)	PsI (4.99) SoI (5.49)	4	16	—	—
4	PsI (2.66) SoI (3.16)	—	—	2	8	—	—
5	Inconsistency	PsC (3.33) SC (4.33)	PsC (4.33) SC (5.33)	4	16	—	—
		Consistencies					
	Conscious	*Preconscious*	*Unconscious*	Ia	Ir	Ia	Ir
6	PsC (3.83) SC (4.83)	—	—	2	8	2	8
7	—	PsC (5.16) SC (6.16)	PsC (6.16) SC (7.16)	4	16	2	8
8	Consistency	PsC (5.49) SC (6.49)	PsC (6.49) SC (7.49)	4	16	2	8
			TOTALS:	28	112	14	56

* For consistency or inconsistency.

Case No. ——————————

SUMMARY CHART
FOR INDIVIDUAL PSYCHODYNAMIC EVALUATION

Inconsistencies

1. Abasement ——————
2. Aggression ——————
3. Chastity ——————
4. Defendence ——————
5. Exhibition ——————
6. Harm Avoidance ————
7. Succorance ——————
8. Achievement ——————
9. Affiliation ——————
10. Counteraction ——————
11. Dominance ——————
12. Nurturance ——————
13. Order ——————
14. Understanding——————
SUM ———

Defensive Consistencies

1. Abasement ——————
2. Aggression ——————
3. Chastity ——————
4. Defendence ——————
5. Exhibition ——————
6. Harm Avoidance ————
7. Succorance ——————
8. Achievement ——————
9. Affiliation ——————
10. Counteraction ————
11. Dominance ——————
12. Nurturance ——————
13. Order ——————
14. Understanding ————
SUM ———

Conflicts

1. Abasement ——————
2. Aggression ——————
3. Chastity — ——————
4. Defendence ——————
5. Exhibition ——————
6. Harm Avoidance ————
7. Succorance ——————
8. Achievement ——————
9. Affiliation ——————
10. Counteraction ——————
11. Dominance ——————
12. Nurturance ——————
13. Order ——————
14. Understanding——————
SUM ———

Consistencies

1. Abasement ——————
2. Aggression ——————
3. Chastity — ——————
4. Defendence ——————
5. Exhibition ——————
6. Harm Avoidance ————
7. Succorance ——————
8. Achievement ——————
9. Affiliation ——————
10. Counteraction ————
11. Dominance ——————
12. Nurturance ——————
13. Order ——————
14. Understanding ————
SUM ———

SUM TOTAL = ———

A. DEGREE OF COMPLIANCE $= \dfrac{\text{Sum Incons.} + \text{Sum Defens. Consist.}}{\text{Sum Total}} = \dfrac{}{100}$

B. DEGREE OF IDENTIFICATION $= \dfrac{\text{Sum Conflicts}}{\text{Sum Total}} = \dfrac{}{100}$

C. DEGREE OF INTERNALIZATION $= \dfrac{\text{Sum Consistencies}}{\text{Sum Total}} = \dfrac{}{100}$

D. INDEX OF ADAPTATION $= \dfrac{C - A}{A + C} =$

E. INDEX OF POSSIBLE GROWTH $= \dfrac{B}{200} =$

F. INDEX OF VOCATIONAL MATURITY $= D + E =$

THE INDEX OF VOCATIONAL MATURITY:
THE REFINEMENT OF ITS MEASUREMENT

The degree of identification — a basic component of the index of vocational maturity — was considered to be a measurement of two processes: internalizing identification and non-internalizing or defensive identification. However, the computational split assigning 50% of the degree of identification to each process did not seem to correspond in every case to the proper amount of defensive/internalizing identification. In fact, such a procedure tended to increase the degree of internalizing identification unrealistically. An analysis of the data confirmed this observation: twenty-eight cases taken at random from our sample yielded a mean discrepancy between degree of internalization and half the degree of identification of 7 with a range of 0 to 21.

Any discrepancy between the degree of internalization and half the degree of identification is a disproportion between the actual internalization of the individual and his capacity to internalize (internalizing identification). Whereas, a low discrepancy is to be considered an asset of the person's psychodynamics, a high discrepancy is to be considered a liability, revealing the predominance of defensive identification.

The assignment of a weight expressive of the above-mentioned asset/liability was made as follows:

for a discrepancy of	0, a weight of	30
	1	20
	2	10
3- 4		— 1
5- 8		— 2
9-15		— 3
16-26		— 4
27 +		— 5

These weights place a premium on the lack of discrepancy between the degree of internalization and identification, and highlight the presence of such discrepancy.

To measure the impact of this discrepancy between actual internalization and the capacity to internalize, another consideration had to be made. Like the impact of the stone depends on its weight as well as on the force that moves it, two stones of equal weight may have a different impact on the target because of the different speed generated by a different force; so the above-mentioned discrepancy (weight) was thought to provide a different impact on the total psychodynamics (the target) according to the different degree of compliance (force on speed) present in the individual. A greater degree of compliance would have to be considered as a greater liability being the provider of a greater force toward defensive identification.

Accordingly, weights were used that minimize the impact of low compliance and maximize the impact of high compliance:

Degree of Compliance	Weight
1- 19	0
20- 39	.25
40- 59	.50
60- 79	.75
80-100	1.00

These two measurements, the weight of the discrepancy between the degree of internalization and half the degree of identification, and the weight of the compliance were combined. The resulting score was algebraically added to the original index of vocational maturity.

388

Appendix C-8

TYPES AND DEGREES OF PERSEVERANCE AND EFFECTIVENESS IN VOCATION FOR THE INTER AND INTRA-PERSONAL DIMENSIONS

Interpersonal Dimension (Ir)

Intrapersonal Dimensions		PsC +N +V (Col. 1)	PsC −A (Col. 2)	SC +N +V (Col. 1)	SC −A (Col. 2)	PsI +N +V (Col. 1)	PsI −A (Col. 2)	SoI +N +V (Col. 1)	SoI −A (Col. 2)
SC +V +A / +N		P3	P5	P3	P5	P3	P1	P3	P1
		E6	E6	E6	E6	E6	E0	E6	E0
PsC +V −A / +N		P1	P3	P1	P3	P1	P-1	P1	P-1
		E2	E4	E2	E2	E2	E-2	E2	E0
PsI +V +A / −N		P-3	P-1	P-3	P-1	P-3	P-5	P-3	P-5
		E0	E0	E0	E0	E0	E0	E0	E0
SoI +V −A / −N		P-1	P1	P-1	P1	P-1	P-3	P-1	P-3
		E-2	E-2	E-2	E-2	E-2	E-2	E-2	E-2

N. B. *For the Intrapersonal Dimension (Ia).*
Positive (+) or negative (−) signs shown above needs (N), values (V), and attitudes (A) indicate self attributes which are respectively consonant or dissonant with vocation.
For the Interpersonal Dimension (Ir).
Positive (+) or negative (−) signs shown above needs (N), values (V), and attitudes (A) indicate self attributes which are respectively fulfilled or not fulfilled by the group. (For *fuller* explanation see text). (Rulla, 1971, p. 128).

Appendix C-9

SCORING PROCEDURE FOR FAMILY CONFLICTS ON THE BIOGRAPHICAL INVENTORY (BI), FAMILY INTERVIEW (FI), AND DEPTH INTERVIEW (DI)

1. On the Biographical Inventory (BI) (subject's self-report):
   + Positive score, i.e., as conflict absent, relationship positive with mother and father, if the subject had circled the polar aspect of the continuum " conflict....harmony " with emphasis on " *harmony* ", part 7, 8, 9 or its equivalent* in Number 55, Task One for description of interaction with mother and Task Two for interaction with father.
   — Negative score, i.e., as conflict present, relationship poor with mother and father, if the subject had circled the polar aspect of " *conflict* " on the same continuum, emphasis on 1, 2, or 3 of the continuum, in Tasks of Number 55 as above. A negative sign was given if there was conflict with *either* or *both* of the parents.
2. On the Family Interview (FI) (cfr. Appendix B-5):
   + Positive score coded, indicating no conflict present if the interviewer, after discussing the family with the subject, had circled a 5, 4 or 3 on the summary sheet for Interactional Conflict, suggesting little conflict. Consideration was also given to scorings for Affection and Communication which were generally indicated as good if they were 4 or 5.
   — Negative score coded, indicating conflict present if the interviewer had circled a 2 or 1 on the summary sheet for inter-

---

* Equivalent elements were used when the subject had circled a 4, 5, or 6 on the continuum. Since this was in the medium range, the other statistically reliable scales were considered : if consistently positively oriented, a positive score was given ; if negatively oriented or confused, a negative score was indicated.

actional conflict, suggesting great conflict at home. Scorings for poor affection and communication (1 or 2) substantiated the conflict scoring.

3. On the Depth Interview (DI):

+ Positive score coded indicating no conflict present if the subject had indicated to the interviewer in discussing family that the family relationships had been favorable and maturing, and there was no contradicting evidence.

— Negative score coded if the subject alone, or on confrontation, had indicated to the interviewer that the relationships at home had been disturbing. Most subjects were not only ready to admit the less ideal situation but also to go on to confirm and extend the confrontation. **

** Note that here family relationships include the relationship of the vocationers with parents, NOT the relationship between parents.

Appendix C-10

THE PREDICTABLE INTERNALIZING CAPACITY: FURTHER PROCEDURES FOR ITS ASSESSMENT

The distinction between the vocationally dissonant and the vocationally more neutral variables used in this assessment is described in Appendix C-2.

The conceptual and operational definitions of " defensive consistencies " given in Appendix C-2 point to the fact that these consistencies function as a defense or as a conflictual gratification of central inconsistencies of dissonant variables. Therefore, dynamically they are strictly tied to these inconsistencies and thus, have a similar dynamic impact upon the total motivation of a person. This impact will quite probably remain the same as long as the inconsistencies which produce and sustain these defenses remain unconscious or deeply preconscious. This reasoning is in line with Hartmann's (1950, 1952, 1955, 1958) conceptualization concerning the function of defenses. Accordingly, in our evaluation of the predictable internalizing capacity of each individual, the percentages over the total scores of his defensive consistencies were added to the percentages of his homonymous central inconsistencies.

The assessment of central inconsistencies and related defensive consistencies presents a relevant question concerning the variable " chastity ", which in our test operational definitions concerns especially the need for or the defense against heterosexual relationships. In this regard, Courtney Murray (1967) has stressed the fact that the three vows of chastity, poverty and obedience may be signs of an outstanding love for God, but may also imply the more or less unconscious avoidance of three basic " encounters " of man with the other sex, with work and its insecurity, with his spirit and its power of free choice.

Now, for chastity, the object and the situations (especially in the sense of the " encounters " connected with a marital, intimate union) which may arouse threats for the vocationer are more or only *out-*

side the vocational commitment; while for the other "encounters", actually for all the other thirteen variables studied here, the threatening object or situation may be both inside or outside such a commitment. In a parallel way of thinking, Schilebeeckx (1968, p. 89 states that Christian celibacy is the only evangelical "counsel" properly so called, while all the other evangelical counsels and the commandments are necessary for perfection in love. Thus, the variable "chastity" should be handled in a special way, at least when it presents central inconsistencies or defensive consistencies. In fact, in *such* cases, the individuals more subconsciously frightened by the outside "encounters" will project a more defensive SI-II produced and sustained especially by their underlying defensive consistencies or inconsistencies for chastity. As a consequence of this greater defensive SI-II, these individuals are driven rather to stay in than to go out of vocation, and this not in spite of but because of their defensive SI-II. If this is the case, then these individuals' lower capacity to internalize is a sign of a force which pushes to be NDO rather than DO and it should be assessed accordingly.

Of course, this type of assessment can be used only if the data available concerning central inconsistencies and defensive consistencies indicate that the individuals or the groups considered are statistically significantly higher in the central inconsistencies and the defensive consistencies for chastity. An analysis of variance between DO and NDO for seminarians, religious men and women, showed that only the NDO male religious were significantly higher than their corresponding DO for central inconsistencies and defensive consistencies of chastity (df within = 20; F = 3.26; p < .04). In the same line, as chart 14 shows, the same male religious are the only ones to be always higher for frequency of defensive consistencies on chastity in comparison with all the other groups of seminarians, female religious and male controls.

GLOSSARY

ADAPTATION, *Index of*: a measurement devised to express the relative weight and therefore the prevalence of the tendency toward internalization over the tendency toward compliance.

ASSESSMENT: 1) a loose general term for measurement. 2) a complex measuring procedure in which several subjects are observed in a sequence of unstructured and structured activities — lasting for hours or days — and are rated by trained observers.

Assessment " of ": the evaluation of the psychodynamics of entering vocationers emphasizing the "understanding" of the mechanics of the entering process.

Assessment " for ": the evaluation of the psychodynamics of entering vocationers emphasizing its "predicting" aspects or its influence upon future vocational perseverence or effectiveness.

Multidimensional model or strategy: based on quantitative variation of dimensions or variables.

Typological model or strategy: based on a qualitative patterning of variables.

ATTITUDE: a mental and neural state of readiness to respond, organized through experience, exerting a directive and/or dynamic influence on mental and physical activities. An attitude includes a cognitive, affective and conative component, and may have the following 4 functions:

1) *Utilitarian function* of an attitude is ˥resent when a particular attitude is adopted because of its specific utility — reward or punishment — to the adopting subject.

2) *Ego-defensive function*: is present when an attitude is adopted in order to defend the subject's self from a conscious or subconscious threat.

3) *Cognitive function*: is present when an attitude is adopted — tsatisfy the desire to know reality.

4) *Value-expressive function*: is present when an attitude is adopted in view of realizing the values held by the subject.

Normative vs. preferential: see under VALUE.

394

Examples of specific attitudes are given in Appendix B-1, p. 338; e.g. " taking the blame for something done by someone I like ". As seen on the same page, specific attitudes can be grouped to indicate general attitudes like " self-depreciation versus self-confidence ", etc.

CENTRALITY: a structural quality of a consistency or inconsistency indicating the functional significance of the same consistency or inconsistency for the psychodynamics of the individual. Three factors contribute to the definition of centrality: a) relevance of a self-attribute for the achievement of one's goals; b) centrality of the same self-attribute for maintaining a positive self-conception or self-esteem; c) adequacy or inadequacy of the person's coping mechanisms in handling the same self-attribute toward the achievement of his goals.

COMPLIANCE: the process of accepting influence from a social agent on the basis of reward or punishment.

CONFLICT: In general, the state of an individual who is prompted to respond simultaneously in different and incompatible ways. Specifically, in this work, three patterns on the intra-actual self consistency/inconsistency continuum (cf. Chart 4, nn. 3, 4, 5) have been designated as " conflicts ". In this sense, they constitute rather preconscious inconsistencies as opposed to consistencies and to unconscious inconsistencies.

CONSCIOUS: the normal field of consciousness that the individual has of himself and things actually present.

CONSISTENCY: is present when an individual is motivated by needs in accordance with vocational values.

Social consistency (SC): when a need, conscious or subconscious, and its corresponding attitude is consonant with vocational values.

Psychological consistency (PsC): when a need conscious or subconscious is consonant with vocational values but is not consonant with the corresponding attitude.

Type of: the pattern taken by the relationship between need, attitude and value. Basically, two types were considered, psychological (PsC) and social (SC) consistency; see, however, TYPOLOGY.

Level of: the fact that a consistency is found at the conscious, preconscious or unconscious level of personality.

Degree of: a quantitative expression of the amount of congruence among the relevant subsystems of the self (cf. Chapter 3 and related Appendices).

CONSTRUCT: a formal concept, a concept that has been systematically defined, delineated, and perhaps related to other constructs.

CORRELATION: the degree of relationship or association between two variables. It is most commonly expressed by a coefficient, like e.g. the Pearson product-moment.

DATA COMBINATION: a basic component of assessment, distinct from data collection, indicating the way in which the data were organized in the assessment procedure.

Clinical combination: when the data are organized largely by the cognizing activity of a clinician.

Statistical combination: when the combining of the data is made by a statistician or a computer.

DATA COLLECTION: see MEASUREMENT.

DEFENSE: a subconscious psychodynamic process which serves to protect the person against danger arising from his impulses or affects.

DEPTH INTERVIEW: an assessment technique used with the subjects of this study after about four years of training. Its procedures are described in Chapter 3.

DEPTH PSYCHOLOGY: the psychology relating to the realm of the subconscious, in contradistinction to the psychology of the conscious part of the mind.

DEVELOPMENTAL MATURITY, *Index of*: a measurement devised to express the degrees of compliance, identification and internalization of an entering vocationer as they can be inferred by his/her capacity to handle, to control his/her major core conflicts.

DISCRIMINANT FUNCTION ANALYSIS: a statistical technique which, providing a partial control for variable intercorrelation, allows a consideration of the magnitude of each variable's contribution to the discrimination between two groups.

EFFECTIVENESS (VOCATIONAL): the visible manifestation and/or social communication of the terminal values, union with God and imitation of Christ.

FAMILY DYNAMICS INTERVIEW: a relatively structured type of interview aimed at clarifying major family conflicts, major familial influences on the subjects and the degree of insight of the subject concerning family dynamics. Its procedures are described in Chapter 3.

FREQUENCY: the number of cases, persons or events in a given distribution or group.

FULFILLMENT: the process of realization of the potentialities as well as of the ideals of an individual.

FUNCTIONAL SIGNIFICANCE: of a consistency/inconsistency: see CENTRALITY.

GERMINATIVE SELF-IDEAL IN SITUATION: the extent to which the self-ideal of individual vocationers is open to growth toward self-transcendence. Concretely, it is the extent to which the self-ideal-in situation shows a prevailing consistency with the actual self of the vocationer.

GOAL: any object appraised as suitable or unsuitable for action. See VALUE.

IDENTIFICATION: the process of accepting influence from a social agent or referent, based on the self-defining value of the relationship with the social agent, person of group.

Internalizing identification: when the process of identification leads to the process of internalization, because the part of the self which is defined is consistent with the values to be internalized.

Non-internalizing identification: when identification does not lead to internalization because the part of the self which is defined is not consistent with the values to be internalized.

INCONSISTENCY: is present when an individual is motivated by needs that are dissonant with vocational values.

Social inconsistency (SoI): when a subconscious need, is dissonant with values but consonant with its corresponding attitude.

Psychological inconsistency (PsI): when a subconscious need is dissonant with values and with its corresponding attitude.

Type of: the pattern taken by the relationship between need, attitude and value. Basically, two types were considered, psychological (PsI) and social (SoI); see however TYPOLOGY.

Level of: the fact that an inconsistency is found at the conscious, preconscious or unconscious level of personality.

Degree of: a quantitative expression of the amount of discrepancy among relevant subsystems of the self (cf. Chapter 3 and related Appendices).

INTERJUDGE RELIABILITY: the generalizability of a procedure over raters or judges, determined from the correlation between their ratings.

INTERNAL CONSISTENCY (statistical): the generalizability estimated from the correlations among the items or other parts of a test. It is commonly labeled as the Kuder-Richardson 20, or simply K-R 20.

INTERNALIZATION: the process of adopting a way of behaving or thinking because it is congruent with one's value system.

INTERNALIZING CAPACITY, Predictable: the more or less unrealistic Self-Ideal-in Situation (SI-II) of expectations of the individual about his future vocational roles. This unrealistic Self-Ideal-in Situation stems from the imbalances between the central inconsistencies and consistencies of needs vs. homonymous attitudes. The unrealistic Self-Ideal-in Situation may influence vocational perseverence and effectiveness because it influences the capacity to internalize vocational values and attitudes.

INVENTORY: a paper-and-pencil test of personality with verbal content, usually measuring more than one variable and implying inclusiveness of coverage.

MEASUREMENT: the assigning of a quantitative ordering to objects in accordance with certain rules. In a more specific way, it is the assigning of scores or indices to persons on the basis of their responses as elicited by a standard procedure.

NEED: action tendency resulting from a deficit of the organism or from natural inherent potentialities which seek exercise or actuality. For examples, see Appendix B-3; page 353; e.g.: ABASEMENT, ACHIEVEMENT, etc.

OPERATIONAL DEFINITION: the empirical measurement or set of measurements taken to express a theoretically relevant concept or construct.

POSSIBLE GROWTH, *Index of:* a measurement which is an elaboration of the Degree of Identification and is intended to express the weight of the internalizing identification on the psychodynamics of the individual.

PREDICTIVE VALIDITY: the correlation between a criterion measure, generally obtained at a later point in time, and a specific test or set of tests.

PSYCHODYNAMICS: the constellation of motivational forces operating within the person which may be expressed by the external behavior.

PSYCHOPATHOLOGY: the branch of science dealing with morbidity or pathology of the mind.

Overt or manifest: when there is evidence of open symptoms, like in schizophrenia or the neuroses.

Covert or latent: in the absence of clear symptoms, like in character disorders or central vocational inconsistencies.

QUESTIONNAIRE: a paper-and-pencil personality test. Its content are questions or implied questions.

RELIABILITY: the extent of the agreement between two or more sets of measurements when essentially the same precedure has been used.

ROLE: the set of prescriptions defining what the behavior of the position member should be.

Role Concept: the perceptions or beliefs of the subjects about his own role, which society offers to him.

Role expectation: the perceptions of a role as held by others in society and offered to an individual for assimilation. These perceptions are organized as social expectations, societal demands or professional requirements.

Role orientation: a way of using the role as an end in itself (rather than using the role as a means to realize values which are both role-transcendent and self-transcendent; see, in contrast, VALUE orientation).

SCORE: a number assigned to a subject and based on the subject's response to one or several items, usually of a test.

SELF or personality: the way the person interacts with the world outside him and the world within him.

Ideal Self: a) as *Institutional Ideal* are the perceptions one has of the ideals his vocational institution values for its members; the individual's role concept (indicated in this work by II); b) as *Self Ideals* are the ideals a person values for himself, e.g. what he would like to be or do.

Actual Self: a) as *Present Behavior* or the manifest self-concepts, e.g. the subject's cognitions about his own present behavior (indicated in this work by PB); b) as *Latent Self:* or the personality characteristics revealed by projective-type instruments. It is assumed that this type of instruments reveals what characteristics, conscious or subconscious, a person actually possesses not merely those which he thinks he has or would like to have (In this work is indicated by LST — prevailingly unconscious — and LSR — prevailiingly preconscious).

SELF ATTRIBUTE: a specific dimensional content (e.g. aggression, succorance) assessed in this study in function of its structural qualities, like centrality, type, level and degree of consistency/inconsistency.

SELF-CONCEPTION: A consistency or an inconsistency of the ideal-self for attitude with the corresponding actual-self, including its subconscious part.

SENTENCE COMPLETION TEST: a semi-unstructured test in which the subject is provided with a series of sentence beginnings which he has to finish in some way.

STABILITY: the generalizability over time estimated from the correlation between scores on a test administered at two different times.

STRUCTURAL APPROACH: a way of considering man as a composite of a definite number of structures, of subsystems of the self: the actual self, the ideal self and their components. The subsystems are distinct but dynamically related among themselves by qualitative patterns. This approach allows one to obtain results which may be transsituational and transtemporal, i.e. valid for people of different cultures, social milieux and vocational institutions.

SUBCONSCIOUS: encompasses the field of psychic experience which is not present to the actual consciousness of the individual and may be:

Preconscious: when the memories can be recalled to consciousness through ordinary rational methods, like reflection, examination of conscience, introspection, meditation etc.

Unconscious: comprehensive of those psychic contents which can be brought to consciousness only through professional intervention, like for instance, psychotherapy.

TEST: a measuring device consisting of a standard set of operations.

Structured: also called objective, when the subject is presented with a structured, organized, specific situation to which to respond.

Unstructured: also called projective, when the subject is presented with a relative unstructured, ambiguous situation to which to respond.

TRANSFERENCE: the process of feeling and behaving toward a person in the same way as one did toward important figures of the past, generally parents, relatives or educators.

Positive: when there is a friendly, attractive attitude toward the other person.

Negative: when there is an unfriendly, hostile attitude toward the other person.

TYPOLOGY: the placing of each subject or variable in one of two or more qualitatively different types within a psychometric model.

Typology of variables: the patterns in which a specific variable can appear in the personal psychodynamics. In this study, 28 patterns were considered (cf. Chapter 3, and Appendix C-5).

Typology of individuals: the patterns of individual intrapsychic dynamics. Only functionally significant vocational consistencies or inconsistencies are considered. In this study, 14 patterns: 8 inconsistencies and 6 consistencies were considered (cf. Chapter 3, and Appendix C-5).

VALIDITY: the extent to which a test or set of tests measure the variable(s) they are intended to measure.

VALUE: enduring abstract ideals of a person, which may be ideal end-states of existence (*terminal* values or ends) or ideal modes of conduct (*instrumental* values or means). A terminal value may be the " Imitation of Christ "; instrumental values may be

400

the three vows of Poverty, Chastity and Obedience or the ones listed in Appendix B-2, pages 351-352.

Norm value to Preference value: a continuum ranging from mandatory to preference based on a matter of taste.

Value orientation: the adopting and use of behaviors or roles as means toward the realization of values or the expression of the same values.

VARIABLE: a quantity that varies; in this work it is used as a general term for a dimension or aspect of personality that varies over people.

Vocationally dissonant: a specific variable which, for its content, is particularly relevant to vocational values (cf. Appendix C-2).

Vocationally neutral: a specific variable which, for its content is not particularly conducive or opposite to vocational values (cf. Appendix C-2).

VOCATIONAL MATURITY, *Index of:* a measurement aiming at expressing the total psychodynamics of the individual in terms of the structural qualities of his consistencies/inconsistencies. It is obtained by finding the algebraic sum of the Index of Adaptation and the Index of Possible Growth.

VOCATIONAL PROBLEMS: different types of impairment in the personality of vocationers : 1) spiritual problems, 2) developmental difficulties, 3) vocational subconscious and latent (the individual appears normal) inconsistencies, 4) more or less manifest non vocational psychopathology.

VULNERABLE SELF-IDEAL IN SITUATION: the extent to which the Self-Ideal of individual vocationers is undermined by subconscious conflicts or inconsistencies.

BIBLIOGRAPHY

Adams, J. F. (Ed.). *Contributions to the understanding of adolescence.*
Rockleigh, N. J. : Allyn and Bacon, Inc., 1968.

Allen, V. L. Role theory and consistency theory. In R. Abelson et
al., *Theories of cognitive consistency* : *A sourcebook.* Chicago :
Rand McNally and Co., 1968, pp. 201-209.

Allport, G. W. Attitudes. In C. Murchison (Ed.), *Handbook of social
psychology.* Worcester, Mass. : Clark University Press, 1935,
pp. 798-884.

—— *Personality* : *A psychological interpretation.* New York : Holt,
Rinehart and Winston, Inc., 1937.

—— Attitudes in the history of social psychology. In G. Lindzey,
(Ed.), *Handbook of social psychology,* Vol. I. Reading, Mass. :
Addison-Wesley Publishing Co., 1954, pp. 43-45.

—— *Patterns and growth in personality.* New York : Holt, Rinehart
and Winston, Inc., 1961.

Arnold, M. B. *Emotion and personality.* 2 vols. New York : Columbia University Press, 1960.

—— Human action and emotion. In T. Mischel (Ed.), *Human
action* : *Conceptual and empirical issues.* New York : Academic
Press, 1961, pp. 167-185.

—— Perennial problems in the field of emotion. In M. B. Arnold
(Ed.), *Feelings and emotion.* New York : Academic Press, Inc.,
1970, pp. 169-185.

Aronson, E. Dissonance theory : progress and problems. In R.
Abelson et al., *Theories of cognitive consistency* : *A sourcebook.*
Chicago : Rand Mc Nally and Co., 1968, pp. 5-27.

—— The theory of cognitive dissonance : A current perspective.
In L. Berkowitz (Ed.), *Advances in experimental social psychology.*
New York : Academic Press, Inc., 1969.

Arrupe, P. Y a-t-il encore des Jésuites ? Réponse à quelque questions. Dossier des *Informations Catholiques Internationales,* 1972,
419, 11-28.

Atkinson, J. W. Motivational determinants of risk taking behavior.
Psychological Review, 1957, 64, 359-372.

Ausubel, D. P. *Ego development and the personality disorders.* New
York : Grune and Stratton, Inc., 1952.

Baars, C. W. and Terruwe, A. *How to treat and prevent the crisis in the priesthood.* Chicago, Ill. : Franciscan Herald Press, 1972.

Bandura, A. and Walters, R. H. *Social learning and personality development.* New York : Holt, Rinehart and Winston, Inc., 1963.

Becker, R. J. Religion and psychological health. In M. P. Strommen (Ed.), *Research on religious development.* New York : Hawthorn Books, 1971, pp. 390-421.

Becker, S. L. and Mittman, A. Student perceptions of SUI, Report No. 1. Unpublished manuscript, 1962.

Becker, W. C. Consequences of different kinds of parental discipline. In M. L. Hoffman and L. W. Hoffman (Eds.), *Review of child development research.* New York : Russel Sage Foundation, 1964, pp. 169-208.

Beier, E. G. The effects of induced anxiety on flexibility of intellectual functioning. *Psychological Monographs,* 1951, 65, No. 9.

Beirnaert, L. (S. J.). Discernement et psychisme. *Christus,* 1954, 4, 50-61.

Berdie, R. F. College expectations, experiences, and perceptions. *Journal of College Student Personnel,* 1966, 7, 336-344.

—— A university is a many-faceted thing. *Personnel and Guidance Journal,* 1967, 45, 768-775.

Berkowitz, L. *The development of motives and values in the child.* New York : Basic Books, Inc., 1964.

—— Social motivation. In G. Lindzey and E. Aronson (Eds.), *The handbook of social psychology,* Vol. III. Reading, Mass. : Addison-Wesley Publishing Co., 1969, pp. 50-135.

Berkun, M., Bialek, H., Kern, R., and Yagi, K. Experimental studies of psychological stress in men. *Psychological Monographs,* 1962, 76, 1-39.

Bier, W. C. (S.J.) (Ed.) *Psychological testing for ministerial selection.* New York : Fordham University Press, 1970.

Bock, D. R. Multivariate analysis of variance of repeated measurements. In C. W. Harris (Ed.), *Problems of measuring change.* Madison : University of Wisconsin Press, 1963.

Bordin, E. S., Nachmann, B., and Segal, S. J. An articulated framework for vocational development. *Journal of Counseling Psychology,* 1963, *10,* 107-117.

Bradburn, N. M. *The structure of psychological well-being.* NORC monographs in social research, no. 15. Chicago : Aldine-Atherton, Inc., 1969.

Brehm, J. M. and Cohen, A. R. *Explorations in cognitive dissonance.* New York : John Wiley and Sons, Inc., 1962.

Brock, T. C. Effects of prior dishonesty on postdecision dissonance. *Journal of Abnormal and Social Psychology,* 1963, *66,* 325-331.

—— Commitment to exposure as a determinant of information receptivity. *Journal of Personal and Social Psychology,* 1965, 2, 10-19.

—— Dissonance without awareness. In R. Abelson et al. (Eds.),

Theories of cognitive consistency : *A sourcebook.* Chicago : Rand McNally and Co., 1968, pp. 408-416.

Brock, T. C. and Blackwood, J. E. Dissonance reduction, social comparison and modification of other's opinions. *Journal of Abnormal and Social Psychology,* 1962, *65,* 319-324.

Brock, T. C. and Grant, L. D. Dissonance, awareness and motivation. *Journal of Abnormal and Social Psychology,* 1963, *67,* 53-60.

Bronfenbrenner, U. Some familial antecedents of responsibility and leadership in adolescents. In L. Petrullo and B. M. Bass (Eds.), *Leadership and interpersonal behavior.* New York : Holt, Rinehart and Winston, Inc., 1961, pp. 239-271.

Brown, R. D. Student characteristics and institutional impact of the large publicly controlled vs. the small private institution. *College and University,* 1967, *42,* 325-336.

Bruning, J. L. and Kintz, B. L. *Computational handbook of statistics.* Glenview, Ill. : Scott, Foresman and Co., 1968.

Buckley, H. D. The relationship between achievement and satisfaction to anticipated environmental press of transfer students in the State University of New York. Unpublished Ph. D. dissertation, Syracuse University, 1969.

Buckley, M. J. (S. J.). The structure of the rules for the discernment of spirits. *The Way,* Supplement 20, Autumn 1973.

Byrne, D. and Blaylock, B. Similarity and assumed similarity of attitudes between husbands and wives. *Journal of Abnormal and Social Psychology,* 1963, *67,* 636-640.

Cameron, N. *Personality Development and Psychopathology. A Dynamic Approach.* Boston : Houghton-Mifflin, 1963.

Campbell, A., Converse, P. E., Miller, W. E., and Stokes, D. E. *The American voter.* New York : John Wiley and Sons, Inc., 1960.

Carroll, D. W. A follow-up study of psychological assessment. In W. C. Bier (S.J.) (Ed.), *Psychological testing for ministerial selection.* New York : Fordham University Press, 1970, pp. 159-189.

Cattell, R. B. et al. *Sixteen Personality Factor Questionnaire.* Champaign, Ill. : Institute for Personality and Ability Testing, 1956.

Chickering, A. W. Faculty perceptions and changing institutional press. Goddard College (Mimeo), n. d.

Clark, R. A. The projective measurement of experimentally induced levels of sexual motivation. *Journal of Experimental Psychology,* 1952, *44,* 391-399.

Cohen, A. R., Greenbaum, C. W., and Mansson, H. H. Commitment to social deprivation and verbal conditioning. *Journal of Abnormal and Social Psychology,* 1963, *67,* 410-421.

Conrad, J. P. The nature and treatment of the violent offender. In C. Spencer (Ed.), *A typology of violent offenders.* California Department of Corrections, Research Report No. 23, 1966.

Cooley, C. H. *Two major works : Social organization and Human nature and the social order.* Glencoe, Ill. : The Free Press, 1956.

Croghan, L. M. Encounter groups and the necessity for ethical guidelines. *Journal of Clinical Psychology*, 1974, *30*, 438-445.
Cronbach, L. J. *Essentials of psychological testing*. New York : Harper and Row Publishers, Inc., 1970.

Dahlstrom, W. G. Personality systematics and the problem of types. From General Learning Press, Morristown, N. J., 1972, pp. 1-27.
Dahlstrom, W. G. and Welsh, G. S. *An MMPI handbook. A guide to use in clinical practice and research*. Minneapolis : University of Minnesota Press, 1960, 1972.
D'Arcy, P. F. Bibliography of psychological, sociological and related studies on the Catholic priesthood and the religious life. In W. J. Coville, P. F. D'Arcy, T. N. McCarthy, and J. J. Rooney, *Assessment of candidates for the religious life*. Washington, D. C. : CARA, 1968.
Darmanin, A. Etude psychologique des séminaristes à travers le *test de Rorschach*. Louvain, Centre de Psychologie de la Religion, Mimeo, 1973.
DeCharms, R., Morrison, R. H., Reitman, W., and McClelland, D. C. Behavioral correlates of directly and indirectly measured achievement motivation. In D. C. McClelland (Ed.), *Studies in motivation*. New York : Appleton-Century-Crofts, Inc., 1955.
Directoria Exercitiorum Spiritualium (1540-1599). Ed. I. Iparraguirre. Rome : Monumenta Historica Societatis Jesu, 1955.
Dittes, J. E. Research on clergymen : Factors influencing decision for religious service and effectiveness in the vocation. *Religious Education* (Research Supplement), 1962, Vol. LVII, 141-165.
—— Psychological characteristics of religious professionals. In M. P. Strommen (Ed.), *Research on religious development*. New York : Hawthorn Books, Inc., 1971, pp. 422-460.
Dollard, J., Doob, L. W., Miller, N. E., Mowrer, O. H., and Sears, R. R. *Frustration and aggression*. New Haven, Conn. : Yale University Press, 1939.
Douglas, W. T. Response. In W. C. Bier (Ed.), *Psychological testing for ministerial selection*. New York : Fordham University Press, 1970, p. 190.
Douvan, E., and Kaye, C. Motivational factors in college entrance. In N. Sanford (Ed.), *The American college : A psychological and social interpretation of the higher learning*. New York : John Wiley and Sons., Inc., 1962, pp. 199-224.

Easterbrook, J. A. The effect of emotion on cue utilization and the organization of behavior. *Psychological Review*, 1959, *66*, 183-201.
Educational Testing Service. *General goals of life inventory*. Princeton, N. J. : 1950.
Edwards J. D., and Ostrom, T. M. Value-bonded attitudes : Changes in attitude structure as a function of value bonding and type

of communication discrepancy. *Proceedings, 77th Annual Convention, American Psychological Association,* 1969, 413-414.

Emmerich, W. Socialization and sex-role development. In P. B. Baltes and K. W. Schaie (Eds.), *Life-span developmental psychology.* New York : Academic Press Inc., 1973, pp. 123-144.

Erikson, E. H. *Childhood and society.* New York : W. W. Norton and Co., Inc., 1950, 1963.

—— Identity and the life cycle. *Psychological Issues,* 1959, *1,* No. 1.

Essen-Möller, E. Individual traits and morbidity in a Swedish rural population. *Acta Psychiat. Scand. Suppl.,* 1956, 100.

Etzioni, A. Basic human needs, alienation and inauthenticity. *American Sociological Review,* 1968, *34,* 870-885.

Fairchild, R. W. Delayed gratification : A psychological and religious analysis. In M. P. Strommen (Ed.), *Research on religious development.* New York : Hawthorn Books, 1971, pp. 155-210.

Feldman, K. A., and Newcomb, T. M. *The impact of college on students.* San Francisco : Jossey-Bass Inc., Publishers, 1969.

Feshback, S. The influence of drive arousal and conflict upon fantasy behavior. In J. Kagan and G. S. Lesser (Eds.), *Contemporary issues in Thematic Apperceptive methods.* Springfield, Ill. : Charles C. Thomas, Publisher, 1961.

Festinger, L. *A theory of cognitive dissonance.* New York : Harper and Row Publishers, Inc., 1957.

—— *Conflict, decision and dissonance.* Stanford, Calif. : Stanford University Press, 1964.

Finney, J. C. Development of a new set of MMPI scales. *Psychological Reports,* 1965, *17,* 706-713.

—— Factor structure with the new set of MMPI scales and the formula correction. *Journal of Clinical Psychology,* 1966, *22,* 443-449.

Fishbein, M. An investigation of the relationships between beliefs about an object and attitude toward that object. *Human Relations,* 1963, *16,* 233-239.

—— A consideration of beliefs, attitudes and their relationship. In I. D. Skiner and M. Fishbein (Eds.), *Current studies in social psychology.* New York : Holt, Rinehart and Winston, Inc., 1965, pp. 107-120.

Fisher, M. S. The relationship of satisfaction, achievement, and attention to anticipated environmental press. Unpublished M. A. thesis, Brigham Young University, 1961.

—— Environment, expectations, and the significance of disparity between actual and expected environment at the University of Utah. Unpublished doctoral dissertation, University of California, Los Angeles, 1966.

Fiske, D. W. *Measuring the concepts of personality.* Chicago : Aldine-Atherton, Inc., 1971.

—— Can a personality construct be validated empirically ? *Psychological Bulletin,* 1973, *80,* 89-92.

Fiske, D. W. and Pearson, P. H. Theory and techniques of personality measurement. In P. H. Mussen and M. R. Rosenzweig (Eds.), *Annual review of psychology*, Vol. 21. Palo Alto, California : Annual Reviews, 1970, pp. 49-86.

Fouriezos, N. T., Hutt, M. L., and Guetzkow, H. Measurement of self-oriented needs in discussion groups. *Journal of Abnormal and Social Psychology*, 1950, *45*, 682-690.

Frankl, V. E. *Der Unbedingte Mesch.* Wien : Deuticke, 1959.

—— *Psychotherapy and existentialism.* New York : Washington Square Press, 1967.

—— *The will to meaning.* New York : The World Publishing Company, 1969.

Fransen, P. Pour une psychologie de la grâce divine. *Lumen Vitae,* 1957, *12*, 209-240.

Freedman, J. L., Wallington, S. A., Bless, E. Compliance without pressure : The effect of guilt. *Journal of Personal and Social Psychology*, 1967, *7*, 117-124.

Freedman, J. L., Carlsmith, J. M., and Sears, D. O. *Social psychology* (2nd Ed.). Englewood Cliffs, N. J. : Prentice-Hall Publishers, 1974.

Freedman, M. B. Personality growth in the college years. *College Board Review*, 1965, *56*, 25-32.

French, J. R. P., Jr. and Sherwood, J. J. Self-actualization and self-identity theory. *Paper No. 107.* Institute for Research in the Behavioral, Economic and Management Sciences. Purdue University, 1965.

Fretelliere, F. A report presented at Lourdes. In *Préparation au Ministère presbytéral.* Paris : Centurion, 1972.

Freud, S. *A general introd ction to psychoanalysis.* Garden City, N. Y. : Garden City Publishing Co., 1943.

Fulkerson, S. C. An acquiescence key for the MMPI. Report No. 58-71. Randolph Air Force Base, Texas : USAF School of Aviation Medicine, July, 1958.

Gaff, J. G. Innovations and consequences : A study of Raymond College, University of the Pacific. Office of Education, U. S. Department of Health, Education, and Welfare Project No. 601257, 1967. (Mimeo)

Ganss, G. E. (S. J.) (Trans.) *The Constitutions of the Society of Jesus,* by St. Ignatius of Loyola. St. Louis : The Institute of Jesuit Sources, 1970.

Ginzberg, E., Ginzberg, S. W., Axelrod, S. and Herma, J. L. *Occupational choice.* New York : Columbia University Press, 1951.

Godin, A. (S. J.) Psychologie de la vocation : un bilan. *Le supplément,* 1975, n. 113, 151-236.

Goldberg, L. R. Seer over sign : the first " good " example ? *Journal. of Experimental Research in Personality*, 1968, *3*, 168-171.

Gough, H. G. *Manual for the California Personality Inventory* (CPI). Palo Alto, California : Consulting Psychologists Press, 1956.

408

Greeley, A. M. *Priests in the United States* : *Reflections on a survey.* Garden City, N. Y. : Doubleday and Co., Inc., 1972.

Guilford, J. *Psychometric methods*, 2nd ed. New York : McGraw-Hill Book Co., 1954.

Harding, L. W. A value-type generalization test. *Journal of Social Psychology*, 1944, *19*, 53-79.

—— Experimental comparisons between generalizations and problems as indices of values. *Journal of General Psychology*, 1948, *38*, 31-50.

Harris, R. E. and Lingoes, J. C. Subscales for the MMPI : An aid to profile interpretation. Mimeographed. San Francisco : Department of Psychiatry, University of California, 1955.

Hartley, R. E. Personal needs and the acceptance of a new group as a reference group. *Journal of Social Psychology*, 1960a, *51*, 349-358.

—— Relationship between perceived values and acceptance of a new reference group. *Journal of Social Psychology*, 1960b, *51*, 181-190.

Hartmann, H. Comments on the psychoanalytic theory of the ego. *Psychoanalytic Study of the Child*, 1950, *V*, 74-96.

—— The mutual influences in the development of the ego and id. *Psychoanalytic Study of the Child*, 1952, *7*, 9-30.

—— Notes on the theory of sublimation. *Psychoanalytic Study of the Child*, 1955, *10*, 9-29.

—— *Ego psychology and the problem of adaptation.* New York : International Universities Press, 1958.

Harvey, J. La vie religieuse : présent incertain-avenir possible. *Relations*, 1973, 383.

Harvey, O. J., Hunt, D. E. and Schroder, H. M. *Conceptual systems and personality organization.* New York : John Wiley and Sons, Inc., 1961.

Hathaway, S. R. and McKinley, J. C. *Minnesota Multiphasic Personality Inventory (MMPI).* New York : The Psychological Corporation, 1951.

Heath, D. *Explorations of maturity.* New York : Appleton-Century-Crofts, Inc., 1965.

Henry, W. E. Guetzkow, H. Group projection sketches for the study of small proups. *J. Social Psychology*, 1951, *33*, 77-102.

Hilgard, E. R. Human motives and the concept of the self. *American Psychologist*, 1949, *4*, 374-382.

Hilliard, A. L. *The forms of value.* New York : Columbia University Press, 1950.

Hoffman, M. L. Development of internal moral standards in children. In M. Strommen (Ed.), *Research on religious development.* New York : Hawthorn Books Inc., 1971, pp. 211-263.

Holland, J. L. *The psychology of vocational choice.* Waltham, Mass. : Blaisdell Publications, 1966.

Hollander, E. P. *Principles and methods of social psychology,* 2nd ed. New York : Oxford University Press, 1971.

* Hollen, C. C. Value change, perceived instrumentality, and attitude change. Unpublished Ph. D. dissertation, Michigan State University Library, 1972.

Holt, R. R. Clinical and statistical prediction : a reformulation and some new data. *Journal of Abnormal and Social Psychology,* 1958, *56,* 1-12.

Homant, R. Values, attitudes and perceived instrumentality. Unpublished Ph. D. dissertation, Michigan State University Library, 1970.

Hovland, C. I. and Rosenberg, M. J. (Eds.). *Attitude organization and change.* New Haven : Yale University Press, 1960.

Ignatius of Loyola, Saint. *The Constitutions of the Society of Jesus.* Trans. by G. E. Ganss, S. J. St. Louis : The Institute of Jesuit Sources, 1970.

—— *Spiritual Exercises.* New York : Catholic Book Publishing Company, 1948 ; or Garden City, N. Y. : Image Books, Doubleday and Company, 1964.

Imoda, F. (S. J.). Sociometric status and personality in training centers for religious. Unpublished Ph. D. dissertation. The University of Chicago, 1971.

Isaacs, K. S. Relatability, a proposed construct and an approach to its validation. Unpublished Ph. D. dissertation, University of Chicago, 1956.

Ismir, A. A. The effects of prior knowledge of TAT on test performance. *Psychological Record,* 1962, *12,* 157-164.

Jackson, D. N. A sequential system for personality scale development. In C. D. Spielberger (Ed.), *Current topics in clinical and community psychology,* Vol. 2. New York : Academic Press Inc., 1970, pp. 61-96.

Janis, I. L., Mahl, G. F., Kagan, J. and Holt, R. *Personality : Dynamics, development and assessment.* New York : Harcourt, Brace Jovanovich, Inc., 1969.

Kaplan, M. F. Freud and modern philosophy. In B. Nelson (Ed.), *Freud and the 20th century.* New York : Meridian Books, 1957.

Kaplan, M. F. and Eron, L. D. Test sophistication and faking in the TAT situation. *Journal of Projective Techniques,* 1965, *29,* 498-503.

Katz, D. The functional approach to the study of attitude change. *Public Opinion Quarterly,* 1960, *24,* 163-204.

—— Motivational basis of organizational behavior. *Behavioral Science,* 1964, *9,* 131-146.

* On p. 164 in the text, the author listed as Holland (1972) is an error; the correct citation is Hollen (1972).

410

Katz, D. and Stotland, E. A preliminary statement to a theory of attitude structure and change. In S. Koch (Ed.), *Psychology : A study of a science*, Vol. 3 : *Formulations of the person and the social context.* Hightstown, N. J. : McGraw-Hill Book Co., 1959, pp. 423-475.

Kauffman, M. Regard statistique sur les prêtres qui quittent le ministère. *Social Compass*, 1970, (4), 495-502.

Kelly, G. A. *The psychology of personal constructs*, Vol. 1. New York : W. W. Norton and Co., Inc., 1955.

—— *A theory of personality : the psychology of personal constructs.* New York : W. W. Norton and Co., Inc., 1963.

Kelman, H. C. Compliance, identification and internalization : three processes of attitude change. *Journal of Conflict Resolution*, 1958, *2*, 51-60.

—— Effects or role-orientation and value-orientation on the nature of attitude change. Paper read t the Eastern Psychological Association, New York, 1960.

—— Three processes of social influence. *Public Opinion Quarterly*, 1961, *25*, 57-78.

Kelman, H. C. and Baron, R. M. Determinants of modes of resolving inconsistency dilemmas : a functional analysis. In R. Abelson, et al. (Eds.), *Theories of cognitive consistency : A sourcebook.* Chicago : Rand McNally and Co., 1968, pp. 670-683.

Keniston, K. The sources of student dissent. *Journal of Social Issues*, 1967, *23*, 108-137.

Kennedy, E. C. and Heckler, V. J. The Catholic priests in the United States : Psychological investigations. Washington, D. C. : United States Catholic Conference, 1971.

Kernan, J. B. and Trebbi, G. G. Attitude dynamics as a hierarchical structure. *Journal of Social Psychology*, 1973, *89*, 193-202.

Klinger, E. *Structure and functions of fantasy.* New York : John Wiley and Sons, Inc., 1971.

Kobler, F. J., Rizzo, J. V. and Doyle, E. D. Dating and the formation of the religious. *Journal of Religion and Health*, 1967, *6*, 137-147.

Kohlberg, L. The development of modes of moral thinking and choice in the years ten to sixteen. Unpublished Ph. D. dissertation, University of Chicago, 1958.

—— Development of moral character and moral ideology. In M.L. Hoffman and L. W. Hoffman (Eds.), *Review of child development research.* New York : Russell Sage Foundation, 1964, pp. 383-432.

—— A cognitive development of children's sex-role concepts and attitudes. In E. Maccoby (Ed.), *The development of sex differences.* Stanford, California : Stanford University Press, 1966.

—— Stage and sequence : the cognitive-developmental approach to socialization. In D. Goslin (Ed.), *Handbook of socialization theory and research.* New York : Rand McNally and Co., 1969.

—— From is to ought : How to commit the naturalistic fallacy

and get away with it in the study of moral development. In
T. Mischel (Ed.), *Cognitive development and epistemology.* New
York : Academic Press Inc., 1971a.
—— Continuities in childhood and adult moral development revisited. In P. B. Baltes and K. W. Schaie, *Life-span developmental
psychology.* New York : Academic Press Inc., 1973, pp. 179-
204.
Kohlberg, L. and Gilligan, C. The adolescent as a philosopher : the
discovery of the self in a postconventional world. *Daedalus,*
1971b, *100,* 1051-1086.
Koval, J. P. and Modde, Sr. M. M. (O. S. F.). Women who have
left religious communities : A study in role stress. Presented
at the annual meeting of the Society for General Systems Research, January 29, 1975.

Laplace, J. Une expérience de la vie dans l'Esprit. Lyon : Chalet,
1972.
Lazarus, R. S. A substitutive-defensive conception of apperceptive
fantasy. In J. Kagan and G. S. Lesser (Eds.), *Contemporary
issues in Thematic Apperceptive methods.* Springfield, Ill.: Charles
C. Thomas, Publisher, 1961.
Lee, J. L. An exploratory search for characteristic patterns and
clusters of seminary persisters and leavers. Unpublished Ph. D.
dissertation, University of Michigan, 1968.
—— Toward a model of vocational persistence among seminarians :
Part I. *National Catholic Guidance Conference Journal,* 1969a,
13(3), 18-29.
—— Toward a model of vocational persistence among seminarians :
Part II. *National Catholic Guidance Conference Journal,* 1969b,
14(1), 33-43.
—— Toward a model of vocational persistence among seminarians :
Part III. *National Catholic Guidance Conference Journal,* 1970a,
14 (2), 104-111.
—— Cognitive dissonance and seminary persistence. An unpub-
lished final research report. University of Wisconsin, 1970b.
Lee, J. L. and Doran, W. J. Vocational persistence among semina-
rians. *National Catholic Guidance Conference Journal,* 1970, *15,*
(2), 55-62.
—— Vocational persistence : An exploration of self-concept and
dissonance theories. *Journal of Vocational Behavior,* 1973, *3* (2),
129-136.
Leighton, D. C., Harding, J. S., Mackling, D. B., Macmillan, A. M.
and Leighton, A. H. *The character of danger.* New York : Basic
Books, 1963.
Levitt, E. E. *The psychology of anxiety.* Indianapolis : The Bobbs-
Merrill Co., 1967.
Levy, D. M. Schumer, F. C., and Zubin, J. The Levy Movement
blots : A study of correlates and validity. In J. Zubin, L. Eron

and F. Schumer (Eds.), *An experimental approach to projective techniques.* New York : John Wiley and Sons, Inc., 1964.

Lewis, C. S. *Surprised by joy.* London : Collins-Clear Type Press, 1955.

Lieberman, M. A., Yalom, I. D., and Miles, M. B. *Encounter groups :* *First facts.* New York : Basic Books, Inc., 1973.

Lindzey, G. and Heinemann, P. S. Thematic Apperception Test : A note on reliability and situational validity. *Journal of Projective Techniques,* 1955, *19*, 36-42.

Loevinger, J. Models and measures of developmental variation. *Annals of the New York Academy of Sciences,* 1966a, *134*, 585-590.

—— The meaning and measurement of ego development. *American Psychologist,* 1966b, *21*, 195-206.

—— Theories of ego development. In L. Breger (Ed.), *Clinical-cognitive psychology.* Englewood Cliffs, N. J. : Prentice-Hall, Inc., 1969, pp. 83-135.

—— Ego development : Syllabus for a course. In B. Rubinstein (Ed.), *Psychoanalysis and contemporary science,* Vol. II. New York : Macmillan Publishing Co., 1973, pp. 77-98.

Loevinger, J. and Wessler, R. *Measuring ego development.* San Francisco : Jossey-Bass, Inc., Publishers, 1970.

Lovejoy, A. O. Terminal and adjectival values. *Journal of Philosophy,* 1950, *47*, 593-608.

Luft, J. *Group processes : An introduction to group dynamics.* Palo Alto, California : National Press, 1966.

MacAndrew, C. The differentiation of male alcoholic out-patients from non-alcoholic psychiatric out-patients by means of the MMPI. *Quarterly Journal of Studies on Alcohol,* 1965, *26*, 238-246.

Maddi, S. R. The pursuit of consistency and variety. In R. Abelson, et al. (Ed.), *Theories of cognitive consistency : A sourcebook.* Chicago : Rand McNally and Co., 1968, pp. 267-274.

Maddi, S. R. and Rulla, L. M. (S. J.). Personality and the Catholic religious vocation, I : Self and conflict in female entrants. *Journal of Personality,* 1972, *40*, 104-122.

Mahl, G. F. Basic concepts of conflict and defense. In I. L. Janis, et al., *Personality : Dynamics, development and assessment.* New York : Harcourt Brace Jovanovich, Inc., 1969, pp. 235-244.

Maitre, J. *Les prêtres ruraux.* Paris : Centurion, 1967.

Marlowe, D. and Gergen, K. G. Personality and social interaction. In G. Lindzey (Ed.), *The handbook of social psychology,* Vol. III. Reading, Mass. : Addison-Wesley Publishing Co., 1969, pp. 590-665.

Maslow, A. H. Self-actualizing people : A study in psychological health. In *Personality,* Symposium No. 1, 1950, pp. 11-34. Revised in A. H. Maslow. *Motivation and Personality.* New York : Harper and Row Publishers, Inc., 1954, Chapter 12.

McClelland, D. C. *Personality.* New York : Dryden Press, 1951.

413

—— Risk-taking in children with high and low need for achievement. In G. W. Atkinson (Ed.), *Motives in fantasy action and society*. Princeton, N. J. : Van Nostrand Reinhold Co., 1958.

—— *The achieving society*. Princeton, N. J. : Van Nostrand Reinhold Co., 1961.

McClelland, D. C., Atkinson, J. W., Clark, R. A., and Lowell, E. L. *The achievement motive*. New York ; Appleton-Century-Crofts, Inc., 1953.

McDougall, W. *An introduction to social psychology*. Boston : John W. Luce, 1926.

McGuire, W. J. Cognitive consistency and attitude change. *Journal of Abnormal and Social Psychology*, 1960, *60*, 345-353.

—— The current status of cognitive consistency theories. In S. Feldman (Ed.), *Cognitive consistency : Motivational antecedents and behavioral consequences*. New York : Academic Press Inc., 1966.

—— The nature of attitudes and attitude change. In G. Lindzey (Ed.), *The handbook of social psychology*, Vol. II. Reading, Mass. : Addison-Wesley Publishing Co., 1969, pp. 136-314.

Mead, G. H. *Mind, self, and society : From the standpoint of a social behaviorist*. Chicago : University of Chicago Press, 1934.

Meehl, P. E. *Clinical vs. statistical prediction : A theoretical analysis and a review of the evidence*. Minneapolis : University of Minnesota Press, 1954.

—— Seer over sign : the first good example. *Journal of Experimental Research in Personality*, 1965, *1*, 27-32.

Meissner, W. W. (S. J.). Psychological notes on the Spiritual Exercises. *Woodstock Letters*, 1964, *2*, 165-191.

Menges, R. J. and Dittes, J. E. *Psychological studies of clergymen : Abstracts of research*. New York : Thomas Nelson Inc., 1965.

Mietto, P. *Maturità Umana e Formazione Sacerdotale*. Bologna : Dehoniane, 1968.

Milanesi, G. and Aletti, M. *Psicologia della religione*. Torino : Leumann Elle Di Ci, 1973.

Miller, D. R. The study of social relationships : situation, identity and social interaction. In S. Koch (Ed.), *Psychology : A study of a science*, Vol. 5 : The process areas, the person, and some applied fields : their place in psychology and in science. New York : McGraw-Hill Book Co., 1963, pp. 639-738.

Modde, Sr. M. M. (O. S. F.). Study on entrances and departures in religious communities of women in the United States, January 1, 1972 — May 1, 1974. Chicago, Illinois : National Sisters Vocation Conference, 1974.

Mönikes, W. *Zur Analyse Von Rollen-konflikten Ehemaliger Priester der Römisch-Katholischen Kirche*. Unpublished Ph. D. dissertation, University of Bonn, West Germany, 1973.

Morgan, C. D. and Murray, H. A. A method for investigating fantasies : The Thematic Apperception Test. *Archives of Neurological Psychiatry*, 1935, *34*, 289-306.

Murray, H. A. *Explorations in personality.* New York: Oxford University Press, 1938, pp. 152-226.

Murstein, B. I. *Theory and research in projective techniques.* New York: John Wiley and Sons, Inc., 1963.

—— Projection of hostility on the TAT as a function of stimulus, background and personality variables. *Journal of Consulting Psychology,* 1965, *29,* 43-48.

National Opinion Research Center (NORC). *American priests.* Chicago: University of Chicago, 1971.

Neal, M. A. The relation between religious belief and structural change in religious orders I: Developing an effective measuring. *Review of Religious Research,* 1970, *12* (1), 2-16; II: Some evidence. Ibidem, 1971, *12* (3), 153-164.

Nel, E., Helmreich, R., and Aronson, E. Opinion change in the advocate as a function of the persuasibility of his audience: A clarification of the meaning of dissonance. *Journal of Personality and Social Psychology,* 1969, *12,* 117-124.

Newcomb, T. M. Interpersonal balance. In R. Abelson, et al., *Theories of cognitive consistency: A sourcebook.* Chicago: Rand McNally and Co., 1968, pp. 28-51.

Nuttin, J. *Psychoanalysis and personality.* New York: Mentor Omega, Books, 1962.

Olabuenaga, J. I. Los ex-sacerdotes y ex-seminaristas en España. Cuernavaca, Mexico: Centro Intercultural (Cidoc), Son Deos, 73, 1970. Also in *Social Compass,* 1970, *17* (4), 503-516.

Orden, S. R. and Bradburn, N. M. Dimensions of marriage happiness. *American Journal of Sociology,* 1968, *73,* 715-731.

—— Working wives and marriage happiness. *American Journal of Sociology,* 1969, *74,* 392-407.

Osler, S. F. Intellectual performance as a function of two types of psychological stress. *Journal of Experimental Psychology,* 1954, *47,* 115-121.

Ostrom, T. M. The relationship between the affective, behavioral, and cognitive components of attitude. *Journal of Experimental Social Psychology,* 1969, *5,* 12-30.

Ostrom, T. M. and Brock, T. C. Cognitive bonding to central values and resistance to a communication advocating change in policy orientation. *Journal of Experimental Research in Personality,* 1969, *4,* 42-50.

Pace, C. R. *Preliminary technical manual: College and university environment scales.* Princeton, N. J.: Educational Testing Service, 1963.

—— When students judge their college. *College Board Review,* 1965-66, No. 58, 26-28.

—— Comparisons of CUES results from different groups of reporters. College Entrance Examination Board Report No. 1. Los Angeles, California: University of California, 1966a.

415

—— The use of CUES in the college admissions process. College Entrance Examination Board Report No. 2. Los Angeles, California : University of California, 1966b.

Paul VI. Encyclical letter, *Sacerdotalis Caelibatus*, Acta Apostolicae Sedis, 1967, 59.

Peck, P. F., and Havighurst, R. J. *The psychology of character development.* New York : John Wiley and Sons, Inc., 1960.

Pervin, L. A. Reality and nonreality in student expectations of college. *Journal of Psychology*, 1966, *64*, 41-48.

Peters, R. S. The education of emotion. In M. B. Arnold (Ed.), *Feelings and Emotion.* New York : Academic Press Inc., 1970, pp. 187-201.

Piaget, J. *The moral judgment of the child.* Glencoe, Ill. : Free Press, 1948. (Originally published, 1932).

—— *The origins of intelligence in children.* New York : W. W. Norton and Co., Inc., 1963.

Pittluck, P. The relationship between aggressive fantasy and overt behavior. Unpublished Ph. D. dissertation, Yale University, 1950.

Potvin, R. and Suziedelis, A. *Seminarians of the sixties* (A national survey). Washington, D. C. : CARA, 1969.

Prelinger, E. and Zimet, C. N. *An ego-psychological approach to character assessment.* New York : The Free Press, 1964.

Pro Mundi Vita. *Le clergé et les séminaires en Espagne.* Bruxelles : Bulletin, 31, 1971.

Pro Mundi Vita. *Le prêtre de 1971 à la recherche de son identité.* Bruxelles : note spéciale, 18, 107-117.

Rabin, A. I. *Projective techniques in personality assessment.* New York : Springer Publishing Co., Inc., 1968.

Rahner, K. (S. J.). *The dynamic element in the Church.* Trans. by W. J. O'Hara. Freiburg : Herder and Herder, Inc., 1964.

——. Uber die evangelische Rate, *Geist und Leben*, 1964, *17*, 17-37.

Rashke, R. Evolution des attitudes envers le ministère pastoral. *Lumen Vitae*, 1973, *28* (4), 617-634.

Reddy, W. B., Lansky, L. M. The group psychotherapy literature : 1973. *International Journal of Group Psychotherapy*, 1974, *24*, 477-517.

Ricoeur, P. *Philosophie de la volonté*, Tome I. Paris : Aubier, 1949, pp. 380, ff.

Ridick, Sr. J. (S. S. C.). Intrapsychic factors in the early dropping out of female religious vocationers. Unpublished Ph. D. dissertation, University of Chicago, 1972.

Roe, A. *The psychology of occupation.* New York : John Wiley and Sons, Inc., 1956.

Roe, A. and Siegelman, M. *The origin of interests.* Washington, D. C. : American Personnel and Guidance Association, 1964.

Rogers, C. R. A theory of therapy, personality, and interpersonal relationships, as developed in the client-centered framework.

In S. Koch (Ed.), *Psychology : A study of a science*, Vol. 3. New York : McGraw-Hill Book Co., 1959, pp. 184-256.
—— *On becoming a person.* Boston : Houghton Mifflin Co., 1961.
Rokeach, M. The nature of attitudes. In *International Encyclopedia of Social Sciences.* New York : The Macmillan Co., 1968a.
—— A theory of organization and change within value-attitude systems. *Journal of Social Issues,* 1968b, *24,* 13-33.
—— *The nature of human values.* New York : The Free Press, 1973.
Rooney, J. J. Psychological assessment in a community of teaching Sisters. *The Catholic Psychological Record,* 1966, *4,* 56-62.
—— Needed research on the psychological assessment of religious personnel. In W. J. Coville, et al., *Assessment of candidates for the religious life.* Washington, D. C. : CARA, 1968.
— — Psychological research on the American priesthood : A review of the literature. In E. C. Kennedy and V. J. Heckler, *The Catholic priest in the United States : Psychological investigations.* Washington, D. C. : United States Catholic Conference, 1972.
Rosenberg, M. J. Cognitive structure and attitudinal affect. *Journal of Abnormal and Social Psychology,* 1956, *53,* 256-261.
Rotter, J. B. *Social learning and clinical psychology.* New York : Prentice-Hall, Inc., 1954.
Rotter, J. B. and Rafferty, J. E. *The Rotter Incomplete Sentences Blank : Manual.* New York : The Psychological Corporation, 1950.
Rulla, L. M. (S. J.). Psychological significance of religious vocation. Unpublished Ph. D. dissertation. The University of Chicago, 1967.
— — *Depth psychology and vocation : A psycho-social perspective.* Rome : Gregorian University Press, and Chicago : Loyola University Press, 1971.
Rulla, L. M. (S. J.) and Maddi, S. R. Personality and the Catholic religious vocation, II : Self and conflict in male entrants. *Journal of Personality,* 1972, *40,* 564-587.

Sacred Congregation of Catholic Education, *Guide to formation in priestly celibacy.* Rome : 1974.
Sampson, E. E. Student activism and the decade of protest. *Journal of Social Issues,* 1967, *23,* 1-33.
Sampson, E. E. and Insko, C. A. Cognitive consistency and conformity in the autokinetic situation. *Journal of Personal. and Social Psychology,* 1964, *68,* 189-192.
Sanford, N., Webster, H., and Freedman, M. Impulse expression as a variable of personality. *Psychological monographs,* 1957, 72, No. 11 (Whole No. 440).
Sawyer, J. Measurement and prediction, clinical and statistical. *Psychological Bulletin,* 1966, *66* (3), 178-200.
Schafer, R. *Aspects of internalization.* New York : International Universities Press, Inc., 1968.

Schallert, E. J. and Kelley, J. M. Some factors associated with voluntary withdrawal from the Catholic priesthood. *Lumen Vitae* (English edition), 1970, *25* (3), 425-460.

Schmidt, C. W., Meyer, J. K., Lucas, J. Sexual deviations and personality disorders. In J. R. Lion (Ed.), *Personality Disorders : Diagnosis and Management.* Baltimore : The Williams and Wilkins Co., 1974.

Schmidtchen, G. *Priester in Deutschland.* Freiburg : Herder und Herder, Inc., 1973.

Scoresby, J. A study to determine the relationship of anticipated and actual perceptions of college environment to attrition and persistence at Brigham Young University. Unpublished M. A. thesis, Brigham Young University, 1962.

Sears, D. O. The paradox of de facto selective exposure without preferences for supportive information. In R. Abelson, et la., *Theories of cognitive consistency : A sourcebook.* Chicago : Rand McNally and Co., 1968, pp. 777-787.

Secord, P. F. Consistency theory and self-referent behavior. In R. Abelson, et al., *Theories of cognitive consistency : A sourcebook.* Chicago : Rand McNally and Co., 1968, pp. 349-354.

Secord, P. F. and Backman, C. W. An interpersonal approach to personality. In B. A. Maher (Ed.), *Progress in experimental personality research,* Vol. 2. New York : Academic Press Inc., 1965.

—— *Social psychology.* New York : McGraw-Hill Book Co., 1974.

Siegel, S. *Non-parametric statistics.* New York : McGraw-Hill Book Co., 1956.

Silber, E., Hamburg, D. A. Coelho, G. V., Murphey, E. B., Rosenberg, M., and Pearlin, L. I. Adaptive behavior in competent adolescents : coping with the anticipation of college. *Archives of General Psychiatry,* 1961, *5,* 354-365.

Simons, G. B. An existential view of vocational development. *Personnel and Guidance Journal,* 1966, *44,* 604-610.

Smith, M. B. The self and cognitive consistency. In R. Abelson, et al., *Theories of cognitive consistency : A sourcebook.* Chicago : Rand McNally and Co., 1968, pp. 366-372.

Smith, M. B., Bruner, J. S., and White, R. W. *Opinions and personality.* New York : John Wiley and Sons, Inc., 1956.

Srole, L., Langer, T. S., Michael, S. T., Opler, M. K., and Rennie, T. A. C. *Mental health in the metropolis.* New York : McGraw-Hill Book Co., 1962.

Standing, G. R. A study of the environment at Brigham Young University as perceived by its students and as anticipated by entering students. Unpublished M. A. thesis, Brigham Young University, 1962.

Standing, G. R. and Parker, C. A. The College Characteristics Index as a measure of entering students' preconceptions of college life. *Journal of College Student Personnel,* 1964, *6,* 2-6.

Stern, G. G. *Preliminary manual* : *Activities Index-College Characteristics Index*. Syracuse : Syracuse University Psychological Research Center, 1958.

—— Recent research on institutional climates : 1. Continuity and contrast in the transition from high school to college. In N. C. Brown (Ed.), *Orientation to college learning — a reappraisal* : *report of a conference on introduction of entering students to the intellectual life of the college*. Washington, D. C. : American Council on Education, 1961, pp. 33-58.

—— Myth and reality in the American college. *American Association of University Professors Bulletin*, 1966a, *52*, 408-414.

—— Studies of college environments. U. S. Department of Health, Education, and Welfare Cooperative Research Project No. 378. Syracuse, New York : Syracuse University, 1966b.

—— *People in context*. New York : John Wiley and Sons, Inc., 1970.

Stryckman, P. *Les prêtres du Québec aujourd'hui*, Vol. I. Québec : Centre de Recherches au Sociologie religieuse (Univ. Laval), 1971.

Sullivan, C., Grant, M. Q., and Grant, J. D. The development of interpersonal maturity : applications to delinquency. *Psychiatry*, 1957, *20*, 373-385.

Sullivan, H. S. *The interpersonal theory of psychiatry*. New York : W. W. Norton and Co., Inc., 1953.

Super, D. E., Starishevsky, R., Matlin, W., and Jordaan, G. P. *Career development* : *Self-concept theory*. New York : College Entrance Examination Board, 1963.

Tannenbaum, P. H. The congruity principle revisited : Studies in the reduction, induction and generalization of persuasion. In L. Berkowitz (Ed.), *Advances in experimental social psychology*, Vol. 3. New York : Academic Press Inc., 1967, pp. 271-320.

—— Comment : Models of the role of stress. In R. Abelson, et al., *Theories of cognitive consistency* : *A sourcebook*. Chicago : Rand McNally and Co., 1968, pp. 432-436.

Thibaut, J. W., and Kelley, H. H. *The social psychology of groups*. New York : John Wiley and Sons, Inc., 1959.

Thomas, E. J. Role theory, personality and the individual. In E. F. Borgatta and W. W. Lambert, *A handbook of personality theory and research*. Chicago : Rand McNally and Co., 1968, pp. 691-727.

Tiedeman, D. V., and O'Hara, R. P. *Career development* : *Choice and adjustment*. New York : College Entrance Examination Board, 1963.

Tutko. In Crown, D. P. and Marlowe, D., *The approval motive*. New York : John Wiley and Sons, Inc., 1964, p. 170.

Van Kaam, A. Sex and existence. In H. M. Ruitenbeek (Ed.), *Sexuality and identity*. New York : Dell Publishing Co., Inc., 1970.

419

Vatican Council II. In W. M. Abbot, S. J. (Ed.), *The documents of Vatican II*. New York : The America Press, 1966.

Vergote, A. Réflexions psychologiques sur le devenir humain et chrétien du prêtre. *Le Supplément*, 1969, *90*, 366-387.

Vroom, V. H. The effects of attitudes on perception of organizational goals. *Human Relations*, 1960, *13*, 229-240.

—— Organizational choice : A study of pre- and post-decision processes. *Organizational Behavior and Human Performance*, 1966, *1*, 212-225.

Wallace, J. An abilities conception of personality : some implications for personality measurement. *American Psychologist*, 1966, *21*, 132-138.

—— What units shall we employ ? *Journal of Consulting Psychology*, 1967, *31*, 56-64.

Wallace, W. L. Peer groups and student achievement : the college campus and its students. Report No. 91. Chicago : National Opinion Research Center, University of Chicago, 1963.

Wallis, W. A. and Roberts, H. V. *Statistics : A new approach*. Glencoe, Ill. : The Free Press, 1956.

Webb, S. C. Eight questions about the Emory environment. Research Memorandum 2-63. Atlanta, Ga. : Testing and Counseling Service, Emory University, 1963.

Webster, H., Sanford, N., Freedman, M. B. *Research manual for Vassar College Attitude Inventory and Vassar College Figure Preference Test*. Vassar College, Mary Conover Mellon Foundation, 1957.

Weigel, G. (S. J.). Theology and freedom. *Thought*, 1960, *35*, 165-178.

Weisgerber, C. A. (S. J.). *Psychological assessment of candidates for a religious order*. Chicago : Loyola University Press, 1969.

—— Validity of psychological testing with religious. In Bier, W. C. (S. J.) (Ed.), *Psychological testing for ministerial selection*. New York: Fordham University Press, 1970.

Weiss, R. F. Student and faculty perceptions of institutional press at St. Louis University. Unpublished Ph. D. dissertation, University of Minnesota, 1964.

Welsh, G. S. Factor dimensions A and R. In G. S. Welsh and W. G. Dahlstrom (Eds.), *Basic readings on the MMPI in psychology and medicine*. Minneapolis : University of Minnesota Press, 1956.

Wiggins, J. S. *Personality and prediction : Principles of personality assessment*. Reading, Mass. : Addison-Wesley Publishing Co., 1973.

Winch, R. F. The theory of complementary needs in mate-selection : a test of one kind of complementariness. *American Sociological Review*, 1955a, *20*, 52-56.

—— The theory of complementary needs in mate-selection : final results on the test of the general hypothesis. *American Sociological Review*, 1955b, *20*, 552-555.

—— *Mate-selection* : *A study of complementarity needs.* New York : Harper and Row Publishers, Inc., 1958.

Wood, P. L. The relationship of the *College Characteristics Index* to achievement and certain other variables for freshman women in the College of Education of the University of Georgia. Dissertation Abstracts, 1963, *24*, 4558.

Wylie, R. C. Some relationships between defensiveness and self-concept discrepancies. *Journal of Personality*, 1957, *25*, 600-616.

Zigler, E., and Child, I. L. Socialization. In G. Lindzey and E. Aronson (Eds.), *The handbook of social psychology*, Vol. III. Reading, Mass. : Addison-Wesley Publishing Co., 1969, pp. 450-589.

Zubin, J., Eron, L. D., and Schumer, F. *An experimental approach to projective techniques.* New York : John Wiley and Sons, Inc., 1965.

AUTHOR INDEX

Kelly, G. A. 168
Kelman, H. C. 36, 65, 115, 116, 117, 168, 236, 237, 244
Keniston, K. 142
Kennedy, E. C. 105, 126, 145, 225
Kern, R. 64
Kernan, J. B. 67, 80, 81
Kiely, B. 233
Kintz, B. L. 132
Klinger, E. 4
Kobler, F. J. 252
Kohlberg, L. 18, 19, 121, 142, 159, 242
Koval, J. P. 162

Langner, T. S. 126
Lansky, L. M. 229
Laplace, J. 263
Lazarus, R. S. 33
Lee, J. L. 163
Leighton, A. H. 126
Leighton, D. C. 126
Levitt, E. E. 64
Levy, D. M. 33, 38
Lewis, C. S. 215
Lieberman, M. A. 226, 229-230, 261
Lindzey, G. 33
Lingoes, J. C. 51
Loevinger, J. 18, 121
Lovejoy, A. O. 10
Lowell, E. L. 33
Lucas, J. 248
Luft, J. 230

MacAndrew, C. 369
Macklin, D. B. 126
Macmillan, A. M. 126
Maddi, S. R. 2, 4, 28, 29, 35, 63
Mahl, G. F. 142
Maitre, J. 148
Mansson, H. H. 11, 78, 201
Marlowe, D. 168
Maslow, A. H. 119, 260, 261
Matlin, W. 3
Matthew, St. 262
McClelland, D. C. 33, 35, 168
McDougall, W. 166

McGuire, W. J. 10, 11, 38, 78, 81, 143, 164, 165, 201
McKinley, J. C. 1, 51
Mead, G. E. 166
Meehl, P. E. 54
Meissner, W. W. (S.J.) 216
Menges, R. J. 169
Meyer, J. K. 248
Michael, S. T. 126
Mietto, P. 252
Milanesi, G. 142
Miles, M. B. 226, 229-230, 261
Miller, D. R. 14
Miller, N. E. 17
Miller, W. E. 63, 74
Mittman, A. 67
Modde, Sr. M. M. (O.S.F.) 161, 162
Monikes, W. 162, 236
Morgan, C. D. 1, 28, 80
Morrison, R. H. 33
Mowrer, O. H. 17
Murphey, E. B. 69
Murray, H. A. 1, 4, 25, 28, 33, 75, 80, 124, 174
Murray, J. C. (S.J.) 392
Murstein, B. I. 33, 38

Nachmann, B. 3
National Opinion Research Center (NORC) 162, 202, 248, 250, 251
Neal, M. A. 162
Nel, E. 166
Newcomb, T. M. 67, 68, 69, 74
NORC see National Opinion Research Center
Nuttin, J. 75

O'Hara, R. P. 3
Olabuenaga, J. I. 162, 248
Opler, M. K. 126
Orden, S. R. 250
Osler, S. F. 64
Ostrom, T. M. 67, 80, 81, 166

Pace, C. R. 68
Parker, C. A. 68
Paul VI 252

425

Wiggins, J. S. 3, 25, 55, 119, 124, 170
Wilcoxon, F. 173, 174, 176, 177, 178, 179, 180, 181, 182, 192, 195
Winch, R. F. 14
Wood, P. L. 68
Wylie, R. C. 32, 63, 79

Yagi, K. 64
Yalom, I. D. 226, 229-230, 261

Zigler, E. 233
Zimet, C. N. 119, 170
Zubin, J. 33, 38

SUBJECT INDEX

predictable internalizing capacity, 173-174, 178-179, 197-198, 200

Interviews
Depth (DI), 51-53

Family Dynamics (FI), 51

Intuitive Analysis, 366ff.

Johari window, 231

Latent Self (LS)
definition of, 10
in female Religious, 88-91
in male Religious, 103-108
in Seminarians, 97-98, 102-105
measurement of, 32

Maturity
affective, 121
and training, 159ff.
definition of, 120
degree of developmental, and family conflicts, 147-149, 153-155
see Index of Developmental (IDM)
see Index of Vocational (IVM)
see Growth and
see Possible Growth

McNemar Test 144-145

Mechanisms of defense
and the Thematic Apperception Test (TAT) 33

Modified Activities Index (MAI) 24-27, 173, 325 ff., 377
and self-concept, 32

Modified General Goals of Life Inventory (GGLI), 27

Motivation
and Erikson's eight stages, 81
and family conflicts, 155-160

and IVM, 120, 123-124, 202
and SI, 81
and values, 81, 164
by needs, 75-76
conscious, for entering, 66-76, 137-140, 202-203
liabilities for, 167-168, 203
patterns for behavior in organizations, 117-118
subconscious, for entering, 77-113, 138-140, 141-143, 202-203
value, 32-33

Multivariate Analysis of Variance, 56, 80, 109

Needs,
and dropping out, 257-259
and Erikson's eight stages, 81
and the entering process, 110
and the predictable internalizing capacity, 173-174
assessment of, 80
attitudes, values and, 12-13, 256-262

Passivity
and growth in commitment, 237-238

Pearson product-moment correlation, 70

Perseverance
and compliance 236-237
and dispositions, 4
and dissonant needs, 14
and internalization, 200-201
and structural aspects of self-conceptions, 193
consistencies/inconsistencies and, 140, 169
difference between effectiveness and, 172
dropouts after Vatican II and, 253-259
intrapersonal (Ia) and interpersonal (Ir) dimensions of

consistencies/inconsistencies
and, 48-49, 384

Personality
definition of, 4
measuring the same variables
at different levels of, 33
of religious vocationers characterized, 9
structural approach to, 34ff.

Phi-coefficient method, 128, 146

Possible growth
Index of, 46

Present Behavior (PB)
as traits, 67
definition of, 9-10, 67
reliability, validity, stability
of MAI-PB, 24-27
of MGGLI-PB, 27
self-concept measured by MAI-
PB, 32

Projective Techniques
Incomplete Sentences Blank
(ISB), 1, 29, 32, 34, 351ff.

Thematic Appearception Test
(TAT), 1, 28-29, 32-34, 351ff.

Pseudovalues, 257-258

Psychodynamics
and entering/leaving, 66ff, 206
and growth in commitment,
241-242
in terms of consistencies, inconsistencies, conflicts, 167-168

Psychological laws of vocations,
259-262

Psychopathology
in formation, 231-233
or inconsistencies, 210-211

Psychosocial Perspective
interpersonal dimension, 35ff.

Questionnaires
and factors differentiating
Dropouts, 239
self-report and reasons for entering, 11
16 Personality Factor, 1

Repression
of family conflicts, 160

Research
the aims of, 1-2
history of, 2-3

Rigidity
see Compliance

Role-concept
definition and measurement of,
37-38
expectations and entering/
dropping out, 205

Role
definition of, 234
— gratification, 241
vocational commitment and
experiencing of, 233-247

Self-actualization, 261-262

Self-concept
in entering male and female
vocationers, 110-111
measured by MAI-PB, 31-32

Self-conceptions
and influence on motivation,
201, 204
definition of, 166
structural patterns of, 130-131,
181, 192

Self-Ideal (SI)
and actual self, 30-32
and group membership, 37-38
and motivation, 81
definition of, 9
MAI-SI and attitudes, 31

TIPOGRAFIA POLIGLOTTA DELLA PONTIFICIA UNIVERSITÀ GREGORIANA
PIAZZA DELLA PILOTTA, 4 - ROMA